Stratford V⁻ ⁻⁻

A visit to Shakespeare's Stratford-upon-Avon prc
the town and countryside, well known to the Ba
visit and this book is a welcome help to anyone
great man during their visit to the town. The St
walks to take visitors and local residents around
outlying countryside.

G000039442

The 12 walks included in this book vary in length from 2 km (1¼ miles) to 17.6 km (11 miles) and offer a variety of scenery and items of interest. All of the walks can start and finish at the Gower Memorial in the beautiful Bancroft gardens by the River Avon in Stratford-upon-Avon. This well known landmark near the approach to Clopton Bridge is conveniently close to shops, buses, car parks and other services. The longer walks into the rolling Warwickshire countryside may be started from other locations, or can sometimes be shortened with the use of public transport to adjust the walk length to your personal preference.

Except where stated, the routes follow public paths marked on the highway authority's definitive map, public roads, or for the Wilmcote walk, the Stratford-upon-Avon Canal towpath. The sketch maps in this book provide a guide for all of the walks. However, just one Ordnance Survey map (Explorer 205 - Stratford-upon-Avon), covers all of the walks and contains more detailed information.

In and around the town of Stratford, the walking will be on pavements or on good footpaths and on these walks normal leisure footwear is suitable. However, when walking any of the longer routes into the nearby countryside walking shoes or boots are recommended.

Every care has been taken to ensure the accuracy of this publication, but the compilers cannot accept responsibility for injury, damage or other misfortune suffered as a result of its use. Particular care should be taken when using river or canal-side paths and public roads without footways. In the latter case, always walk so as to face the oncoming traffic.

Inevitably, public paths and their surroundings undergo change. Apart from naturally-produced problems of undergrowth and overgrowth, paths may be officially diverted, hedges removed, or new buildings erected. Users of this guide are invited to report any difficulties that they encounter, or suggestions for the improvement of the form or content of this publication. Such comments, which will be valuable in the preparation of any future edition, should be sent to the Stratford-upon-Avon Group of Ramblers.

Contact Stratford Ramblers at **www.stratfordramblers.com**
or follow the link at **www.ramblers.org.uk**

Contents

Twelve walks around Shakespeare's beautiful Stratford-upon-Avon. The walks, which all start from the Gower Memorial in Bancroft Gardens, provide an opportunity to explore Stratford-upon-Avon and visit the countryside and villages around the historic town.

The Walks

Walks Location Map

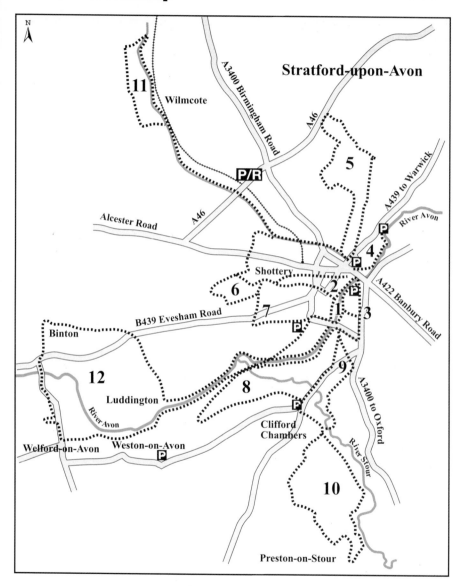

Walk 1 - Riverside Stroll to Holy Trinity Church

An easy stroll along the east bank of the lovely river Avon followed by the opportunity to visit Holy Trinity Church where Shakespeare is buried. The return journey passes through attractive gardens and by the Royal Shakespeare Theatre.

Distance   2.4 km (1½ miles)
Time   Allow 1 to 1¼ hours
Terrain   Easy walking on street pavements and tarmac footpaths
Car Parking   Bridgefoot multi-storey P&D Park – toilets/Parking by Butterfly Farm
Refreshments There are very many good eating places to visit in Stratford
O.S. Map   Explorer 205: Stratford-upon-Avon & Evesham

From the Gower Memorial, proceed across the tramway bridge over the river Avon pausing to enjoy a fine view over the lovely river with Holy Trinity Church to the south. At the end of the bridge, go right and descend a clear footpath down to the banks of the Avon where you will arrive opposite the famous Royal Shakespeare Theatre. Continue along the riverside path for the next km (about ½ a mile) passing by the small passenger ferry and some very attractive weirs until you arrive at Mill Bridge.

Go over the pedestrian bridge by the side of the A4390 road bridge. Immediately at the end of the bridge, turn right to ascend a footpath which becomes Mill Lane - there are a number of attractive buildings to admire. In 150 m you will reach the gateway to Holy Trinity Church. Enter the churchyard and go right before the church to enjoy the view from the west bank of the Avon. Proceed along the bank until the end of the churchyard and then go left to exit the churchyard at its main front entrance onto the pavement. Go right and then right again through a gateway to enter RSC Gardens where you can visit a fine Brass Rubbing Centre. Go on past the chain ferry then entering the Memorial Theatre Gardens at the rear of the Royal Shakespeare Theatre - the view over the old buildings at the rear is very attractive and you can stroll the river bank once again.

Continue along the theatre terrace by the river to arrive back in the Bancroft Gardens near to the front of the Theatre. Continue along the river bank and then cross over the new canal bridge (a plaque refers to the old Prisoners' Bridge) back to the Gower Memorial.

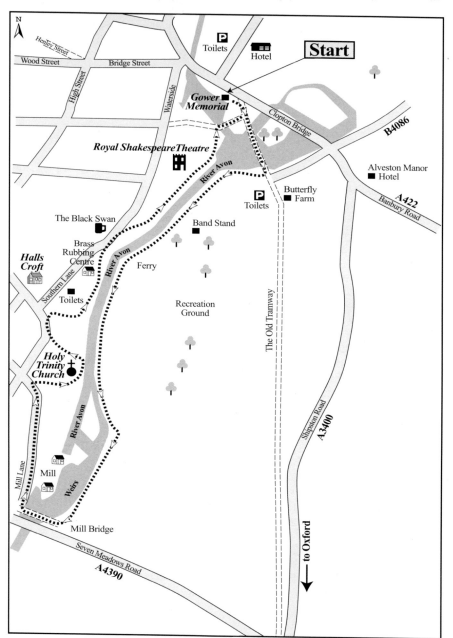

Walk 2 – The Shakespeare Tour of Stratford–upon–Avon

An easy stroll around Stratford-upon-Avon to see the many Shakespeare attractions in the historic town. You will pass by Shakespeare's Birthplace and can visit Holy Trinity Church where he is buried. The return journey allows you to stroll along the west bank of the lovely river Avon passing through attractive gardens and by the Royal Shakespeare Theatre.

Distance	3.2 km (2 miles)
Time	Allow 1 to 2 hours for the walk
Terrain	Easy walking on street pavements
Car Parking	Bridgefoot multi-storey P&D Park - toilets
Refreshments	There are very many good eating places to visit in Stratford
O.S. Map	Explorer 205: Stratford-upon-Avon

From the Gower Memorial, cross over the new canal footbridge and meander through the middle of Bancroft gardens to reach Waterside near to the Swan fountain. Go left along Waterside until you reach Chapel Lane, then go right up Chapel Lane. About half way up the lane you pass the New Place Gardens (access is via Nash's House in Chapel Street) and then proceed to the Guild Chapel.

Go right along Chapel Street and you will pass by the black & white Shakespeare Hotel and the attractive Town Hall before you enter High Street with The Garrick Inn on your left and immediately next to it, with a flagpole, Harvard House (the home of Mary Harvard, mother of John, who founded Harvard University). Proceed past the Barclays bank building (with a small clock tower) at the top of Bridge Street and bear left into Henley Street. Towards the top of this Street you will find the Shakespeare Centre and the Shakespeare Birthplace; opposite turn left to stroll through The Minories to arrive near to the American Fountain in Rother Street.

Walk down Rother Street by the market place passing by Ely Street before going left into Scholars Lane. At the end of the Lane you will enjoy the picture post card scene of the Guild Chapel, the Grammar School and the Almshouses as you go down Church Street. At the end of Church Street, go left and meander through Old Town. Soon you will pass by Hall's Croft (open to the public) and will go past Southern Lane to arrive at Holy Trinity Church where William Shakespeare is buried.

Be sure to walk around the fine church for a pleasing view over the River Avon and then return to the Church entrance. Now proceed towards Southern Lane but go right through a gate to enter the RSC Gardens. Here you can enjoy a quiet stroll to the Brass Rubbing Centre. Go on past the chain ferry before entering the Memorial Theatre Gardens. Exit onto Waterside near to the RSC and Swan Theatre and walk along Waterside. Go right at Bridgefoot and return to the Gower Memorial.

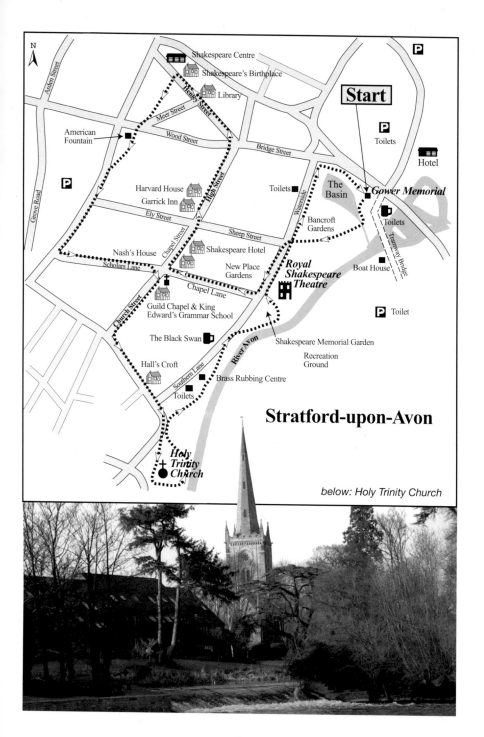

below: Holy Trinity Church

Walk 3 – The Tramway and River Avon Stroll

An easy stroll that will enable you to get your bearings in the locality. The route goes along the old Tramway which was part of the old Stratford to Moreton-in-Marsh Railway when it carried freight in horse drawn trucks from 1826 to the beginning of the 20th century. There is an opportunity to visit the Butterfly Farm and there are pleasing views from the Tramway before you return by gently strolling through the Recreation Ground.

Distance	2.0 km (1¼ miles) or 2.7 km (1¾ miles)
Time	Allow 1 to 1½ hours of walking
Terrain	Easy walking - the shorter walk is suitable for wheelchair users
Car Parking	Bridgefoot multi-storey P&D Park - toilets
Refreshments	Café in Recreation Ground
O.S. Map	Explorer 205: Stratford-upon-Avon & Evesham

From the Gower Memorial, proceed towards the brick built Tramway Bridge (just below the 15th century Clopton Bridge) over the river Avon. Before the bridge spare a minute to look at the memorial to the firemen who died attending a warehouse fire in 2007 in nearby Atherstone on Stour. Continue across the bridge and straight ahead to cross the road to the Recreation Ground, and proceed south along the Tramway embankment. You will soon pass by the Butterfly Farm with the Stratford Sports Club Grounds below to your right and then proceed above the gardens of the houses in Shipston Road (to the left). There are steps down to the Old Tramway pub.

Shorter Walk

Walk the tramway for about 500 m then bear right down a clear footpath with railings that leads down to the Recreation Ground. Follow the path until you arrive by the river Avon near to the Weir. Here you can go right for the Final Part of the Walks (below).

Longer Walk

Walk the tramway for about 1 km then cross over the busy A4390 Seven Meadows Road with care. Now go right to walk the clear footpath that runs parallel with the road and you will soon arrive near Mill Bridge and the river Avon. Go right under the road bridge and continue along the riverside footpath past the attractive weirs.

Final Part of the Walks

Walk the footpath that meanders along the banks of the River Avon. You will pass by a chain ferry and soon the Shakespeare Theatre will be on the bank opposite. Now bear right past the boat clubhouse to reach the tramway once again where you go left over the bridge to return to the Gower Memorial.

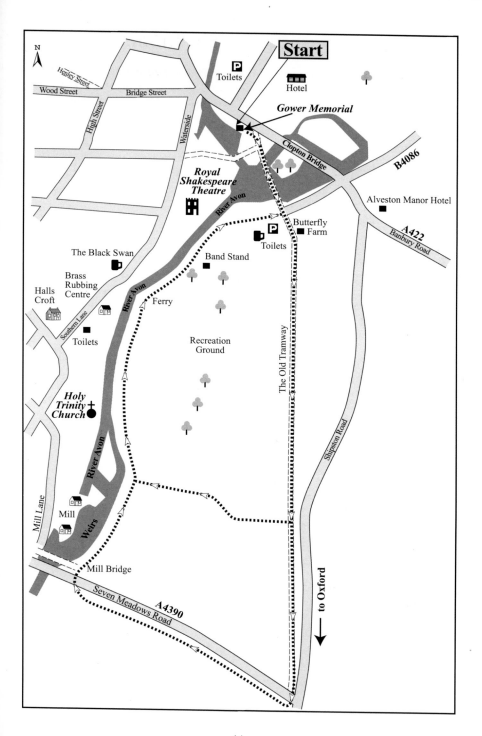

Walk 4 – Fishermen's Car Park Stroll

This easy stroll offers an opportunity to meander the banks of the River Avon between the Gower Memorial and Fishermen's Car Park. Because parking is easier at the Fishermen's Car Park it may be better to start your walk from there, especially for wheelchair users.

Distance	3.2 km (2 miles)
Time	Allow 1 to 1.5 hours
Terrain	Easy walking - suitable for wheelchair users
Car Parking	Either Bridgefoot multi-storey P&D Park (toilets) or park free in the Fishermen's Car park in Warwick Road
Refreshments	Cox's Yard, Stratford-upon-Avon
O.S. Map	Explorer 205: Stratford-upon-Avon & Evesham

From the Gower Memorial turn left then right to cross over the main A3400 road by the pelican crossings and an island. Go diagonally right on a tarmac path across a grassed area, then right on a roadway which runs between the Holiday Inn Hotel and the Marina. After passing by the Marina you will soon go over a footbridge and then can meander along the river bank taking time to enjoy the water activities with colourful boats and the occasional fisherman to entertain you.

The route will take you to a large free car park where you can pause to drink any liquid refreshment you have with you. When you are ready merely retrace your steps back to the Gower Memorial.

Royal Shakespeare Theatre

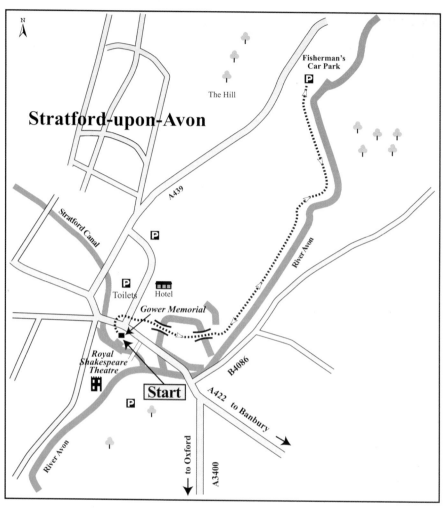

Stratford-upon-Avon

Passenger chain ferry near The Black Swan

Walk 5 – The Welcombe Hills

Visit Stratford's traditional recreation area where there is abundant wildlife. The Obelisk is a landmark in the area and provides the opportunity for a fine view over Stratford and the surrounding area.

Distance	5.6 km (3½ miles) or 8 km (5 miles)
Time	Allow 2 or 3 hours
Terrain	Easy walking through the town but with a couple of hills to ascend - unsuitable for wheelchair users
Car Parking	Bridgefoot multi-storey P&D Park - toilets
Refreshments	There are very many good eating places to visit in Stratford
O.S.Map	Explorer 205: Stratford-upon-Avon & Evesham

From the Gower Memorial, cross over the new canal bridge and go around the edge of the canal basin. Proceed beneath the canal bridge and stroll along the towpath. After going beneath Canal Bridge No. 68 ascend to the pavement of Warwick road. Go left past the Grosvenor Hotel and in about 200 m bear left again up Welcombe Road and stroll past the pleasing gardens of this rather nice residential road. In about 500 m where the road bends to the left, continue ahead through a kissing gate (signpost: Public footpath to Ingon 2) and maintain your walk line up a clear path that leads onto the Welcombe Hills Country park as you proceed along the back of houses. This is pleasant walking as you progress through a kissing gate - to the left you will have a good view of Clopton Tower while a large obelisk stands proudly on the hill ahead - there is a golf course over the hedge to your right.

As you progress through The Dingles you will approach the impressive building of the Welcombe Hotel. This vast Victorian building was erected in 1867 (at a cost of £35,000) as a private residence for a Mr. Mark Philips, a cotton manufacturer from Manchester, and supposedly the model for Mr. Millbank in Disraeli's novel 'Coningsby'. In 1931 the building was bought by the LMS Railway and it is now the Welcombe Hotel and Golf Course.

Continue beyond the hotel over the undulating ground aiming for a field stile in the top right hand corner of the park. Go over the stile and ascend to visit the impressive monument/obelisk on the skyline and to see the topograph. The stile can be avoided by going straight ahead and through a kissing gate then turning right to go through a bridle gate to the monument thus making this a stile-less walk. *The Welcombe Monument was erected by a Robert Needham Philips, a 'Merchant and manufacturer', as a memorial to his elder brother Mark Philips. Pause to read the inscription on the base of the monument which cost £4,000 to build in 1876.* From the monument return to the field corner and now go through the farm gate to the right of the stile you went over earlier and walk the clear track to the right of the field hedge until you reach a metal farm gate.

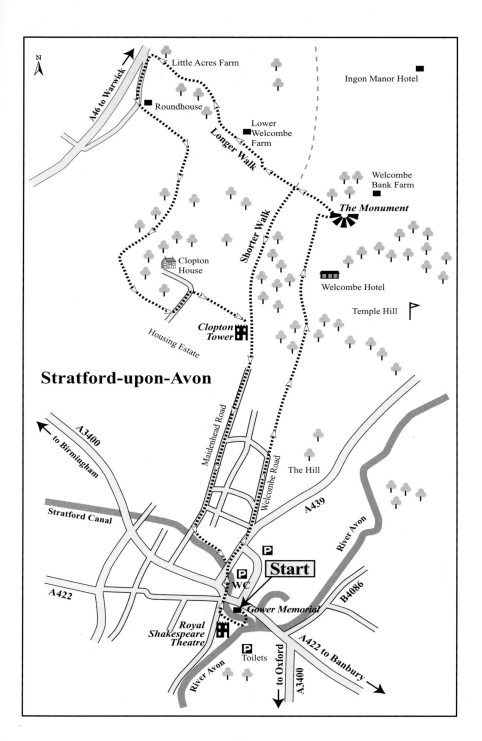

The Obelisk on The Welcombe Hills

Shorter Walk

Go left and descend the clear track through the trees of Welcombe Hills. The pleasant track is easy walking down to Clopton Tower.

Longer Walk

Go through the metal farm gate and continue on the clear wide bridleway going generally north west. A further farm gate will allow you to go to the left of Lower Welcombe farm with its large new farm house to continue in the same direction. Proceed along the farm track that takes you past woodland and soon you will walk near to Little Acres farm before you arrive at the busy Stratford by-pass, the A46 road. Here, go left and walk-onto King's Lane - so called because Charles II supposedly passed this way in disguise in 1651 after the Battle of Worcester. In about 300 m, go left after passing by Roundhouse Farm and walk the clear track to the right of the field hedge with a wire fence to your right - there is a pleasing view over Stratford-upon-Avon towards the south-west. At the field end turn right, through a wooden gate and walk with the hedge on your left, south downhill. In about 120 m, before a small wood, go left through a kissing gate and continue on the other side of the field hedge - the field is part of the Welcombe Hills Country Park. Descend the footpath to the left of the field hedge going through a couple of kissing gates until you reach the field corner.

Here, go through a kissing gate onto a short wide track and turn left for 40 m then right through a kissing gate. Go diagonally across a large field aiming for a kissing gate in a post and rail fence. Go through onto a tarmac footpath and turn left behind the houses. After walking this footpath for about 200 m you will reach a residential road. From here there is a fleeting view of Clopton House set in the trees.

Clopton House *is a 17th century manor house which belonged to the Clopton family - leading citizens of Stratford. They were Lords of the Manor from the 13th to 18th centuries and several members of the family are buried in the Lady Chapel (often referred to as the Clopton Chapel) in Holy Trinity Church. Clopton House was probably one of the meeting places of the conspirators in the Guy Fawkes gunpowder plot of 1605 and legend has it that a girl called Charlotte Clopton was entombed somewhat prematurely during the plague of 1564 and that her fate gave Shakespeare ideas for 'Romeo and Juliet'.*

At the road go left over a cattle grid and walk the road to a junction of lanes/paths. Where the road bears left go right onto an earth track passing through a farm gate and meander along the lovely avenue of horse chestnut trees - in spring they are ablaze with white and pink blossom. Go through the gateway by Clopton Tower (now a modernised home) and stroll past the house then go right through a kissing gate.

Final Part of the Walks

Walk the waymarked public footpath across the field to a metal kissing gate and a tarmac footpath at the back of houses into Maidenhead Road. Stroll the pavement of Maidenhead Road passing by some very attractive houses. In about 1 km (about ½ mile) you will reach the bridge over the Stratford canal. Here, descend to the peaceful canal towpath and go left to arrive back at the Bancroft Basin and the Gower Memorial.

Anne Hathaway's Cottage at Shottery

Walk 6 – Shottery and Anne Hathaway's Cottage

An easy walk that takes you through Stratford and over Shottery Fields to the village of Shottery and the historic Anne Hathaway's Cottage. A 2 km (1¼ mile) loop to Hansell Farm goes into the countryside providing a fine view over Stratford before returning to the town.

Distance	7 km (4½ miles)
Time	Allow 2 to 2.5 hours
Terrain	Easy walking through the town and along generally good footpaths. Suitable for wheelchairs, but not the loop to Hansell Farm
Car Parking	Bridgefoot multi-storey P&D Park - toilets
Refreshments	The Bell Inn, Shottery or The Cottage Restaurant and Tea Gardens, Shottery
O.S. Map	Explorer 205: Stratford-upon-Avon & Evesham

From the Gower Memorial, cross the canal footbridge and walk through the middle of Bancroft Gardens to reach Waterside, near to the Swan fountain. Cross the road and proceed up Sheep Street, straight over High Street into Ely Street until you arrive in Rother Street. Turn left and walk for 50 m before crossing over the busy street to enter the small triangular shaped gardens. Bear left through these pleasant gardens into Grove Road. Cross over Grove Road and proceed up Albany Road. Turn left onto a path between houses numbered 77 and 79 with a footpath sign to Anne Hathaway's Cottage on the opposite side of the road. Shortly, bear left again and keep straight ahead until you reach a road closed off with bollards and an entrance to Stratford High School. Turn left through the bollards and immediately right onto a footpath that leads into Shottery Fields following the Anne Hathaway's Cottage sign. After walking past the children's play area turn right. Follow the signs towards Anne Hathaway's Cottage via Tavern Lane. This will take you past some very attractive period houses to arrive by a road island near to The Bell Inn in Shottery.

Ahead of you is Cottage Lane but, to the right, you can normally go up a few steps to go along 'Jubilee Walk' which leads through pleasant gardens down to a footbridge over Shottery Brook and a lovely view of Anne Hathaway's Cottage. If the gate to Jubilee Walk is locked you can walk the pavement of Cottage Lane to the Cottage. Continue along Cottage Lane and about 250 m after passing the Cottage and just after passing Hathaway Hamlet, a settlement of timber-framed houses on your right, go left up the tarmac drive to the signposted Hansell Farm.

The drive climbs steadily and as you approach the farm buildings go left through a kissing-gate that leads you to the top of the field and another gate. Just through the gate there is a stone memorial to Charles Turriff who lived on the farm for 40 years and from here there is a good bird's-eye view of Stratford.

You can probably pick out the Royal Shakespeare Tower and Theatre and Holy Trinity Church. On the skyline is the Welcombe Monument (you may have visited this if you have already walked Walk No 5).

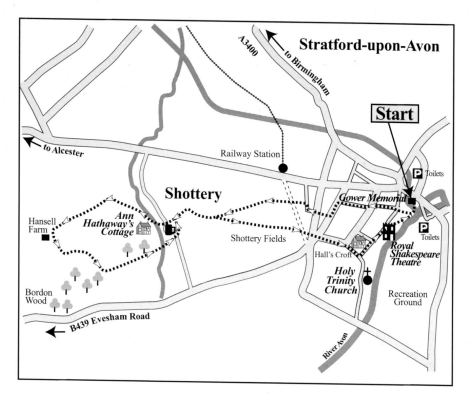

Turn left and follow the field path as it bends right, still enjoying the lovely view over Stratford-upon-Avon. The path enters trees and in about 50 m, turn left on a wooded path heading back to Shottery with fields on either side of the trees and then a conifer plantation. After going over a small bridge over Shottery Brook you will arrive at the road by Shottery St. Andrew's Primary School. Go left and at the next road junction you will again see the inviting building of The Bell Inn, where you may choose to stop for refreshments.

Turn right along Shottery to return to Stratford-upon-Avon. At the sharp right bend, look left to see the attractive thatched cottages in Tavern Lane and cross the road with care. Turn left down a lane and footpath between houses and gardens and right along the footpath which will take you back to Shottery Fields. At the field entrance keep straight ahead with Trinity Church steeple just visible in the distance. This path will lead you along the back of houses, crossing 3 residential roads and a cycle track, until you arrive back in Stratford-upon-Avon at Evesham Place. Cross over the two roads and proceed down Chestnut Walk to pass by Hall's Croft and then go left along Southern Lane, past the Royal Shakespeare Theatre and Tower and back to the Gower Memorial.

Walk 7 – Stratford and Shottery Urban Stroll

A gentle walk through quiet parts of Stratford, along the old Tramway and past the Racecourse to Shottery. If possible allow time to visit Anne Hathaway's Cottage before returning to Bancroft Gardens alongside the Stratford-upon-Avon canal.

Distance	8 km (5 miles)
Time	Allow 2½ to 3 hours
Terrain	Easy walking along good footpaths. Some steps make it unsuitable for wheelchairs
Car Parking	Bridgefoot multi-storey Car Park - toilets
Refreshments	The Bell Inn, Shottery and The Cottage Restaurant and Tea Gardens, Shottery
O.S. Map	Explorer 205: Stratford-upon-Avon & Evesham

Proceed across the old Tramway Bridge over the River Avon and continue along the Tramway, enjoying good views of the Royal Shakespeare Theatre and later Holy Trinity Church. Stay on the Tramway footpath heading south, passing the Butterfly Farm and the Stratford Sports Grounds. After passing some tennis courts bear right and descend a footpath that leads across the Recreation Grounds to the river. Turn left and walk along the river bank, looking across to the attractive weir before crossing the footbridge over the Avon.

Once over the footbridge, turn left and immediately right onto a tarmac path with houses on the right and the busy A4390 on your left. Follow the path round to the right and left before crossing Avon Meadow Close and bearing slightly left onto another footpath, which leads onto Old Town Mews. Keep left along this residential road until you reach the A4390 roundabout. Cross carefully and walk into the housing area down Wetherby Way. Stay on the pavement and tarmac path to go straight ahead on the path between houses for just over 1 km (²/₃ mile). After passing a cemetery on your right, continue ahead on the public footpath through the housing area, with very occasional glimpses of Stratford Racecourse to your left. Cross over the residential roads until the path eventually leads out onto Luddington Road, next to the Racecourse entrance.

Turn right and walk the pavement of Luddington Road until you reach the busy B439, Evesham Road. Cross over the road with great care and walk straight ahead along the clearly signed footpath, following to the right of Shottery Brook, and leading onto Hogarth Road. Walk on the pavement past attractive houses to the end of Hogarth Road and briefly rejoin the footpath alongside Shottery Brook, before bearing right onto a track, leading away from Brookfield Nurseries on the other side of the brook. At St. Andrews Primary School turn left up Hathaway Lane and left again to go round the Bell Inn, Shottery. Cross over Cottage Lane at the mini-roundabout and turn left up the steps into Jubilee Walk, which you can normally walk in daylight hours. Go through the pleasant gardens to a footbridge over Shottery Brook for a good view and possible visit to Anne Hathaway's Cottage across Cottage Lane.

Turn right to walk up Cottage Lane, past the Cottage Restaurant and Tea Gardens, where you can take refreshments and use the toilets, and then walk on past Hathaway Hamlet, a settlement of timber-framed houses. At the top of Cottage Lane, turn right onto South Green Drive. Keep straight ahead and when the road bends left, turn right past rows of lock-up garages and left along a path leading between houses and up to the busy A422 Alcester Road.

Turn right and walk along the pavement to the bollards in the middle of the road, before Church Lane. Cross carefully and continue in the same direction for about 30 m. Opposite Church Lane, turn left down a very narrow path and then walk to the left of Shottery Brook through a pleasant grassed area. At the end of this path, go left up to a residential road. Turn right and in a few metres, just before the end of the cul-de-sac, turn left onto a footpath and almost immediately right to walk between houses. Continue straight ahead through a wooded area with Shottery Brook still on your right. Cross over a road and walk over a grassy play area to the right of Trevelyan Close and go over a footbridge to cross the Brook for the last time. Keep straight ahead and walk past industrial buildings down Mason's Road for about 350 m.

Go left over Timothy's Bridge to cross the canal and very shortly take the path on the right to descend onto the towpath of the Stratford-upon-Avon canal. Go left, keeping the canal on your right, for about 2 km (about 1¼ miles) back to the Canal Basin in Bancroft Gardens. You will pass a number of colourful moored narrowboats and attractive canal-side houses before going under the final road bridge and into Bancroft Gardens near the Gower Memorial.

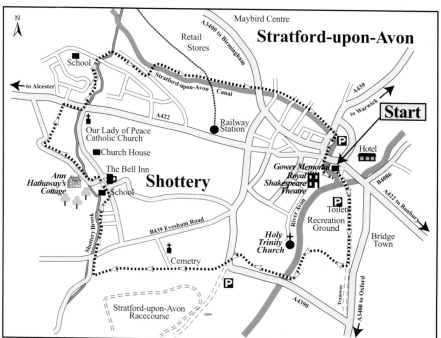

Walk 8 – The Greenway Walk

An easy walk along a disused railway line known as The Greenway and a fine farm track eventually returning past the attractive village of Clifford Chambers. The Greenway is a walkway suitable for wheelchairs and being high above the neighbouring fields offers good views all around as you progress past Stratford Racecourse into attractive Warwickshire countryside.

Distance	9.7 km (6 miles)
Time	Allow 2 to 3 hours
Terrain	Easy walking through the town and along generally good footpaths. The Greenway is suitable for wheelchair users between The Greenway Car Park and Long Marston. No stiles.
Car Parking	Bridgefoot multi-storey Car Park (toilets) or The Greenway Car Park
Refreshments	The New Inn at Clifford Chambers
O.S. Map	Explorer 205: Stratford-upon-Avon & Evesham

Walk to Mill Bridge footbridge following the route suggested in Walk 2.

After crossing Mill Bridge footbridge, go left under the road bridge to the A4390, then walk a tarmac path as it arcs right to run parallel with Seven Meadows Road (the A4390). In about 500 m you will be able to bear left to join The Greenway.

Stroll the Greenway for the next 3 km (1.9 miles) to Chambers Crossing Halt. You will pass by Stratford Racecourse and go over Stannell's Bridge en route to Chambers Crossing Halt. Here, go left and walk a clear wide bridleway. This is also easy walking and you will pass by Burnt House Farm with pleasing views over Bordon Hill to your left.

After some 2 km (about 1¼ miles) of pleasant walking you will pass by Milcote Hall Farm (on your left) and arrive at the B4632 road with the village of Clifford Chambers opposite.

Go left, with care, along the narrow pavement of the B4632 crossing over the River Stour where you may see fishermen enjoying their sport. You will pass by Clifford Bank Farm and then in about 400 m bear left through a gate into a narrow field. Cross the field to another gate. Go through and turn right onto a farm track. Follow the track as it progresses north in a fairly straight line for about 300 m. At a farm gate take a kissing gate on the right and follow a hedged tarmac footpath in the same direction as it descends through fields to reach a junction with a further path coming in from the right. Continue down to the embankment to the A4390 road and here bear left to walk parallel with the road. At the River Avon, go right beneath the road bridge and follow the directions in Walk 2 to return to the Gower Memorial.

opposite: A view over Stratford-upon-Avon Racecourse

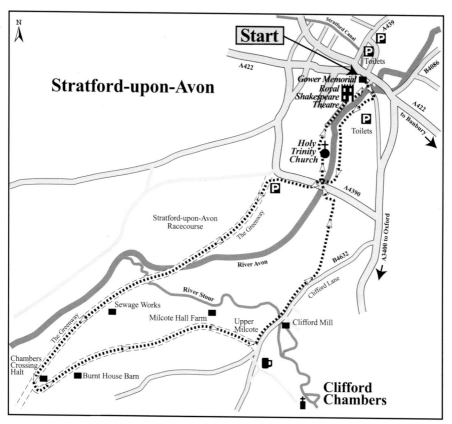

Stratford-upon-Avon

Start

Stratford Canal

A439

B4086

A422

Gower Memorial
Royal
Shakespeare
Theatre

Toilets

A422

to Banbury

Holy
Trinity
Church

Toilets

A4390

Stratford-upon-Avon
Racecourse

The Greenway

A3400 to Oxford

River Avon

B4632

River Stour

Clifford Lane

Sewage Works

The Greenway

Milcote Hall Farm

Upper
Milcote

Clifford Mill

Chambers
Crossing
Halt

Burnt House Barn

Clifford
Chambers

Walk 9 – The Clifford Chambers Walk

An easy walk to visit a nearby attractive village.

Distance   8 km (5 miles) from the Gower Memorial
Time   Allow 2 to 3 hours
Terrain   Easy walking through the town and along generally good footpaths. There are a few stiles
Car Parking   Bridgefoot multi-storey P&D Park - toilets
Refreshments The New Inn at Clifford Chambers
O.S. Map   Explorer 205: Stratford-upon-Avon & Evesham

Commence with Walk 3 to the Mill Bridge near to the A4390 road.

Proceed under the road bridge and go immediately left up a fenced footpath. In about 80m, go right through a gate and walk a clear footpath towards the hill. Just by some trees, after 150 m, go left up the waymarked footpath for 250 m then veer left between the buildings of Cross O' th' Hill farm and over a stile. Cross the field to a second stile onto the B4632 road near a bend.

Cross over this busy road with great care and go over the stile opposite to walk diagonally over a cultivated field to a marker. At the field end, go right with hedge on your left and proceed along a path that becomes a farm track as you pass by Springfield House. Continue along this wide earth track walking parallel with overhead power lines and you will soon arrive at the building complex of the Clifford Park.

Go left between the buildings of the complex and then you go right and then left before a gate to cross a stile and walk with the fence on your left. At end of the field go through a gate and veer away from the left fence across pasture land of horses to a kissing gate. Go in the same direction to a marker post, then right across a footbridge over the River Stour. This leads you up a footpath into the attractive village of Clifford Chambers. At the road go right and meander through the picturesque village. At its end you will pass by The New Inn where you may get refreshments.

Cross over the B4632 road with care and then go right along the roadside pavement. You will cross over the bridge over the River Stour where you may see fishermen enjoying their sport. You will pass by Clifford Bank Farm and then in about 400 m bear left through a gate into a narrow field. Cross the field to another gate. Go through and turn right onto a farm track. Follow the track as it progresses north in a fairly straight line for about 300 m. At a farm gate take a kissing gate on the right and follow a hedged tarmac footpath in the same direction as it descends through fields to reach a junction with a path coming in from the right, (the one you will have walked up as you passed Cross O' th' Hill farm). Continue down to the embankment to the A4390 road and here bear left to walk parallel with the road. At the River Avon, go right beneath the road bridge and follow the directions to Walk 2 to return to the Gower Memorial.

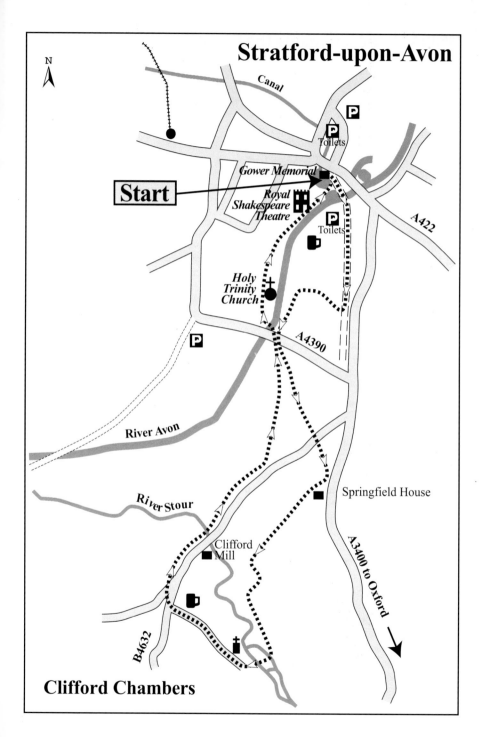

Walk 10 – Villages along the River Stour

A scenic walk into beautiful Warwickshire countryside which takes you through the picturesque village of Preston on Stour. There are lovely views to enjoy throughout the walk, including Alscot Park House, the Cotswolds, Ilmington Downs and Meon Hill.

Distance	15.2 km (9½ miles) from Gower Memorial, or 8.5 km (5¼ miles) from Clifford Chambers
Time	Allow 4½ to 5 hours from Gower Memorial, or 2½ hours from Clifford Chambers
Terrain	Easy walking along good footpaths but unsuitable for wheelchair users
Car Parking	Bridgefoot multi-storey Car Park – toilets, or near New Inn at Clifford Chambers
Refreshments	The New Inn, Clifford Chambers
O.S. Map	Explorer 205: Stratford-upon-Avon & Evesham

If you are walking from Stratford follow Walk 9 to reach Clifford Chambers and then walk up the village main street from the New Inn. After passing the church on your left, pause to admire Clifford Manor before turning right to walk a hedged track alongside the manor wall. In about 80 m go left, following the Shakespeare Way marker, along a narrow footpath, with a fence to your right and garden hedge to your left. In about 300 m the path widens to become a farm track with the village of Atherstone on Stour visible ahead. Pass to the right of a metal farm gate and soon enter the village. Bear left onto the road and pass the former village church, now a private residence.

After leaving the village, where the road bends sharp left, turn right and follow the Shakespeare Way marker. Walk along the left edge of the field and then, following the same direction, through a wooded area. Bear left into another field, keeping the wood on your left and go through a kissing gate into another field, now with a fine view of Alscot Park House and a glimpse of the river Stour over to your left. Continue across the field and through a gate into a small wooded area before emerging on a road leading up to the green in the centre of the photogenic village of Preston on Stour. *Delightful looking black and white houses mingle with properties belonging to Alscot estate, home of the West family for centuries.*

At the village green, with St. Mary's church up to your right, turn left and descend a lane, which narrows and soon bends round to the right, passing more lovely houses. Shortly after two black and white houses on opposite sides of the lane, go left along a hedged path and track to reach Preston Lane near to the bridge over the Stour. Turn right, but spare time to walk onto the bridge and enjoy the tranquil, rural scene before walking up the lane to a road junction. *Here the 146 miles long Shakespeare Way goes left on its way to the Globe Theatre in London, a route that William Shakespeare may have taken on some of his journeys from his home to the capital.*

Proceed straight across the junction, signposted to Admington and Radbrook, and in 200 m go right along a lane, in the direction of Radbrook. In 100 m, as the road bears left, go right over a stile, partly hidden by the hedge, and walk across the field back towards the village of Preston on Stour. Aim slightly left to go through the cross-fence opening and to the right of the barely visible church tower and to the right of the row of cottages, when these come into view. Go over the stile, beside a gate, onto a wide grass track and turn left up the track, keeping the church on your right until you reach a lane and one of the lodges of the Alscot estate.

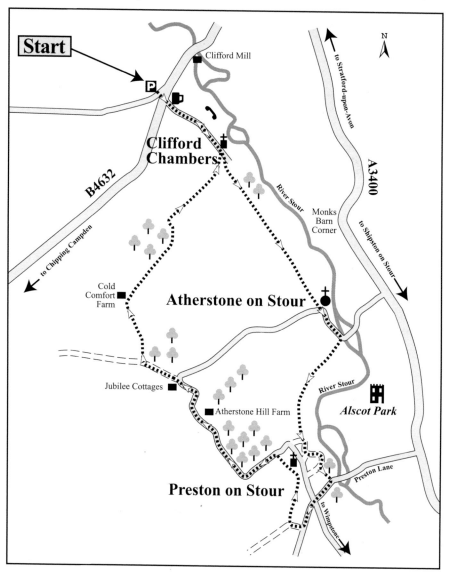

The Village Green at Preston on Stour

Turn left and walk the lane for the next 1.3 km (about ¾ mile). This normally quiet lane zigzags first alongside a wood and then past Atherstone Hill Farm, with lovely views to your left, stretching away to the Cotswold Hills. At Jubilee Cottages, where the lane goes right, turn left and immediately right along a wide track, before descending by a small copse on your right. At the end of the copse, go right over a stile and walk through a field heading towards Cold Comfort Farm. At the other side of the field, cross another stile and keep straight ahead, with a large hedge on your left as you approach Cold Comfort Farm. Follow the path through a gate and climb the hill until, at the top, you can stop to admire the beautiful views all around. There is a trig point (85 m) in the field over to your left. Continue on the footpath over the top of the hill, keeping the hedge and then a small wood on your left. At the end of the wood, bear right descending gently and enjoy some final views of the Stour and Avon valleys. Follow the path for 1.2 km (¾ mile) back to the village, crossing a farm track and going down a wooded lane, before arriving in the village alongside Clifford Manor again. Turn left to walk back up the main street to the New Inn and follow the directions in Walk 9, if you are walking back to Stratford.

The Old Mill at Clifford Chambers

Walk 11 – Wilmcote and Mary Arden's House

A lovely 6 km (3¾ miles) walk along the towpath of the Stratford-upon-Avon Canal to the village of Wilmcote to visit Mary Arden's House. The walk can be extended by a 4 km (2½ miles) loop beyond Wilmcote into delightful countryside. The return to Stratford can be a walk back along the canal, by train or by bus.

Distance	15 km (9½ miles)
Time	Allow 4½ to 5 hours
Terrain	Easy walking along towpath and good footpaths. Suitable for wheelchairs to Wilmcote
Car Parking	Bridgefoot multi-storey Car Park – toilets
Refreshments	The Mason's Arms and Mary Arden Hotel, Wilmcote
O.S. Map	Explorer 205: Stratford-upon-Avon & Evesham

From the Gower Memorial go across the canal bridge and around the canal basin in Bancroft Gardens. Proceed through the canal tunnel under the main road on the towpath of the Stratford-upon-Avon Canal. This canal, which was originally completed in 1816, was re-opened in 1964 after years of abandonment and neglect. Staying on the towpath you will walk under many attractive bridges and pass locks which have been repaired and rebuilt, before arriving at Bridge No. 60 near to the village of Wilmcote.

After Lock No.52, as you leave Stratford, pass a number of colourful narrowboats moored at the boatyard and continue on the towpath to Bishopton Lane Bridge No. 63, where the path is wider and goes under the A46. *At Bishopton there was once a Spa, with a hotel and Victorian Spa Baths, opened in 1837 and intended to rival Leamington Spa as an inland mineral spa resort. This was not to be, but note that Bridge No. 62A is named 'Chalybeate Bridge', a reference to the old Spa days and the iron rich waters.*

At lock No. 50 you reach the renowned Wilmcote flight of locks, which enable the canal to rise up about 30 metres from the level of the Avon valley. Just past the top lock, No. 40, there is a Lock Keeper's old cottage, and shortly Bridge No. 60, where you turn left to cross the canal and walk a good wide track leading to the outskirts of Wilmcote. Wilmcote Manor and the gardens of more modern houses can be seen over to your left, before the track bends left and onto a quiet road, Manor Drive.

After a slight incline, turn right onto the main road, keeping to the right hand side and taking care, because at first there is no pavement. When the pavement starts on the left side of the road, cross over and walk past Wilmcote Primary School and St. Andrews Church, a typical village church and worth sparing a few minutes to visit. Continue along Church Road, until just before the Villages Stores, and turn right into Station Road to visit Mary Arden's house and the half-timbered Tudor house, now known as Palmer's Farm, just beyond.

Mary Arden's House

For over 300 years the Tudor House was thought to have been the home of Mary Arden, William Shakespeare's mother, before she married John Shakespeare, and moved with him into Stratford-upon-Avon. In November 2000 researchers announced that the next door house, long known as Glebe Farm, was in fact the Arden family home, belonging to Robert Arden, William's grandfather. As well as these two most interesting houses, there are attractive gardens, falconry displays and other fascinating reasons to make a visit.

If you are continuing on the walk beyond Wilmcote, return to the junction of Station Road and Church Road and turn right in front of the Village Stores. Just before Chapel House, turn right and go over a stile beside the gate to walk the path, which goes between the rear of the Mason's Arms on your left and the grassland belonging to the Shakespeare properties on your right. Continue along the path – you may see owls, eagles and other birds of prey, as well as donkeys – and over two more stiles, before walking along the right-hand edge of a normally beautifully maintained paddock. Keep heading in the same direction over two more stiles and out into open pastureland following the path on the left edge of the next two fields with a hedge and fence to your left. Before the end of the second field, where another path comes over a stile on your left, turn right (heading east) to go through a gate and across another field heading for the metal gate at the far side. Go through the gate, bending slightly left for a few metres, before bearing right to walk along the right hand edge of the next field, with the canal soon visible again on your right behind the hedge.

About 30 m before you reach the end of the field, turn right over a final stile and cross the attractive cast iron bridge over the canal. *The gap in the bridge was introduced to save the cost of providing a towpath underneath, allowing the rope from the boat to the towing horse to pass through the slit unhindered.* Once over the bridge, turn right and walk along the peaceful towpath back to Wilmcote. The rural tranquillity is broken only by the occasional sound of a train passing over to your left or a narrowboat on your right.

Once back in Wilmcote, after passing the moorings, you have three alternative ways to return to Stratford-upon-Avon.

1. Catch a train from Wilmcote station (30 m to the left of canal bridge No. 59)

2. Catch a bus, including one of the tourist sightseeing buses which stop at Mary Arden's house

3. Walk back along the towpath, retracing your route after bridge No. 60

opposite: Palmer's Farm, Wilmcote

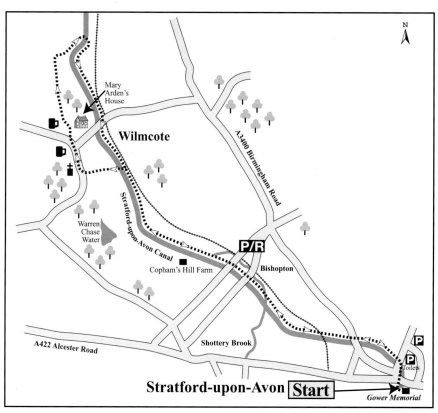

Mary
Arden's
House

Wilmcote

A3400 Birmingham Road

N

Stratford-upon-Avon Canal

Warren
Chase
Water

Copham's Hill Farm

P/R

Bishopton

A422 Alcester Road

Shottery Brook

P

P
Toilets

Stratford-upon-Avon **Start**

Gower Memorial

Walk 12 – Villages near River Avon

This is an easy riverside walk to visit some very attractive Warwickshire villages. Picturesque houses in Welford-on-Avon, a fine bridge over the Avon, an interesting church to visit in Binton and excellent pubs for refreshment add up to a super day's walking.

Distance	17.6 km (11 miles) from Gower Memorial
Time	Allow 5 to 5½ hours
Terrain	Easy walking but unsuitable for wheelchair users
Car Parking	Bridgefoot multi-storey Car Park – toilets
Refreshments	There are three pubs in Welford – the Bell Inn, The Four Alls and the Shakespeare Inn
O.S. Map	Explorer 205: Stratford-upon-Avon & Evesham

Walk to the Mill Bridge (see Walk 2) following the left bank of the river. Proceed under the road bridge and go through the kissing gate to walk along the footpath close to the river. The walk out to Welford-on-Avon follows the Avon River Walk signs for most of the way. Just before reaching the river lock, bear left and ascend a flight of steps away from the river into the trees. Continue on the clear path through the woodland and eventually come out into fields at the top. Continue downstream following the hedge line on a well trodden path along the right-hand edge of a series of riverside fields. About 100 m after passing a disused railway bridge (Stannell's Bridge), proceed through an underpass and continue on the other side of the embankment maintaining the same direction as before, with the embankment now on the left.

Cross over a bridge over the River Stour (it joins the Avon near here), turn left and shortly walk along a well-defined path between the embankment on your left and a field on your right. About 400 m after going over the Stour you will reach the field end and here go right down to the Avon river bank. Now go left over a footbridge and continue along the river bank over the next two fields. *On your left you will see Milcote Manor Farm, once the site of a fortified manor house destroyed in the Civil War.* Continue along the river bank with a view of Luddington village on the far bank of the river. After passing by a lock and weir, continue until you reach the bridleway/Marcliff signpost. Turn right onto this bridleway and soon you will be passing the small church of Weston-on-Avon.

Just past the church the track joins a road where you go right and follow the road to its end. Here go left, leaving the Avon River Walk and very shortly go right onto a track with houses on the right. In 50m bear left and walk along a wide well-surfaced path, which narrows before entering Welford. At the end of the path, turn right into Pool Close and immediately left into Chapel Street. Turn right at the famous Maypole and walk through the centre of the lovely village with many delightful houses to admire. Just before reaching the flower adorned Bell Inn, go left down Church Street to see the much photographed timber-framed buildings. Just before the church, go right along Church Lane, walking to its end, then go left and walk a pleasant footpath, at the back of houses, until you emerge on the Welford to Binton road. Go left and walk the pavement past The Four Alls Inn and cross Binton Bridges over the Avon, ascending

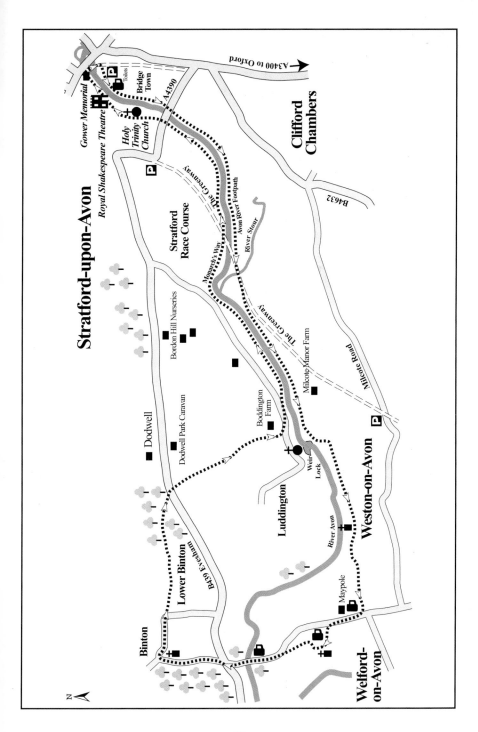

33

gently up to the main road (the B439 Evesham Road). Cross over the busy road with care, go right for about 75 m and then go left up the minor road signposted to Binton. After about 700 m, turn right along the road signposted to Lower Binton and then go through the gate to visit Binton Church. *The lovely stained glass West window depicts the 1912 Antarctic expedition of Captain Scott, whose brother-in-law was the rector at Binton and there may be an exhibition in the church.* Continue, exiting the churchyard by another gate, and proceed along the quiet road for about a quarter of a mile. About 20 m after the road turns sharp right, just after the first house, go left through a hedge gap on a footpath that leads to a stile.

Maintain the same walk line, aiming for another stile in the right hand fence, then go over another stile onto a private road. Where this road bears left, turn right and go over a stile to the left of a metal gate. Once over this stile, turn right and immediately left to walk alongside a hedge on your left and a paddock on your right. Go over another stile, heading in the same direction and through a gap in the hedge ahead. Turn right and in 20 m go left, with a ditch and hedge on your right. Go over the stile, just left of the field corner, and go straight on heading for the wood beyond a farm bridge over a stream and then go over a stile under power lines. The route now meanders gently through small tree plantations where the wild flowers are lovely in springtime. Follow the path through the plantations and eventually emerge on the main Evesham to Stratford road.

Cross the road and proceed through the kissing gate, walking on grassland to the right of a small industrial estate of modern buildings and then over scrubland. Maintain this walking line until you arrive in the village of Luddington. This is a pleasing stretch of walking with appealing views over Meon Hill and the Cotswold Hills. The footpath is sometimes on the left of the field hedge and sometimes on the right. It crosses a bridge over the dismantled railway line from Stratford to Broom junction. When you are within sight of Luddington the path skirts round an enclosure with a pool in it. Aim to the right of a bungalow garden and go through a gate and down a driveway to emerge in Luddington Lane. Go left along the lane for about 100 m and with farm buildings on your left, go right through a kissing gate by a large metal gate following the way marker directions until you arrive in a river meadow.

Go left and walk the attractive riverbank footpath, which takes you virtually all the way back to Stratford. The path (a Public Right of Way) crosses the bottom of a series of private gardens – this is delightful walking with very attractive houses and gardens to admire. After crossing a bridge over a stream the path follows the river towards Stannell's Bridge. Go beneath the bridge to continue along the riverbank footpath on the left of the Avon. This pleasant riverside path eventually arrives back at Mill Bridge in Stratford. From this point you can return to the town centre by either of the routes of Walk No.2.

Jane Suthering, Dip NCHEE, trained at the Birmingham College of Food and Domestic Arts. She spent four years working at the Good Housekeeping Institute and later for other publishing enterprises.

In 1979 Jane went freelance, specializing in food styling for photography and cookery writing. Her books include *Delicious Desserts* and *Step-by-Step Cake Decorating*, and she has been invited to speak a number of times on BBC Radio 4's *Woman's Hour*.

Sue Lousley, BSc, SRD, was until recently Research Nutritionist at the Department of Community Medicine and General Practice, Radcliffe Infirmary, Oxford. In this post and previously as Chief Dietitian at the Radcliffe Infirmary, she worked with Dr Jim Mann in the diabetic unit where the new high-fibre, low-fat diabetic diet was developed. She collaborated with the development of recipes in the bestselling title – *The Diabetics' Diet Book*, also in the Positive Health Guide series.

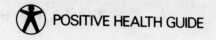

POSITIVE HEALTH GUIDE

DIABETIC DELIGHTS
Cakes, biscuits and desserts

Jane Suthering
and
Sue Lousley, BSc, SRD

MARTIN DUNITZ

© Jane Suthering and Sue Lousley 1986

First published in the United Kingdom in 1986 by
Martin Dunitz Ltd, 154 Camden High Street, London NW1 0NE

British Library Cataloguing in Publication Data

Suthering, Jane
    Diabetic delights: cakes, biscuits and
    desserts.—(Positive health guide)
    1. Diabetes—Diet therapy—Recipes
    2. Confectionery 3. Desserts
    I. Title II. Lousley, Sue III. Series
    641.8'6   RC662

    ISBN 0-948269-07-3

Phototypeset by Book Ens, Saffron Walden, Essex
Printed in Singapore by Toppan Printing Company (S) Pte Ltd

Front cover photograph shows: Coconut milk jelly with tropical fruits (top, see page 99);
Crispy crunchies and Walnutties (centre left, see pages 56 and 57); Fresh stuffed figs
(centre, see page 113); Surprise hazelnut plait (centre right, see page 40); Australian
cake (bottom, see page 36)
Back cover photograph shows: Cranberry and pineapple shimmer (top right, see page
101); Sunshine bread pudding (bottom left, see page 75); Sarah's summer salad (bottom
right, see page 90)

CONTENTS

INTRODUCTION

People with diabetes know that sugar-containing foods are to them what the apple was to Eve – forbidden fruit. The results of giving way to temptation may not be as drastic for diabetics, but it is generally believed that diabetics should avoid foods with a high sugar content, such as sweets and cakes. The reasons for this are well founded: besides having a high sugar content which can cause hyperglycaemia (see page 14), this type of food also tends to have a high fat and, therefore, a high energy content; that is, it is fattening.

So why are we producing a cookery book specially for people with diabetes that is full of cakes, biscuits and desserts?

We are not suggesting that the situation has altered in any way. Sugar-containing foods should *not* become a regular part of your diet (except those foods that may be substituted into your diet as prescribed by your doctor or dietitian). As this book will demonstrate, it is possible to devise a wide variety of delicious recipes for cakes, biscuits and desserts that do not contain sugar and that can be eaten by diabetics in varying quantities within their calorie- and/or carbohydrate-controlled diet. Indeed many people find it extremely difficult and unpleasant to cut out 'sweet' foods altogether, and there is a very real danger that these diabetics will go to the other extreme and eat exactly what they want. The answer is to find a happy medium for all. Within the confines of your controlled diabetic diet, you can still allow yourself the occasional high-fibre, low-fat 'sweet' food. Knowing this should help you to keep to your diet and enjoy good health and good diabetic control.

A diet that is controlled but varied, and permits the occasional treat is the one most likely to succeed in achieving a balance between healthy and enjoyable eating, as well as being acceptable in the long term.

Controlling your blood glucose levels
Everyone, diabetic or not, needs a balanced diet in order to remain healthy. Diet means the pattern of food and drink you consume, not necessarily food which is advised or not advised for the treatment of an illness. If you have diabetes, you will know that your diet has to be modified to achieve good diabetic control. In other words, to keep your blood glucose (blood sugar) level close to that of non-diabetics, you must be careful about what you

eat and drink. To do this, it helps to know about the major nutrients and to be able to recognize the foods you can and cannot eat.

Food – its structure and function

Food is made up of a number of components, all of which are essential for your health. The three major nutrients are carbohydrate, fat and protein and they provide you with energy (measured in kilocalories or kilojoules) and essential raw materials for growth and repair within your body. In addition to these, fibre, vitamins, minerals and water are also essential in the diet to provide bulk and essential chemical elements.

Different foods contain different proportions of these components; for example, butter is nearly all fat whilst milk is made up of fat, protein, carbohydrate and water; milk does not contain fibre, but butter beans contain fat, protein carbohydrate and large quantities of fibre. It is important to eat a variety of foods to obtain a balanced diet. The diagram opposite illustrates examples of common foods containing carbohydrate, protein and fat.

Carbohydrate

There are two forms of carbohydrate in the diet – sugar and starch. Together they form your body's main immediate energy source (as opposed to fat which is your body's main energy store). All carbohydrates are digested and absorbed as glucose, but the rate at which this happens depends on the structure and type of carbohydrate:

Sugar is a very simple carbohydrate which is easily and rapidly broken down and absorbed into the bloodstream. There are various types of sugar, including glucose, sucrose (table sugar), fructose (fruit sugar) and lactose (milk sugar). Sugar is present in large quantities in manufactured foods, such as confectionery, preserves and desserts. Foods, such as potatoes, bread, rice and fruit, contain smaller quantities of simple sugars and larger quantities of starch.

Starch is a more complex carbohydrate; that is, it is made up of many chemical chains of sugar molecules bound together in complicated structures. It takes longer for starch to be absorbed than sugar because it has to be separated and broken down to simple sugar – glucose – before it can be absorbed. The rate of digestion and subsequent rise in blood glucose will vary with the length and conformation of the chemical chains that make up different types of starch.

Fibre

In addition to the physical structure of complex carbohydrate in food, the presence of dietary fibre is a very important factor in

Examples of common foods containing carbohydrate, fat and protein	
CARBOHYDRATE 4 kcal/g	Potatoes, cereals, pasta, plain biscuits, fruit, bread
Carbohydrate and fat	Crisps, fried potatoes, fried bread, shortbread
FAT 9 kcal/g	Suet, lard, butter, oil, cream, margarine
Fat and protein	Cheese, fried eggs, sardines
PROTEIN 4 kcal/g	Fish, meat, cottage cheese, boiled and poached egg, poultry
Protein and carbohydrate	Skimmed milk, yoghurt, dried beans and pulses
Carbohydrate, fat and protein	Whole milk, sausages, peanuts

determining the rate of absorption of nutrients in the gut. All food derived from plants contains some fibre, unless it has been highly refined like table sugar. It is now well established that fibre, when mixed with starch, delays the process of digestion and absorption. Generally, the higher the fibre content of a food, the slower the rate of absorption, but this is not always the case. It is now realized that there are two forms of fibre and that the physical nature of the fibre, as well as the quantity, determines the effect fibre has on the rate of digestion and absorption:

> **Insoluble fibre,** found in wheat bran, does not appear to have a significant effect on absorption, although it is important in the prevention of many intestinal disorders, such as constipation, haemorrhoids and diverticular disease.
> **Soluble or viscous fibre,** found in legumes, is far more potent in delaying absorption and reducing blood glucose levels.

The finer details of this process are still not understood fully.
The physical state of food is also directly related to the rate of absorption because cooking alters the fibre composition of food. Raw food is more slowly digested than solid cooked food, which in turn is more slowly digested than puréed cooked food.

So, generally speaking, the refined simple carbohydrates are far more rapidly broken down and absorbed than the unrefined complex carbohydrates, and those with a high soluble fibre content are likely to be absorbed very slowly.

With this information on carbohydrate and fibre, it would be of great benefit to be able to compile a list or league of foods, ranging from foods absorbed at the fastest rate to those absorbed very slowly. This has been attempted in the past in Great Britain by Dr Jenkins who introduced the concept of the glycaemic index. This was based on test meal experiments that measured the effect of 50 g of a variety of carbohydrate foods on blood glucose levels. The simple sugar, glucose, was given a glycaemic index of 100 because it is absorbed very quickly, whereas high-fibre complex carbohydrates, absorbed more slowly, were given a lower index; for example, lentils have a glycaemic index of 29. Although the Jenkins system is a true measure of what happens to blood glucose levels after eating a meal of one food, it does not accurately represent the glycaemic effect of eating mixed meals over a prolonged period. The latter is, of course, the real life situation where many other influences affect the rate of digestion and absorption.

At this stage, the glycaemic index cannot be used to list individual foods in order of preference for day to day eating, although it certainly has its uses in medical research. But it is possible to group foods into those which are high or low in fibre and to divide the high-fibre foods into those that contain soluble fibre and those that contain insoluble fibre (see diagram opposite). As a general rule, you should aim to eat a diet that contains a high percentage of complex carbohydrates to get the beneficial effects that fibre has on delaying absorption and preventing intestinal disorders.

For further details on fibre in the diabetic diet, see *The Diabetics' Diet Book*, another title in this series.

Protein

Proteins are necessary for the production of hormones and antibodies in the body, and for the continuous process of growth and repair of body cells; they are therefore particularly important in children's diets. Excess protein, not needed for these processes, is stored in the body as fat.

Fat

Energy is stored in the body as fat. It is a very concentrated source of energy, providing 9 kcal of energy/g fat – more than twice the amount of energy supplied by a gram of carbohydrate or protein (an important point to remember if you are trying to lose weight). The most obvious sources of fat in the diet are the so-called visible fats – butter, lard, margarine and fat on meat – but there are other important sources of fat that many people forget about, namely, the invisible fats. These include oils, milk, cheese, eggs, lean meat and nuts.

Although fat forms an important part of the structure of the body, and certain fats contain essential vitamins, most fat can be

High-sugar foods	Low-fibre starchy foods	High-fibre starchy foods	
Sugar	White bread	Dried beans eg. butter beans, red kidney beans, soya beans	
Meringue	Wheatgerm		
Syrup	White flour		
Treacle	Cornflour	Lentils	⎫ Soluble fibre
Jam	Custard powder	Peas	
Marmalade	White pastry	Fruit	
Honey	White pasta eg. spaghetti, macaroni	Oats	
Lemon curd		Soya flour	⎬ Soluble and insoluble fibre
Sweets	White polished rice	Oatcakes	
Chocolates	Dessert cereals eg. semolina, tapioca, sago	Muesli	
Drinking chocolate		All Bran	
Ovaltine		Puffed Wheat	
Horlicks	Cornflakes	Weetabix	
Bournvita	Special K	Wholemeal bread	
Marzipan	Rice Krispies	Rye bread	
Condensed milk	Plain biscuits eg. Cream crackers, Water biscuits	Wholemeal flour	⎬ Insoluble fibre
Sugar-coated cereals		Rye flour	
Cakes		Wholemeal pastry	
Sweet biscuits	Sweet biscuits eg. Rich Tea, Morning Coffee	Wholegrain pasta	
Instant desserts		Wholegrain rice	
Sweetened desserts		Nuts	
Fruit tinned in syrup		Wholemeal biscuits eg. crispbreads, digestive biscuits	
Fruit squash			
Coca-Cola			
Sweetened fizzy drinks			

Different types of carbohydrate in common foods

made by the body from other nutrients, such as protein, when supplies of fat-containing foods are short.

There are three categories of fat in the diet:

Saturated fat – hard, animal fats, such as butter, fat on meat.

Polyunsaturated fat – soft or oily vegetable fats which contain the highest number of essential fatty acids and for this reason are sometimes called essential polyunsaturates.

Monounsaturated fat – such as olive oil.

Cholesterol, which is often put in the same category as the three types of fat, is in fact a fat-like, waxy material, present in the blood and most tissues in the body, especially nervous tissue. Cholesterol is both made in the body and eaten in our diet – for example, in eggs and offal.

Polyunsaturated fat is now regarded as healthier than saturated fat because it helps to lower levels of cholesterol in the blood. This is very significant because high levels of cholesterol in the blood will cause cholesterol to be deposited on the walls of blood vessels thus restricting the passage of blood to the heart. This condition is called coronary heart disease which can cause heart attacks and is the commonest cause of death in all people over thirty-five years of age. Diabetics are particularly at risk from heart disease. Saturated fat tends to increase the levels of cholesterol in the blood and therefore increase the risk of heart disease; polyunsaturated fat helps to reduce the risk of heart disease by lowering levels of cholesterol in the blood. Therefore, in addition to reducing your total fat intake, you should eat polyunsaturated fat in preference to saturated fat which seems to serve no useful purpose in the body apart from providing energy.

For further details about fats and heart disease, I recommend you read *The Healthy Heart Diet Book*, another title in the Positive Health Guide series.

Why do diabetics need to reduce sugar in the diet?

As we have seen, sugar is rapidly absorbed into the blood stream because of its simple chemical structure. Starch, being more complex in structure, is usually absorbed more gradually into the blood. The addition of fibre, especially soluble fibre, will further delay the breakdown of starchy carbohydrates to glucose. This information can be directly related to glucose levels in the blood:

The diagram opposite shows the sharp peaks in blood glucose levels after eating sugar compared to the less extreme and more gradual rise in blood sugar after eating foods which are pre-

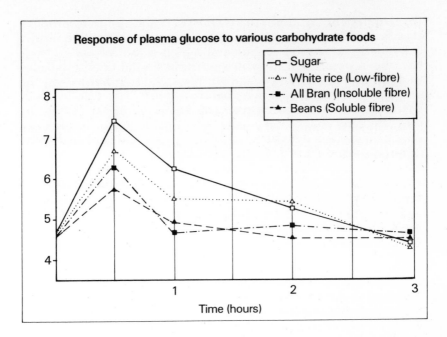

Response of plasma glucose to various carbohydrate foods

—□— Sugar
···△··· White rice (Low-fibre)
-■- All Bran (Insoluble fibre)
-▲- Beans (Soluble fibre)

Time (hours)

dominantly starch. Therefore, eating too much sugar can completely disrupt diabetic control.

- A rapid rise in blood glucose in a non-diabetic will be counteracted by the immediate release of the hormone, insulin, from the pancreas. Insulin regulates blood glucose at a fairly constant level by helping to remove excess amounts of glucose from the blood to the tissues where it is used to provide energy.
- Insulin regulation is impaired in people with diabetes: some diabetics cannot produce insulin at all, others do not produce enough. Therefore they cannot control blood glucose levels without the help of a specially modified diet and, in most cases, either insulin injections or special tablets.

Your type of diabetes

As you are probably aware, there are two types of diabetes: Insulin dependent diabetes mellitus (IDDM) and non-insulin dependent diabetes mellitus (NIDDM). Although NIDDM in theory should be easier to control than IDDM, a suitable diet including sugar restrictions is important for everyone with diabetes, whether dependent on insulin or not.

Insulin dependent diabetics (IDDs) lack the ability to produce significant amounts of insulin in the pancreas. If you are insulin dependent, an insulin regime and a high-carbohydrate diet will have been prescribed for you and these should counterbalance each other and blend in with your life style. In other words, the amount of insulin you take before a meal will automatically balance the amount of glucose you are likely to eat during the meal, keeping your blood glucose levels stable. A true balance can only be maintained if you have regular meals and eat roughly the same type and quantity of food from day to day. You will probably have been given a carbohydrate exchange list to make this easier for you. This list will include the complex carbohydrate foods but not the concentrated sugary foods.

If you eat a lot of sugar-containing food, your blood glucose levels will rise very rapidly because the insulin from your injection will not be able to cope with such a sudden increase – that is, you will become *hyper*glycaemic (high blood sugar). After such a rapid rise in blood sugar, there will be a correspondingly rapid fall in blood glucose as the sugar is absorbed quickly into the tissues. Insulin is supplied to your body at a fixed rate for a fixed time. This will depend on the type of insulin you use, regardless of what you eat. So if there is a rapid fall in blood glucose, *hypo*glycaemia (low blood sugar) will result because the insulin will continue to act for a fixed time despite blood glucose reaching normal levels. So your blood glucose levels will swing from one extreme to the other before your next meal. A controlled diet, which counter-balances your insulin injections, is very important in the treatment of diabetes.

Non-insulin dependent diabetics (NIDDs) Although your pancreas produces some insulin and your body can cope with a gradual rise in blood glucose, it cannot effectively maintain your blood glucose within its normal range; you may be taking hypoglycaemic tablets to help your pancreas in addition to a special diet. If you eat too much food, particularly concentrated carbohydrates, not only will hyperglycaemia result but you will also put a further strain on your pancreas. Many NIDDs are also overweight and, since sugar-containing food tends to have a high energy content, this is a further reason for avoiding it where possible.

More recently, some studies have suggested that the picture of diabetes may not be that simple. Some research studies in France, the United States and Sweden have suggested that, after meals containing simple sugar, hyperglycaemia and glycosuria (sugar in the urine) are no worse than after meals containing complex carbohydrates. But only a few such studies have been conducted and the majority of them have only looked at the effect of a single meal on blood levels. No one yet knows what would happen if diabetics ate sugar for a long time. In practice, most diabetics regularly consume some foods which contain some sugar, for example, breakfast cereals. It may be that if a large proportion of unrefined carbohydrate is eaten as well as some sugar to ensure a high-fibre intake, this may protect against the effect of the sugar in the diet. However, research into this is at far too early a stage to draw any conclusion at the moment, and sugar must remain a food to avoid.

Although sugar and starch have the most direct effect on diabetic control, the protein and fat content of a diet is also very important. Both protein and, in particular, fat are sources of energy, so if you eat more than your body requires you will put on weight. It is now well known that being overweight causes a deterioration in diabetic control and puts you at high risk from heart disease (see page 12). If you are overweight and then lose weight, your blood glucose levels can improve significantly. Many overweight diabetics who are taking oral hypoglycaemic tablets to achieve good diabetic control could in fact achieve the same results by diet alone if they lost weight. In addition, neither fat nor protein contains fibre and thus foods which have a high protein or fat content will equally have a low-fibre content. As we have seen, fibre is increasingly being recognized as essential for a healthy diet and has clearly been shown to help keep blood glucose levels down in people with diabetes.

To control your blood glucose levels, you should:

- Avoid becoming overweight, or lose weight if you are already overweight.
- Avoid simple sugar.
- Eat plenty of unrefined, high-fibre carbohydrate food – though go steady if you are overweight because all food is fattening if you eat too much of it.
- Eat moderate amounts of protein food.
- Carefully watch the amount of fat you eat, particularly saturated fat, as not only does it have a high energy content but also a high risk association with heart disease. Eat essential polyunsaturated fat in moderation.

How much sugary food can you eat?
This is the sixty-four thousand dollar question! Although there is no hard and fast rule, there are certain general guidelines which should be of some help; for example, exercise will affect the amount of sugar you can, and should, eat.

Being diabetic does not mean that you have to omit all foods containing sugar from your diet. This would not only be extremely difficult to do but, in point of fact, it would not be of great benefit either. Many foods contain some sugar (even bread, for example) but, if eaten in reasonable quantities, they should not upset your diabetic control unless they are very concentrated sources. This is especially true if they also contain a fairly high percentage of fibre, for example, All Bran and other wholegrain cereals, wholegrain biscuits, fruit and even baked beans. The actual quantity of these various foods that can be eaten without ill effect depends on the individual. As people differ in almost every other aspect of their make-up, so they differ in terms of their reaction to diet. People seem to vary in their sensitivity to sugar; for example, some individuals can eat four oranges or more a day quite happily while others find that even one upsets their control. This is equally true of other foods, such as biscuits and cereals. If you test your urine/blood regularly you will soon find out if you are overdoing things. A controlled diet fitted to your individual requirements should control your weight as well. But if you have a tendency to put on weight, exercise and general activity will undoubtedly help to keep your diabetes under control.

Exercise
Regular exercise is extremely good for you; it keeps you fit and improves diabetic control by increasing the efficiency of insulin action. Exercise facilitates the entry of glucose into the body cells thereby helping to remove excessive glucose from the blood. If you are fit and active, you will need a higher energy intake than someone who leads a sedentary life.

Exercise for NIDDs   If you are non-insulin dependent and are not taking oral hypoglycaemic tablets, taking exercise simply enables you either to eat more or to lose weight.

Exercise for IDDs   If you are insulin dependent and/or are taking oral hypoglycaemic agents, the situation is not as simple. For everyday activities, like shopping, walking or riding a bike to work, your diet will have been planned to provide for your needs. However, for more strenuous exercise, such as spring cleaning or a round of golf, where extra glucose is needed to provide the necessary energy, your normal diet will not be adequate. You will need to supplement your diet with complex carbohydrate foods. The amount of extra carbohydrate needed varies from person to person but, normally, 20–30 g carbohydrate before starting your exercise should be sufficient. You can alter this amount as you become used to your own requirements, which in turn will vary depending on the type of exercise you are taking.

Prolonged activity for IDDs and those taking oral hypoglycaemic tablets   If you are taking exercise over a prolonged period, you should eat extra carbohydrate before you start. For example, if you are digging the garden, going for a long vigorous walk or doing exercises, you should eat high-carbohydrate food, such as a sandwich or an apple and a biscuit, as an extra snack before starting. The carbohydrate snack which, as we have seen, should contain starch, smaller amounts of sugar, and plenty of fibre, will sustain you over a prolonged period because the glucose from the carbohydrate will be released slowly. It is important to remember that you should not take extra energy in the form of concentrated sugar for prolonged exercise because you require a long-lasting energy source, not a sudden burst of energy. If the prolonged work is extremely strenuous, you may need to take an extra carbohydrate snack after exercise to prevent hypoglycaemia (see page 14).

Strenuous exercise for IDDs and those taking hypoglycaemic tablets Extremely active sports, such as badminton, squash and judo, require a great deal of energy expenditure over a relatively short period of time. This type of exercise uses up glucose in your body extremely rapidly and the only way to supply glucose at the same rate is to eat simple sugars as a significant part of your extra carbohydrate snack before exercise. In these circumstances, a bar of chocolate, chocolate biscuits, a glass of lemonade or a glucose drink, or similar foods made with sugar (not sweeteners) may be suitable. They will not cause high blood glucose levels because, once the sugar is broken down to glucose, it is immediately transported to the muscle cells to provide energy.

Illness
The only other time that you are likely to need to eat concentrated sugar-containing food is when you are ill and have lost your appetite. In these circumstances, you are still taking either your tablets or your insulin (in fact insulin requirements are often increased during illness) so you still need to eat carbohydrate to balance this insulin. If you are too ill to eat solid food, or your appetite is very poor, it is best to drink small quantities of sugary food regularly (every 20 minutes or so) throughout the day. You should not worry about consuming the correct quantity of carbohydrates as long as the quantity is regular and small. This will prevent hypoglycaemia.

Exercise and illness are special circumstances when a quick release of energy in the form of simple sugars is essential. But in your normal daily life, simple sugars must be avoided and this can prove limiting. Although we have established that it is acceptable to eat foods containing some sugar (a general rule is that if sugar or glucose is not in the first three foods on the list of ingredients, the food is acceptable), this is never the same as being able to eat the very sweet tasting foods, such as cakes and puddings that help to add a little sweet variety to what can become a rather monotonous savoury diet. One obvious solution to this problem is to find sweet alternatives to sugar.

Sweet alternatives

There are a variety of ways of sweetening food without actually using table sugar (sucrose). Sweetening agents are available in their natural form or as commercially prepared products.

Natural alternatives
All dried fruit and some fresh fruit and fruit juice impart a sweet flavour that is distinct and pleasant, and derived from the sugar in fruit called fructose. Fructose is also available in powder form as an artificial bulk sweetener (see page 21). Unlike refined sugar, fruit has the advantage of providing vitamins, minerals, and fibre with all its associated benefits (see page 8). But it must be remembered that because all forms of fruit contain sugar, albeit natural and unrefined, they do have to be counted as part of your daily carbohydrate or calorie allowance. This is also true of honey which can be used in very small amounts as a sweetener in cooking. Fruit sugar and honey have therefore been included in recipe analyses when they have been used in the recipe.

Dried fruit and mashed fresh fruit are excellent for sweetening cakes and teabreads, whilst small quantities of fruit juice can be used to sweeten desserts. When it is not suitable or practical to use fruit, artificial sweeteners can be used.

Artificial sweeteners
There are two forms of artificial sweetener now available which can be used as a substitute for sugar:

- Intense, or non-nutritive sweeteners
- Less concentrated, bulk sweeteners.

The type that you use is determined largely by what you are sweetening, but it is important to stress here that *you should use intense sweeteners in preference, wherever possible.*

Intense sweeteners
These occur both naturally and as chemically produced sweetening agents. They are so concentrated and impart such a sweet flavour that only a minute quantity is required to sweeten food satisfactorily. Thus they are effectively calorie- and carbohydrate-free and contribute nothing to your diet apart from a sweet taste (hence the term, non-nutritive). They are suitable for all diabetics, regardless of the type of diet you are on.

In Britain there are four types of intense sweeteners on the market: Aspartame (Nutrasweet), Saccharin, Thaumatin, and Acesulfame potassium (Acesulfame K, Sweetex Plus or Diamin):

Aspartame is a chemically produced sweetener that is a protein. It is used in the body like other proteins you eat and similarly, it provides 4 kcal of energy/g protein. It does not tolerate heat well. Since it is about 200 times sweeter than sugar, you only need to use very small amounts to sweeten food and drink. It is available in tablet and powder form: one tablet contains less than 1 kcal of energy and a negligible amount of carbohydrate; the powdered form, called Canderel, contains lactose and dextrose as bulking agents which make it slightly less concentrated. Consequently more powder has to be used to provide the equivalent sweetness. One sachet of Canderel provides approximately 4 kcal of energy and 1 g carbohydrate. The tablet form can be used freely, but Canderel should be used more carefully because of its calorie and carbohydrate content.

Thaumatin is an extract of a fruit found in West Africa. It is a protein, almost 2,000 times sweeter than sugar. It is mainly used as a flavour enhancer, although it is becoming more widely used as a sweetener.

Acesulfame potassium is a chemical that is almost 200 times sweeter than sugar. It is available in tablet form and powder form (Diamin). Unlike Aspartame, it tolerates heat well.

Saccharin has been available for many years in tablet and liquid form, and is over 500 times sweeter than sugar. It is now available in powdered form as well, achieved by mixing it with small quantities of a bulking agent. As a result, the powdered forms are slightly less concentrated and contain some calories so they should be used in moderation. The powdered forms of saccharin are:

- **Sweet 'n' Low** – a mixture of saccharin and lactose, available in sachets or a packet. One sachet is as sweet as two teaspoonfuls of sugar but contains only 3.5 kcal (compared to 40 kcal in sugar) and 1 g carbohydrate.
- **Hermesetas Sprinkle Sweet** – a mixture of saccharin and maltodextrin. One teaspoonful can replace one teaspoonful of sugar but provides less than 2 kcal compared to 20 kcal of sugar.
- **Sugar Twin** – again a saccharin and maltodextrin mix. As sweet as sugar but provides less than 2 kcal per teaspoonful.

These powders are useful for sprinkling on food, but they have a limited use in cooking because, like the other intense sweeteners, they cannot be used in large enough quantities to provide bulk. This characteristic is in fact the main drawback of the intense sweeteners. Being so concentrated that they can only be used in small quantities, they provide sweetness but not volume. Sugar is used in cooking not only to sweeten but also to act as a bulking agent to give structure to cakes, meringues, preserves and so on.

When this quality is needed, a different type of sweetener is necessary.

Bulk sweeteners

These can be used to provide both sweetness and volume. The two most commonly available types are fructose and sorbitol. Their use should be limited to those recipes where sugar would normally be used to provide bulk as well as sweetness. They should never be used neat, for example, to sweeten drinks. The British Diabetic Medical Advisory Committee now recommends that a *maximum* of 25 g/1 oz of one or a combination of these sweeteners should be used per day. You should remember that this not only relates to home cooking, but also to bulk sweeteners used in commercial products. There are some important reasons for restricting your intake of bulk sweeteners:

- They all contain carbohydrate and their energy content is very similar to that of sugar. If you are on a weight-reducing diet, you should not use them except perhaps on special occasions. If you are not overweight, you should still remember that bulk sweeteners contain the same quantity of calories as sugar. As long as you do not exceed the BDA recommendations (see above), you do not have to include their carbohydrate content in your daily allowance. In recipes containing fructose, their analysis includes the calorie content but not carbohydrate content, and this is in keeping with the recipe books produced by the BDA (with the exception of their book on preserves where the recipes contain larger quantities of fructose).
- All bulk sweeteners have a laxative effect and can cause diarrhoea if eaten in large quantities. Individuals vary in their sensitivity but it is certainly wise to keep within the limits recommended by the BDA.
- Bulk sweeteners can sometimes adversely affect diabetic control even though they are generally considered suitable for diabetics. Normally fructose and sorbitol are broken down in the liver by a mechanism independent of insulin, and for this reason, fructose and sorbitol are considered to be better than sugar for people with diabetes. But if there is an insulin deficiency in the body, for example, in untreated or poorly controlled diabetes, there can be a highly significant conversion of these bulk sweeteners to glucose which obviously results in raised blood glucose levels and a further deterioration of diabetic control. It is therefore important that you do not use bulk sweeteners if your control is poor or even if you are unsure. For people with good control, the evidence is that they are well tolerated in the quantities recommended by the BDA.

Fructose, also referred to as fruit sugar (brand name, Dietade or Fructofin) is found naturally in a variety of plants, fruits and berries and also in honey (see page 18). It is sweeter than sucrose although the degree of sweetness depends on its preparation and can vary from 15–80 per cent sweeter than sucrose. Generally, if you use approximately one-third less fructose than you would sugar, it will provide sufficient bulk and sweetness. Consequently it is possible to reduce the calories in a recipe slightly since both fructose and sugar (sucrose) provide approximately 4 kcal/g. The drawbacks we already know, and it should be remembered that fructose in its refined, powdered form is similar to sugar because it contains virtually no minerals, no vitamins and no fibre. If eaten in its natural state in fruit, you will get the benefit of all of these.

Sorbitol is a naturally occurring sugar alcohol found in a variety of fruits, vegetables and berries. Like fructose, it is produced commercially in powdered form; unlike fructose, it is only about 50 per cent as sweet as sugar. Since it still provides approximately 4 kcal/g, it follows that recipes using sorbitol are likely to be higher in calories than those using fructose or sugar. Sorbitol is combined with saccharin in commercially produced products, such as Sionon, Sweetex powder and Boots' Diabetic Sweetening Powder. Sionon is as sweet as sugar, and Sweetex powder four times as sweet. Both can be used in baking so they are a useful means of reducing the calorie content.

In summary, fructose and sorbitol should only be used as sugar substitutes in recipes where sugar would normally be used to provide structure as well as sweetness. They can provide much needed variety in cooking and are excellent in preserves, cakes, crumbles and meringues. If you are not overweight and your control is satisfactory, there is no reason why you should not use up to 25 g/day per person of either one or a combination of these sweeteners.

Unsuitable sweeteners
There is a further type of sweetener available that is not suitable for people with diabetes because it contains sugar. This type includes Slimcea Sweet 'n' Slim, Sucron, and Boots' Sugar Lite. The number one rule when buying sweeteners is the same as that for buying any commercially prepared food – always read the list of ingredients first. If sugar is among the first two or three ingredients, the product is usually not suitable for diabetics. As so many canned and packed foods contain sugar, excluding any product containing sugar would be impractical, but try to use fresh ingredients whenever possible and be sensible about the food you buy.

Proprietary diabetic foods

A wide variety of foods specially prepared for diabetics is now available, including jams, cakes, biscuits, sweets and drinks. These do not have to form a necessary part of any diabetic diet and, in addition, they tend to be expensive. Fructose and sorbitol are invariably used as sweetening agents in proprietary products, raising their calorie content to a similar, if not greater, level to that of their sugar-containing counterparts. Low-calorie dietary or slimming foods, such as low-sugar jam or low-calorie squash and carbonated drinks, are of considerably more use because they tend to be less expensive, are suitable for all diabetics, and have the positive advantage of being sweet, low in calories and having no effect on diabetic control.

Of course this does not mean that diabetic food should not be bought; from the large number of products now being sold, it is obvious that there *is* a demand for diabetic foods. They are pre-packed, convenient, quick and easy, and include foods, such as sweets, that you are unlikely to want to prepare yourself. But their main disadvantage is their expense. Also many people consider that cakes, biscuits, preserves and so on, taste better cooked at home although that is a matter of taste, how good a cook you are, and how good the recipes are!

Diabetic sweets

The selection of diabetic sweets now ranges from bars of chocolate to boiled sweets and chewing gum. The chocolates tend to contain fructose as a sweetener, while pastilles generally are sweetened with sorbitol or a sorbitol–saccharin mix. Chewing gum is sweetened with saccharin or zylitol and mannitol. All these products list their ingredients and the quantity of fructose or sorbitol used, so you can easily calculate how much you can eat and keep within the limits recommended by the BDA (see page 20). Remember to count the number of calories provided by the sugar substitute in each sweet, but not the carbohydrate values. Also remember that sweets are probably the most unnecessary food that we consume. They contain little or no fibre, few vitamins and minerals and are often very high in calories. Many people find them an irresistible temptation and disastrously easy to nibble in between meals – a major cause of weight increase in children and adults, and a contributory factor in tooth decay. Most people are brought up on the adage that sweets are bad for them but they still continue to eat them; likewise, most diabetics know that sweets are very bad for them but many continue to eat both the diabetic and sugared varieties. Incidentally, the occasional ordinary sweet is probably better than a lot of diabetic sweets.

Diabetic children

It is often taken for granted that the majority of people, especially children, like, and often cannot do without, sweet tasting food. This may be the case but it should not be an automatic assumption. You cannot want or miss something that you have not known – and this is not as obvious as it sounds. Parents feeding their children will tend to encourage them to do what they did as children; for example, if they had sugar on cereal, their children will automatically have sugar on cereal. This principle can be applied to so many things – sugar in tea, sugar on fruit, sugar in puddings, sweets after a meal. None of these things is necessary, but it is sometimes assumed that without them the child will not like and therefore will not eat the food. It is far harder to stop children from eating food, such as sugar, that they are used to than to prevent them from eating it in the first place.

A major problem is that *what* you eat and *when* you eat is largely determined by social factors, whether it is a family meal, a social dinner, or a trip to the local chip shop at lunch time. It is not simply determined by your physical needs. As one grows older, it becomes easier (though never easy) to deviate from the norm and to tell other people that you cannot eat something like sugar because you are on a special diet. Indeed for many women, this *is* the norm! But it can be extremely difficult and very upsetting for a child to opt out of going to the shops with friends to buy sweets. Coping with the facts of diabetes is difficult enough, but for many children the diet is far more of a problem than the insulin injections. Undoubtedly, missing the taste of sweet food is part of the problem, but other major factors contribute, such as having to eat set quantities at set times and the dislike, or even fear, of feeling different and apart from other children and not being able to join in with friends. There is no magic answer to this very real problem and all diabetic children must be made aware of the importance of their diet. Meals and snacks cannot be omitted; high-fat and high-sugar foods should be avoided. One of the hardest facts they have to accept is that they cannot simply go out with their friends and buy a whole bar of chocolate or a bag of boiled sweets and eat all of it.

The ideal course of action, therefore, is for parents to bring up their children on unsweetened foods right from the start; sugar is not needed by any child and is of no benefit to anyone, diabetic or not. But we can discard such an unrealistic solution and consider more practical suggestions. We are stuck with the paraphernalia of sweets, cakes, biscuits and puddings – and we like them.

The best we can do is to suggest ways of controlling your child's sugar intake within the home environment. Having accepted this, it is important to give your child foods he or she likes to eat and not to make life too difficult:

- Remove sugar from home cooking. You will find it far easier to make changes in the home environment than outside the home. But there is nothing worse than having a different meal or dish cooked specially for one person. A diabetic diet is a healthy diet so, if one member of the family is diabetic, it should be family policy to keep off the sugar, have lots of high-fibre and low-fat foods and even to use sweeteners in cakes and biscuits. This at least provides a united front with which to face the outside world!

- Try to find alternatives to the unsuitable foods. This is not an easy thing to do, especially having to convince your child that they are unsuitable, but there are compromises. Fruit is an excellent alternative to sweets for snacks and lunches; it is generally sweet tasting, it contains fibre, vitamins and minerals and is certainly the healthier choice. Fruit should be one alternative but variety is important. Home baking is an ideal way of helping your child. What better way of making the diet acceptable than to make delicious sugar-free (preferably low-fat, high-fibre) biscuits that can be shared with friends at school – though always make sure that your child eats the correct carbohydrate allowance and, if necessary, wrap his or her portion separately. Extra fruit in a lunch box that can be shared with friends is also a possibility although this sort of generosity can get rather expensive! If your child does want to buy snacks with friends, recommend the least harmful alternatives. Fruit, again, is the ideal choice but packets of nuts and raisins are a suitable and often preferrable alternative. Packets of crisps and savoury biscuits, although very low in fibre and high in fat, are unlikely to cause hyperglycaemia and are therefore better than sweets. Sugarless chewing gum can also be bought as long as it is understood that chewing gum is an extra and cannot be used to replace a snack. The carbohydrate content of all these foods is given in the BDA's *Countdown* book.
- At all times you should aim to adjust your child to the taste of unsweetened foods and this may be easier than you think – after just one or two weeks, many children are quite used to not having sugar.
- Of course, there are circumstances when diabetics can have sugar. Exercise should be a part of every child's daily routine and should be actively encouraged (though *not* used as a bribe to eat sweets!). The more exercise children get, the more fit and healthy they will be and the more they will be able to eat, including the occasional confectionery bar, before very strenuous exercise.
- One last, very practical point to remember – there will be times when children cheat, for whatever reason. If it is simply that they fancy a packet of sweets and nothing more complex, there is no need to worry. In these circumstances, a little down-to-earth advice on eating a little at a time and eating slowly and at the end of a main meal will probably do as much good as anything. If it starts to become a habit, a

harder line should be taken. Each child in each circumstance is different, and you and your medical advisers will find the best way to cope.

If you and your child follow these suggestions, plus think of ideas for yourselves, you should be able to cope with and enjoy the diabetic diet. Do remember that your doctor or dietitian is there to help with any problem.

THE RECIPES

Analyses
Each recipe has been analysed for its energy, carbohydrate, fibre, protein and fat content. The analysis for fructose is included in the calorie value, not the carbohydrate value. The carbohydrate values have been rounded to the nearest 5 grams. The figures are given per serving where possible. The energy content is given in kilocalories (kcal) and their metric equivalent, kilojoules (kJ). (neg = negligible)

Measurements
Ingredients are given in both metric and imperial measurements, but only use one system yourself; do not combine the two. When spoonfuls are referred to, level spoons are meant.

1 tsp (teaspoon) = 5 ml
1 tbsp (tablespoon) = 15 ml

To ensure success, check the size of the spoons you are using. Australian users should remember that, as their tablespoon has been converted to 20 ml and is therefore larger than the tablespoon measurements used in the recipes in this book, they should use 3 × 5 ml tsp where instructed to use 1 × 15 ml tbsp.

Recipe coding
Each recipe has been clearly coded into one of four categories which relates to the nutritional content of the recipe and therefore how frequently or infrequently it should be included in your controlled diet. All recipes have been made as low in fat and as high in fibre as possible.

★ ★ ★ = This signifies that the recipe is high in carbohydrate and fibre and that its percentage fat content is low. It can therefore be eaten regularly within the confines of your calorie allowance.

★ ★ = This signifies that the recipe has a higher percentage fat content and a correspondingly lower carbohydrate and fibre content. It can be eaten in moderate amounts.

★ = This signifies that the recipe should be treated with great respect and only eaten on very special occasions, such as birthdays or feast days, because it is higher in fat and therefore has a high calorie content.

⊞ = This signifies that the recipe is very low in calories and therefore can be eaten regularly even if you are on a weight-reducing diet.

Try to keep to your personal carbohydrate plan at all times. If you are on a weight-reducing diet, remember that the very low calorie recipes are clearly marked. There are a number of other recipes that have a reasonably low calorie content and can be eaten as long as they are calculated in your daily allowance. Choose those recipes coded with three stars in preference. With their higher fibre content, you will find them more satisfying as well as being better for you.

Suitable for all the family
The wide variety of recipes in this book includes those suitable for everyday cooking and those for special occasions. The appearance and taste of a dish has been an important factor in the development of these recipes. Since the diabetic diet contains little or no sugar (sucrose) and is low-fat and high-fibre, it is very healthy and can be adopted by all members of the family, especially those on a weight-reducing diet.

Sweeteners (see page 18)
The type of sweetening agent used does vary from one recipe to another, but use intense sweeteners in preference to bulk sweeteners wherever possible.

Sugar (sucrose) in non-diabetic cooking provides sweetness and texture, and is used as a preservative and a bulking agent. Alternative sweeteners can provide both sweetness and bulk to recipes, but they do not act as such effective preservatives, and do not provide the expected texture of recipes using sugar – for example, biscuits made with artificial sweeteners are often soft, not crisp.

- Artificially sweetened food may not keep as well so try to eat cakes, biscuits and desserts within 1 or 2 days of cooking. Cakes will not keep well even in an airtight container so any cakes not eaten can be frozen in a freezer or the freezer compartment of a fridge until required. Biscuits and bread can be freshened and crisped in a warm oven before eating.

● Other recipes, such as Spiced mincemeat and Christmas pudding (see pages 116 and 114), should be frozen until required and then kept in the refrigerator for no more than 1–2 days before use.

Frozen desserts

These present the biggest problem in diabetic cooking. Traditional ice cream recipes require eggs, sugar and double cream to achieve good results, while sorbets require a large amount of sugar and some egg whites. Sugar and high-fat ingredients, such as cream, are not suitable for a diabetic diet, so ice cream recipes have been omitted and sorbet recipes have been adapted to achieve similar results.

General tips on ingredients and food preparation for a healthy diet

● **To ensure you eat a high-fibre diet:** use wholemeal flour in preference to white flour (or half wholemeal/half white); try to introduce the interesting nutty flavours of wholegrain products as well as wholemeal flour – for example, add oats and breadcrumbs to a crumble topping; eat plenty of fruit, nuts, cereals and grains; leave skins on fresh fruit where possible; a wide variety of frozen and canned fruit is available and can be substituted for fresh fruit, but check that canned fruit is canned in natural juice and not sugar syrup; use an electric blender for processing food rather than a sieve to ensure you do not lose valuable fibre – also, do not blend to too fine a purée to keep fibre intact.

● **To ensure you eat a low-fat diet:** use polyunsaturated margarines, low-fat spreads, polyunsaturated oils, such as corn, soya and sunflower, but use them all sparingly; since fat in pastry and baking recipes provides moisture and some crispness, try to eat the recipes on the day of cooking to retain freshness – they are often better warmed in the oven; use skimmed milk or reconstituted dried skimmed milk instead of whole milk; use low-fat skimmed milk cheeses, such as cottage cheese, low-fat curd cheese and Fromage blanc – these are often good for fillings, toppings and alternatives to cream; use low-fat plain yoghurts or low-fat fruit yoghurts without added sugar. Instead of glazing pastry, be creative with the pastry trimmings and decorate the top of the pie or flan with pastry leaves and roses instead.

● Use Pear and apple spread as an alternative sweetener. This is a commerical product available from most health food stores and is particularly good in cakes.

SPONGE AND FRUIT CAKES

SPONGE CAKES

Whisked sponge cake ★ ★

Serves 8
Each serving: 105 kcal/442 kJ, 15 g carbohydrate, 1 g fibre, 4 g protein, 2 g fat

polyunsaturated margarine, for greasing
3 eggs, separated
40 g/1½ oz fructose
30 ml/2 tbsp water
75 g/3 oz wholemeal flour

¼ tsp cream of tartar
90 ml/6 tbsp sugar-free strawberry jam
1 tsp icing sugar or powdered sweetener, to sprinkle

Heat the oven to 190°C/375°F/gas 5 and grease and base-line with greaseproof paper two 20 cm/8 inch sandwich tins. Using an electric mixer or hand whisk, whisk the egg yolks, fructose and water in a large bowl until pale and foamy. Fold in the flour.

Whisk the egg whites and cream of tartar in another large bowl until peaks form. Fold the egg whites into the flour mixture. Divide the mixture between the prepared sandwich tins.

Bake for 10–15 minutes until risen and firm to the touch. Cool on a wire tray. Peel off the paper and sandwich the cakes together with the jam. Dredge the top with the icing sugar or powdered sweetener, and serve.

Lemon sandwich cake ★

Serves 8
Each serving: 211 kcal/886 kJ, 20 g carbohydrate, 1 g fibre, 4 g protein, 12 g fat

115 g/4 oz polyunsaturated margarine, plus extra for greasing
50 g/2 oz fructose
2 eggs
75 g/3 oz self-raising wholemeal flour

grated rind and juice of 1 lemon
75 g/3 oz self-raising flour
½ tsp baking powder
a little skimmed milk
45 ml/3 tbsp sugar-free jam

Heat the oven to 170°C/325°F/gas 3 and lightly grease and base-line with greaseproof paper two 18 cm/7 inch sandwich tins.

Cream the margarine and fructose together in a bowl until pale and fluffy. Beat in the eggs, one at a time, adding a little wholemeal flour, if necessary, to prevent the mixture curdling. Stir in the lemon rind.

Sift the white flour and baking powder together and fold into the mixture with the remaining wholemeal flour. Stir in the lemon juice and sufficient skimmed milk to give a dropping consistency.

Divide the mixture between the prepared tins. Level the surface and bake for about 20 minutes until risen and firm to the touch. Leave to cool slightly in the tins, then remove from the tins and cool on a wire tray. Peel off the greaseproof paper and sandwich the cakes together with the jam.

Carrot and nut sponge cake

Makes 12 slices   see photograph, page 33
Each slice: 108 kcal/453 kJ, 5 g carbohydrate, 2 g fibre, 3 g protein, 7 g fat

polyunsaturated margarine, for greasing   *75 g/3 oz fructose*
115 g/4 oz shelled hazelnuts or   *150 g/5 oz carrots, grated*
*   almonds, or a mixture of both*   *25 g/1 oz wholemeal flour*
25 g/1 oz desiccated coconut   *½ tsp baking powder*
3 eggs, separated   *grated rind of ½ lemon or orange*

Heat the oven to 180°C/350°F/gas 4 and grease and base-line with greaseproof paper an 18 cm/7 inch round cake tin. Place the nuts on a baking sheet and toast in the oven for 10–15 minutes until golden. Add the coconut after 5 minutes and toast for a further 5 minutes until golden. Cool slightly. Grind the mixed nuts in a food processor or rotary grater.

Whisk the egg yolks with two-thirds of the fructose in a bowl until pale and thick. Stir in the ground nuts, grated carrots, flour, baking powder and lemon or orange rind.

In another bowl, whisk the egg whites until stiff, then continue whisking while adding the remaining fructose, a little at a time. Fold the egg white mixture into the cake mixture until evenly mixed. Spoon the mixture into the prepared cake tin. Bake for 40–45 minutes until risen and firm to the touch. Cool in the tin, then transfer to a wire tray to go cold.

Poppy seed cake

Serves 16
Each slice: 205 kcal/860 kJ, 10 g carbohydrate, 2 g fibre, 5 g protein, 14 g fat

115 g/4 oz poppy seeds
225 ml/8 fl oz skimmed milk
3 eggs, separated
115 g/4 oz fructose

150 ml/¼ pt sunflower oil, plus extra
  for greasing
225 g/8 oz wholemeal flour
2 tsp baking powder
pinch of salt

Heat the oven to 170°C/325°F/gas 3 and grease and line with greaseproof paper a 20 cm/8 inch cake tin. Put the poppy seeds and milk in a saucepan and bring to the boil. Remove from heat and leave to stand for 15 minutes.

In a mixing bowl, beat the egg yolks and fructose, then mix in the sunflower oil. Gradually add the dry ingredients, mixing well. Beat in the poppy seeds and milk.

In another bowl, whisk the egg whites with a pinch of salt until stiff, then carefully fold into the mixture.

Pour into the prepared cake tin and bake for about 1¼ hours, until risen and firm. Test by inserting a thin skewer into the centre of the cake. If it comes out clean, the cake is ready. Leave in the tin for 10 minutes then turn out on to a wire tray and leave to go cold.

Serve in slices.

Moist gingerbread   ★ ★

Serves 16

see photograph, page 33

Each serving: 172 kcal/722 kJ, 25 g carbohydrate, 3 g fibre, 4 g protein, 6 g fat

225 g/8 oz Pear and apple spread (see
  page 28)
300 ml/½ pt skimmed milk
10 ml/2 tsp lemon juice
115 g/4 oz white polyunsaturated
  vegetable fat, plus extra for greasing
4 tsp ground ginger

1 tsp ground cinnamon
350 g/12 oz wholemeal flour
50 g/2 oz sultanas
2 tsp bicarbonate of soda
30 ml/2 tbsp boiling water
25 g/1 oz flaked almonds

Heat the oven to 180°C/350°F/gas 4 and grease and line with greaseproof paper a 20 cm/8 inch square cake tin. Place the Pear and apple spread, skimmed milk, lemon juice, fat and spices in a saucepan and heat gently until melted.

Mix together the flour and sultanas in a large bowl. Mix together the bicarbonate of soda and boiling water and add to the flour with the skimmed milk mixture. Beat well until evenly mixed, then pour into the prepared cake tin. Sprinkle with the almonds and bake for about 45 minutes until risen and firm to the touch. Cool in the tin, then transfer to a wire tray until cold. Cut in squares to serve.

Plum and almond squares

Makes 9
Each square: 125 kcal/525 kJ, 10 g carbohydrate, 1 g fibre,
2 g protein, 7 g fat

50 g/2 oz polyunsaturated margarine,
  plus extra for greasing
50 g/2 oz fructose
1 egg
25 g/1 oz self-raising wholemeal
  flour
50 g/2 oz self-raising flour

25 g/1 oz ground almonds
few drops almond or vanilla essence
30–45 ml/2–3 tbsp skimmed milk
4–5 dessert plums, stoned, and cut in
  quarters
15 ml/1 tbsp flaked almonds

Heat the oven to 170°C/325°F/gas 3 and lightly grease and base-
line with greaseproof paper a 19 cm/7½ inch shallow square cake
tin. Put the margarine and fructose in a bowl and cream until pale
and fluffy. Beat in the egg then fold in the dry ingredients. Stir in
the almond or vanilla essence and sufficient milk to mix to a dropping consistency.

Spread the mixture over the base of the prepared tin. Top with
the quartered plums and sprinkle with the flaked almonds. Bake
for about 25 minutes until risen and firm to the touch. Cool in the
tin, then cut into squares.

FRUIT CAKES

Fruit cake loaf

Serves 12
Each serving: 288 kcal/1212 kJ, 40 g carbohydrate, 7 g fibre,
5 g protein, 14 g fat

90 ml/6 tbsp skimmed milk
550 g/1¼ lb mixed dried fruits (eg.
  currants, sultanas, raisins, dates,
  prunes, apricots, pears, apples),
  roughly chopped
225 g/8 oz wholemeal flour

2 tsp baking powder
pinch of salt
2 eggs
150 ml/¼ pt sunflower oil, plus extra
  for greasing

Pour the milk into a bowl. Add the fruit and leave to soak for at
least 30 minutes. Heat the oven to 170°C/325°F/gas 3 and grease
and line with greaseproof paper a 900 g/2 lb loaf tin.

Mix together the dry ingredients. Beat the eggs and oil together
in a bowl. Stir in the dry ingredients and fruit with any milk that
has not been absorbed.

Pour the mixture into the prepared loaf tin. Level the surface

---

Moist gingerbread (*top*, see page 31); Carrot and nut sponge (*centre left
and bottom*, see page 30); Plum and almond squares (*centre right*)

and bake for 1 hour. Reduce the heat to 150°C/300°F/gas 2 for about 30 minutes. Cover the cake with foil to prevent over brown-ing, if necessary. Test by inserting a thin skewer into the centre of the cake. If it comes out clean, the cake is cooked. Cool the cake in the tin, then transfer to a wire tray. Leave to go cold. Serve in slices.

Boiled fruit cake

Makes 16 slices
Each slice: 171 kcal/719 kJ, 25 g carbohydrate, 3 g fibre, 3 g protein, 5 g fat

300 ml/½ pt freshly made tea
175 g/6 oz currants
175 g/6 oz sultanas
15 ml/1 tbsp ground mixed spice
115 g/4 oz polyunsaturated
  margarine, plus extra for greasing

50 g/2 oz fructose
275 g/10 oz plain flour (preferably
  half wholemeal, half white)
2 tsp bicarbonate of soda
1 large egg, beaten

Place the tea, currants, sultanas, and spice in a saucepan and bring to the boil. Reduce the heat and simmer for 20 minutes. Stir in the margarine and leave to cool. Heat the oven to 170°C/325°F/gas 3 and grease and base-line with greaseproof paper a 20 cm/8 inch round cake tin.

Mix together the fructose, flour and bicarbonate of soda in a bowl. Add the fruit mixture and the egg and beat well until evenly mixed.

Spoon the mixture into the cake tin, level the surface and bake for about 1 hour until risen and firm to the touch. Cool in the tin then transfer to a wire tray and leave until completely cold.

Boil-in-pan fruit cake

Serves 10
Each serving: 148 kcal/621 kJ, 25 g carbohydrate, 3 g fibre, 4 g protein, 5 g fat

50 g/2 oz sultanas
50 g/2 oz raisins
50 g/2 oz currants
50 g/2 oz stoned dates, chopped
50 g/2 oz polyunsaturated margarine,
  plus extra for greasing
150 ml/¼ pt skimmed milk

1 egg, beaten
150 g/5 oz wholemeal flour
2 tsp baking powder
1 tsp ground cinnamon
1 tsp ground nutmeg
about 60 ml/4 tbsp skimmed milk

➡

Cornish saffron bread (*top*, see page 39); Chunky apple cake (*left*, see page 36); Cranberry and pecan teabread (*right*, see page 42)

Heat the oven to 180°C/350°F/gas 4 and grease and line with greaseproof paper an 18 cm/7 inch cake tin. Put the dried fruit, margarine and milk in a saucepan and bring to the boil. Reduce the heat and simmer gently, covered, for 10 minutes. Remove from the heat and allow to cool. Stir in the egg. Gradually mix in the flour, baking powder and spices and sufficient skimmed milk to give a dropping consistency.

Pour the mixture into the prepared cake tin and bake for about 30 minutes, until risen and firm to the touch. Cool on a wire tray.

Australian cake

Serves 16
Each serving: 232 kcal/974 kJ, 30 g carbohydrate, 8 g fibre, 6 g protein, 11 g fat

polyunsaturated margarine, for greasing
175 g/6 oz stoned dates
50 g/2 oz ready-to-eat stoned prunes
115 g/4 oz dried pears, quartered
175 g/6 oz dried peaches or apricots, quartered
grated rind and juice of 1 large orange
50 g/2 oz raisins
75 g/3 oz unblanched almonds

175 g/6 oz shelled walnuts
75 g/3 oz shelled hazelnuts
175 g/6 oz wholemeal flour
pinch of salt
1 tsp baking powder
3 eggs, beaten
1 tsp vanilla essence
30 ml/2 tbsp sugar-free apricot jam, sieved and warmed

Heat the oven to 150°C/300°F/gas 2 and grease and line with greaseproof paper a 900 g/2 lb loaf tin.

Mix all the fruit and nuts together. Mix the flour, salt and baking powder in a bowl. Add the fruit and nut mixture to the flour and toss well to coat evenly.

Add the eggs and vanilla essence and mix well. Spoon the mixture into the prepared tin and press down with the back of a spoon.

Bake for about 1 hour, until firm and golden. Test by inserting a skewer into the centre of the cake. If it comes out clean the cake is cooked. Cool in the tin. Turn out the cake and glaze the top with the apricot jam.

Chunky apple cake

Makes 12 slices   see photograph, page 34
Each slice: 185 kcal/776 kJ, 15 g carbohydrate, 3 g fibre, 3 g protein, 10 g fat

200 g/7 oz wholemeal flour
pinch of salt
½ tsp ground cinnamon
½ tsp bicarbonate of soda
100 ml/4 fl oz sunflower oil, plus extra
    for greasing
75 g/3 oz fructose

1 large egg
450 g/1 lb cooking apples, peeled,
    cored and thinly sliced
50 g/2 oz raisins
25 g/1 oz shelled walnuts, chopped
15 ml/1 tbsp skimmed milk or water

Heat the oven to 180°C/350°F/gas 4 and lightly grease a 24 cm/ 9½ inch ring tin (1.5 litre/2½ pt capacity). Mix together the flour, salt, cinnamon, and bicarbonate of soda.

Put the oil and fructose in a bowl and beat together until well mixed. Beat in the egg until the mixture is creamy. Stir in the flour mixture, apples, raisins, walnuts and milk or water. The mixture will be very 'chunky'.

Spoon the mixture into the prepared tin and bake for about 40 minutes or until risen and firm to the touch. Allow to cool in the tin, then turn out and serve either at room temperature or cold, cut in slices.

Orange, raisin and almond cake ☒ ☒

Makes 12 squares
Each serving: 136 kcal/573 kJ, 15 g carbohydrate, 1 g fibre, 6 g protein, 6 g fat

75 g/3 oz raisins, very finely chopped
15 ml/1 tbsp grated orange rind
50 g/2 oz polyunsaturated margarine,
    plus extra for greasing
40 g/1½ oz skimmed milk powder
1 egg
150 g/5 oz plain flour
1½ tsp baking powder
100 ml/4 fl oz orange juice

50 g/2 oz flaked or nibbed almonds,
    toasted

Sauce:
60 ml/4 tbsp fructose
60 ml/4 tbsp orange juice
12 fresh orange segments, to decorate
    (optional)

Heat the oven to 170°C/325°F/gas 3 and grease and base-line a 20 cm/8 inch square cake tin. Mix together the raisins and orange rind. Cream the margarine and skimmed milk powder in a bowl. Beat in the egg, and then the raisin mixture.

Sift the flour and baking powder together and fold in alternating with the orange juice. Fold in the almonds.

Spoon the mixture into the prepared cake tin, level the surface and bake for about 30 minutes until risen and firm to the touch.

To make the sauce, put the fructose and orange juice in a small saucepan and bring to a rapid boil. Prick the top of the cake with a fine skewer and pour the orange sauce over. Leave to go cold in the tin, then cut into squares to serve. Decorate with fresh orange segments if wished.

Orange and caraway towers   ☒

Makes 10
Each tower: 160 kcal/673 kJ, 15 g carbohydrate, 1 g fibre,
3 g protein, 9 g fat

75 g/3 oz polyunsaturated margarine,   *115 g/4 oz self-raising flour*
  plus extra for greasing   *(preferably half white, half*
50 g/2 oz fructose   *wholemeal)*
105 ml/7 tbsp sugar-free marmalade   *1–2 tsp caraway seeds*
grated rind of 1 orange   *about 45 ml/3 tbsp desiccated coconut*
2 eggs, beaten

Heat the oven to 170°C/325°F/gas 3 and lightly grease ten dariole
moulds. Put the margarine and fructose in a bowl and cream until
pale and fluffy. Beat in 30 ml/2 tbsp of the marmalade, and the
grated orange rind. Gradually beat in the eggs. Fold in the flour
and caraway seeds.

Divide the mixture between the prepared moulds. Bake for
about 20–25 minutes, until risen and firm to the touch. Remove
from the moulds and leave to cool on a wire tray. Warm and sieve
the remaining marmalade. Brush each cake with the marmalade
and roll in the desiccated coconut to cover evenly.

BREADS, TEABREADS AND PASTRIES

BREADS

Cornish saffron bread ☒ ☒ ☒

Makes 16 slices see photograph, page 34
Each slice: 138 kcal/579 kJ, 25 g carbohydrate, 2 g fibre,
3 g protein, 3 g fat

3 generous pinches of saffron strands *450 g/1 lb strong plain flour*
150 ml/¼ pt boiling water *1 tsp salt*
25 g/1 oz fresh yeast or 15 g/½ oz *50 g/2 oz polyunsaturated margarine,*
dried yeast *plus extra for greasing*
150 ml/¼ pt lukewarm skimmed *115 g/4 oz currants*
milk *finely grated rind of 1 lemon*
15 ml/1 tbsp fructose

Grease a 20 cm/8 inch round cake tin. Soak the saffron in the boiling water. Put the yeast in a small bowl with the milk and, if using dried yeast, stir in the fructose at this stage. Leave in a warm place for about 15 minutes until frothy.

Put the flour, salt (and fructose if using fresh yeast) in a large bowl. Rub in the margarine then add the currants and lemon rind. Mix to a soft dough with the saffron liquid and the yeast. Knead quickly on a lightly floured surface. Press the dough into the prepared cake tin, cover with oiled polythene and leave in a warm place for about 1 hour until the mixture has risen almost to the top of the tin. Heat the oven to 200°C/400°F/gas 6.

Bake for 30 minutes. Reduce the heat to 180°C/350°F/gas 4 and bake for a further 30 minutes. Turn out and cool on a wire tray. When cold, serve in slices spread lightly with polyunsaturated margarine or low-fat spread.

Cottage cheese bread

Makes 14 slices
Each slice: 94 kcal/394 kJ, 15 g carbohydrate, 1 g fibre, 4 g protein,
2 g fat

➡

175 g/6 oz cottage cheese, sieved
1 egg
grated rind of 1 orange
225 g/8 oz plain flour
2 tsp baking powder
pinch of salt

30 ml/2 tbsp finely chopped dried
figs
15 ml/1 tbsp raisins
15 ml/1 tbsp nibbed almonds
15 g/½ oz polyunsaturated margarine,
melted, plus extra for greasing

Heat the oven to 180°C/350°F/gas 4 and lightly grease a baking sheet. Put the cottage cheese, egg and orange rind in a bowl and beat well. Sift the dry ingredients into another bowl. Stir in the figs, raisins and almonds. Add the cheese mixture and mix to a firm dough.

Knead on a lightly floured surface. Shape to an oval about 20 cm/8 inch long and 2.5 cm/1 inch deep. Place the dough on the baking sheet and bake for 30 minutes. Reduce the heat to 170°C/325°F/gas 3 and cook for a further 20 minutes. Cover with foil if the bread becomes too brown.

Transfer the bread to a wire tray and brush the surface with margarine. Leave until completely cold. Serve cut in thin slices and spread thinly with polyunsaturated margarine or low-fat spread.

Soda bread   ☒ ☒ ☒

Serves 8
Each serving: 195 kcal/817 kJ, 40 g carbohydrate, 5 g fibre, 9 g protein, 1 g fat

polyunsaturated margarine, for greasing
450 g/1 lb wholemeal flour
½ tsp salt

½ tsp bicarbonate of soda
½ tsp cream of tartar
300 ml/½ pt buttermilk

Heat the oven to 220°C/425°F/gas 7 and lightly grease a baking sheet. Mix together all the dry ingredients in a bowl. Stir in the buttermilk and mix to a firm dough. Knead on a lightly floured surface. Shape into a round about 20 cm/8 inch in diameter. Place the dough on the baking sheet and cut a deep cross through the centre.

Bake for about 30 minutes, until risen and firm. To check if the bread is cooked through, tap the underside with your knuckles; it should sound hollow. Allow to cool on a wire tray. Serve fresh on the day of making.

Surprise hazelnut plait

Makes 16 slices
Each slice: 87 kcal/364 kJ, 10g carbohydrate, 1 g fibre, 2 g protein, 4 g fat

175 g/6 oz plain flour
25 g/1 oz wheatgerm
pinch of salt
40 g/1½ oz polyunsaturated margarine,
plus extra for greasing
15 g/½ oz fresh yeast, or 7 g/¼ oz
dried yeast
15 g/½ oz fructose

50 ml/2 fl oz lukewarm skimmed
milk
1 egg, beaten

Filling:
50 g/2 oz shelled hazelnuts, toasted
and chopped
25 g/1 oz raisins, roughly chopped
30 ml/2 tbsp sugar-free cherry jam
(or any other flavour)

Lightly grease a baking sheet. Sift the flour into a bowl. Stir in the wheatgerm and salt. Rub in 25 g/1 oz of the margarine. Mix the yeast with the fructose and milk in a cup and leave in a warm place for 15 minutes or until frothy.

Add the yeast mixture and egg to the flour and mix to a soft dough. Knead on a lightly floured surface for 5 minutes. Return the dough to the lightly oiled bowl, cover and leave in a warm place to rise for about 30–45 minutes or until doubled in size. Turn out the dough, knead for a minute or two then roll out to a rectangle 30 × 23 cm/12 × 9 inch and mark into three sections crossways.

Mix the ingredients for the filling and spread this over the central section of dough. Cut the two outside sections into 1.5 cm/¾ inch wide slanting strips. Fold in the top and bottom pieces of dough then fold in the strips alternately to give a plaited effect. Place the plait on the baking sheet. Cover and leave in a warm place for 15 minutes. Heat the oven to 220°C/425°F/gas 7. Bake for 10 minutes, reduce the heat to 190°C/375°F/gas 5 and bake for a further 10–15 minutes.

Brush with the remaining margarine to glaze. Cool on a wire tray. Serve fresh, cut in slices.

TEABREADS

Banana walnut teabread ☒ ☒

Makes 12 slices
Each slice: 180 kcal/756 kJ, 20 g carbohydrate, 2 g fibre, 3 g protein, 8 g fat

75 g/3 oz polyunsaturated margarine,
plus extra for greasing
75 g/3 oz fructose
1 egg, beaten
2 large ripe bananas, mashed

225 g/8 oz plain flour (preferably half
white, half wholemeal)
pinch of salt
15 ml/1 tbsp baking powder
50 g/2 oz shelled walnuts, chopped

➡

Heat the oven to 170°C/325°F/gas 3 and grease and base-line with greaseproof paper a 900 g/2 lb loaf tin. Put the margarine and fructose in a bowl and beat until pale and fluffy. Beat in the egg and bananas. Mix the flour, salt and baking powder together and fold in with the nuts. Spoon the mixture into the prepared loaf tin. Level the surface.

Bake for about 50 minutes until risen and firm to the touch. Cool in the tin, then transfer to a wire tray. Leave until completely cold. Serve in slices.

Apricot and almond teabread

Makes 12 slices
Each slice: 182 kcal/763 kJ, 20 g carbohydrate, 3 g fibre, 4 g protein, 8 g fat

75 g/3 oz polyunsaturated margarine,   *115 g/4 oz dried apricots, finely*
  plus extra for greasing   *chopped*
75 g/3 oz fructose   *50 g/2 oz nibbed almonds*
1 egg   *225 g/8 oz self-raising flour*
½ tsp almond essence   *100 ml/4 fl oz skimmed milk*

Heat the oven to 170°C/325°F/gas 3 and grease and base-line with greaseproof paper a 900 g/2 lb loaf tin. Put the margarine and fructose in a bowl and cream until pale and fluffy. Beat in the egg and almond essence. Fold in the apricots, almonds and flour, and mix to a soft dough with the milk.

Transfer the mixture to the prepared tin. Level the surface and bake for about 50 minutes until risen and firm. Cool in the tin, then transfer to a wire tray and leave until completely cold. Serve in slices, spread thinly with polyunsaturated margarine or low-fat spread.

Cranberry and pecan teabread

Makes 16 slices

see photograph, page 34
Each slice: 126 kcal/529 kJ, 10 g carbohydrate, 1 g fibre, 3 g protein, 5 g fat

225 g/8 oz plain flour (preferably half   *115 g/4 oz fructose*
  wholemeal, half white)   *115 g/4 oz cranberries*
2 tsp baking powder   *75 g/3 oz pecan nuts, chopped*
50 g/2 oz polyunsaturated margarine,   *1 egg, beaten*
  plus extra for greasing   *100 ml/4 fl oz skimmed milk*

Heat the oven to 170°C/325°F/gas 3 and grease and base-line with greaseproof paper a 900 g/2 lb loaf tin. Mix together the flour and baking powder in a bowl and rub in the margarine. Stir in the fructose, cranberries, two-thirds of the pecans and mix to a soft dough with the egg and milk. Transfer the mixture to the loaf tin and level the surface.

Sprinkle with the remaining pecans and bake for about 1 hour until risen and firm to the touch. Cool in the tin, then place on a wire tray. Serve in slices, spread thinly with polyunsaturated margarine or low-fat spread.

Spicy fruit teabread

Makes 12 slices
Each slice: 162 kcal/680 kJ, 35 g carbohydrate, 3 g fibre, 4 g protein, 1 g fat

polyunsaturated margarine, for greasing
115 g/4 oz each currants, sultanas and raisins
freshly made tea, to soak
175 g/6 oz wholemeal flour
175 g/6 oz self-raising flour

2 tsp baking powder
25 g/1 oz fructose
2 tsp ground mixed spice
¼ tsp aniseed
grated rind of ½ lemon
1 egg, beaten

Grease and base-line with greaseproof paper a 900 g/2 lb loaf tin. Put the dried fruit in a bowl and cover generously with freshly made tea. Cover and leave to soak for at least 12 hours. Heat the oven to 190°C/375°F/gas 5.

Drain the fruit, reserving 150 ml/¼ pt of the soaking liquid for this recipe*. Place all the ingredients in a bowl and beat well for 2 minutes until evenly mixed. Transfer the mixture into the prepared loaf tin. Level the surface and bake for about 1¼ hours, until risen and firm to the touch. To test if the loaf is cooked, insert a metal skewer into the centre; if it comes out clean the teabread is ready.

Allow to cool, then transfer to a wire tray. Leave until completely cold, then serve in slices, with a thin spreading of polyunsaturated margarine or low-fat spread.

* Do keep the rest of the liquid – chilled, it makes a delicious drink, either on its own, or with added soda.

PASTRIES

Basic wholemeal pastry

Makes 350 g/12 oz
Total recipe: 1382 kcal/5804 kJ, 135 g carbohydrate, 19 g fibre, 27 g protein, 85 g fat ➡

200 g/7 oz wholemeal flour
2 tsp baking powder

100 g/3½ oz polyunsaturated
　margarine
45 ml/3 tbsp cold water

Put the flour and baking powder in a bowl and rub in the margarine until the mixture resembles fine crumbs. Stir in the water and mix to a firm dough.
Chill and use as required.

Quick bread pastry dough　

Makes 350–400 g/12–14 oz
Total recipe: 769 kcal/3230 kJ, 150 g carbohydrate, 23 g fibre, 31 g protein, 10 g fat

225 g/8 oz plain flour (all wholemeal
　or half wholemeal and half white)
pinch of salt

5 ml/1 tsp polyunsaturated oil
1 tsp easy blend dried yeast
about 150 ml/¼ pt lukewarm water

Place the flour, salt, oil and dried yeast in a bowl. Mix in sufficient water to make a manageable dough. Knead on a lightly floured surface, then wrap in a polythene bag and refrigerate until required.

Raspberry profiteroles　

Makes 20　　　　　　　　　　**see photograph, page 51**
Each profiterole: 73 kcal/307 kJ, 10 g carbohydrate, 1 g fibre, 2 g protein, 4 g fat

150 ml/¼ pt water
50 g/2 oz polyunsaturated margarine
65 g/2½ oz wholemeal flour
pinch of salt
2 medium eggs, beaten

Filling:
1 quantity Pastry cream (see page 110)

Sauce:
150 ml/¼ pt orange or any other
　fruit juice
150 ml/¼ pt water
2 tsp arrowroot
50 g/2 oz chocolate, broken into
　pieces
20 fresh raspberries or cherries, to
　decorate

Heat the oven to 200°C/400°F/gas 6 and grease a baking tray.
　In a saucepan, heat the water and margarine, until the margarine melts and the water boils. Remove from the heat and beat in the flour and salt. Cool slightly and beat in the eggs. Continue beating until the mixture is smooth and glossy. Spoon or pipe twenty walnut-sized pieces of pastry on to the baking tray. Bake for 10 minutes, then reduce the temperature to 180°C/350°F/gas 4 and bake for a further 25 minutes. Make a slit in each bun to release the steam and ensure the pastry remains crisp.

To make the sauce, mix the orange juice and water together in a saucepan. Whisk in the arrowroot and cook, stirring, until thickened. Remove from the heat and whisk in the chocolate to make a smooth sauce.

To serve, pipe or spoon the cold Pastry cream into each choux bun. Decorate each with a fresh raspberry or cherry. Pour some sauce over the buns and serve the remainder separately.

Amanda's apple strudel

Serves 8
Each serving: 160 kcal/674 kJ, 20 g carbohydrate, 3 g fibre, 4 g protein, 7 g fat

115 g/4 oz wholemeal flour
15 ml/1 tbsp polyunsaturated oil
1 small egg, beaten
30–45 ml/2–3 tbsp water

Filling:
25 g/1 oz polyunsaturated margarine

25 g/1 oz toasted breadcrumbs
25 g/1 oz ground almonds
50 g/2 oz raisins
2 tsp ground cinnamon
450 g/1 lb cooking or dessert apples, peeled, cored and thinly sliced

Heat the oven to 200°C/400°F/gas 6.

Place the flour in a bowl, add the oil, egg and sufficient water to mix to a fairly soft, yet manageable dough. Roll out the dough on a lightly floured clean tea towel as thinly as possible to a large rectangle. Spread with a generous half of the margarine and then sprinkle with the breadcrumbs, ground almonds, raisins and cinnamon. Place the apple slices along the length of the pastry. Fold in the ends, then fold over first one side, and then the other to encase the apples completely. Press the edges well to seal.

Transfer the apple strudel to a non-stick baking tray, spread with the remaining margarine and bake for about 25 minutes until the apples are tender when tested with a skewer, and the pastry is crisp. Serve warm or cold cut in slices.

MUFFINS, SCONES AND BUNS

MUFFINS

English muffins ⊠ ⊠ ⊠

Makes 12   see photograph, page 51
Each muffin: 155 kcal/651 kJ, 25 g carbohydrate, 4 g fibre,
7 g protein, 3 g fat

450 g/1 lb wholemeal flour   *150 ml/¼ pt skimmed milk*
1 tsp salt   *150 ml/¼ pt water*
1 standard pkt easy blend dried   *1 egg, beaten*
  yeast   *30 ml/2 tbsp semolina*
25 g/1 oz polyunsaturated white fat,
  plus extra for greasing

Lightly grease a baking sheet. Mix together the flour, salt and
yeast in a bowl. Rub in the fat. Heat the milk and water together
until just tepid. Add to the flour with the egg and mix to a dough.
Turn out and knead well for at least 10 minutes. Alternatively,
work the dough in a food processor until smooth and elastic.
  Transfer to a lightly oiled bowl, cover with oiled polythene and
leave in a warm place for 45–50 minutes to rise until doubled
in size.
  On a lightly floured surface, roll out the dough to about 2 cm/
¾ inch thick. Stamp out twelve 7.5 cm/3 inch rounds, using the
trimmings and rerolling as necessary. Sprinkle the baking sheet
with half the semolina and arrange the muffins on it. Sprinkle the
remaining semolina over the muffins and cover with oiled
polythene. Leave in a warm place to rise for about 30 minutes.
Heat the oven to 200°C/400°F/gas 6 and bake for 15 minutes until
firm to the touch and hollow-sounding when tapped. Serve
warm.

Bran and raisin muffins

Makes 9
Each muffin: 106 kcal/444 kJ, 15 g carbohydrate, 2 g fibre,
3 g protein, 4 g fat

100 g/3½ oz oat germ and oat bran
40 g/1½ oz wholemeal flour
¼ tsp salt
1½ tsp baking powder
1 tsp mixed spice

50 g/2 oz raisins
1 egg, beaten
125 ml/4½ fl oz skimmed milk
25 ml/1½ tbsp sunflower oil, plus
   extra for greasing

Heat the oven to 200°C/400°F/gas 6 and lightly oil nine muffin tins. Mix all the dry ingredients together in a bowl. Add the raisins and mix well. Mix in the egg, milk and oil and leave to stand for a short while.

Pour the batter into the muffin tins; they should be only two-thirds full. Bake for about 15 minutes, or until golden and firm to the touch. Serve warm.

Blueberry muffins

Makes 12   see photograph, page 51
Each muffin: 90 kcal/378 kJ, 10 g carbohydrate, 1 g fibre, 3 g protein, 3 g fat

175 g/6 oz wholemeal flour
1½ tsp baking powder
25 g/1 oz fructose
1 egg, beaten

30 ml/2 tbsp sunflower oil, plus extra
   for greasing
60–75 ml/4–5 tbsp skimmed milk
115 g/4 oz blueberries, defrosted if
   frozen

Heat the oven to 200°C/400°F/gas 6 and lightly oil twelve patty tins. Put the flour, baking powder and fructose in a bowl and mix until evenly combined. Add the egg, sunflower oil and skimmed milk to give a soft dropping consistency. Stir in the blueberries.

Divide the mixture between the patty tins and bake for 10–15 minutes until risen and firm to the touch. Remove from the tins and serve warm.

SCONES

St Clement's scones

Makes 16
Each scone: 75 kcal/317 kJ, 10 g carbohydrate, 1 g fibre, 2 g protein, 3 g fat

115 g/4 oz self-raising flour
115 g/4 oz wholemeal flour
1½ tsp baking powder
50 g/2 oz polyunsaturated margarine,
   plus extra for greasing
25 g/1 oz fructose

grated rind of ½ orange
grated rind of ½ lemon
1 egg, beaten
45–60 ml/3–4 tbsp skimmed milk
   or buttermilk

Heat the oven to 220°C/425°F/gas 7 and lightly grease two baking sheets. In a bowl, mix together the flours and baking powder. Rub in the margarine until the mixture resembles fine crumbs. Add the fructose and the orange and lemon rind and mix well. Mix in the beaten egg and milk or buttermilk to make a firm dough.

On a lightly floured surface, roll out the dough to about 1–2 cm/ ½–¾ inch thickness and stamp out rounds with a 6 cm/2½ inch cutter. Arrange on the baking sheets and bake for about 10 minutes until golden and firm to the touch. Cool on a wire tray.

Note: Best served on the day of making.

Yoghurt scones   ⊠ ⊠ ⊠

Serves 8
Each scone: 104 kcal/438 kJ, 20 g carbohydrate, 2 g fibre, 4 g protein, 1 g fat

polyunsaturated margarine, for greasing
225 g/8 oz plain flour (preferably half wholemeal, half white)
½ tsp baking powder
¼ tsp bicarbonate of soda

pinch of salt
15 ml/1 tbsp fructose
150 g/5 oz low-fat plain yoghurt
45–60 ml/3–4 tbsp cold water

Heat the oven to 190°C/375°F/gas 5 and lightly grease a baking sheet. Mix together the dry ingredients in a bowl. Mix to a smooth dough with the yoghurt and water. Knead on a lightly floured surface. Pat into an 18 cm/7 inch round. Place on the baking sheet, and mark into eight sections with a sharp knife.

Bake for 25–30 minutes until risen and firm. Break into wedges and serve warm.

Sultana scone triangles   ⊠ ⊠ ⊠

Makes 8
Each triangle: 155 kcal/652 kJ, 25 g carbohydrate, 3 g fibre, 4 g protein, 3 g fat

225 g/8 oz self-raising flour (either all wholemeal or half wholemeal, half white)
25 g/1 oz polyunsaturated margarine

25 g/1 oz fructose
75 g/3 oz sultanas
150 ml/¼ pt buttermilk

Heat the oven to 200°C/400°F/gas 6. Put the flour in a bowl and rub in the margarine. Stir in the fructose and sultanas and mix to a

firm dough with the buttermilk. Knead quickly, on a lightly floured board. Shape to a 20 cm/8 inch circle. Cut out eight triangles and place on a non-stick baking sheet.
Bake for 10–15 minutes until risen and golden.

Note: Best served on day of making, preferably while still warm.

Lemon drop scones

Makes 12
Each scone: 53 kcal/222 kJ, 5 g carbohydrate, 1 g fibre, 2 g protein, 2 g fat

115 g/4 oz wholemeal flour
1 tsp baking powder
¼ tsp salt
15 g/½ oz polyunsaturated margarine,
  plus extra for greasing

25 g/1 oz fructose
1 egg, beaten
90–105 ml/6–7 tbsp skimmed milk
½ tsp grated lemon rind

In a mixing bowl, mix the flour, baking powder and salt together. Add the margarine, fructose and beaten egg. Mix together well and beat in enough milk to make a thick batter. Finally mix in the lemon rind.

Heat a lightly greased griddle. Drop spoonfuls of the batter on to the griddle and cook, turning once, for about 5 minutes, until golden on both sides.

Note: Drop scones are best eaten while still warm.

Singing hinny

Serves 10
Each serving: 169 kcal/710 kJ, 20 g carbohydrate, 2 g fibre, 3 g protein, 8 g fat

225 g/8 oz plain flour (preferably half
  wholemeal, half white)
pinch of salt

115 g/4 oz polyunsaturated
  margarine, plus extra for greasing
75 g/3 oz currants
60–75 ml/4–5 tbsp skimmed milk

Put the flour and salt in a bowl. Rub in the margarine until the mixture resembles fine crumbs. Stir in the currants and mix to a firm dough with the milk. Turn out and knead gently. Flatten to a 18–20 cm/7–8 inch round shape, about 1 cm/½ inch thick.

Heat and lightly grease a heavy-based frying pan or griddle. Place the hinny in the pan and prick all over with a fork. Cook over medium heat, turning once, for about 15 minutes. Serve warm, cut in wedges.

BUNS

Spice buns

Makes 12
Each bun: 198 kcal/832 kJ, 35 g carbohydrate, 4 g fibre, 6 g protein,
4 g fat

225 g/8 oz wholemeal flour	*50 g/2 oz sultanas*
225 g/8 oz strong plain flour	*50 g/2 oz stoned dates, chopped*
1 tsp salt	*¼ tsp grated orange rind*
1 pkt easy blend dried yeast	*¼ tsp grated lemon rind*
15 ml/1 tbsp ground mixed spice	*150 ml/¼ pt skimmed milk*
50 g/2 oz polyunsaturated white	*150 ml/¼ pt water*
vegetable fat, plus extra for greasing	*1 egg, beaten*
50 g/2 oz currants	

Lightly grease a baking sheet. Mix together the flours, salt, yeast, and mixed spice in a bowl. Rub in the fat. Add the currants, sultanas, dates and orange and lemon rind.

Warm the milk and water together and add to the dry ingredients with the beaten egg. Mix to a dough and knead for at least 10 minutes until smooth. Alternatively, omit the fruit and work the dough in a food processor, until smooth and elastic, then work in the fruit.

Place the dough in a lightly oiled bowl. Cover with oiled polythene and leave in a warm place for 45–60 minutes or until doubled in size. Punch down the dough, turn out on to a lightly floured surface and knead well. Shape into twelve buns. Place on the baking sheet and cover with oiled polythene. Leave to rise in a warm place for 20–30 minutes. Heat the oven to 200°C/400°F/gas 6. When well risen, bake the buns for about 15 minutes or until firm, and hollow sounding when tapped on the base. Cool on a wire tray.

Hot cross buns

Makes 12
Each bun: 255 kcal/1073 kJ, 40 g carbohydrate, 4 g fibre, 7 g protein, 8 g fat

To make Hot cross buns, follow the recipe for Spice buns (see above) and make half quantity of Basic wholemeal pastry (see page 43). Roll the pastry out on a lightly floured surface and cut twenty-four long thin strips. Shape the buns then press two strips

---

Raspberry profiteroles (*top*, see page 44); Blueberry muffins (*centre*, see page 47); English muffins (*bottom*, see page 46)

of pastry on to each bun to form a cross. Cover and leave to rise, then brush lightly with beaten egg.

Bake as described for Spice buns (see opposite).

BISCUITS

Oatcakes

Makes 24
Each oatcake: 50 kcal/210 kJ, 5 g carbohydrate, 1 g fibre, 1 g protein, 2 g fat

200 g/7 oz fine oatmeal
25 g/1 oz plain flour
½ tsp baking powder
¼ tsp salt

50 g/2 oz polyunsaturated margarine, melted
about 60 ml/4 tbsp boiling water

Heat the oven to 180°C/350°F/gas 4.

Mix the dry ingredients together in a bowl. Stir in the margarine and sufficient boiling water to mix to a firm dough.

Sprinkle the work surface with a little fine oatmeal and roll out the dough to about 3 mm/⅛ inch thickness. Stamp out twenty-four 6 cm/2¼ inch rounds, using the trimmings and rerolling as required. Arrange on a non-stick baking tray and bake for about 20 minutes. Cool on a wire tray.

Hazelnut cookies

Makes 18
Each cookie: 69 kcal/292 kJ, 5 g carbohydrate, 1 g fibre, 1 g protein, 4 g fat

75 g/3 oz polyunsaturated margarine, plus extra for greasing
50 g/2 oz dried apricots, minced
2 egg yolks

60 ml/4 tbsp unsweetened pineapple juice
25 g/1 oz hazelnuts, coarsely ground
140 g/4½ oz wholemeal flour

Heat the oven to 170°C/325°F/gas 3 and lightly grease two baking sheets. Put the margarine and apricots in a bowl and mix together. Beat in the egg yolks and pineapple juice. Add the nuts and flour and blend thoroughly. ➡

Cinnamon cherry sandwiches (*top*, see page 55); Hazelnut cookies (*centre left*); Chocolate chip crunchies (*centre right*, see page 55); Oatcakes, served with low-fat Cheddar cheese (*bottom*)

Place tablespoonfuls of the mixture on to the baking sheets and bake for about 25 minutes, until firm and golden. Cool on a wire tray.

Oat and nut cookies

Makes 18
Each cookie: 63 kcal/267 kJ, 5 g carbohydrate, 1 g fibre, 1 g protein, 4 g fat

75 g/3 oz rolled oats
25 g/1 oz desiccated coconut
50 g/2 oz ground almonds
25 g/1 oz polyunsaturated margarine

1 egg
30 ml/2 tbsp Pear and apple spread
- (see page 28)
½ tsp vanilla essence

Heat the oven to 170°C/325°F/gas 3.
Combine all the ingredients together in a bowl until evenly mixed. Shape into eighteen balls, then flatten each one on to a non-stick baking sheet. Bake for about 15 minutes until golden at the edges. Cool on a wire tray.

Peanut butter cookies

Makes 24
Each cookie: 77 kcal/323 kJ, 10 g carbohydrate, 1 g fibre, 2 g protein, 4 g fat

50 g/2 oz polyunsaturated margarine,
plus extra for greasing
50 g/2 oz peanut butter
115 g/4 oz raisins, minced
1 egg, beaten
60 ml/4 tbsp water

1 tsp vanilla essence
200 g/7 oz wholemeal flour
½ tsp baking powder
1 tsp bicarbonate of soda
a little skimmed milk
50 g/2 oz salted peanuts, chopped

Heat the oven to 170°C/325°F/gas 3 and lightly grease two baking sheets.
In a mixing bowl, mix together the margarine, peanut butter and raisins. Add the egg, water and vanilla essence, beating well. Then mix in the flour, baking powder and bicarbonate of soda, until well blended. Place spoonfuls on the baking sheets and flatten slightly. Brush with skimmed milk.
Divide the chopped peanuts between the cookies, pressing them well into each one. Bake for about 15 minutes until firm and golden. Cool on a wire tray.

Country crisp biscuits

Makes 18
Each biscuit: 66 kcal/276 kJ, 10 g carbohydrate, 1 g fibre, 2 g protein, 3 g fat

175 g/6 oz granary or wholemeal
  flour
40 g/1½ oz coarse oatmeal
1 tsp baking powder

pinch of salt
25 g/1 oz fructose
50 g/2 oz polyunsaturated margarine
30 ml/2 tbsp skimmed milk

Heat the oven to 180°C/350°F/gas 4.

Mix together the flour, oatmeal, baking powder, salt and fructose in a bowl. Rub in the margarine and mix to a firm dough with the milk. Turn out on to a lightly floured surface, and roll out as thinly as possible. Stamp out eighteen 7.5 cm/3 inch rounds, using the trimmings and rerolling as required.

Place on non-stick baking sheets and bake for 15–20 minutes until golden. Cool on a wire tray. Serve with cheese.

Cinnamon cherry sandwiches

Makes 12   see photograph, page 52
Each biscuit: 103 kcal/433 kJ, 10 g carbohydrate, 1 g fibre,
2 g protein, 4 g fat

50 g/2 oz polyunsaturated margarine
50 g/2 oz fructose
1 egg
½ tsp vanilla essence
1 tsp grated lemon rind
1 tsp ground cinnamon
115 g/4 oz plain flour
50 g/2 oz wholemeal flour

pinch of salt
90 ml/6 tbsp sugar-free cherry or
  raspberry jam

Topping:
1 tsp fructose
½ tsp ground cinnamon

Heat the oven to 190°C/375°F/gas 5. Put the margarine and fructose in a bowl and cream together until light and fluffy. Beat in the egg, vanilla essence and lemon rind. Mix in the remaining ingredients, except the jam, to make a dough.

Roll out the dough on a lightly floured surface and stamp out twenty-four 7.5 cm/3 inch fluted rounds, using the trimmings and rerolling as necessary. Place on two non-stick baking sheets. To make the topping, mix together the fructose and cinnamon and sprinkle over half the rounds.

Bake for about 10 minutes until lightly browned. Cool on a wire tray. Sandwich the biscuits together with a little of the jam, using all the cinnamon-sprinkled biscuits as the top of each sandwich.

Chocolate chip crunchies

Makes 12   see photograph, page 52
Each biscuit: 136 kcal/570 kJ, 10 g carbohydrate, 1 g fibre,
3 g protein, 7 g fat

75 g/3 oz polyunsaturated margarine,
  plus extra for greasing

50 g/2 oz fructose
few drops vanilla essence

1 egg, beaten   *1 tsp baking powder*
175 g/6 oz wholemeal flour   *50 g/2 oz chocolate chips*

Heat the oven to 170°C/325°F/gas 3 and lightly grease a baking tray.

In a mixing bowl, cream the margarine and fructose until light and fluffy. Add a few drops of vanilla essence and the egg. Beat well, then add the flour and baking powder. Continue beating until well mixed. Mix in the chocolate chips.

Put spoonfuls of the mixture on to the baking tray. Flatten out slightly then bake for about 20 minutes, until golden brown and firm to the touch. Cool on a wire tray.

Crispy crunchies

Makes 24
Each biscuit: 64 kcal/271 kJ, 5 g carbohydrate, neg fibre, 1 g protein, 4 g fat

115 g/4 oz polyunsaturated margarine   *50 g/2 oz wholemeal flour*
75 g/3 oz fructose   *75 g/3 oz self-raising flour*
few drops vanilla essence   *½ tsp baking powder*
1 egg yolk   *25 g/1 oz Special K or other cereal*

Heat the oven to 180°C/350°F/gas 4.

Put the margarine, fructose and vanilla essence in a bowl and cream until pale. Beat in the egg yolk, then work in the flours and baking powder. Form the mixture into twenty-four balls. Roll each one in Special K and place on a non-stick baking tray.

Bake for about 15 minutes until firm and golden. Cool on a wire tray.

Bumble bees

Makes 16   see photograph, page 62
Each biscuit: 69 kcal/289 kJ, 10 g carbohydrate, 1 g fibre, 1 g protein, 3 g fat

50 g/2 oz polyunsaturated margarine   *50 g/2 oz Special K, or Rice Krispies*
225 g/8 oz stoned dates, finely chopped *few drops vanilla essence*

Melt the margarine in a saucepan and leave to cool. Stir in the remaining ingredients and squeeze into sixteen 'barrels' with your fingers. Leave to go cold.

Walnutties

Makes 20
Each biscuit: 84 kcal/353 kJ, 5 g carbohydrate, 1 g fibre,
2 g protein, 5 g fat

50 g/2 oz polyunsaturated margarine,   *150 g/5 oz plain flour*
plus extra for greasing   *¼ tsp baking powder*
50 g/2 oz fructose   *50 g/2 oz shelled walnuts, finely*
1 egg   *chopped*
1 tsp vanilla essence   *20 walnut halves*

Heat the oven to 180°C/350°F/gas 4 and lightly grease two baking
sheets. Put the margarine and fructose in a bowl and cream
together until pale and fluffy. Beat in the egg and vanilla essence.
Sift the flour and baking powder over the creamed mixture and
fold in with the chopped walnuts.
 Drop the mixture in spoonfuls on to the baking sheets. Press a
walnut half on top of each one. Bake for about 20 minutes until
golden. Cool on a wire tray.

PIES AND CRUMBLES

Rhubarb and raspberry pie

Serves 8
Each serving: 209 kcal/879 kJ, 20 g carbohydrate, 5 g fibre,
4 g protein, 13 g fat

175 g/6 oz wholemeal flour   *30 ml/2 tbsp ground rice*
25 g/1 oz ground almonds   *225 g/8 oz rhubarb, trimmed and cut*
25 g/1 oz fructose (optional)   *in 2.5 cm/1 inch lengths*
115 g/4 oz polyunsaturated margarine   *225 g/8 oz raspberries*
1 egg yolk   *liquid sweetener, to taste*
30 ml/2 tbsp water

Heat the oven to 200°C/400°F/gas 6.
 Put the flour, ground almonds and fructose, if using, into a
bowl. Rub in the margarine until the mixture resembles fine

crumbs. Add the egg yolk and water and mix to a firm dough. Lightly knead the pastry. Roll out half the pastry on a lightly floured surface and line a 20 cm/8 inch pie dish. Sprinkle the base with 15 ml/1 tbsp ground rice.

Mix together the rhubarb, raspberries, liquid sweetener, to taste, and the remaining ground rice. Fill the pastry case with the fruit. Roll out the remaining pastry and top the pie. Trim and seal the edges well. Crimp the edges to give a decorative effect. Make a slash in the top of the pie.

Bake for 15 minutes. Reduce the heat to 180°C/350°F/gas 4 and bake for a further 25–30 minutes until the fruit is tender and the pastry crisp. Serve warm or cold.

Traditional apple crumble

Serves 4
Each serving: 362 kcal/1520 kJ, 45 g carbohydrate, 6 g fibre, 5 g protein, 16 g fat

Topping:
75 g/3 oz polyunsaturated margarine
175 g/6 oz wholemeal flour
40 g/1½ oz fructose

1 tsp ground coriander

450 g/1 lb cooking apples, peeled, cored and sliced thinly

Heat the oven to 200°C/400°F/gas 6.

Make the topping by rubbing the margarine into the flour, until the mixture resembles coarse breadcrumbs. Add the fructose and coriander and mix together. Set aside.

Put the prepared apples into a 900 ml/1½ pt ovenproof dish. Sprinkle the topping over the apples and bake for 25–30 minutes until the fruit is tender when tested with a skewer.

Crunchy topped crumble

Serves 4
Each serving: 298 kcal/1252 kJ, 25 g carbohydrate, 10 g fibre, 6 g protein, 21 g fat

Topping:
75 g/3 oz mixed flakes (e.g. wheat, oat or barley)
25 g/1 oz flaked almonds
25 g/1 oz desiccated coconut

25 g/1 oz sunflower seeds
50 g/2 oz polyunsaturated margarine

450 g/1 lb mixed fruit (e.g. apple, blackberries etc.)

Heat the oven to 200°C/400°F/gas 6. Mix together all the ingredients for the topping.

Put the prepared fruit into a 900 ml/1½ pt ovenproof dish. Cover the fruit with the topping mixture and bake for 25–30 minutes, until the fruit is tender when tested with a skewer.

Blackcurrant and apple crunch ☒ ☒

Serves 4   see photograph, page 61
Each serving: 282 kcal/1183 kJ, 35 g carbohydrate, 8 g fibre,
5 g protein, 12 g fat

225 g/8 oz cooking apples, peeled,   Topping:
  cored and thinly sliced   *115 g/4 oz sugar-free crunchy muesli*
225 g/8 oz blackcurrants   *50 g/2 oz wholemeal flour*
liquid sweetener, to taste   *50 g/2 oz polyunsaturated margarine*
                     25 g/1 oz fructose

Heat the oven to 180°C/350°F/gas 4. Mix together the apples,
blackcurrants and liquid sweetener and place in a 900 ml/1½ pt
ovenproof dish.
   Mix together the ingredients for the topping and sprinkle over
the fruit. Bake for about 30 minutes, or until the fruit is tender.
Serve warm with Pouring custard (see page 112).

Variation: Use 450 g/1 lb of any other fruit or mixture of fruits
prepared as necessary instead of blackcurrants and apples.

TARTS AND FLANS

TARTS

Baked cheese tart ☒

Serves 10
Each serving: 126 kcal/530 kJ, 10 g carbohydrate, 1 g fibre,
5 g protein, 8 g fat

½ quantity Basic wholemeal pastry   *50 g/2 oz mixed dried fruit*
  (see page 43)   *1 egg*
200 g/7 oz low-fat skimmed milk   *generous pinch of ground nutmeg*
  cheese, or cottage cheese   *½ tsp grated lemon rind*
25 g/1 oz polyunsaturated margarine   *ground cinnamon, to sprinkle*
25 g/1 oz fructose (optional)

Heat the oven to 190°C/375°F/gas 5.
  Roll out the pastry and use to line a 19 cm/7½ inch flan tin. Beat
together all the remaining ingredients, except the cinnamon, and
pour into the flan tin. Sprinkle the cinnamon over the top and
bake for about 25 minutes until just firm. Best served fresh, on the
day of making.

Rhubarb and banana tart

Serves 8
Each serving: (without topping) 120 kcal/506 kJ, 15 g carbohydrate, 3 g fibre, 2 g protein, 6 g fat
(With topping) 128 kcal/537 kJ, 15 g carbohydrate, 3 g fibre, 3 g
protein, 6 g fat

½ quantity Basic wholemeal pastry   *liquid sweetener, to taste*
(see page 43)
175 g/6 oz rhubarb, cut in 2.5 cm/   Optional topping:
  1 inch lengths   *1 egg white*
30 ml/2 tbsp water   *few drops fresh lemon juice*
2 tsp cornflour   *15 ml/1 tbsp fructose*
1 egg yolk   *½ tsp arrowroot*
2 ripe bananas, mashed

Heat the oven to 200°C/400°F/gas 6.
  Roll out the pastry and use to line a 19 cm/7½ inch flan tin. Chill
for 15–20 minutes. Then bake blind in the oven for 15 minutes.
Remove the baking beans and bake for a further 5 minutes. Leave
to go cold.
  Put the rhubarb with half the water in a saucepan and simmer
until just tender. Mix together the cornflour, remaining water and
egg yolk and stir into the rhubarb. Bring to the boil, stirring all the
time. Lower the heat and simmer until thickened. Leave to go
cold, stirring from time to time. When cold, add the bananas and
liquid sweetener, to taste. Spoon into the flan case and serve or
cover with the topping.
  To make optional topping, whisk the egg white until stiff, then
whisk in remaining ingredients. Pipe or spoon decoratively on top
of the flan and brown under the grill.

Lemon mallow tart

Serves 8
Each serving: 180 kcal/757 kJ, 10 g carbohydrate, 1 g fibre,
4 g protein, 12 g fat

½ quantity Basic wholemeal pastry   *finely grated rind and juice of 2*
(see page 43)   *lemons*
15 ml/1 tbsp cornflour   *40 g/1½ oz fructose*
100 ml/4 fl oz skimmed milk   *50 g/2 oz polyunsaturated margarine*
2 eggs, separated   *1 tsp arrowroot*

Rhubarb and banana tart (*top*); Blackcurrant and apple crunch (*bottom*,
see page 59)
Overleaf: Raspberry lattice flan (*top left*, see page 66); Pumpernickel
fool (*top right*, see page 104); Kiwi cups (*bottom left*, see page 91);
Bumble bees (*bottom right*, see page 56)

Heat the oven to 200°C/400°F/gas 6.

Roll out the pastry and use to line a 19 cm/7½ inch flan tin. Chill for 15–20 minutes. Then bake blind in the oven for 15 minutes. Remove the baking beans and return to the oven for a further 5 minutes. Leave to go cold.

In a saucepan, mix the cornflour with the milk and egg yolks. Stir in the lemon rind and juice, 15 g/½ oz of the fructose, and the margarine. Cook, stirring, over gentle heat until thickened. Remove from the heat and leave to go cold. Spread the lemon filling over the base of the pastry case.

Put the egg whites in a bowl and whisk until stiff. Whisk in the remaining fructose, and the arrowroot, a little at a time. Using a medium star nozzle, pipe the topping over the lemon filling. Brown under a medium grill until golden.

FLANS

Fruit flan

Serves 8

Each serving: 159 kcal/666 kJ, 15 g carbohydrate, 1 g fibre, 4 g protein, 6 g fat

½ quantity Basic wholemeal pastry (see page 43)
1 quantity Pastry cream with bay leaf flavouring (see page 110)

411 g/14½ oz can fruit salad, in fruit juice
½ tsp arrowroot

Heat the oven to 200°C/400°F/gas 6.

Roll out the pastry and use to line a 20 cm/8 inch flan tin. Chill for 15–20 minutes. Bake blind for 20 minutes. Leave to cool. When cold spread the base with the pastry cream. Drain the fruit salad, reserving the juice, and arrange the fruit over the pastry cream. Simmer the fruit juice in a saucepan until reduced by half. Whisk in the arrowroot and cook, stirring, until thickened. Cool slightly then brush over the fruit to glaze. Serve on the day of assembling.

Tropical fruit flan

Serves 8

Each serving: 125 kcal/527 kJ, 10 g carbohydrate, 1 g fibre, 7 g protein, 5 g fat

2 eggs, separated
30 ml/2 tbsp hot water

25 g/1 oz Pear and apple spread (see page 28)

➡

Tropical fruit flan

25 g/1 oz polyunsaturated margarine, plus extra for greasing
50 g/2 oz wholemeal flour
1 tsp baking powder

Filling:
grated rind of 1 lemon

225 g/8 oz cottage cheese, sieved
liquid sweetener, to taste
285 g/10½ oz can guava halves in fruit juice, drained, juice reserved
½ paw paw, peeled, seeded and sliced
1 kiwi fruit, peeled and sliced
½ tsp arrowroot

Heat the oven to 190°C/375°F/gas 5 and lightly grease a 20 cm/ 8 inch sponge flan tin. Put the egg yolks in a bowl and whisk until thick and creamy. Whisk in the hot water and pear and apple spread. Beat in the margarine, then the flour and baking powder.

In another bowl, whisk the egg whites until stiff, then fold into the flour mixture. Pour the mixture into the flan tin. Bake for 10 minutes until risen and firm to the touch. Cool on a wire tray.

To make the filling, mix the lemon rind with the cottage cheese and add liquid sweetener, to taste. Spread the mixture over the cooled flan, then arrange the fruit on top. Pour the reserved juice into a saucepan and boil until reduced by half. Whisk in the arrowroot and cook, stirring until thickened. Lightly brush the fruit and flan case with this mixture to glaze.

Raspberry lattice flan

Serves 10 see photograph, page 62
Each serving: 120 kcal/505 kJ, 15 g carbohydrate, 4 g fibre, 2 g protein, 6 g fat

½ quantity of Basic wholemeal pastry (see page 43)

liquid sweetener, to taste
25 g/1 oz polyunsaturated margarine

Filling:
1 tsp ground cinnamon
45 ml/3 tbsp semolina
411 g/14½ oz can raspberries in fruit juice

Topping:
1 egg white
15 ml/1 tbsp fructose
few drops lemon juice

Heat the oven to 200°C/400°F/gas 6.

Roll out the pastry and line a 19 cm/7½ inch flan tin. Chill for 15–20 minutes. Then bake blind for 15 minutes. Remove the baking beans and bake for a further 5 minutes. Leave to cool. Reduce the oven to 180°C/350°F/gas 4.

To make the filling, add the cinnamon and semolina to the raspberries in a saucepan, bring to boil and simmer for 5 minutes. Cool, then add liquid sweetener, to taste, and the margarine. Spread the raspberry mixture in the flan case.

To make the topping, whisk the egg white in a bowl until stiff. Whisk in the fructose a little at a time, and the lemon juice. Using a medium star nozzle, pipe the egg white in a lattice effect on top of the flan. Return to the oven for 7–8 minutes to brown. Serve just warm or cold.

Individual apple pizzas

Serves 4
Each pizza: 204 kcal/857 kJ, 40 g carbohydrate, 5 g fibre, 4 g protein, 5 g fat

½ quantity Quick bread pastry dough (see page 44)
4 tsp polyunsaturated margarine

2 large dessert apples, quartered, cored and thinly sliced
60 ml/4 tbsp sugar-free jam or marmalade, sieved

Heat the oven to 200°C/400°F/gas 6. Divide the dough into four equal portions. Knead each one lightly on a floured surface, then roll out to a round about 12–15 cm/5–6 inch in diameter. Spread each round with a little margarine and place on a non-stick baking sheet. Make a cartwheel of apple slices on top of each round of dough. Place 15 ml/1 tbsp of jam or marmalade in the centre of each cartwheel.
 Bake for about 20 minutes until the dough is crisp and the apple tender. Using a knife, spread the remaining jam or marmalade evenly over the apples to glaze. Serve warm.

Warm peach cartwheel

Serves 4
Each serving: 237 kcal/997 kJ, 40 g carbohydrate, 8 g fibre, 6 g protein, 6 g fat

115 g/4 oz wholemeal flour
1 tsp baking powder
½ tsp ground mixed spice
pinch of salt
25 g/1 oz polyunsaturated margarine, plus extra for greasing

411 g/14½ oz can peach slices in fruit juice, drained and juice reserved
30 ml/2 tbsp thick set plain yoghurt
ground cinnamon

Heat the oven to 200°C/400°F/gas 6 and lightly grease a baking tray. Mix together the flour, baking powder, mixed spice and salt in a bowl. Rub in the margarine. Stir in sufficient peach juice to mix to a firm dough. On a lightly floured surface, knead the dough gently and roll out to a 20 cm/8 inch round.
 Place the round on the baking tray. Crimp the edges, and arrange the peach slices in a pattern on top. Dot with yoghurt and sprinkle with cinnamon. Bake for 20–25 minutes. Transfer to a serving plate and serve warm in wedges.

Fruit and cheese slice

Makes 16 pieces
Each piece: 120 kcal/504 kJ, 15 g carbohydrate, 1 g fibre,
6 g protein, 3 g fat

15 g/½ oz fresh yeast (or 7 g/¼ oz
  dried yeast)
90 ml/6 tbsp lukewarm skimmed
  milk
15 ml/1 tbsp fructose
225 g/8 oz plain flour
pinch of salt
25 g/1 oz polyunsaturated margarine,
  plus extra for greasing
½ egg, beaten

Topping:
350 g/12 oz low-fat soft cheese
1½ eggs, beaten
15 ml/1 tbsp cornflour
grated rind of ½ lemon
25 g/1 oz fructose
2 × 411 g/14½ oz cans fruit
  cocktail in fruit juice, drained

Lightly grease a 33 × 23 cm/13 × 9 inch Swiss roll tin. Cream the
yeast with the milk and fructose in a small bowl and leave in a
warm place for about 15 minutes or until frothy.

Sift the flour and salt into a bowl and rub in the margarine. Add
the yeast mixture and beaten egg and mix to a dough. Knead the
dough on a lightly floured surface for 5 minutes. Return the
dough to a lightly oiled bowl, cover with oiled polythene, and
leave in a warm place for 40–60 minutes or until risen and doubled
in size. Heat the oven to 220°C/425°F/gas 7.

Meanwhile make the topping. Mix together the cheese, eggs,
cornflour, lemon rind and fructose.

Punch down the dough, knead lightly and roll out to fit the base
of the prepared tin. Spread the cheese mixture on top and sprinkle
with the fruit cocktail.

Bake for 20–25 minutes. Allow to cool slightly then cut in slices
and serve warm.

PUDDINGS

BAKED PUDDINGS

Strawberry Clafoutis

Serves 8
Each serving: 130 kcal/548 kJ, 10 g carbohydrate, 2 g fibre,
5 g protein, 6 g fat

40 g/1½ oz polyunsaturated margarine, plus extra for greasing
3 eggs
25 g/1 oz fructose
65 g/2½ oz wholemeal flour
pinch of salt
300 ml/½ pt skimmed milk
225 g/8 oz strawberries
30 ml/2 tbsp sugar-free strawberry jam, warmed and sieved

Heat the oven to 200°C/400°F/gas 6 and lightly grease a 23 cm/ 9 inch pottery flan dish. Put the eggs and fructose in a bowl and whisk together. Put the flour and salt in another bowl. Heat the milk and pour over the flour. Beat to a smooth mixture. Add the eggs and fructose and mix well. Pour the batter into the flan dish and arrange the strawberries on top.

Bake for about 30 minutes, until risen and golden. Brush the top of the clafoutis with the strawberry jam and serve at once.

David's date pudding ☒ ☒ ☒

Serves 6
Each serving: 208 kcal/872 kJ, 40 g carbohydrate, 7 g fibre, 6 g protein, 4 g fat

225 g/8 oz stoned dates
300 ml/½ pt water
grated rind of 1 orange
175 g/6 oz wholemeal breadcrumbs
300–350 ml/10–12 fl oz skimmed milk
25 g/1 oz desiccated coconut or long thread coconut
15 ml/1 tbsp sesame or sunflower seeds or 1 tsp poppy seeds

Heat the oven to 190°C/375°F/gas 5 and grease a 900 ml/1½ pt ovenproof serving dish. Place the dates in a saucepan with the water and orange rind. Simmer gently for about 15 minutes and mash to a soft purée. Spread the date purée over the base of the prepared dish and cover with the breadcrumbs. Pour over enough of the milk until it just starts to show through the crumbs. Sprinkle with the coconut and seeds and bake for about 45 minutes until the surface is crisp and golden. Serve warm.

Apple and almond pudding ☒

Serves 4
Each serving: 248 kcal/1041 kJ, 10 g carbohydrate, 4 g fibre, 7 g protein, 16 g fat

30 ml/2 tbsp polyunsaturated margarine, plus extra for greasing
30 ml/2 tbsp wholemeal flour
100 ml/4 fl oz skimmed milk
40 g/1½ oz fructose
2 eggs, separated
¼ tsp almond essence
50 g/2 oz blanched almonds, toasted and chopped
1 medium cooking apple (about 175 g/ 6 oz), peeled, cored and coarsely grated

➡

Heat the oven to 180°C/350°F/gas 4 and lightly grease a 750 ml/
1¼ pt ovenproof serving dish. Melt the margarine in a saucepan.
Stir in the flour and cook, stirring, for 1 minute. Stir in the milk
and bring to the boil. Remove from the heat. Stir in the fructose,
egg yolks and almond essence and beat well. Stir in the almonds
and grated apple. Stiffly whisk the egg whites and fold through the
almond apple mixture.
   Pour into the dish and bake for about 40 minutes until risen and
firm to the touch. Serve warm.

Sweet potato pudding

Serves 8
Each serving: 194 kcal/813 kJ, 20 g carbohydrate, 3 g fibre,
4 g protein, 10 g fat

2 medium sweet potatoes (about 500 g/
   1 lb 2 oz), peeled and roughly
   chopped
50 g/2 oz polyunsaturated margarine,
   plus extra for greasing
50 g/2 oz raisins, minced

50 g/2 oz sugar-free muesli
grated rind and juice of ½ orange
grated rind and juice of ½ lemon
¼ tsp ground nutmeg
2 eggs, separated
50 g/2 oz shelled walnuts, chopped

Lightly grease a 900 ml/1½ pt ovenproof serving dish. Steam or
boil the sweet potatoes for about 20 minutes until tender. Drain
well and mash.   Beat in all the remaining ingredients, except the
egg whites and walnuts.   Heat the oven to 170°C/325°F/gas 3.
   Stiffly whisk the egg whites and fold into the sweet potato
mixture. Spoon the mixture into the prepared dish. Sprinkle with
the chopped walnuts and bake for about 45 minutes until just firm
to the touch.

Baked chocolate provençale

Serves 4
Each serving: 160 kcal/674 kJ, 10 g carbohydrate, 1 g fibre,
7 g protein, 7 g fat

150 ml/¼ pt skimmed milk
15 ml/1 tbsp polyunsaturated
   margarine, plus extra for greasing
25 g/1 oz cocoa or carob powder

40 g/1½ oz fructose
2 eggs, separated
50 g/2 oz fresh wholemeal breadcrumbs

Heat the oven to 180°C/350°F/gas 4 and lightly grease a 750 ml/
1¼ pt ovenproof serving dish. Place the milk, margarine, cocoa or

carob powder and fructose in a saucepan. Heat gently and mix well. Remove from the heat and stir in the egg yolks and then the breadcrumbs. Leave to cool. Stiffly whisk the egg whites and fold into the chocolate mixture until evenly incorporated.

Transfer to the dish and bake for 25–30 minutes until risen and just firm to the touch. Serve warm with Pouring custard (see page 112).

Rice pudding

Serves 4
Each serving: 220 kcal/926 kJ, 30 g carbohydrate, 1 g fibre, 10 g protein, 7 g fat

*115 g/4 oz short-grain brown rice,
washed
900 ml/1½ pt skimmed milk
2 thinly pared twists of lemon or orange
rind*

*30 ml/2 tbsp polyunsaturated margarine
pinch of ground nutmeg
liquid sweetener, to taste*

Place the rice in a saucepan with the remaining ingredients, except the sweetener, and bring to the boil. Reduce the heat, cover the pan and simmer, stirring occasionally for about 1 hour, until tender. Remove the lemon or orange rind and add sweetener to taste. If you like, transfer to a heatproof serving dish and brown under the grill for several minutes.

Variation: About 10 minutes from the end of cooking time, stir in 50–75 g/2–3 oz chopped dates or figs, sultanas or raisins instead of the sweetener.

Poppy seed pudding

Serves 4
Each serving: (without jam) 122 kcal/513 kJ, 20 g carbohydrate, neg fibre, 8 g protein, 2 g fat
(With jam) 159 kcal/668 kJ, 30 g carbohydrate, 1 g fibre, 8 g protein, 2 g fat

*2 tsp poppy seeds
600 ml/1 pt skimmed milk
60 ml/4 tbsp ground rice
1 egg, beaten*

*liquid sweetener, to taste
squeeze of lemon juice
60 ml/4 tbsp sugar-free jam (optional)*

Place the poppy seeds in a heavy-based saucepan and cook over medium heat until they start to jump. Cool the pan slightly before adding the milk and stirring in the ground rice. Simmer, stirring frequently, for about 5 minutes, until thickened. Remove from the heat and beat in the egg. Stir in liquid sweetener and lemon juice to taste. Serve at once, with a spoonful of sugar-free jam, if wished.

STEAMED PUDDINGS

Steamed chocolate chip pudding

Serves 4
Each serving: 375 kcal/1574 kJ, 30 g carbohydrate, 3 g fibre,
8 g protein, 20 g fat

50 g/2 oz polyunsaturated margarine,   *pinch of salt*
   plus extra for greasing   *1 tsp baking powder*
50 g/2 oz fructose   *50 g/2 oz chocolate, cut in small*
2 eggs   *pieces*
115 g/4 oz wholemeal flour   *25 g/1 oz shelled walnuts, chopped*

Lightly grease a 900 ml/1½ pt pudding basin. Place all the
ingredients in a bowl and beat well with a wooden spoon for 1–2
minutes until evenly mixed. Transfer the mixture to the pudding
basin. Cover the basin with a piece of greased foil with a pleat in it
to allow for expansion. Tie down securely with string.
    Place the basin in a large saucepan. Pour in boiling water to
come at least half-way up the sides of the basin. Cover with a lid
and simmer gently for about 1¾ hours until the pudding has risen
and is firm to the touch. Add more boiling water if necessary.
Unmould the pudding on to a serving plate and serve at once with
Pouring custard (see page 112).

Cottage cheese and lemon dumplings with peach sauce

Serves 4
Each serving: 332 kcal/1393 kJ, 25 g carbohydrate, 7 g fibre,
10 g protein, 23 g fat

50 g/2 oz wholemeal breadcrumbs   *grated rind of ½ lemon*
25 g/1 oz polyunsaturated margarine   *50 g/2 oz ground almonds*
1 egg, beaten   *liquid sweetener, to taste*
50 g/2 oz cottage cheese   *50 g/2 oz desiccated coconut, toasted*
25 g/1 oz self-raising flour   *411 g/14½ oz can peach slices in fruit*
pinch of salt   *juice, puréed*

Cottage cheese and lemon dumplings with peach sauce (*top*); Steamed
chocolate chip pudding with Pouring custard (*bottom*); Pouring custard
(see page 112)

Put the first nine ingredients into a bowl and beat until well mixed. Shape the mixture into twelve even-sized ovals with two spoons. Arrange well apart in a steamer and steam for about 10 minutes until firm to the touch. Roll immediately in the toasted coconut and serve at once with the peach purée, either warm or cold.

BREAD PUDDINGS

Sunshine bread pudding ☒ ☒

Serves 6
Each serving: 180 kcal/756 kJ, 20 g carbohydrate, 3 g fibre, 7 g protein, 8 g fat

40 g/1½ oz polyunsaturated margarine
4 large thin slices wholemeal bread
60 ml/4 tbsp sugar-free orange
  marmalade

450 ml/¾ pt skimmed milk
2 eggs, beaten
½ tsp vanilla essence
freshly ground nutmeg

Use 15 g/½ oz margarine to grease a 1.1 litre/2 pt ovenproof serving dish. Spread the bread evenly with the remaining margarine and then with the marmalade. Cut each slice into four triangles. Arrange the bread in the dish.

Heat the milk to just below boiling point. Beat in the eggs and vanilla and pour over the bread slices. Leave to soak for 30 minutes. Heat the oven to 180°C/350°F/gas 4.

Place the dish in a roasting tin. Pour in enough hot water to come half-way up the sides of the dish. Sprinkle with nutmeg and bake for about 45 minutes until set and crisp on top.

Spiced bread pudding ☒ ☒

Serves 4
Each serving: 355 kcal/1490 kJ, 45 g carbohydrate, 7 g fibre, 12 g protein, 15 g fat

225 g/8 oz wholemeal bread, cubed
450 ml/¾ pt skimmed milk
50 g/2 oz polyunsaturated margarine,
  plus extra for greasing
50 g/2 oz each sultanas and currants
1 tsp ground ginger

1 tsp ground cinnamon
½ tsp ground nutmeg
2 eggs, beaten
a little powdered sweetener to
  sprinkle (optional)

➡

Summer pudding (see page 77)

Heat the oven to 180°C/350°F/gas 4 and grease a 28 × 18 cm/ 11 × 7 inch ovenproof baking dish. Place the bread in a bowl. Bring the milk to the boil, stir in the margarine and pour over the bread. Leave to soak for 15 minutes. Add the remaining ingredients and beat well. Transfer to the baking dish and bake for 45 minutes until golden, and firm to the touch.

Serve cut in squares and sprinkled with sweetener, if wished. Any leftover pudding may be eaten cold.

MOULDED PUDDINGS

Savarin

Serves 8
Each serving: 152 kcal/639 kJ, 20 g carbohydrate, 2 g fibre, 6 g protein, 7 g fat

15 g/½ oz fresh yeast
45 ml/3 tbsp lukewarm skimmed
  milk
50 g/2 oz wholemeal flour
50 g/2 oz strong plain flour
pinch of salt
15 g/½ oz fructose
2 medium-sized eggs, beaten

50 g/2 oz polyunsaturated margarine,
  plus extra for greasing
411 g/14½ oz can pears (or other
  fruit), in fruit juice
30 ml/2 tbsp sugar-free apricot jam,
  warmed and sieved
115 g/4 oz fresh strawberries, hulled
  and halved

Lightly grease an 18 cm/7 inch ring mould. Crumble the yeast into a bowl. Stir in the milk and dissolve the yeast. Add 25 g/1 oz of the wholemeal flour and blend together until smooth. Leave in a warm place for about 20 minutes or until frothy.

Stir in the remaining flours, salt, fructose, eggs and margarine. Beat together for 3–4 minutes. Spoon the mixture into the prepared mould. Cover with greased polythene and return to a warm place for 30–40 minutes or until the dough has almost risen to the top of the mould. Heat the oven to 200°C/400°F/gas 6. When risen remove the polythene and bake for 15–20 minutes until the savarin is golden brown in colour.

Invert the savarin on to a wire tray. Cool slightly and prick all over with a fine skewer. Drain the pears. Put the juice in a saucepan and boil until reduced to 100 ml/4 fl oz. Pour the reduced juice over the savarin. Brush the jam over the surface of the savarin. Fill the centre of the savarin with the drained pears and the strawberries, reserving about twelve to fourteen strawberries for decoration.

Apricot rice ring with raspberry sauce

Serves 4 ☒ ☒ ☒

Each serving: 218 kcal/918 kJ, 45 g carbohydrate, 14 g fibre, 7 g protein, 2 g fat

75 g/3 oz pudding rice
300 ml/½ pt skimmed milk
411 g/14½ oz can apricot halves in
* fruit juice, drained and juice reserved*
15 ml/1 tbsp custard powder
1 egg yolk

liquid sweetener, to taste

Sauce:
225 g/8 oz raspberries
30 ml/2 tbsp sugar-free raspberry jam,
* or liquid sweetener to taste*

Wash the rice well. Put the rice and milk in a saucepan and simmer for about 25 minutes until the rice is tender and all the milk has been absorbed.

Mix the apricot juice with the custard powder in a saucepan and simmer gently until thickened. Immediately stir in the rice and egg yolk. Beat well, then leave to cool. Stir in the sweetener to taste. Press the rice mixture into a 450 ml/¾ pt mould or spoon into four individual serving dishes. Chill until required.

To make the sauce, purée the raspberries then pass them through a sieve to remove the seeds. Stir in the jam or sweetener to taste. Unmould the rice ring on to a serving plate and decorate with the apricot halves. Spoon a little raspberry sauce over the top and hand the remaining sauce separately.

Summer pudding

☒ ☒ ☒

Serves 8   see photograph, page 74

Each serving: 80 kcal/336 kJ, 15 g carbohydrate, 6 g fibre, 3 g protein, 1 g fat

8 large slices wholemeal bread,
* crusts removed*
700 g/1½ lb mixed summer fruits (e.g.
* raspberries, strawberries,*
* redcurrants and cherries)*

60 ml/4 tbsp low-calorie lemon and
* lime drink*
1 tsp gelatine
liquid sweetener, to taste
reserve 1 or 2 pieces of fruit for garnish

Use about 7 slices of the bread to line the base and sides of a 1.1 litre/2 pt pudding basin.

In a large saucepan, combine the fruits and lemon and lime drink. Simmer gently for about 5 minutes until tender. Spoon the fruit into the prepared basin, reserving the juice in the pan. Sprinkle the gelatine over the juice in the pan and heat gently to dissolve. Cool, then add the liquid sweetener to taste. Pour the juice over the fruit in the basin. Cover the fruit with the remaining bread, cutting to shape as required. Cover loosely with cling film or greaseproof paper and weight down. Chill for several hours, or overnight. Unmould on to a serving dish and decorate with reserved fruit.

CHEESECAKES AND PANCAKES

CHEESECAKES

Quick pineapple cheesecake

Serves 8   **see photograph, page 84**
Each serving: 195 kcal/820 kJ, 15 g carbohydrate, 3 g fibre, 12 g protein, 9 g fat

Base:
50 g/2 oz desiccated coconut
50 g/2 oz wheatgerm
25 g/1 oz polyunsaturated margarine, melted
30 ml/2 tbsp sugar-free apricot jam, or marmalade

Filling:
225 g/8 oz can pineapple in fruit juice

450 g/1 lb cottage cheese
25 g/1 oz fructose
½ tsp lemon juice
15 g/½ oz gelatine (or 15 ml/ 1 tbsp)

Topping:
225 g/8 oz can pineapple in fruit juice
1 tsp arrowroot
scented geranium leaves, to decorate

Line the base and sides of an 18 cm/7 inch loose-bottomed cake tin with greaseproof paper.

Toast the coconut and wheatgerm in a non-stick frying pan over a gentle heat. Mix together with the margarine and jam or marmalade and press into the base of the prepared tin. Put into the refrigerator to chill.

To make the filling, drain the pineapple and reserve the juice. Place the pineapple, cheese, fructose and lemon juice in a food processor, or blender, and purée until smooth. Dissolve the gelatine in the reserved juice, then stir into the cheese mixture. Spoon the mixture into the cake tin and return to the refrigerator until set.

To make the topping, drain the pineapple and put the juice into a saucepan. Stir in the arrowroot and bring to the boil, stirring. Cook gently until thickened. Remove from the heat and allow the glaze to cool. Transfer the cheesecake to a serving dish. Arrange the pineapple pieces around the outside edge and brush with glaze; then spoon the remaining glaze into the centre. Chill until required. Decorate with scented geranium leaves and serve.

Orange cheesecake   ⊠

Serves 6
Each serving: 204 kcal/858 kJ, 20 g carbohydrate, 2 g fibre, 10 g protein, 10 g fat

Base:
50 g/2 oz toasted breadcrumbs
25 g/1 oz shelled walnuts or hazelnuts, finely chopped
25 g/1 oz chocolate
25 g/1 oz polyunsaturated margarine, plus extra for greasing

Topping:
225 g/8 oz low-fat soft cheese
100 ml/4 fl oz low-fat plain yoghurt
2 eggs, separated
25 g/1 oz flour
50 g/2 oz fructose
2 large oranges

Mix together the breadcrumbs and walnuts or hazelnuts. In a saucepan, melt the chocolate and margarine and stir into the breadcrumb mixture. Press on to the base of a lightly greased 20 cm/8 inch spring release cake tin and chill.

To make the topping, beat together the cheese, yoghurt, egg yolks, flour, fructose and grated rind of 1 orange. Gently whisk the egg whites and fold into the mixture. Pour the mixture into the cake tin and bake at 180°C/350°F/gas 4 for 25–30 minutes until set. Leave to go cold, then remove from the tin.

Peel the rind and pith from the oranges and carefully remove each orange segment. Use to decorate the cheesecake.

Gooseberry cheesecake

Serves 12
Each serving: 113 kcal/473 kJ, 10 g carbohydrate, 1 g fibre, 6 g protein, 6 g fat

Base:
115 g/4 oz digestive biscuits, crushed
50 g/2 oz polyunsaturated margarine, plus extra for greasing

Topping:
30 ml/2 tbsp custard powder
300 ml/½ pt skimmed milk

225 g/8 oz gooseberries, topped and tailed
30 ml/2 tbsp water
15 g/½ oz gelatine (or 15 ml/ 1 tbsp)
225 g/8 oz cottage cheese, sieved
liquid sweetener, to taste
1 egg white

Mix together the digestive biscuits and margarine and press into the base of an 18 cm/7 inch lightly greased loose-bottomed (or spring release) cake tin, and chill.

To make the topping, mix the custard powder with a little milk in a bowl. Heat the remaining milk, and pour on to the custard powder. Return to the pan and cook, stirring, until thickened. Cool, stirring occasionally to prevent a skin forming.

Put the gooseberries with the water in a saucepan and cook over gentle heat until soft. Drain the gooseberries and pour the juice into a small saucepan. Sprinkle the gelatine on top of the gooseberry juice and dissolve over gentle heat.

Combine the custard, gooseberries, gelatine and cottage cheese, and beat well. Cool, then add liquid sweetener to taste.

Whisk the egg white until stiff then fold into the gooseberry mixture. Pour the mixture on to the chilled base. Return to the refrigerator until set. Unmould on to a serving plate.

Strawberry cheesecake

Serves 12
Each serving: 83 kcal/349 kJ, 10 g carbohydrate, 1 g fibre, 3 g protein, 4 g fat

Base:
50 g/2 oz wholemeal flour
50 g/2 oz rolled oats
50 g/2 oz polyunsaturated margarine, plus extra for greasing
15 ml/1 tbsp sugar-free strawberry jam

Topping:
225 g/8 oz strawberries

15 g/½ oz gelatine (or 15 ml/ 1 tbsp)
45 ml/3 tbsp water
175 g/6 oz curd cheese
150 ml/¼ pt Greek strained yoghurt
liquid sweetener, to taste
1 egg white
12 strawberries, to decorate

Heat the oven to 200°C/400°F/gas 6.

Mix together the flour, oats, margarine and jam and press into the bottom of an 18 cm/7 inch lightly greased loose-bottomed cake tin. Bake for 10 minutes. Set aside to cool while preparing the filling.

Crush the strawberries in a bowl. Put the gelatine and water in a small saucepan and dissolve over very low heat. Add the gelatine to the crushed strawberries and mix in the curd cheese, yoghurt and liquid sweetener, to taste.

Whisk the egg white until stiff and fold into the strawberry mixture. Pour the mixture over the prepared base. Chill for several hours, then remove from the tin and decorate with the reserved strawberries.

PANCAKES

Pancake batter

Makes 8

Each pancake without filling: 64 kcal/270 kJ, 10 g carbohydrate, 1 g fibre, 4 g protein, 2 g fat

50 g/2 oz wholemeal flour
pinch of salt (optional)
1 egg
65 ml/2½ fl oz soda water

65 ml/2½ fl oz skimmed milk
a little polyunsaturated oil, for
  frying (optional)

In a bowl, whisk together the flour, salt, egg, soda water and milk to make a smooth batter. Alternatively, process all the ingredients in a blender or food processor.

To cook the pancakes, heat a non-stick 15 cm/6 inch frying pan until very hot. Pour in 15 ml/1 tbsp of the batter and tilt the pan so that the batter runs all over the base. After about 30 seconds when the bottom of the pancake is cooked, flip it over and cook the other side. Transfer the pancake to a plate and cook the other pancakes in the same manner. If you are using a traditional frying pan, brush the base lightly with oil before frying each pancake.

Spicy apple filling

Serves 8

Each serving: 126 kcal/529 kJ, 10 g carbohydrate, 1 g fibre, 8 g protein, 5 g fat

225 g/8 oz cottage cheese
50 g/2 oz raisins
1 dessert apple, cored and finely
  chopped

1 tsp ground cinnamon
30 ml/2 tbsp polyunsaturated margarine
  or low-fat spread
ground cinnamon, to sprinkle

Method (as for Tropical fruit filling).

Tropical fruit filling

Serves 8

Each serving: 121 kcal/508 kJ, 15 g carbohydrate, 3 g fibre, 4 g protein, 6 g fat

115 g/4 oz cottage cheese
115 g/4 oz grapes, halved or quartered
  and pips removed
25 g/1 oz toasted desiccated coconut

2 bananas, chopped
30 ml/2 tbsp polyunsaturated margarine
  or low-fat spread

Combine all the ingredients for the filling of your choice and divide between the pancakes. Fold the edges in to make neat envelopes. Place the stuffed pancakes in a heatproof serving dish in a single layer. Spread with a little polyunsaturated margarine or low-fat spread and sprinkle with cinnamon, if using. Heat through under a medium grill for 5–10 minutes until crisp on the surface. Serve at once.

Banana pancakes

Makes 8
Each pancake: 67 kcal/283 kJ, 10 g carbohydrate, 1 g fibre, 2 g protein, 3 g fat

45 ml/3 tbsp wholemeal flour
pinch of salt
90 ml/6 tbsp skimmed milk
1 egg

2 ripe bananas, chopped
25 g/1 oz polyunsaturated margarine
sugar-free jam, to serve

Place the flour, salt, skimmed milk, egg and bananas in a food processor or blender and process until smooth.

Heat a little of the margarine in a 15 cm/6 inch frying pan. When very hot, pour in one-eighth of the batter. Tilt the pan so that the batter covers the base. Cook for about 30 seconds or until the bottom is golden. Turn the pancake over and cook the other side. Transfer to a plate and keep warm while you make the remaining pancakes. Serve at once with a little jam.

Raspberry omelette

Serves 2
Each serving: 178 kcal/746 kJ, 10 g carbohydrate, 5 g fibre, 9 g protein, 12 g fat

25 g/1 oz wholemeal breadcrumbs
60 ml/4 tbsp skimmed milk
2 eggs
½ tsp vanilla essence

liquid sweetener, equivalent to 2 tsp
sugar
115 g/4 oz fresh raspberries
15 g/½ oz polyunsaturated margarine

Mix the breadcrumbs and milk together in a bowl and leave to soak for 10 minutes. Add the eggs, vanilla essence and liquid sweetener. Purée three-quarters of the raspberries and add liquid sweetener to taste, if wished. Melt the margarine in a small omelette pan. Pour on the egg mixture and, using a fork, work the mixture into the centre as it begins to cook. When almost cooked, place under the grill and brown quickly.

Transfer to a serving plate and pour over the raspberry purée. Decorate with reserved raspberries.

Sesame crusted pear (*top*, see page 88); Banana pancakes (*bottom*)
Overleaf: Watermelon and ginger jelly (*top left*, see page 99); Chocolate fruit cups (*top right*, see page 90); Blueberry islands (*bottom left*, see page 98); Quick pineapple cheesecake (*bottom right*, see page 78)

Prune fritters   ☒   ☒

Serves 4
Each fritter: 298 kcal/1251 kJ, 40 g carbohydrate, 9 g fibre,
4 g protein, 14 g fat

16 prunes, pitted, soaked overnight in
  boiling water
sunflower oil, for deep-frying
powdered sweetener, to sprinkle
  (optional)

40 g/1½ oz wholemeal flour
15 g/½ oz semolina
1 tsp baking powder
1 tsp ground cinnamon
150 ml/¼ pt water or skimmed milk

Batter:
50 g/2 oz rice flour

Simmer the prunes in the soaking water for 15 minutes. Leave to
go cold in the liquid. Drain and dry on absorbent kitchen paper
towels (reserve the juice for another recipe).
    Put all the dry ingredients for the batter in a bowl. Beat in
sufficient water or milk to make a coating batter. Heat the oil in a
deep frying pan to 180°C/350°F. If you do not have a ther-
mometer, drop in a cube of stale bread; if it browns within 1
minute the oil is hot enough. Dip the prunes in the batter, coating
them well then deep-fry until crisp and golden. Drain on absorbent kitchen paper towels and serve at once. Sprinkle with
powdered sweetener, if wished.

Note: Other bite-size pieces of prepared fresh fruit may be used,
such as apple, pineapple or banana.

BAKED, FRESH AND DRIED FRUIT

BAKED FRUIT

Baked apples   ☒   ☒   ☒

Serves 4
Each serving: 91 kcal/381 kJ, 20 g carbohydrate, 3 g fibre,
1 g protein, 1 g fat

4 dessert apples
115 g/4 oz Spiced mincemeat (see

page 116)
60 ml/4 tbsp water

Winter fruit medley (*top*, see page 91); Guava custards with toasted
coconut (*bottom*, see page 101)

Heat the oven to 200°C/400°F/gas 6.

Wash and core the apples and make a cut round each circumference. Stand the apples in a baking dish and fill the centres with the mincemeat. Add the water to the dish and bake for 25 minutes, until the apples are tender.

Baked pears

Serves 4

Each serving: 128 kcal/538 kJ, 20 g carbohydrate, 3 g fibre, 1 g protein, 3 g fat

4 fairly ripe Conference pears, peeled,   *30 ml/2 tbsp flaked almonds*
* halved and cored*   *150 ml/¼ pt unsweetened white grape*
60 ml/4 tbsp sugar-free apricot jam   * juice or medium-dry white wine*

Heat the oven to 180°C/350°F/gas 4. Place the pears in a baking dish and spoon a little jam into the centre of each. Sprinkle with flaked almonds. Pour the grape juice or white wine carefully round the pears and bake for about 20 minutes, until just tender. Serve warm.

Baked apples in pastry cases

Serves 4

Each serving: 455 kcal/1909 kJ, 55 g carbohydrate, 8 g fibre, 9 g protein, 24 g fat

4 dessert apples, washed and cored   *1 quantity Basic wholemeal pastry*
115 g/4 oz Spiced mincemeat (see   * (see page 43)*
* page 116)*   *1 egg, beaten*

Heat the oven to 200°C/400°F/gas 6. Make a cut round the circumference of each apple. Fill the centres with the mincemeat.

Cut the pastry into four. Roll out each piece of pastry thinly and stamp out a circle large enough to enclose each apple. Place an apple in the middle of the pastry circle. Lift and work the pastry to enclose the apple completely. Put the apples on a non-stick baking sheet. Use any trimmings to cut out some leaves and stalks for decoration; brush the pastry-covered apples with water and press the pastry leaves and stalks on to the apples.

Brush with beaten egg and bake for 25 minutes, until the apples are tender and the pastry crisp and golden.

Sesame crusted pears

Serves 4   see photograph, page 83

Each pear: 257 kcal/1079 kJ, 30 g carbohydrate, 7 g fibre, 8 g protein, 11 g fat

4 medium-sized ripe dessert pears (eg. Williams)	½ quantity Quick bread dough (see page 44)
½ quantity Almond paste (see page 111)	1 egg white, beaten
	30 ml/2 tbsp sesame seeds

Heat the oven to 200°C/400°F/gas 6. Wash and dry the pears, leaving the stalks in place. Cut a small slice from the base of each pear so that they stand upright. Using a small sharp knife, remove the core starting from the base so that the pears remain whole.

Roll the almond paste into four 'barrel' shapes, and press one piece into each pear to fill the cored area. Divide the dough into four equal pieces. Roll each piece on a lightly floured surface until it is large enough to enclose a pear completely. Brush the edges of the dough with egg white and carefully encase each pear, pressing the edges together to seal. Reserve trimmings to make eight leaves. Put the pears on a non-stick baking sheet. Brush the outside of each covered pear with egg white and sprinkle with the sesame seeds. Attach leaves and bake for about 30 minutes until golden and tender when tested with a skewer.

Sautéed bananas

Serves 4

Each serving: 169 kcal/710 kJ, 25 g carbohydrate, 4 g fibre, 2 g protein, 7 g fat

25 g/1 oz polyunsaturated margarine	¼ tsp ground cinnamon
4 bananas, thickly sliced	30 ml/2 tbsp toasted chopped
120 ml/8 tbsp orange juice	hazelnuts or pistachio nuts
25 g/1 oz raisins or sultanas	

Melt the margarine in a large non-stick frying pan and sauté the bananas until golden on both sides. Add the orange juice, raisins or sultanas and cinnamon. Cover and simmer for 5 minutes until the bananas are just tender. Sprinkle with chopped nuts and serve at once.

FRESH FRUIT

Fresh fruit platter

One of the nicest desserts to serve when on a diet is a fresh fruit platter – a beautiful arrangement of prepared fruit served on a plate (glass or china), rather than a fruit salad served in a syrup.

The choice of fruits is very important– choose interesting fruits with a good combination of flavours and colours, or keep to one colour for a dramatic effect. For example, for a platter of yellow fruit, choose mango, paw paw, oranges, apricots and yellow plums. To prepare the mango, hold it upright on a plate. Using a sharp knife, and keeping it as close to the central stone as possible, cut downwards to slice off one 'cheek'. Then turn the fruit around and slice off the other 'cheek'. Cut the cheeks in half, then peel. Cube or cut the flesh in strips. Cut the flesh off the stone. Prepare paw paws as you would melon.

Other combinations may include pineapple, strawberries and banana (banana discolours easily so add it at the last moment or dip in lemon juice); or for an all red mixture, use raspberries, strawberries, red plums and cherries.

A little soft cheese or a scoop of sorbet may be added as well. Serve lightly chilled, but not ice-cold.

Sarah's summer salad

Serves 4
Each serving: 27 kcal/114 kJ, 5 g carbohydrate, 3 g fibre, 1 g protein, 0 g fat

½ medium-sized melon
115 g/4 oz strawberries or raspberries
1 kiwi fruit, peeled and sliced

Remove the seeds from the melon and, using a melon baller, make as many melon balls as possible. Using a spoon, scrape out the remaining melon and purée in a blender. Hull the strawberries and slice or halve, or pick over the raspberries, if using. Place the melon balls and purée in a serving dish. Carefully stir in the strawberries, or raspberries, and the kiwi fruit. Chill until required.

Chocolate fruit cups

Serves 4   see photograph, page 84
Each serving: 102 kcal/427 kJ, 15 g carbohydrate, 3 g fibre, 1 g protein, 4 g fat

50 g/2 oz chocolate   *grapefruit, orange, pomegranate,*
200 g/7 oz prepared fresh fruit,   *passion fruit)*
  chopped (e.g. plums, mango, dates,

Break the chocolate into pieces and put in a heatproof bowl. Place the bowl over a pan of very gently simmering water. Stir to melt the chocolate. When melted, brush the chocolate on the inside of four paper cake cases. Apply a thin layer, then place the cases in the freezer for about 10 minutes. Brush the remaining chocolate inside the cases and return to the freezer.

When set hard, remove the paper and divide the prepared fruit between the chocolate cups. Serve immediately.

Kiwi cups ☒ ☒ ☒

Serves 4 see photograph, page 62
Each serving: 75 kcal/316 kJ, 10 g carbohydrate, 3 g fibre,
5 g protein, 1 g fat

4 large firm kiwi fruit *4 small strawberries, to decorate*
½ quantity Lemon delight (see
  (page 105)

Cut a small slice from the stalk end of each kiwi fruit so that they
stand upright. Using an apple corer, carefully remove the centre
core, and discard. Using a small sharp knife or potato peeler, peel
the fruit.
  Stand each fruit on a small plate. Spoon the Lemon delight mixture into the centre of each kiwi. Decorate with slices of fresh
strawberry and serve at once.

Note: The kiwi fruit and Lemon delight can be prepared well in
advance. However they should be filled just before serving.

Redcurrant and raspberry kissel ☒ ☒ ☒

Serves 6

Each serving: 110 kcal/460 kJ, 10 g carbohydrate, 6 g fibre,
1 g protein, 0 g fat

225 g/8 oz fresh or frozen raspberries *115 g/4 oz fructose*
225 g/8 oz fresh or frozen redcurrants *50 g/2 oz ground rice*
300 ml/½ pt water

Pick over the fruits and place in a saucepan with the water. If
frozen, bring slowly to the boil.
  Mix the fructose and ground rice in a bowl. Pour on a little of
the liquid from the saucepan, stirring all the time. Return this
mixture to the saucepan and simmer gently, stirring frequently,
for 5 minutes until thickened. Pour into individual ramekin dishes
or small glasses and chill until required. If wished, decorate with a
sprig of redcurrants and two fresh raspberries.

DRIED FRUIT

Winter fruit medley ☒ ☒ ☒

Serves 8 see photograph, page 86
Each serving: 108 kcal/453 kJ, 25 g carbohydrate, 7 g fibre,
2 g protein, 0 g fat ➡

250 g/9 oz pkt dried fruit salad (eg.   *1 large orange*
  apricots, apples, prunes, etc)   *1 large pink grapefruit*
75 g/3 oz dried figs   *1 pomegranate*
600 ml/1 pt boiling water

Place the dried fruit salad and figs in a large bowl. Cover with the water and leave to soak for at least 12 hours.

Cut the larger pieces of fruit in half, if wished, then transfer the fruits and their juice to a saucepan and bring to the boil. Reduce the heat, cover and simmer for 15 minutes. Remove from the heat and leave to cool.

Peel the orange and grapefruit with a serrated knife, ensuring that all the white pith is removed. Carefully remove each segment from the central membrane. Squeeze the juice from the skin and peelings and add this to the fruit salad with the orange and grapefruit segments.

Cut the pomegranate in half and, using a teaspoon, scoop out all the seeds and juice. Add to the fruit salad. Mix well, then transfer to a serving dish. Chill until required, but do not serve too cold.

Pecan-stuffed prunes

Serves 4
Each serving: 170 kcal/714 kJ, 25 g carbohydrate, 10 g fibre, 3 g protein, 8 g fat

24 large prunes (about 225 g/8 oz)   *squeeze of lemon juice*
300 ml/½ pt freshly made weak tea   *few drops of rosewater (optional)*
24 pecan or walnut halves

Wash the prunes and place in a shallow dish or roasting pan. Pour the tea over to cover the prunes completely and leave to soak for at least 12 hours. Drain the prunes, reserving the liquid. Using a small sharp knife, remove the prune stones and replace with the pecan or walnut halves. Arrange in a serving dish. Add the lemon juice and rosewater, if using, to the reserved tea liquid and carefully pour over the prunes.

If you prefer a softer texture, place the prunes in a saucepan, cover with the tea, lemon juice and rosewater and simmer gently for 5 minutes. Transfer to a serving dish and leave to go cold.

Winter compote

Serves 4
Each serving: 77 kcal/323 kJ, 20 g carbohydrate, 3 g fibre, 1 g protein, 0 g fat

150 ml/¼ pt unsweetened apple juice
2 dessert apples, preferably Cox's
orange pippins, cored and thinly
sliced

25 g/1 oz stoned dates, finely chopped
2 oranges

Place the apple juice and apple slices in a wide, shallow saucepan and bring to the boil. Reduce the heat, cover and simmer for about 5 minutes, until just tender. Remove from the heat and sprinkle the dates over the apple slices. Cover and leave to one side while you prepare the oranges.

Using a sharp knife, peel the oranges, removing all the white pith with the rind. Carefully remove each segment of orange from the inner membrane. Squeeze the juice from the peelings and the membrane and reserve. Transfer the apples to a serving dish and carefully stir in the orange segments and juice. Cover and chill until required.

SOUFFLÉS, PUFFLES AND MERINGUES

SOUFFLÉS

Chestnut and chocolate soufflé   ☒

Serves 4
Each serving: 182 kcal/765 kJ, 15 g carbohydrate, 2 g fibre, 5 g protein, 7 g fat

15 ml/1 tbsp cornflour
100 ml/4 fl oz skimmed milk
15 ml/1 tbsp polyunsaturated
margarine, plus extra for greasing
2 eggs, separated

15 ml/1 tbsp cocoa powder
50 g/2 oz fructose
½ tsp vanilla essence
115 g/4 oz unsweetened chestnut
purée

Heat the oven to 190°C/375°F/gas 5 and grease a 750 ml/1¼ pt soufflé dish.

In a cup, mix the cornflour to a smooth paste with a little of the milk. Bring the remaining milk to the boil in a saucepan. Stir in the cornflour and margarine and simmer, stirring all the time, until thickened. Beat in the egg yolks, cocoa powder, fructose, vanilla essence and chestnut purée until smooth.

Put the egg whites in a bowl and whisk until stiff. Fold the egg whites into the chestnut mixture. Pour the mixture into the soufflé dish. Place the dish in a roasting tin. Pour in enough hot water to come half-way up the sides of the dish. Bake for 40–45 minutes until risen and firm when shaken slightly. Serve at once.

Chilled pineapple and banana soufflé

Serves 10   ★ ★ ★
Each serving: 83 kcal/349 kJ, 5 g carbohydrate, 1 g fibre, 6 g protein, 1 g fat

polyunsaturated margarine, for greasing
300 ml/½ pt pineapple purée, made from about 225–350 g/8–12 oz prepared fresh pineapple
2 bananas, mashed
225 g/8 oz skimmed-milk soft cheese
liquid sweetener, to taste

45 ml/3 tbsp water
15 g/½ oz gelatine (or 15 ml/ 1 tbsp)
3 egg whites
tiny pieces of fresh pineapple and lemon balm or scented geranium leaves, to decorate

Prepare a 750 ml/1¼ pt soufflé dish by tying a double layer of greased greaseproof paper around the dish so that it extends about 7.5 cm/3 inches above the top to form a collar.

Simmer the pineapple purée for about 5 minutes in a covered saucepan. Cool. Mix in the bananas, cheese and liquid sweetener, to taste. Put the water in a saucepan, sprinkle the gelatine on top and heat gently until it dissolves. Stir the gelatine into the pineapple mixture.

Whisk the egg whites until stiff and carefully fold into the pineapple mixture. Pour the mixture into the prepared soufflé dish and leave to set for at least 4 hours in the refrigerator.

Carefully remove the paper collar and decorate with small pieces of fresh pineapple and lemon balm or scented geranium leaves.

PUFFLES

Lemon and pineapple puffle

Serves 4
Each serving: 135 kcal/568 kJ, 10 g carbohydrate, neg fibre, 4 g protein, 6 g fat

15 ml/1 tbsp cornflour
100 ml/4 fl oz skimmed milk
15 ml/1 tbsp polyunsaturated

margarine, plus extra for greasing
2 eggs, separated
40 g/1½ oz fructose

Sparkling grape jellies (*top*, see page 100); Chilled pineapple and banana soufflé (*bottom*)

115 g/4 oz pineapple, finely chopped   *1 tsp grated lemon rind*
(use either fresh or canned in fruit   *30 ml/2 tbsp lemon juice*
juice, drained)

Heat the oven to 190°C/375°F/gas 5 and lightly grease a 750 ml/
1¼ pt ovenproof serving dish.
Mix the cornflour to a smooth paste with a little of the milk.
Bring the remaining milk to the boil in a saucepan. Stir in the
cornflour and margarine and simmer, stirring all the time, until
thickened. Beat in the egg yolks, fructose, chopped pineapple,
lemon rind and half the lemon juice.
Stiffly whisk the egg whites in a bowl. Whisk in the remaining
lemon juice. Fold the egg whites into the custard until evenly
combined, then transfer the mixture to the prepared serving dish.
Place the dish in a roasting tin. Pour boiling water into the tin to
come half-way up the sides of the dish. Bake for about 40 minutes
until risen and firm when shaken slightly. Serve at once.

Prune puffle

Serves 4
Each serving: 58 kcal/244 kJ, 10 g carbohydrate, 4 g fibre,
3 g protein, 0 g fat

polyunsaturated margarine, for greasing   *⅛ tsp salt*
115 g/4 oz ready-to-eat pitted prunes   *⅛ tsp cream of tartar*
150 ml/¼ pt water   *15 ml/1 tbsp fructose*
3 egg whites   *1 tsp grated lemon rind*

Heat the oven to 180°C/350°F/gas 4 and lightly grease a 750 ml/
1¼ pt ovenproof serving dish. Put the prunes and water in a
saucepan and bring slowly to the boil. Reduce the heat, cover and
simmer for 15 minutes. Leave to cool. Purée the prunes and their
liquid in a blender.
In a bowl, whisk the egg whites until stiff with the salt and cream
of tartar. Whisk in the fructose and lemon rind. Fold the prune
purée into the egg whites and transfer to the ovenproof dish. Bake
for 25–30 minutes until risen and golden. Serve at once.

MERINGUES
Floating islands

Serves 4
Each serving: 126 kcal/530 kJ, 10 g carbohydrate, neg fibre,
8 g protein, 4 g fat

Tangy lime mousse (*top left*, see page 103); Mango water ice (*top right*,
see page 107); Fruit and cheese dessert with Carob sauce (*bottom*, see
page 106)

2 eggs, separated
25 g/1 oz fructose
few drops fresh lemon juice
600 ml/1 pt skimmed milk
pared rind of ½ orange

2 tsp cornflour
liquid sweetener, to taste
2 tsp long-thread coconut, toasted
orange peel, cut into julienne strips,
  to decorate

Put the egg whites in a bowl and whisk until stiff. Whisk in the fructose a spoonful at a time, and then the lemon juice.

Heat the milk in a large shallow pan to simmering point. Using two teaspoons, shape the egg white mixture into sixteen ovals. Drop them into the milk – you may need to do this in two batches – and poach gently for 5 minutes, until firm and puffed. Lift out with a slotted spoon and drain well on kitchen paper towels.

Add the orange rind to the milk. Mix the cornflour and egg yolks together in a bowl and stir in a little hot milk. Pour back into the pan and cook, stirring, until the custard has just thickened. Strain and add liquid sweetener, to taste. Pour the custard on to four individual plates. Arrange four 'islands' on top of each plate of custard and sprinkle with coconut and orange strips.

Variation: Add 50 g/2 oz broken pieces of chocolate to the strained custard. Stir until melted.

Blueberry islands ⊞ ⊞ ⊞

Serves 4   see photograph, page 84
Each serving: 69 kcal/291 kJ, 15 g carbohydrate, neg fibre, 2 g protein, 0 g fat

2 egg whites
25 g/1 oz fructose
few drops fresh lemon juice
225 g/8 oz blueberries or other soft
  fruit

60 ml/4 tbsp low-calorie orange squash
2 tsp arrowroot
150 ml/¼ pt water
orange peel, cut into julienne strips,
  to decorate

Put the egg whites in a bowl and whisk until stiff. Whisk in the fructose a little at a time, and then the lemon juice.

Bring a large shallow pan of water to simmering point. Add a few drops of lemon juice. Using two teaspoons, shape the egg white into sixteen ovals. Drop them into the simmering water and poach them gently for 5 minutes until firm and puffed – you may have to do this in two batches. Lift out with a slotted spoon and drain well on kitchen paper towels. Combine the blueberries, orange squash, arrowroot and water in a saucepan. Heat gently, stirring all the time, until thickened. Spoon the blueberry sauce on to four individual plates. Arrange the 'islands' on top of the sauce and decorate with strips of orange peel.

JELLIES, CUSTARDS AND MOUSSES

JELLIES

Watermelon and ginger jelly ⊞ ☒ ☒ ☒

Serves 6
Each serving: 24 kcal/102 kJ, 5 g carbohydrate, 1 g fibre, 2 g protein, 0 g fat

see photograph, page 84

450 g/1 lb prepared watermelon, puréed
½ tsp ground ginger
25 g/1 oz stem ginger, finely chopped (optional)

15 ml/1 tbsp lemon juice
15 g/½ oz gelatine (or 15 ml/ 1 tbsp)
45 ml/3 tbsp low-calorie lemon squash

Combine the first four ingredients in a bowl. In a small saucepan, dissolve the gelatine in the lemon squash over gentle heat. Remove from the heat and stir in a little of the melon purée. Stir into the watermelon purée in a bowl. Pour the mixture into a 600 ml/1 pt dampened jelly mould and chill until set. Unmould on to a dampened plate.

Note: Any other well-flavoured melon may be used instead of watermelon.

Coconut milk jelly with tropical fruits ☒ ☒ ☒

Serves 4
Each serving: 88 kcal/370 kJ, 15 g carbohydrate, 2 g fibre, 5 g protein, 2 g fat

300 ml/½ pt skimmed milk
2 thin strips lemon rind
15 g/½ oz desiccated coconut
liquid sweetener, to taste
1½ tsp gelatine

30 ml/2 tbsp water
225 g/8 oz prepared tropical fruits (eg. pineapple, mango, kiwi, papaya, banana)

Place the milk and lemon rind in a saucepan and heat very gently for 10 minutes to infuse. Add the coconut and liquid sweetener and leave to cool.

➡

In a small saucepan, dissolve the gelatine in the water. Remove the lemon rind from the milk and add the milk to the gelatine. Stir well and chill until the mixture has the consistency of unbeaten egg white. Stir well and pour into a 300 ml/½ pt dampened ring mould. Chill until set.

Unmould the jelly on to a flat dish and fill the centre with a mixture of tropical fruits.

Sparkling grape jellies   ☒ ☒

Serves 6 see photograph, page 95
Each serving: 87 kcal/364 kJ, 20 g carbohydrate, neg fibre, 3 g protein, neg fat

600 ml/1 pt unsweetened white grape juice
15 g/½ oz gelatine (or 15 ml/ 1 tbsp)

115 g/4 oz small green or black grapes, halved and pips removed
90 ml/6 tbsp low-fat plain yoghurt, sweetened to taste with fructose or liquid sweetener (optional)

Pour about one quarter of the grape juice into a small saucepan. Sprinkle with the gelatine and dissolve over very gentle heat. Stir in the remaining grape juice and chill until the mixture has the consistency of unbeaten egg white. Stir in the grapes and divide the jelly between four tall glasses. Chill until set.

If wished, top with a little sweetened yoghurt.

Fresh coffee jellies

Serves 4   ⊞ ☒ ☒ ☒
Each serving: without cream – 26 kcal/109 kJ, 5 g carbohydrate, 0 g fibre, 2 g protein, 1 g fat   ☒
With cream – 62 kcal/260 kJ, 5 g carbohydrate, 0 g fibre, 3 g protein, 4 g fat

450 ml/¾ pt freshly made black coffee
liquid sweetener, to taste

2 tsp gelatine
60 ml/4 tbsp single cream (optional)
4 tsp grated chocolate

Combine the coffee and liquid sweetener, to taste Place 60 ml/ 4 tbsp of the coffee in a saucepan and sprinkle with gelatine. Heat very gently to dissolve. Add the remaining coffee and transfer to individual glasses. Chill until set.

If wished, pour 15 ml/1 tbsp cream on top of each and sprinkle with grated chocolate just before serving.

Apricot and grape jelly   ☒ ☒ ☒

Serves 4
Each serving: 115 kcal/481 kJ, 25 g carbohydrate, 8 g fibre, 5 g protein, 0 g fat

115 g/4 oz dried apricots
300 ml/½ pt unsweetened white
  grape juice
15 g/½ oz gelatine (or 15 ml/
  1 tbsp)

To decorate:
grapes, small mint, balm or scented
  geranium leaves

Wash the apricots and place in a bowl, cover generously with boiling water and leave to soak for at least 12 hours. Drain the apricots, reserving 150 ml/¼ pt of soaking liquid. Purée the apricots and reserved liquid in a food processor or blender. Mix in all but 45 ml/3 tbsp of the grape juice. Place the remaining grape juice in a small saucepan and sprinkle with the gelatine. Dissolve over gentle heat and stir into the apricot mixture. Pour the mixture into a 600 ml/1 pt dampened jelly mould and chill until set.

Unmould and decorate with black or green grapes and the leaves.

Note: This jelly can also be used for spreading on bread, scones, or as a cake filling.

Cranberry and pineapple shimmer

★ ★ ★

Serves 4
Each serving: 61 kcal/256 kJ, 15 g carbohydrate, 1 g fibre, 2 g protein, 0 g fat

300 ml/½ pt pineapple or apple juice
  (or a mixture of the two)
115 g/4 oz cranberries
1½ tsp gelatine

115 g/4 oz prepared pineapple,
  finely chopped
liquid sweetener, to taste

Place half the juice in a saucepan. Add the cranberries and simmer gently until they burst and are softened.

In another saucepan, sprinkle the gelatine over the remaining juice and heat gently until dissolved. Mix all the ingredients together and transfer to four individual glasses. Chill until set.

CUSTARDS

Guava custards with toasted coconut ⊠ ⊠

Serves 4
see photograph, page 86
Each serving: 113 kcal/476 kJ, 10 g carbohydrate, 4 g fibre, 5 g protein, 6 g fat

285 g/10½ oz can guavas in fruit
  juice
150 ml/¼ pt skimmed milk
2 eggs

½ tsp vanilla essence
¼ tsp ground ginger
¼ tsp ground nutmeg
60 ml/4 tbsp long-thread coconut,
  toasted

➡

Heat the oven to 170°C/325°F/gas 3.

Purée the contents of the can of guavas in a blender with the skimmed milk, eggs, vanilla essence, ginger and nutmeg. Pour the mixture into four individual ramekin dishes of about 250 ml/ 8 fl oz capacity.

Place the dishes in a roasting tin. Pour boiling water into the tin to come half-way up the sides of the dishes. Bake for 45 minutes until lightly set. Remove the custards from the tin. Sprinkle each one with a little coconut and serve just warm.

Mango and coconut custards

Serves 4

Each serving: 75 kcal/315 kJ, 10 g carbohydrate, 1 g fibre, 2 g protein, 3 g fat

225 ml/8 fl oz thick coconut milk   *liquid sweetener, to taste (optional)*
(from a can)   *175 g/6 oz chopped fresh mango*
2 tsp cornflour   *ground nutmeg*
2 egg yolks

Heat the oven to 170°C/325°F/gas 3.

Whisk the coconut milk, cornflour and egg yolks together. Add liquid sweetener to taste, if using. Spoon the prepared mango into four individual ramekin dishes. Pour the custard carefully on top and sprinkle with ground nutmeg.

Place the dishes in a roasting tin. Pour boiling water into the tin to come three-quarters of the way up the sides of the dishes. Bake for about 30 minutes until just firm. Remove from the oven. When cool, chill in the refrigerator.

Variation: Pour the custard mixture into four ramekin dishes and sprinkle with cinnamon. Bake as above. Chill and just before serving, top each one with 50 g/2 oz fresh raspberries.

MOUSSES

Strawberry cheese mousse

Serves 10

Each serving: 72 kcal/304 kJ, 5 g carbohydrate, neg fibre, 9 g protein, 1 g fat

411 g/14½ oz can strawberries in   *1 quantity Low-calorie topping (see*
fruit juice   *page 111)*
225 g/8 oz skimmed-milk soft cheese   *fresh strawberries or raspberries, to*
15 g/½ oz gelatine (or 15 ml/   *decorate*
1 tbsp)

Drain the strawberries. Reserve the juice and roughly mash the fruit in a bowl. Stir in the cheese.

Put the gelatine and the reserved fruit juice in a small saucepan and heat gently to dissolve. Stir into the strawberry cheese mixture. Fold the Low-calorie topping into the strawberry mixture. Pour the mixture into a serving dish. Chill until set. Decorate with sliced fresh strawberries or whole raspberries.

Tangy lime mousse

Serves 6   see photograph, page 96
Each serving: 115 kcal/484 kJ, 10 g carbohydrate, neg fibre, 6 g protein, 2 g fat

25 g/1 oz cornflour   *grated rind and juice of 2 large limes*
450 ml/¾ pt skimmed milk   *2 tsp gelatine*
2 eggs, separated   *fresh lime slices, to decorate*
75 g/3 oz fructose

In a bowl, mix the cornflour to a smooth paste with a little of the milk. Beat in the egg yolks. Heat the remaining milk in a saucepan and stir into the egg yolk mixture. Return to the pan and cook, stirring, until the mixture thickens. Remove the pan from the heat and stir in the fructose and lime rind.

In a small saucepan, dissolve the gelatine in the lime juice over gentle heat. Stir into the custard. Whisk the egg whites until stiff and fold into the lime custard. Transfer to a serving dish and chill until required. Decorate with fresh lime slices.

Variation: Use two small lemons or oranges instead of the limes.

Apricot fool

Serves 4
Each serving: 75 kcal/317 kJ, 15 g carbohydrate, 8 g fibre, 3 g protein, 1 g fat

115 g/4 oz dried apricots   *15 g/½ oz fructose*
115 g/4 oz sheep's milk yoghurt *chopped toasted hazelnuts, to decorate*
1 egg white   *(optional)*

Wash the apricots and place in a bowl, cover generously with boiling water and leave to soak for at least 12 hours. Drain and reserve the juice for another recipe. Purée the apricots roughly and stir in the yoghurt.

In another bowl, whisk the egg white until stiff and continue whisking as you sprinkle in the fructose, a little at a time. Fold the egg white into the apricot mixture. Transfer to four individual dishes and chill until required. Decorate with the hazelnuts, if using.

Pumpernickel fool

Serves 4　　　　　　　　　　　　see photograph, page 62
Each serving: 134 kcal/563 kJ, 25 g carbohydrate, 3 g fibre,
6 g protein, 1 g fat

350 g/12 oz low-fat plain yoghurt　*liquid sweetener, to taste*
115 g/4 oz pumpernickel, grated　*1 tsp ground mixed spice*
50 g/2 oz raisins, roughly chopped　*4 strawberries*
grated rind of 1 lemon

Mix all the ingredients, except the strawberries, together and
spoon into individual dishes. Decorate each one with a whole
strawberry.

Note: This dessert will thicken on standing so thin it with a little
skimmed milk if necessary.

Chestnut fool

Serves 4
Each serving: 171 kcal/719 kJ, 30 g carbohydrate, 4 g fibre,
3 g protein, 4 g fat

225 g/8 oz unsweetened chestnut　*150 g/5 oz low-fat plain yoghurt*
* purée*　　　　　　　　　　　　*25 g/1 oz chocolate, chopped*
25 g/1 oz fructose

In a bowl, beat together the chestnut purée, fructose and yoghurt
until smooth. Transfer to four small serving dishes and sprinkle
with a little chocolate.

Rhubarb snow

Serves 4
Each serving: 30 kcal/122 kJ, neg carbohydrate, 2 g fibre,
3 g protein, 0 g fat

225 g/8 oz rhubarb, cut in short　*liquid sweetener, to taste*
* lengths*　　　　　　　　　　*2 egg whites*
60 ml/4 tbsp orange juice　　*15 ml/1 tbsp fructose*
1½ tsp gelatine

Put the rhubarb and half the orange juice into a saucepan. Simmer
gently until tender. Dissolve the gelatine in the remaining orange
juice and stir into the rhubarb. Allow to cool then sweeten to taste
with liquid sweetener.
　Whisk the egg whites until stiff in a bowl and whisk in the fructose. Fold the rhubarb mixture into the egg whites. Transfer to
four individual glasses and chill until set.

YOGHURT AND SOFT CHEESE DESSERTS

Lemon delight with strawberries

Serves 4 ★ ★ ★

Each serving: 89 kcal/373 kJ, 10 g carbohydrate, 1 g fibre, 9 g protein, 2 g fat

25 g/1 oz skimmed milk powder
175 g/6 oz curd cheese
grated rind and juice of ½ large
*   lemon*
75 ml/5 tbsp low-fat plain yoghurt

liquid sweetener, to taste
ground nutmeg (or cinnamon), to
*   sprinkle*
225 g/8 oz fresh strawberries, hulled

In a food processor or blender, combine the milk powder, curd cheese, lemon rind and juice, yoghurt and sweetener and process until smooth.

Transfer to four small ramekin dishes or glasses, sprinkle with nutmeg or cinnamon and top with sliced strawberries.

Real muesli with yoghurt and fresh fruit ★ ★

Serves 4

Each serving: 177 kcal/743 kJ, 25 g carbohydrate, 5 g fibre, 6 g protein, 6 g fat

60 ml/4 tbsp rolled oats, toasted
50 g/2 oz hazelnuts, toasted and
*   chopped*
225 g/8 oz low-fat plain yoghurt
1 dessert apple, cored and grated
1 banana, sliced

115 g/4 oz strawberries, hulled and
*   sliced*
50 g/2 oz raspberries
liquid sweetener, to taste
skimmed milk, as required

Mix the oats, hazelnuts, yoghurt and apple together. Fold in the fruits and sweeten to taste. If the mixture stands it may need thinning with milk.

Fruit and cheese desserts ☒ ☒

Serves 8   see photograph, page 96
Each serving with Carob sauce: 173 kcal/726 kJ, 20 g carbohydrate,
6 g fibre, 10 g protein, 6 g fat

450 g/1 lb skimmed milk soft cheese   *½ tsp rosewater*
115 g/4 oz sheeps' milk yoghurt   *grated rind and juice of 1 tangerine*
50 g/2 oz almonds, toasted and   *1 quantity Carob sauce (see below –*
  coarsely chopped   *optional), to serve*
250 g/9 oz dried fruit salad, chopped

In a large bowl, mix all the ingredients together. Use the mixture
to fill eight dariole or coeur a la crème moulds. If using the latter,
line the moulds with muslin before filling with the mixture.
Refrigerate for 2–3 hours.

Unmould on to plates and serve with the carob sauce, if
using.

Carob sauce   see photograph, page 96

115 g/4 oz carob bar
60 ml/4 tbsp skimmed milk

Break the carob bar into a saucepan. Add the milk and heat gently,
whisking all the time, to make a smooth sauce. Allow to cool
before serving.

Chilled apple and orange dessert

Serves 6
Each serving: 121 kcal/509 kJ, 20 g carbohydrate, 3 g fibre,
4 g protein, 4 g fat

450 g/1 lb cooking apples, peeled,   *liquid sweetener, to taste*
  cored and sliced   *50 g/2 oz coarse oatmeal*
grated rind and juice of 1 large   *50 g/2 oz hazelnuts, roughly chopped*
  orange   *225 g/8 oz low-fat plain yoghurt*
25 g/1 oz sultanas

Place the apples, orange juice and sultanas in a saucepan and
simmer, covered, over very gentle heat for about 15 minutes until
soft. Cool, then add liquid sweetener to taste.

Toast the oatmeal and hazelnuts until golden, then leave to
go cold.

Mix the yoghurt with the orange rind and further liquid
sweetener, to taste.

Layer the three mixtures in one large or six individual dishes,
finishing with a layer of yoghurt. Serve lightly chilled.

Coffee and banana dessert

Serves 4
Each serving: 111 kcal/466 kJ, 25 g carbohydrate, 3 g fibre,
4 g protein, 1 g fat

2 tsp instant coffee powder
15 ml/1 tbsp boiling water
225 g/8 oz sheep's milk yoghurt

liquid sweetener, to taste
2 large ripe bananas, roughly mashed
(reserve a few slices for decoration)

In a bowl, mix the instant coffee powder with the water to dissolve. When cool, beat in the yoghurt and sweeten to taste. Stir in the mashed bananas.

Transfer to four individual glasses and top with slices of banana. Serve at once.

Raspberry cheese delight

Serves 4
Each serving: 121 kcal/510 kJ, 5 g carbohydrate, 4 g fibre,
12 g protein, 3 g fat

350 g/12 oz cottage cheese
25 g/1 oz fructose
225 g/8 oz fresh raspberries

Sieve the cottage cheese into a bowl. Mix in the fructose. Purée a scant half of the raspberries and sieve to remove the seeds. Stir into the cheese. Spoon the mixture into a glass serving dish. Top with the remaining raspberries.

Variation: Use any other soft fruit available.

ICES AND SORBETS

Mango water ice

Serves 4   see photograph, page 96
Each serving: 105 kcal/441 kJ, 15 g carbohydrate, 1 g fibre,
2 g protein, 0 g fat

350 ml/12 fl oz mango purée
(2 medium–large mangoes)
100 ml/4 fl oz soda water
15 ml/1 tbsp fresh lime or lemon
juice

2 egg whites
50 g/2 oz fructose
slices of mango or peach, to serve
(optional)

➤

Mix together the mango purée, soda water and lime or lemon juice in a bowl. In another bowl, whisk the egg whites until stiff, then whisk in the fructose a little at a time. Fold the mango mixture into the egg whites until evenly mixed.

Pour into a rigid container, cover and freeze for about 2 hours or until 'slushy'. Turn out into a large bowl and beat thoroughly – a hand-held electric beater is the most efficient. As soon as the mixture becomes pale and expanded, return to the container and freezer.

Allow the water ice to soften for 30 minutes in the refrigerator before scooping on to plates, or dishes. Decorate with slices of fresh fruit, if wished.

Coconut water ice   ⊞ ☒ ☒ ☒

Serves 4
Each serving: 55 kcal/230 kJ, neg carbohydrate, neg fibre, 2 g protein, 0 g fat

225 ml/8 fl oz can thick coconut milk
10 ml/2 tsp fresh lime juice

150 ml/¼ pt soda water
2 egg whites
50 g/2 oz fructose

Stir together the coconut milk, lime juice and soda water. Whisk the egg whites until stiff in a bowl. Whisk in the fructose a little at a time. Fold the coconut mixture into the egg whites.

Transfer to a rigid container, cover and freeze for about 2 hours or until 'slushy'. Turn out into a large bowl and beat well. Return to the container and freeze until required.

Allow to soften for 30 minutes in the refrigerator before serving. Serve in scoops.

Note: If wished, serve with a decoration of thinly sliced pineapple and a cherry or strawberry for colour.

Rhubarb and strawberry ice   ⊞ ☒ ☒ ☒

Serves 4
Each serving: 16 kcal/69 kJ, 5 g carbohydrate, 2 g fibre, 2 g protein, 0 g fat

175 g/6 oz prepared rhubarb, cut in 2.5 cm/1 inch lengths
15 ml/1 tbsp water
125 g/4 oz ripe strawberries, hulled
1 tsp gelatine

45 ml/3 tbsp low-calorie orange squash
liquid sweetener, to taste
4 strawberries, to decorate

Put the rhubarb and water in a saucepan and simmer until just tender. Remove from the heat. Roughly crush the strawberries and add to the rhubarb. Dissolve the gelatine in the orange squash and stir into the fruit. Leave to go cold. Add liquid sweetener to taste.

Transfer the mixture to a rigid container. Cover and freeze for about 2 hours or until 'slushy'. Turn the mixture out into a large bowl and beat well. Return to the container and freeze until required.

Allow to soften to room temperature and roughly crush. Transfer to glasses and serve topped with a strawberry.

Pear sorbet   ⊞ ☒ ☒ ☒

Serves 4
Each serving: 54 kcal/228 kJ, 10 g carbohydrate, 2 g fibre, 0 g protein, 0 g fat

411 g/14½ oz can pears in fruit juice
1 tsp gelatine

45 ml/3 tbsp low-calorie lemon and lime squash
1 egg white

Purée the pears with their juice in a blender. Dissolve the gelatine in the fruit squash over gentle heat. Remove from the heat and add the pear purée.

When cold pour the mixture into a rigid container. Cover and freeze for about 2 hours or until the mixture is 'slushy'. Turn the mixture out into a large bowl. Stiffly whisk the egg white and fold into the pear mixture. Return to the container and freeze until required.

Allow to soften in the refrigerator for 30 minutes before serving.

Watermelon granita   ⊞ ☒ ☒ ☒

Serves 4
Each serving: 35 kcal/147 kJ, 10 g carbohydrate, 1 g fibre, 1 g protein, 0 g fat

450 ml/¾ pt watermelon purée (made from about 450–600 g/1–1¼ lb melon)

1½ tsp cornflour
15 ml/1 tbsp fresh lime juice
liquid sweetener, to taste

Mix together about one-quarter of the melon purée with the cornflour and lime juice. Cook, stirring until thickened. Remove from the heat and stir in the remaining melon purée. Cool, then add liquid sweetener to taste.

Freeze in a rigid container for about 2 hours until 'slushy'. Spoon into individual glasses and serve at once.

Note: The granita can also be stored in the freezer. Allow it to soften in the refrigerator to a 'slushy' consistency before serving.

FILLINGS AND TOPPINGS

Apricot cheese filling

Sufficient to fill and top a 20 cm/8 inch cake
Total recipe: 278 kcal/1168 kJ, 45 g carbohydrate, 24 g fibre, 18 g protein, 4 g fat

115 g/4 oz dried apricots, washed and   *115 g/4 oz low-fat soft cheese*
  soaked overnight   *liquid sweetener, to taste*

Just cover the apricots with water in a saucepan and bring to the boil. Cover and simmer for about 25 minutes until soft. Drain, reserving the juice for another dish. Purée the apricots in a bowl. Cover and put in the refrigerator to chill. Fold in the soft cheese and add liquid sweetener to taste.

Pastry cream

Makes about 300 ml/½ pt
Total recipe: 376 kcal/1579 kJ, 55 g carbohydrate, 1 g fibre, 18 g protein, 10 g fat

2 egg yolks   *1 vanilla pod (or a few drops vanilla*
30 ml/2 tbsp cornflour   *essence)*
15 ml/1 tbsp plain flour   *liquid sweetener, to taste*
350 ml/13 fl oz skimmed milk

Put the egg yolks in a bowl and whisk until pale. Beat in the cornflour and flour and sufficient milk to make a smooth paste.

Heat the remaining milk in a saucepan with the vanilla pod to just below boiling point. Remove from the heat and leave to infuse for 5 minutes. Stir the milk into the egg yolk mixture and return to the pan. Cook, stirring all the time, until thickened.

Strain and add liquid sweetener to taste. Cover and chill until required. Use as a filling or spread. It will keep in the refrigerator for two to three days, covered.

Note: If using vanilla essence, add with the liquid sweetener.

Variations
Orange or lemon – omit the vanilla pod; use a few strips of pared orange or lemon rind.

Bay or rosemary – omit the vanilla pod; use a fresh bay leaf or sprig of fresh rosemary.

Almond – omit the vanilla pod; add a few drops of almond essence.

Chocolate – add 50 g/2 oz grated chocolate, stir until melted.

Date and banana spread ☒ ☒ ☒

Makes 350 g/12 oz
Total recipe: 517 kcal/2170 kJ, 110 g carbohydrate, 13 g fibre, 12 g protein, 5 g fat

115 g/4 oz stoned dates *½ quantity Pastry cream (see*
1 banana *opposite)*

Mince or purée the dates in a food processor or blender. Mash the banana and beat all the ingredients together until evenly combined.

Use at once as bananas discolour quite soon.

Note: Serve on bread or as a filling for a sandwich cake.

Almond paste ☒

Makes about 175 g/6 oz
Total recipe: 616 kcal/2588 kJ, 5 g carbohydrate, 14 g fibre, 19 g protein, 58 g fat

115 g/4 oz ground almonds *1 tsp lemon juice*
25 g/1 oz fructose *¼ tsp almond essence*
1 egg yolk

Mix the ground almonds and fructose in a bowl. Add the remaining ingredients and work together to make a firm paste.

Use as an icing or filling.

Note: The paste will store in the refrigerator for up to one week, well wrapped.

Low-calorie topping ☒ ☒ ☒

Makes about 600 ml/1 pt
Total recipe: 268 kcal/1126 kJ, 20 g carbohydrate, 0 g fibre, 27 g protein, 0 g fat

1½ tsp gelatine *30 ml/2 tbsp fructose*
150 ml/¼ pt iced water *¼ tsp vanilla essence*
40 g/1½ oz skimmed milk powder

➤

In a small saucepan, dissolve the gelatine in about one-quarter of the water over a gentle heat. Leave to cool.

Whisk together the remaining water and milk powder using a hand-held electric whisk for about 2 minutes until frothy and increased in volume. Slowly whisk in the gelatine, fructose and vanilla and continue whisking until soft peaks form. Use immediately.

Note: Do not refrigerate this topping because it will set to a foam jelly.

Variation
Coffee – add 30 ml/2 tbsp fructose and 2 tsp instant coffee dissolved in 30 ml/2 tbsp hot water.
Lemon, orange or lime – omit the vanilla essence and add 1–2 tsp grated lemon, lime or orange rind. You may wish to increase the amount of sweetening, to taste.

Pouring custard

Makes about 300 ml/½ pt   see photograph, page 73
Total recipe: 185 kcal/779 kJ, 25 g carbohydrate, 0 g fibre, 13 g protein, 5 g fat

300 ml/½ pt skimmed milk   *few drops vanilla essence*
1 egg yolk   *liquid sweetener, to taste*
2 tsp cornflour

Place most of the milk in a saucepan and bring to just below boiling point.

In a bowl, combine the remaining milk with the egg yolk and cornflour and blend to a smooth paste. Pour the hot milk over the egg mixture, stir well and return to the saucepan. Heat gently, stirring constantly, until the mixture thickens. Remove from the heat and stir in the vanilla essence and liquid sweetener. Serve immediately.

'SWEETS'

Orange coconut nuggets

Makes 18
Each nugget: 105 kcal/443 kJ, 10 g carbohydrate, 1 g fibre,
1 g protein, 6 g fat

100 g/3½ oz polyunsaturated
margarine, plus extra for greasing
65 g/2½ oz fructose
25 g/1 oz desiccated coconut
1 tsp grated orange rind

15 ml/1 tbsp orange juice
175 g/6 oz self-raising flour
45 ml/3 tbsp long-thread or desiccated
coconut, to decorate

Heat the oven to 190°C/375°F/gas 5 and lightly grease a baking
sheet. Put the margarine and fructose in a bowl and cream until
light and fluffy. Stir in the coconut, orange rind and juice and
work in the flour. Drop spoonfuls of the mixture on to the baking
sheet. Sprinkle each one with a little coconut and press gently.
Bake for about 15 minutes until golden. Cool on a wire tray.

Prune and pecan bites

Makes 12
Each one: 35 kcal/148 kJ, 5 g carbohydrate, 2 g fibre, 1 g protein,
2 g fat

115 g/4 oz ready-to-eat prunes, soaked
for 5 minutes in boiling water

50 g/2 oz shelled pecan nuts (or
walnuts)

Place the prunes and pecans in a grinder or food processor until
finely chopped. Divide the mixture into twelve pieces and form
each into a small ball. Leave on greaseproof paper to dry out for a
few hours. Serve in petits fours cases.

Fresh stuffed figs

Serves 4
Each serving: 84 kcal/355 kJ, 10 g carbohydrate, 1 g fibre,
5 g protein, 4 g fat

8 fresh figs, washed
115 g/4 oz skimmed-milk soft cheese
finely grated rind of 2 tangerines

25 g/1 oz pistachio nuts, chopped
25 g/1 oz raisins, chopped
liquid sweetener, to taste

➡

Cut the stalks off the figs. Without cutting right through the fruit, make three cuts in each fig so that it opens out into six petals. Combine the remaining ingredients and divide between the figs. Draw up the 'petals' around the filling. Arrange on individual serving plates.

Coconut bars

Makes 4
Each bar: 121 kcal/510 kJ, 10 g carbohydrate, 4 g fibre, 2 g protein, 9 g fat

40 g/1½ oz desiccated coconut　　　*50 g/2 oz raisins*
20 g/¾ oz unsalted cashew nuts or　*15 g/½ oz fresh pineapple*
peanuts

Heat the oven to 200°C/400°F/gas 6.
　Put the coconut and cashew nuts on a non-stick baking sheet and toast in the oven for about 10 minutes, or until golden brown.
　Place all ingredients in a grinder or food processor and work the mixture until it holds together well. Roll out between two sheets of non-stick paper to a rectangle 15 × 10 cm/6 × 4 inches. Cut into four bars. Leave overnight to dry out.

Date bars

Makes 12
Each bar: 132 kcal/554 kJ, 15 g carbohydrate, 2 g fibre, 4 g protein, 6 g fat

100 g/3½ oz polyunsaturated　　*75 g/3 oz self-raising flour*
margarine, plus extra for greasing　*25 g/1 oz rolled oats*
50 g/2 oz fructose　　　　　　*pinch of salt*
150 g/5 oz stoned dates, finely chopped

Heat the oven to 180°C/350°F/gas 4 and lightly grease a 20 cm/8 inch shallow square tin. Put the margarine and fructose in a bowl and cream together until pale and fluffy. Stir in the remaining ingredients. Press the mixture into the tin. Bake for about 30 minutes until golden. Allow to cool in the tin, then cut into bars.

FESTIVE DESSERTS

Christmas pudding ★

Makes 2 puddings (550 g/1¼ lb, each pudding serves 4)
Each serving: 301 kcal/1264 kJ, 40 g carbohydrate, 7 g fibre, 7 g protein, 15 g fat

115 g/4 oz wholemeal flour
1 tsp baking powder
50 g/2 oz wholemeal breadcrumbs
50 g/2 oz ground almonds
50 g/2 oz polyunsaturated margarine, plus extra for greasing

1 large carrot, finely grated
3 eggs
550 g/1¼ lb Spiced mincemeat (see page 116)

Lightly grease two 750 ml/1¼ pt pudding basins. Combine all the ingredients in a bowl and beat well until evenly mixed. Divide the mixture between the pudding basins. Cover each basin with a greased round of foil with a central pleat to allow for expansion. Tie securely with string. Steam or, alternatively, place the pudding basins in two large saucepans; pour in boiling water to come half-way up the sides of the basins, cover with a lid and simmer for 2 hours. Add more boiling water, if necessary. Remove the basins from the pans and leave to go cold.

Remove the puddings from the basins and wrap well in grease-proof paper and foil. Store in the refrigerator or, if keeping for more than two days, freeze. To reheat, unwrap the puddings, return to the pudding basins and steam or boil for 1 hour. Serve with Pouring custard (see page 112).

Mince pies ★

Makes 18
Each pie: 108 kcal/455 kJ, 15 g carbohydrate, 2 g fibre, 2 g protein, 6 g fat

1 quantity Basic wholemeal pastry (see page 43)
275 g/10 oz Spiced mincemeat (see page 116)

Heat the oven to 200°C/400°F/gas 6. Roll out the pastry on a lightly floured surface and stamp out rounds to fit eighteen patty tins. Fill each one with the mincemeat.

Reroll the pastry trimmings and stamp out eighteen lids. Dampen the edges of the pastry and seal each pie carefully. Using a sharp knife, make a small slit in each pie. Bake for 20 minutes. Serve warm or cold.

Spiced mincemeat ★

Makes about 1.5 kg/3½ lb
Total recipe: 3013 kcal/12655 kJ, 555 g carbohydrate, 75 g fibre,
24 g protein, 92 g fat

225 g/8 oz cooking apples, peeled,
cored and grated
grated rind and juice of 1 lemon
grated rind and juice of 1 orange
50 g/2 oz polyunsaturated margarine
225 g/8 oz currants
225 g/8 oz sultanas
225 g/8 oz raisins

115 g/4 oz dried figs, chopped
300 ml/½ pt apple juice
½ tsp ground cinnamon
½ tsp ground nutmeg
½ tsp ground mixed spice
½ tsp ground mace
¼ tsp ground cloves
125 g/4 oz shelled walnuts, chopped

Place all the ingredients except the walnuts in a large saucepan
and bring to the boil. Reduce the heat, cover the pan and simmer,
stirring occasionally, for 1 hour.

Allow the mincemeat to cool then stir in the walnuts. Spoon
into jars or rigid plastic containers, cover and store in the
refrigerator. It will keep in the refrigerator for up to one
week.

ACKNOWLEDGMENTS

I am very grateful to Anne Hildyard for her help with the recipes, to Louise Pickford for assisting with the food photography, and to Nova Pilbeam for typing the recipes.

Jane Suthering   *1986*

I should like to thank the following for their help and advice: Pat Butler, Jackie Edington, Joanna Lousley, Jill Metcalfe (from the British Diabetic Association), Margaret Thorogood and David Yeates.

Sue Lousley   *1986*

The publishers would like to thank Peter Myers and his assistant, Neil Mersh, for the photography, and Penny Markham for the styling. The food was prepared for photography by Jane Suthering.

INDEX

Page numbers in *italic* refer to the illustrations

Other books for diabetics in the Positive Health Guide series:

DIABETES: A PRACTICAL NEW GUIDE TO HEALTHY LIVING
Dr James Anderson
Written especially for those with newly diagnosed diabetes, this book is packed with information on diet, insulin, exercise, and coping with everyday life – the best help for diabetics is self-help, and this book provides it.

THE DIABETICS' DIET BOOK
Dr Jim Mann and the Oxford Dietetic Group
The first book to explain how a high-carbohydrate and fibre diet can lead to better control of diabetes, including over 140 mouthwatering recipes which the whole family will enjoy.

THE DIABETICS' COOKBOOK
Roberta Longstaff, SRD, and Dr Jim Mann
The sequel to the bestselling *The Diabetics' Diet Book*, this book not only contains wholesome everyday meals, but also exciting dishes for dinner and drinks parties, children's meals, and food for festive occasions.

THE DIABETICS' GET FIT BOOK
Jacki Winter and Dr Barbara Boucher
At last – a complete home workout routine written by an insulin dependent diabetic specially for diabetics. Here's how to get fit and stay fit whatever your age and ability.

THE HEALTHY HEART DIET BOOK
Enjoy delicious low-fat, high-fibre recipes
Roberta Longstaff, SRD, and Dr Jim Mann

BEAT HEART DISEASE
A cardiologist explains how you can help your heart and enjoy a healthier life
Prof Risteard Mulcahy

THE SALT-FREE DIET BOOK
An appetizing way to help reduce high blood pressure
Dr Graham MacGregor

CARING FOR AN ELDERLY RELATIVE
A guide to home care
Dr Keith Thompson

THE VEGETARIAN'S HEALTHY DIET BOOK
150 nutritious recipes
Colin Spencer
Introduction by Dr Tom Sanders

COOKING FOR KIDS THE HEALTHY WAY
Wholesome recipes with child appeal
Joanna Pay, SRD

EYES: THEIR PROBLEMS AND TREATMENTS
Michael Glasspool, FRCS

KEEPING BABIES AND CHILDREN HEALTHY
A parents' practical handbook to common ailments
Dr Bernard Valman

THE HYPERACTIVE CHILD
A parents' guide
Dr Eric Taylor

CHILDREN'S PROBLEMS
A parents' guide to understanding and tackling them
Dr Bryan Lask

Curriculum and Teaching Dialogue

Volume 10, Numbers 1 and 2

Curriculum and Teaching Dialogue

edited by

Barbara Slater Stern
James Madison University

Information Age Publishing, Inc.
Charlotte, North Carolina • www.infoagepub.com

ISBN 13: 978-1-59311-989-8 (pbk.)
ISBN 13: 978-1-59311-990-4 (hardcover)

Printed in the United States of America

CONTENTS

PRESIDENT'S MESSAGE

Raising a Professor:
A Tribute to Mentorship

Karen L. Riley

Every professor who reads this modest message can identify in some way with the following story. As you read along, assume that I am speaking directly to you as a colleague. For some of you, this story will be a recent event, for others, it will bring back memories. For all of us, it is a story that represents a defining moment in our academic, professional, and often, in our private lives.

The dissertation defense is over and you passed. The fear and trepidation of presenting your research to a committee of five university professors, any one of whom is capable of holding your life's career hostage, now takes leave of your body in one long, heaving sigh. You are not sure whether to smile, laugh, cry, whistle, or go to bed for 3 days. You anxiously wait for the euphoria to set in. After all, you have spent endless hours in the library, eaten countless cheap meals in order to afford a new computer on which to write your great work, and waited patiently for the next chapter to be returned to you by Fed Ex by your dissertation chair so that you can make those dozens, perhaps hundreds, of changes as you

Curriculum and Teaching Dialogue
Volume 10, Numbers 1 & 2, 2008, pp. xi–xiii
Copyright © 2007 by Information Age Publishing
xi

slowly grind your way to the finish line. Yet, the longed-for euphoria is nowhere in sight. That hoped-for emotional high has been replaced by a leaden feeling of dread. Dread that others will be able to tell that you really aren't a "real" professor. After all, 5 minutes before your dissertation chair shook your hand and said "congratulations Dr. so and so," you were a lowly graduate student, grateful for any acknowledgement by one of your professors that you just might have what it takes to one day take your place in the temple. Well the time has come. You have been congratulated by your chair and committee members. Now it is time to seek out a position in higher education and make your family, friends, and most of all, your major professor proud. Where do you begin? How can the landscape change so suddenly? From a graduate student handbook with pages of dos and don'ts and a verbal list of what you need to do from your major professor, to the uncertain world of job hunting where you will seemingly be all alone. While you are focused on your career dilemma, there is someone else who is busy behind the scenes helping to pave your career path—that individual is called your major professor, dissertation chair, mentor, or all three.

The doctoral experience from start to finish and then beyond is a shared experience. While few will argue with the notion that the dissertation stage of a doctoral program can be a lonely endeavor, there is always someone who figuratively walks beside you—your mentor. If you reflect upon the doctoral experience you can probably name one or two professors who not only advised you on what courses to take, but also shaped the professional that you would become. This person is called a mentor. Good mentors are individuals who model the behavior expected in any given field that leads to success. As a doctoral student, your mentor undoubtedly insisted that you write proposals, attend this or that conference, and sat in the audience as you presented your work. He or she may have co-presented with you. In addition, your mentor introduced you to the "stellar lights" in education. You know, those folks whose books we all read as graduate students, who became our academic heroes and heroines. Your mentor saw to it that your work was considered for publication through his or her network of professional friends and put you in touch with publishers who might consider your work. When a letter from this or that journal arrived inviting you to become a member of the editorial board, you may have thought that somehow the word was out that a new "brilliant professor" has just entered the ranks of academe and should be appointed to the board; however, it is likely that your mentor used his or her connections to have you appointed to the editorial board, thus giving you a boost up the higher education ladder. More importantly, your major professor/mentor taught you what was expected of you as a new professor, such as how to balance committee work with your teaching load and research. He or she provided you with opportunities to serve as program chairs at conferences and in general introduced you to the world of academe.

The debt that most of us owe to our dissertation chairs, major professors, mentors, or whatever name we give to the individual/s who shaped our intellectual lives, is one that can never be repaid. Some of us are more fortunate than others. Not all major professors or dissertation chairs make the lifelong personal investment in their students that many of ours made in us. Not all major professors or dissertation chairs paved the way to success for their students as many of ours did for us. A number of years ago, what became apparent to the leadership of The American Association of Teaching and Curriculum (AATC) was that this unique organization was founded and is comprised today of some of the leading professionals in the fields of teaching and curriculum who not only mentored their own students through the doctoral experience, but also have served as mentors to many of you who hail from other institutions. AATC is dedicated to fostering collegiality and mentorship. As president, I am indebted to my colleagues who share their talents and expertise with all of us and most especially to my own mentors Marcella L. Kysilka and O. L. Davis, Jr., who understand fully the importance of mentorship to doctoral students and beginning professors. They have helped to shape the success of many of us in this organization. The success of AATC is largely due to the collegial nature of our organization, the successful mentoring offered by our senior professors and the quality of scholarship that each of you contributes to this very fine organization. Now, the challenge to the AATC membership is to carry forward the work initiated by the founders of this organization that is dedicated to the fields of teaching and curriculum.

EDITOR'S NOTES

Searching for Truth(s)

Barbara Slater Stern

As I was arranging and rearranging the table of contents for this volume of *Curriculum and Teaching Dialogue* I thought back to my time as a high school teacher. During those years I was privileged to have had several preservice teachers assigned to my social studies classroom. One day, the university supervisor observed one my student teachers and me as we were co-teaching. His comment during our debriefing after the class has stayed with me across the years. Of course I am paraphrasing, but the gist of what he told me is "I love coming to watch your classes, they always involve students in a search for the Truth." I understood that he was speaking of a metaphysical construct, Truth with a capital T. I also understand that in a complex field such as education Truths might be the more applicable term. Either way, I like to think of each edition of this journal as a collection of authors; educators with a wide variety of experiences and research interests, engaged on a search to uncover Truth(s). As such, each of these articles represents an invitation to the reader to join with the authors on their quests.

Curriculum and Teaching Dialogue
Volume 10, Numbers 1 & 2, 2007, pp. xv–xxi
Copyright © 2008 by Information Age Publishing

We begin the journeys which comprise Volume 10, with an essay by Alan Garrett, the American Association of Teaching and Curriculum's (AATC) past president, that explores the broad relationship between scholarship and school practice. The intriguing thing about his article is that Alan wears two hats: one as a professor and educational scholar, and the other as a school board member. Thus, "The Games People Play: Educational Scholarship and School Practice," represents a search toward understanding how the academy could move towards having more influence in the real world of schooling. Kai-Ju Yang narrows this quest by exploring "Teacher and Parent Beliefs on Tracking: A Taiwanese Perspective." This article focuses on what teachers and parents think about tracking as measured by the three dimensions of tracking identified by Jeannie Oakes (1992)—the technical, the normative, and the political. Despite the research on the benefits of untracking, the author reveals teachers and parents have hold a different truth. Will these findings point us toward different Truth(s)? Next, Mary McGlamery hones in to the more particular by trying to improve the curriculum in early elementary classrooms with her article The "Case for Social Skills Training in the Primary School Curriculum: A Follow Up Study of Attention and Theory of Mind Skills in First Grade Boys."

Switching to the teacher education level, Jackie Bach's article, "Project Teach: Using Reality Shows as a Framework for Teaching Methods Courses" grows out of a comment made during a "conversation session" at an AATC annual conference when Madeleine Grumet discussed *Project Runway*, airing on cable television's Bravo channel, as an ideal curriculum project. Bach states:

> I am not sure if she thought anyone in the audience would take her comment seriously … but I spent quite a bit of time pondering her suggestion … Grumet's suggestion is somewhat related to problem-based learning (PBL), and I could see how this television-inspired approach might enrich students' engagement with education courses' texts and topics.

I am particularly intrigued by this search on how to improve methods classes as I, too, have been pondering Grumet's comments about *Project Runway* since I heard them in that same session! Staying on the quest for improving teacher education, we move to Christine Moseley, Stacey Reeder, and Neill Armstrong's article "I Don't Eat White: The Transformational Nature of Student Teaching Abroad." This qualitative study focuses on three preservice teachers and details the importance of cultural immersion in a foreign country and culture as a means of learning about one's self. Since there are many Truths to be learned about preservice teaching, taking us on a different search is Heidi Mullins with her article, "At the Crossroads of Preservice Teacher Education, NAEA, and Terry Barrett: Exploring Metaphors of Meaning, Narratives of Hope." Mullins' also focused on three preservice teachers. Here, by exposing them to several pieces of art and observing how they constructed new meanings of art that challenged their preconceived notions that art was not relevant to the elementary school classroom.

One of the two featured speakers at the 2007 annual conference was Suzanne Wilson. It is an AATC tradition to invite articles that were part of a retrospective panel on our guest speaker's career. Yonghee Suh's article is about the impact of Suzanne Wilson on Suh's career as a future educator. This article reinforces Karen Riley's President's Message about the debt we owe to our teachers and mentors. Suh's article, "How Doctoral Mentoring Supported A Cultural Transformation from Peripheral Observer to Active Learner: Learning to Teach and Research from Suzanne Wilson," demonstrates how a teacher can assist her students on their quest for knowledge. Sometimes our search for Truth comes from those who can no longer actively mentor us, but they can still teach us. Benjamin Welsh and Nancy Brooks take us on an historical quest by exploring the work of Mary Sheldon Barnes, (1850–1898), the first female professor of Stanford University. Their aim is to understand both how Barnes formed and was formed by the intellectual and educational milieu of her times. In their article, "The Con/text of Mary Sheldon Barnes (1850–1898): A Hermeneutic Inquiry," Welsh and Brooks suggest that the influence of Barnes' work, especially in the teaching of history, continues to linger in current educational thought and practice.

History as an academic subject found its place in the curriculum as a means of fostering citizenship. There are multiple ways to search for Truths about citizenship preparation. In their article, "Citizens of Today and Tomorrow: An Exploration of Preservice Social Studies Teachers' Knowledge and Their Professors' Experiences With Citizenship," Chara Haeussler Bohan, Frans Doppen, Joseph Feinberg, and Carolyn O'Mahony examine preservice teachers' knowledge about citizenship through their performance on the United States Citizenship and Immigration Services Naturalization Test. The study found that many teachers, particularly at the elementary school level, were unable to answer correctly questions associated with the U.S. Constitution and the different branches of government. All teachers, not only those in the disciplines of social studies and history, are charged with preparing their students to take their places in our society as future citizens. We all know that preservice teachers are looking forward to the day when they have their own classrooms. Thus, many teachers are searching for Truth(s) about service learning as a vehicle to assist in that area. Marjori Krebs explores this in "Service-Learning: What Motivates K–12 Teachers to Initiate Service-Learning Projects?" Krebs states: "By involving my students in service-learning activities, I was able to catch a glimpse of the positive effects these activities had on the lives of my students. This method had a positive impact on their personal development as well as their academic achievement." Thus far, the first half of volume 10 has taken us on a variety of searches for Truth(s) from elementary through doctoral levels of education.

The second featured speaker at the 2007 annual conference was Carl Glickman. Our journeys transition to the second half of Volume 10 opening with Glickman's personal essay "The Story Behind the Presentation: Forrest Gump and Uncloistered Scholarship." Here Glickman considers how his career has focused on the purpose of education in a democratic society concluding that "democracy must be first seen as a practice of learning before it can become a practice of self government. In essence, we can't close learning gaps until we close participation gaps. And it has to be simultaneously played out at every level of education, starting with ourselves." Rather than a retrospective panel, Carl Glickman requested a response panel. Thus, on the morning following his presentation, the Professors of Curriculum sponsored a discussion of invited reactions to his speech and several of the panel members were asked to formalize their remarks for this edition of CTD. Bill Schubert's response, "Perspectives on the Pedagogy of Democracy," leads him to conclude that, in terms of democratic pedagogy, "the most revolutionary thing we can do ... is encourage learners, educators, and the general (including oppressed) public to ask and act on basic curriculum questions." The quest that Schubert is calling for would result in teaching each person to be his or her own curriculum director.

Quests are seldom direct lines from start to finish, rather they are circuitous journeys that hopefully wind up revealing the Truth(s) we are seeking. So we return to several topics we began to explore in the first half of Volume 10. The struggle to bridge theory and practice recurs with "Connections, Constructions and Collages: Initiating Dialogues on Diversity in Teacher Education Courses" by Pamela Thompson and Richard Biffle. These authors highlight the culturally competent practice of dialogic learning activities in a university level classroom, as supported by Freire's (1995) definition of dialogue. Thompson and Biffle designed hands-on, self-expressive activities that incorporate selected ideas from Banks (2000), Eisner (1994), and Gay (2000). Amy Masko continues our explorations about the importance of searching for Truth(s) related to diversity with her article, "Resistance at City Middle School: Critical Race Theorizing in Educational Research." Her ethnographic study seeks to understand how race permeates an urban middle school at three levels: the systemic level, the classroom level, and among youth. Masko's conclusion cites Solórzano and Yosso (2002) to remind us that "Critical Race methodology in education recognizes that multiple layers of oppression and discrimination are met with multiple forms of resistance" (p. 22). In my quest to organize this journal, I decided to respond to discussions of oppression and resistance by seeking a different approach for teachers; Kevin Cloninger's article "Giving Beyond Care: An Exploration of Love in the Classroom." This critical ethnography explores the effects of care, love, empathy, and trust in a classroom environment. Creating care, love, empathy, and trust in a classroom requires a deep understanding of the students in that classroom. David Callejo Perez takes on that quest with his article "Enacted Curriculum and the Search for Identity: Angst and the Cuban search for Meaning after the Cuban Revolution." Cajello Perez states:

> There is hope that within the schooling and its curriculum there are still gray spaces where individuals can address the concepts of social justice and equality ... and by referencing traditional authors in comparison to Cuban authors, teachers and curriculum developers might be able to incorporate Cuban literature to illustrate required themes while appealing to the multiple identity issues of diverse minority students.

Thus, these articles reinforce the searches for Truth(s) that bridge the theory/practice gap that all educators face when dealing with the complex realities of school and schooling.

The final articles in this section of the journal are more concerned with how we search for Truth(s)—our multiple ways of knowing and learning— that is, the many paths that may lead us to finding our Truth(s). In "Leveraging Eclectic Arts as a Rationale for Multiple Modes of Inquiry," Brian Schultz provides a "theoretical basis for applying Schwab's notion of eclectic arts as a rationale and a justification for using a multiplicity of modes for conducting educational inquiry." Then, Jeong-Hee Kim follows with "A Romance with Narrative Inquiry: Toward an Act of Narrative Theorizing." Kim seeks to identify some of the challenges that narrative inquiry faces in the current political era and find ways to overcome them. This article affirms the importance of narrative research in teaching and learning and suggests that doing narrative research is a poetizing and sacred act transcending the limit of doing research. Last, Mark Seaman looks carefully at terms that are frequently misunderstood in his article, "Birds of a Feather? Communities of Practice and Knowledge Communities." Seaman's quest is to clarify two distinct theories concerning communities that have emerged in regard to group efforts to improve practice: communities of practice (Lave & Wenger, 1991; Wenger, 1998a) and knowledge communities (Craig, 1992, 1995). By comparing these two theories educators may better understand their similarities and differences should they choose to utilize such communities in their research and/or practice.

Curriculum and Teaching Dialogue, Volume 10, closes with an invited book review. Robert Boostrom cheerfully accepted the rather daunting task I assigned and his article, "Transdimensional Curriculum: A Review of The SAGE Handbook of Curriculum and Instruction (2007)" edited by Michael Connolly with Ming Fang He and JoAnn Phillion is required reading for anyone involved with the field of curriculum. Bob certainly has my thanks for rising to the challenge and providing a thoughtful and comprehensive review for a compendium as large and diverse as the new Sage Handbook which is, of course, another search for Truth(s) about the complex and fascinating field of curriculum.

I close the editor's notes with thanks to all those institutions and individuals who have assisted with bringing Volume 10 to completion. My thanks go first to AATC for renewing my editorship for a second term. I continue to be grateful that the organization is committed to providing funding for a graduate student to assist the editor. Heartfelt thanks to this year's able graduate students, Greg Thompson and Jill Miller, who have spent many hours working to insure a successful volume. I also wish to thank our membership, the peer reviewers for the submissions. Each manuscript is sent to three reviewers. Often, I send articles to members who have not indicated that they wish to review and they never let me down. A list of those reviewers is at the back of the journal. I could not do this job without them. James Madison University has continued to provide course release in the spring to enable me to complete the editing of the journal and that is greatly appreciated. George Johnson and his staff at Information Age Publishing work hard to produce a professional publication and to market the journal both at professional meetings and through their advertising brochures, Web sites, and so forth. We owe them thanks for their efforts. Lynne Bailey and her graduate students took over the task of mailing journals to members and authors who were unable to attend the AATC annual conference. That is a large task and it was cheerfully undertaken—I thank you, as does Marcella Kysilka who formerly handled that job as executive secretary.

Last, I wish to thank James Moore, our associate editor. Jim completed his work in an efficient and timely manner. I also appreciate the assistance given by Cleveland State University which enabled Jim to attend our journals talks session at AERA (American Educational Research Association). Jim will be stepping down from his position to pursue other interests and he will be missed. I am happy to announce that David Flinders will be the new associate editor beginning with Volume 11. I hope the membership will congratulate David as he steps into his new role with AATC.

As always, I encourage the membership to provide feedback to the journal—book reviews, responses to articles, and so forth. Simply e-mail ctdjournal@jmu.edu or contact me personally at sternbs@jmu.edu. The call for manuscripts is at the close of this volume. Please submit by October 31st of the calendar year.

May the articles in this journal help each and every reader as they search for Truth(s)—Happy reading.

PART I

CHAPTER 1

THE GAMES PEOPLE PLAY

Educational Scholarship and School Practice

Alan W. Garrett

This essay, based on the 2007 AATC presidential address, explores the relationship between educational scholarship and school practice using the ecology of games metaphor, considers the problem of theory largely divorced from reality, and offers alternatives for consideration by educational scholars who desire more influence in the development and implementation of public school policy.

The purpose of the American Association for Teaching and Curriculum (AATC), "to promote the scholarly study of teaching and curriculum," is focused and clear (AATC, 2006). This statement describes not only what AATC is but also what it is not. Despite the limited scholarly purpose of AATC, its members by and large also are deeply concerned with the practice of schooling and how it might be improved. Our scholarly studies often lead us to ideas or insights that might elude those individuals engaged in the hectic daily challenges of schooling or policymakers distantly removed from the realities of classrooms, students, and teachers. Despite our potential contributions, our voices are largely unheard in the world of "real school" practice and policy. A complaint commonly heard from attendees at AATC conferences and other scholarly gatherings is

Curriculum and Teaching Dialogue
Volume 10, Numbers 1 & 2, 2008, pp. 3–11
Copyright © 2008 by Information Age Publishing
All rights of reproduction in any form reserved.

that everything they have to offer, their ideas, theories, and suggestions for school improvement, routinely are ignored.

Former AATC president David Flinders (personal communication, 2004) bluntly described the bulk of the work performed by a majority of educational scholars when he noted that we spend most, if not all, of our time writing for each other in our journals of limited circulation and talking to each other at conferences attended by individuals who share similar interests and perspectives and have backgrounds much like our own. Our influence in the real world of schools, more often than not, is indirect and hopeful. We hope that our former and current students will use their public school positions to put into practice at least some of what we have taught them in our classes. In reality, we live in a rather insulated world that we understand and find comfortable. Unfortunately, our safe world seems to be surrounded by what might best be described as a sort of differentially permeable membrane, allowing information and ideas in with relative ease while, at the same time, allowing little of the results of our work to escape. Critics of education do not appear to face this problem. They tend to understand better how the larger world works and disseminate their messages in ways that are much more likely to sway opinion and influence policy. Arthur Bestor (1953, 1955) and Hyman Rickover (1959, 1963), for example, remain widely known for their mid-twentieth century critiques of public education. They got their messages across, yet their contemporaries—our professional ancestors—engaged in the scholarly study of education, and today remain largely unknown, except, perhaps, to select individuals in organizations such as AATC.

How can educational scholars enhance their influence in the ways in which school is conducted? Clearly, we have the potential to bring understandings and perspectives to the debate that is currently absent. This essay will frame the current situation within the context of an ecology of games; explore the allure of theory, a mainstay of our existence, as well as its limits; and suggest a possibility that opens the door for AATC members, as well as other educational scholars, to have greater influence in the conduct of schooling while maintaining our organizational integrity and scholarly purpose.

DIFFERENT GAMES, DIFFERENT RULES

The ecology of games metaphor provides an elegant and useful framework for the consideration of the various parties that seek to influence American public education. Norton E. Long (1958), who first suggested analyzing local communities as ecologies of games, proposed the following:

[That] the structured group activities that coexist in a particular territorial system can be looked at as games. These games provide the players with a set of goals that give them a sense of success and failure. They provide them determinate roles and calculable strategies and tactics. In addition, they provide the players with an elite and general public that is in varying degrees able to tell the score. (p. 252)

William A. Firestone (1989) extended Long's notion of an ecology of games to the development of educational policy. Firestone's initial analysis was limited to four games, "the state legislative game, the state government administration game, the district and school administration game, and the teaching game" (p. 19). To these, the "university faculty member game" must be added for the present discussion.

Long's (1958) insight was the linkage between different games taking place simultaneously. He noted the following:

Sharing a common territorial field and collaborating for different and particular ends in the achievement of overall social functions, the players in one game make use of players in another and are, in turn, made use of by them. (p. 253)

Thus, legislators can make use of schools to win public favor, enhancing their chances for reelection through the passage of legislation with the apparent intent of improving public education. Administrators may lobby legislators to pass acts that they believe would result in the better operation of schools. At the same time, both groups are dependent on teachers for carrying out each school's work—the improvement of student learning. Teachers depend directly on administrators and legislators to provide them the resources necessary to do their jobs. Additionally, through their professional organizations, teachers can have a significant impact on both legislation passed and the political futures of individual legislators. University faculty members help to educate new teachers and administrators and sometimes provide assistance at the classroom or district level, yet the vast majority of them remain largely centered in their own game. Work in schools can provide the data necessary for publication and presentation, both requirements for tenure and promotion, and both prerequisites for most players to remain active in the "university game." Overall, most encounters between university faculty members and "real schools" likely prove far more beneficial to the former than to the latter.

Long (1958) also observed the following:

Individuals may play in a number of games, but, for the most part, their major preoccupation is with one, and their sense of achievement is through success in one. Transfer from one game to another is, of course, possible,

and the simultaneous playing of roles in two or more games is an important
manner of linking separate games. (p. 253)

Thus, university faculty members might consider themselves players in
both the "university game" and the "real school game," but, more often
than not, they and others view their major, if not only, role as that of a
university faculty member. They may be in schools at times, but they
rarely are considered players in the "real school" game.

Given their backgrounds and the differing rules of their primary
games, university faculty members are likely to approach schools and
school problems differently than educational administrators or teachers.
Clearly, all are concerned with improving opportunities for student learning. The realities of today's "real school game," however, are apt to
encourage administrators and teachers to place a far greater emphasis on
the importance of test scores as evidence of such learning than would university faculty members. The current rules of the "real school game" by
and large have made test scores a major determinant in the selection of
winners and losers. Administrators and teachers, unfortunately, often
seek dubious and quick means of helping them achieve their goal of
higher test scores. On the other hand, university faculty members are
more likely to be less concerned with the outcomes of any single assessment. They might advocate more robust means for long-term school
improvement as measured by multiple means. Their suggestions and proposals almost invariably have well-grounded theoretical bases, for theory
is valued and enjoys widespread acceptance by other players of the "university faculty" game, especially those from other disciplines. Unfortunately, such suggestions and proposals may fail to alleviate the "real
school" sense of urgency for practicality, familiarity, and near immediate
results.

THE ALLURE AND LIMITS OF THEORY

University faculty members in education departments easily can be drawn
in two directions—toward the very practical world of schooling, from
which many came, and toward the sometimes esoteric world of theory, a
staple of university culture. Such directions need not be diametrical oppo-
sites. As Joseph Schwab (1969) pointed out, the deliberations leading to
answers for the practical problems encountered in schools should be
informed, but not controlled, by theory. Clearly, theories that promote
practical solutions to real problems through deliberations—in Schwab's
(1983) words to curriculum professors, "enquiries which would inform,
advise and refresh their former students working in schools" (p. 263)—at

least stand a chance of entering the "real school game." The potential impact of such inquiries and their resultant theories, however, would most likely be limited to a single district, school, or even classroom. Such a limitation is not a problem in the Schwabbian world, but today's increasingly centralized, top-down approach to public education can make even such localized influence problematic.

Added to that problem is the unfortunate fact that many fellow players in the "university game" appear to pursue theory for its own sake. They invoke words such as "education," "schools," "teachers," "students," and "learning," yet their work is of limited or no value in today's "real school game." This observation can be easily confirmed by even the most cursory perusal of any recent American Educational Research Association conference program. These colleagues make rhetorical appeal to schools but are firmly centered in the "university game." Their efforts are valued and rewarded in most universities, and they are often viewed as successful by their colleagues. Although appreciated by like-minded individuals playing the same game, they are largely irrelevant to those regularly and directly involved in the "real school game." Their esoteric work can even lead to a questioning of the credibility of all educational scholars. Such an infatuation with theory to the extent that one escapes the presumed bases of his or her supposed field of inquiry is by no means unique to education; it is similar to the case of string theory in the field of physics.

String theory is a branch of theoretical physics that has grown to significant prominence since its initial development in the early 1980s. According to Brian Greene (1999/2003), a string theorist who has popularized the field through nontechnical books on the subject as well as a television program in the *Nova* series, string theory holds that subatomic quarks, of which protons, neutrons, and electrons are composed, "are actually tiny loops of vibrating string" (p. 14). String theorists contend that their work so far has united the separate theories of general relativity and quantum mechanics and may well provide the basis for a "Theory of Everything," long sought by many physicists. Such a theory would unite the four basic forces, gravitational, electromagnetic, weak, and strong, with a single underlying explanation. Since its inception, string theory has garnered significant influence and visibility. The theory's critics, however, point to its one inescapable shortcoming.

Physicist Lee Smolin (2006) was not alone when he recognized that string theory so far is untested, untestable, and unfalsifiable. In other words, it is not "science" as the term commonly is understood. As Peter Woit (2006) observed, "The problem is that superstring theory is not really a theory, but rather a set of hopes that a theory exists" (p. 204). With this idea in mind, Woit titled his critique of string theory *Not Even Wrong*, a phrase physicist Wolfgang Pauli invoked to describe an assertion that "is so incomplete and ill-defined that it can't be used to make firm predictions whose failure would show it to be wrong" (Woit, 2006, p. xii). Despite such a glaring flaw, string theory continues to garner attention and support, especially through university hiring practices and external funding, in large part due to the herd-like mentality of many physicists (Smolin, 2006). While it is not the only theoretical physics game in town, many physicists have determined string theory to be the best at this time, at least partly because of the distinct career advantages it currently offers.

Lacking strong experimental evidence, some string theorists take an almost metaphysical stance, claiming that the theory must be correct due to its "beauty and elegance," despite its failure to provide any predictions that can be verified or refuted by observational data (Woit, 2006, p. 261). Perhaps all of this will change in the future with a refined string theory or enhancements in data collection capabilities. On the other hand, string theory could become a sort of alchemy for the late twentieth and early twenty-first centuries, an endeavor with a mere patina of science. String theorists clearly are doing something, but whether or not that something is science remains uncertain. That some scientists in a well-established discipline such as physics could become so enamored with theory that they potentially lose sight of the reality they presumably set out to describe should serve as a reminder for educational scholars to remain alert and not to forget their own real world of schools. How many people "in education" at universities are not "doing education" in a way that is meaningful or even recognizable to those individuals in the "real school game," the very people they supposedly wish ultimately to influence with their results? Several options are open to educational scholars who wish to alter this situation.

THE EDUCATIONAL SCHOLAR AND SCHOOL PRACTICE

What follows is not a call to change the nature of AATC, whose purpose is the "scholarly study of teaching and curriculum" (AATC, 2006). This is a worthy and important purpose that must continue. Likewise, it is not a call for all educational scholars to follow a single path in their study and research. Free and open inquiry in a variety of directions remains critical for both the better understanding and improved practice of education. However, those individuals who wish to wield greater influence on educational policy and the conduct of schooling must recognize that the status quo in their professional lives will not suffice. They have two courses of action.

One option would be to provide input through studies that could be useful in deliberations at the national, state, district, or school level, as suggested by Schwab (1983). Many AATC members and others already do this. Unfortunately, those educators and others normally involved in such deliberations seldom, for whatever reason, make use of such works. The most likely explanations involve a lack of knowledge of or access to reports of these studies. While this option complies with all of the expectations of the "university game," and thus, is rewarded in that game, it almost certainly ensures faculty members at best a marginal status in the "real school game."

A potentially more productive option for educational scholars desiring to have a greater positive influence on schooling would be for at least some of them, for at least a portion of their careers, to engage more fully in the "real school game." Theodore Roosevelt (1910/2004) offered his unvarnished support of this course of action, noting its value and risks:

> It is not the critic who counts; not the man who points out how the strong man stumbles, or where the doer of deeds could have done them better. The credit belongs to the man who is actually in the arena, whose face is marred by dust and sweat and blood; who strives valiantly; who errs, and comes short again and again, because there is no effort without error and short-coming; but who does actually strive to do the deeds; who knows the great enthusiasms, the great devotions; who spends himself in a worthy cause; who at the best knows in the end the triumph of high achievement, and who at the worst, if he fails, at least fails while daring greatly, so that his place shall never be with the cold and timid souls who know neither victory nor defeat. (pp. 781–782)

At least three means beyond their customary research in schools exist for educational scholars who wish to enter the "arena."

First, educational scholars can write for a different audience than to which they are accustomed. For example, newspaper editorials or articles directed toward teachers or school administrators that are submitted to publications they read are likely to garner a larger readership and a readership more involved in the day-to-day world of schooling than any peer-refereed manuscript. Such works never will be cited, but they offer the potential of a far greater impact. Second, educational scholars can speak to groups such as school boards and legislative committees, groups that are in no way scholarly but whose membership is directly involved in the development of educational policy. Finally, educational scholars can become regularly involved with committees and other groups that inform policy decision making at the local, state, or national level, or even become members of those groups that ultimately make such decisions. Each of these alternatives serves to link more directly the "university game" with the "real school game," and provides participants in the latter with ideas and perspectives that otherwise likely would be ignored. Each of these alternatives would serve to enrich deliberation and improve schools.

Clearly, none of the above represents actions that would serve to enhance a junior faculty member's argument for tenure or promotion at most universities, nor should they be. To maintain credibility in the "university game" as well as to remain true to shared academic values, education faculty members ultimately must play the "university game" and be judged by rules similar to those used by other players. Thus, junior faculty members would be wise not to become overly involved in the "real school game" until they have their own careers in order. Likewise, many senior faculty members would find such endeavors unappealing. They must be allowed and encouraged to continue contributing to a better understanding of education in their own ways. There remain, however, some senior faculty members who have earned tenure and promotion and should consider entering the "arena." They can take on the risks required with minimal personal or professional consequences. Additionally, only a few members are needed in order to begin to bring the perspectives of many educational scholars to the discussion, and thus, to begin to help influence the decisions ultimately made.

Educational scholars who have waited for educational policymakers to seek the benefit of their insight and wisdom have not enjoyed great success. There is no reason to believe that continued waiting will result in anything other than an extended exercise in futility. Those educational scholars who choose to devote part of their time during a portion of their careers to the "real school game" by entering the "arena" can be satisfied with the knowledge that they contributed to the dialogue and improved schooling, that they made a difference. The alternative is that we largely continue writing for and talking to each other.

REFERENCES

American Association for Teaching and Curriculum. (2006). *Constitution* (Amended October 13, 2006). Retrieved September 9, 2007, from http://www.aatchome.org/AATC/Constitution.htm.

Bestor, A. E. (1953). *Educational wastelands: The retreat from learning in our public schools*. Urbana: The University of Illinois Press.

Bestor, A. (1955). *The restoration of learning: A program for redeeming the unfulfilled promise of American education*. New York: Alfred A. Knopf.

Firestone, W. A. (1989). Educational policy as an ecology of games. *Educational Researcher, 18*, 18–24.

Greene, B. (2003). *The elegant universe: Superstrings, hidden dimensions, and the quest for the ultimate theory*. New York: W. W. Norton. (Original work published 1999)

Long, N. E. (1958). The local community as an ecology of games. *American Journal of Sociology, 64*, 251–261.

Rickover, H. G. (1959). *Education and freedom.* New York: E. P. Dutton.

Rickover, H. G. (1963). *American education—A national failure: The problem of our schools and what we can learn from England.* New York: E. P. Dutton.

Roosevelt, T. (1910/2004). Citizenship in a republic. In L. Auchincloss (Ed.), *Theodore Roosevelt: Letters and speeches* (pp. 778–798). New York: Library of America. (Original work published 1910)

Schwab, J. J. (1969). The practical: A language for curriculum. *School Review, 78*, 1–23.

Schwab, J. J. (1983). The practical 4: Something for curriculum professors to do. *Curriculum Inquiry, 13*, 239–265.

Smolin, L. (2006). *The trouble with physics: The rise of string theory, the fall of a science, and what comes next.* Boston: Houghton Mifflin.

Woit, P. (2006). *Not even wrong: The failure of string theory and the search for unity in physical law.* New York: Basic Books.

CHAPTER 2

TEACHER AND PARENT BELIEFS ON TRACKING

A Taiwanese Perspective

Kai-Ju Yang

This paper explores what teachers and parents think about tracking as measured by the three dimensions of tracking identified by Oakes (1992)—the technical, normative, and political considerations. Questionnaires and interviews are used to collect data. Results show what teachers and parents believe about tracking agrees with Oakes' three dimensions of tracking. Results also reveal three additional findings: (1) teachers believe parents have a significant influence on tracking; (2) teachers believe tracking is inequitable but efficient; and (3) parents believe tracking is equitable and efficient.

I was assigned to the low-track classes in junior high school. Recalling my educational experiences during that period, I still feel vividly the unfairness of tracking at my school. For example, my school assigned veteran teachers to high-track classes to help students achieve high academic performance. However, the school paid little attention to low-track students or to helping these students learn academics content. As a researcher, I am now interested in what the teachers assigned into low-track classes

Curriculum and Teaching Dialogue
Volume 10, Numbers 1 & 2, 2008, pp. 13–26
Copyright © 2008 by Information Age Publishing

could do to improve their students' academic performance. Yet, whatever recommendations may stem from research, they must be informed by the views that teachers already hold.

HISTORICAL BACKGROUND ON TRACKING

Tracking has a long history that directly ties it to the purposes of education. As the educational philosopher Nel Noddings (1995) notes, Socrates provides one of the earliest examples that link differentiated education directly to social needs. In *The Republic*, Socrates argues that society requires three classes of citizens. Using the analogy of citizens as bronze, silver or gold, these classes included: (1) artisans or workers; (2) guardians; and (3) rulers. Education was differentiated based on the specific skills required by each role in the hierarchical structure.

Socrates' "Myth of the Metals" seems quaint but his conceptions of the role of education were not entirely undemocratic. In particular, Socrates believed that individuals would be happiest if they were able to use their natural abilities and were assigned to the role of worker, guardian, or ruler according to these abilities. A person's station in life was not inherited on the basis of family position or wealth. In making these points, Socrates anticipated that questions of fairness and equality would remain central in debates over how education should be used to address social needs.

In the United States, tracking as a widespread practice can be traced back to an era of urbanization, industrialization, and the resulting growth of the common school. As early as the mid-nineteenth century, educational leaders argued vigorously that tracking was efficient for what historian David Tyack (1994) called "the one best system" and Joel Spring (1989) refers to as the "sorting machine." As schools became larger and more bureaucratic, educational leaders sought practical forms of school organization. Yet, beyond efficiency, tailoring instruction and curriculum to the abilities of varying pupils may have been viewed as morally justifiable based on the argument that the same levels of education for all was a disadvantage to both faster-learning and slower-learning students.

THE LOGIC OF TRACKING

Why is tracking needed? The logic of tracking can be traced from two different perspectives--the pedagogical and the public.

Pedagogical Perspective

In a heterogeneous class, students differ widely in their intellectual abilities, and these differences are reflected in their educational outcomes. Theorists such as Bloom (1971) and Block (1974) claimed that students could achieve equitable outcomes if educators employ the method of mastery learning in their instruction. Mastery learning is an instructional technique for the teaching and learning of hierarchical, sequential materials. Materials to be learned are subdivided into units. Students are given a test at the end of each unit. If students do not receive a mastery grade on the test, they are provided with more time and teaching until they can achieve a mastery grade on a retest. Hopefully, this will allow all students to master the material and reduce the degree of inequality.

However, the equality of educational outcomes among students in a heterogeneous classroom is rarely attained if teaching time is the same for all students. This occurs because students are different in their learning speed and abilities. To diminish the inequality of educational outcomes among students, teachers have to provide extra teaching time for slower-learning students to master each unit, which causes the inequality of time among students and creates dilemmas. Just as Arlin (1984) observed,

> Given individual differences among students and a relationship between these differences and time needed to learn, the more we provide equality of time to students, the more we will obtain inequality of achievement; and the more we obtain equality of achievement, the more we will have to provide inequality of time to students. (p. 66)

If the extra teaching time for slower-learning students is needed, will teachers have to neglect fast-learning students? Will faster-learning students be held back while waiting for slower-learning students? Or will the slower-learning students be left behind? Tracking, an approach in which students are assessed based on their prior achievement or measured intelligence, and then placed into different level of homogeneous groups (Oakes, 2005), is often viewed as a way to avoid disadvantaging particular groups (see Figure 2.1).

Public Perspective

Policymakers and the public at large may view tracking as necessary for three reasons. First, students vary in their abilities. Second, education should address diverse social needs. And third, schools can best accommodate all students and prepare them for productive careers by tracking.

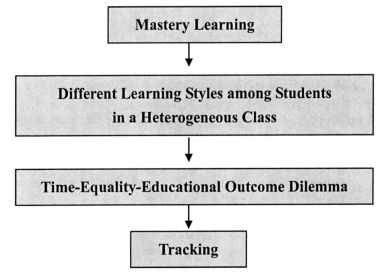

Figure 2.1.   The logic of tracking.

In short, tracking is seen as a way to produce the skills and knowledge needed for a differentiated work force.

CONCEPTUAL FRAMEWORK

Oakes (1992) suggested that tracking should be viewed as neither equitable nor an effective instructional management on three dimensions—the technical, normative, and political. In the technical dimension of tracking, content knowledge, teaching strategies, and school resources (including teachers) are different among tracks. However, that differentiation results in the inequality of learning opportunities and educational outcomes among students. In the normative dimension of tracking schools both accommodate different individual abilities and accomplish social purposes, such as work-force preparation, by sorting students into different tracks and providing students with a specific curriculum. In the political dimension, tracking produces an inequality of school resources and learning opportunities between high-track and low-track classes (Figure 2.2).

Drawing on Oakes' (1992) views, the research questions that emerged and are being investigated in this study are: From the perspective of the school teachers, what is tracking? Do their definitions include the technical, normative, and political views? Do they hold other ideas of tracking not mentioned by Oakes?

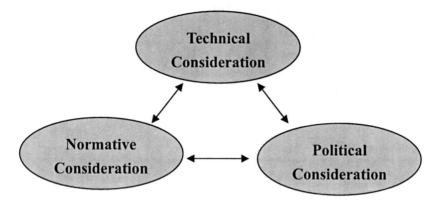

Figure 2.2.   Three dimensions of tracking. Tracking practice is neither equitable nor efficient.

METHODOLOGY

In order to select participants, I used five criteria. First, participating teachers were English, math, or science teachers because those subjects are more important than others in schools that track students. For example, Taiwanese schools make significant efforts to achieve high performance in English, math, and science. Second, participating teachers are from different junior high schools thus providing a broader range of sources. Third, participating teachers had at least 5 years of teaching experience. Fourth, the schools in which they teach implemented tracking practices. Finally, participating teachers went through tracking practices when they were in junior high school. In short, I sought teachers who had both professional and personal experiences with tracking. I surveyed and interviewed a total of six teachers—Chris, Peter, Mary, Jimin, Vicky, and Annie (see Table 2.1). Because the sample is small, it provides only a snapshot portrait of beliefs. Nevertheless, this sample still provides important insights into the concerns of practicing teachers.

The purpose of the questionnaire was to investigate *what* teachers think about tracking. The questionnaire included eleven questions that used a 4-point Likert scale. The questions focused on the technical, normative, and political dimensions of tracking practices mentioned by Oakes (1992). I also included questions on parental influence, drawing upon my own experience as a Taiwanese teacher and student. Completion of the questionnaires was facilitated by a 30-minute phone conversation with each participant.

Table 2.1.   The Information of Participating Teachers

Name	Subject	Years of Teaching	Location
Chris Wang	Math	15	suburban
Peter Chen	English	6	rural
Mary Sung	English	8	suburban
Jimin Lee	Math	17	urban
Vicky Hu	Science	15	urban
Annie Chan	English	12	urban

The purpose of the additional face-to-face interviews was to further explore *why* participants held the beliefs they did. The questionnaire thus served as a framework for the interview. Each teacher was interviewed twice, with each interview ranging from 60 to 90 minutes. Because my participants were in Taiwan, I returned to that country to conduct the interviews. Interviews were taped to increase the study's descriptive validity. As a follow-up to the teacher data, I also interviewed six Taiwanese parents from different social classes and parent viewpoints will be reported briefly in the second part of this study.

Table 2.2.   Questionaire Results

	Issues	SA	A	D	DA
Technical	Curriculum	83%	17%		
	Academic performance	66%	34%		
	Teacher assignment	17%	83%		
Normative	Work force		50%	50%	
	SES	34%	66%		
Political	School resource		100%		
	Equitable			100%	
Parental	Educational background		50%	50%	
	Parents at home	100%			
	Parents at school	34%			

A. Technical Dimension of the Tracking

Three statements (see Table 2.2) focused on the technical consideration of tracking practices. (1) Tracking produces differentiated curricula that are appropriate for different ability levels—83% strongly agree and 17% agree; (2) Tracking increases the gap in academic achievement between high-track students and low-track students—66 % strongly agree and 34% agree; and (3) More experienced teachers are assigned into high-track classes and new teachers are assigned into low-track classes—17% strongly agree and 83% agree. One of the participants, Mary Sung mentioned:

> Of course, tracking produces different curriculum which are appropriate for different ability levels.... I mean ... In a heterogeneous class, it would be unfair that faster-learning students are held back while waiting for slower-learning students to catch up.

In short, these teachers seem to agree that curricula, teaching strategies, and school resources (including teachers) differ among tracks.

B. Normative Dimension of the Tracking

Two statements (see Table 2.2) focused on the normative dimension of tracking. (1) Tracking has a positive impact on preparing students for productive work-force participation—50% agree and 50% disagree, and (2) More students in high-track classes are from middle or upper income families and more students in low-track classes are from low income families—34% strongly agree and 66% agree. One of the participants, Peter Chen reported:

> I think tracking has an impact on preparing students for productive work-force participation. For example, my school has the partnership with some factories. And some of the students in low-track classes go to the factory to learn some working skills. But I think it is too early to let them choose what they want to do in the future.

This is one of the two areas in which teachers seemed ambivalent. In particular, teachers disagreed over whether or not schools can both accommodate different individual abilities and accomplish social purposes, such as work-force preparation, by sorting students into different tracks with different curriculum.

C. Political Dimension of the Tracking

Two statements (see Table 2.2) focused on the political dimension of tracking. (1) Tracking strongly influences the school resources that students receive—100% agree; and (2) Tracking is an equitable instructional method—100% disagree. One of the participants, Chris Wang said:

Yeah, tracking influence the school resources that students receive, such as teachers or equipment. Take my school as an example. Teachers give extra instruction to high-track students from 7:00 am to 8:00 am while no teachers go to low-track classroom.

Here the teachers seemed in general agreement: Tracking produces an unequal distribution of school resources and learning opportunities.

EMERGENT THEMES

Two additional themes emerge from interviewing teachers (see Figure 2.3). First, these teachers believe that tracking is an inequitable but efficient form of instructional and curricular management. Second, they believe that parental influence is significant on tracking practices.

A. Inequitable but Efficient

At the end of the last interview, I asked each teacher "Is tracking an efficient instructional management device although it is not equitable?" The teachers all agree—Tracking is an inequitable but efficient practice. This finding is important because it conflicts with Oakes' (1992) conclusion that tracking is inefficient. Teachers explained that in their opinions regarding academic achievement, it is necessary for schools to track students. But they also admitted that tracking may decrease low-track stu-

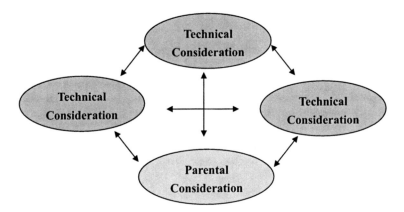

Figure 2.3.   Four dimensions of tracking. Tracking practice is inequitable but efficient.

dents' self-esteem and produce disparities in learning opportunities between low-track and high-track students. Chris said:

> In my opinion, tracking is a good instructional strategy to manage academic diversity among students, because it allows teachers to tailor their instructional approaches to students' abilities. Tracking also permits students to make progress commensurate with their abilities. For faster-learning students, it helps to maintain their learning interests because they do not have to wait for slower-learning students to catch up; on the other hand. For slower-learning students, it makes them participate more in the homogeneous class.

B. Parental Influence

Three survey statements (see Table 2.2) focused on parent involvement. (1) Parental educational background influences their child's track placement—50% agree and 50% disagree; (2) Parents play a significant role in their child's academic performance—100% strongly agree; and (3) Parents play a significant role in school activities when a school implements tracking—34% strongly agree and 66% agree.

During interviews, teachers indicated that parental involvement is not determined by track placement, but in how parents educate their children at home. This includes staying with the children at home to do homework and creating an environment at home which supplies appropriate forms of motivation. The teachers also indicated that parental involvement in school activities (such as attending Parent-Teacher Association meetings) gives students a feeling of care, love, and safety, which in turn leads to higher academic performance. Mary argued:

> Under tracking practices, parents play a very significant role in their child's schooling. If I distribute the percentage of influence to teachers, students, parents, and school administrator, I would say parents account for 40%, teachers 30%, students 20%, and school administrators 10%.

Because parental influence seemed so important in the teachers' eyes, I conducted interviews with parents to determine what they thought of tracking in the second part of this study. Six parents from different social classes were interviewed (see Table 2.3). Each interview was taped and lasted around 60 minutes. Every parent had at least one child in junior high school (seventh to ninth grade) at the time of the interview and these children attended different junior high schools. Three of these six parents (May Yen, Tom Chang, and Amy Xie), had children who recently completed the Senior High School National Entry Exam. May's son and

Table 2.3.   The Information of Participating Parents

Name	Profession	Educational Background
May Yen	Crime scene investigator	Doctoral degree
Tom Chang	Taxi driver	Elementary school diploma
Amy Xie	Vice CEO	Bachelor degree
Yo Chang	Secretary	Senior high school diploma
Paul Yen	Senior high school teacher	Bachelor degree
Suri Chan	Housewife	Junior high school diploma

Table 2.4.   Tracking Practice at School

	Tracking Practice at School?	
	Yes	No
May Yen	★	
Tom Chang		★
Amy Xie		★
Yo Chang		★
Paul Yen		★
Suri Chen		★

Tom's son had excellent grades and were accepted into some famous public schools in Taiwan. But Amy's daughter did not perform well, so Amy decided to send her daughter to a famous "cram" school for another year to better prepare her for next year's senior high school national entry exam. In other words, a student's academic performance in this national-wide exam determines the school to which they will be assigned.

In Taiwan, tracking has been utilized was implemented for 30 years. However, now it cannot be implemented in all schools because the Department of Education abandoned this instructional approach in 2000. However, there are still a few junior high schools using this instructional management, on an informal basis. This is particularly evident in those schools that are noted for their high academic standards. In my data, only May's son went to a junior high school that used tracking (see Table 2.4 above). This is also another reason why I wanted to interview parents to hear their views on tracking since they attended junior high schools that tracked students. However, now their children were attending junior high schools that do not practice tracking. How do these six parents feel about tracking in junior high school? Are there any differences between schools that practice tracking and schools that do not practice tracking? Which schools are better for their children? It is important to hear parents' voices regarding tracking practices.

The interview questions included: What are tracking practices? Do you think tracking is necessary for your child and why do you think so? Do you think tracking is or is not an effective form of instructional management and why do you think so? Do you think tracking is or is not an equitable form of instructional management and why do you think so? Do you think you self as a parent have an influence on your child's academic performance under tracking? What kinds of roles do parents play under tracking practices? How should schools best implement tracking?

Tracking Practices are Necessary for Your Child?

In general, the six parents agreed that tracking is the instructional management technique that assigns students into different level of homogeneous groups based on their prior achievement or measured intelligence. When I asked whether or not tracking practices are necessary for the child, five out of six parents agreed with this view (see Table 2.5). May said:

> Tracking is necessary for my child because it motives my son's learning interests. I think my son is a smart child but he does not like to study. After my son is assigned into high-track class, he told me that he wants to attend the cram school to increase more academic knowledge to get better academic performance because he does not want to be left behind in the class. Maybe you will think that learning should not be built on the competition, but in reality, my son is indeed learning something.

Amy also said the similar opinion:

> My daughter's school does not implement the tracking practice so my daughter is placed in a heterogeneous class. Based on what I have heard from my daughter and what I have known about the teaching and learning

Table 2.5. Interview Results

Issues	Agree	Disagree
Tracking practices are necessary for your child?	83%	17%
Tracking practices are effective?	83%	17%
Tracking practices are equitable?	50%	50%
Parents are influential on tracking practices?	100%	0%

in her class, I feel that my daughter did not learn much as I expected. I mean … she never asks me that she wants to attend the cram school to learn more academic knowledge. Even though I hired math tutor and English tutor for her, she did not pay much attention at learning. Everyday after she came back from school, she just sits down on the couch and watched TV. She did not spend much time at studying. In the other words, I think the heterogeneous class kind of decreases my daughter's motivation to learn.

Tracking Practices are Effective?

I asked each parent whether tracking is an effective instructional management strategy. Five parents agreed with this view (please see Table 5). Paul said:

I think tracking is an effective instructional management because it gives what child needs based on his ability. For example, if the child is smart enough to learn advanced math, then why keeps this child at the basic level for learning simple math? Oppositely, if the child has difficult at learning, then why forces this child to learn something that he cannot afford just because he is in a heterogeneous class?

As part of this interview question, I asked (1) when to assign students and (2) how to assign them. All of the parents think that the best time for children to be assigned into different levels of homogeneous groups is when the children are in the eighth grade (the second year of the junior high school) instead of the seventh grade. The criteria for placing students into different categories should be based on a students' IQ (intelligence quotient) test and academic performance, without taking teachers' recommendations into consideration. The parents interviewed believed that sometimes teachers' recommendations would not be able to reflect students' learning ability. For example, some wealthy parents might influence the teacher to write "beneficial" words to place their child into a high-track class. They believe that only an IQ test and academic performance could reflect most accurately students' learning ability.

Are Parents Influential on Tracking Practices?

All six parents reported that as a parent, they have influence on their child's academic performance. They all agreed that parental educational background is strongly related to the child's academic performance (see Table 2.5). They also think that parents should play the role of "friend" to their child, without placing undue pressure on academic performance. In addition, parents should also communicate frequently with their children and discuss what happens to them at home and at school. Suri said:

> I do not have higher educational degree so I might not be very helpful in academics for my daughter while other parents with higher educational degree help their child in academics, such as checking their child's home-work or answering their child's question. However, I frequently talk to the teacher a lot to understand my daughter's learning circumstance at school. Also, I do not give her much pressure on academic performance. I become her good friend. When she fails to the standardized test, I comfort her by giving her encouraging words instead of blaming her not studying well.

Tracking Practices are Equitable?

I asked each parent that whether tracking is an equitable form of instructional management. Three of the six parents agreed with this view (see Table 2.5). Amy said:

> Some people might think that tracking is not an equitable instructional management because the educational resources, such as teachers and learn-ing materials, are not fairly distributed into different groups. Well...in my opinion, I do think this kind of distribution is fair for both high-track stu-dents and low-track students. I mean, assigning a veteran experienced teacher into high-track class is appropriate to do because this teacher will be beneficial for these high-track students at learning. As for the low-track class (for example, a low-track class whose students are interested in cooking), then assign a teacher who is professional at cooking. From this perspective, I think tracking practice is an equitable instructional management because it meets students' needs.

Parent interview data suggested four results: (1) Tracking is viewed as necessary for their child, because it motivates students' to learn; (2) The best time to assign children to tracks is the eighth grade (seventh grade is now the typical practice in Taiwan). In addition, an IQ test and academic performance should be regarded as the only criteria for tracking place-ment; (3) Parental educational background strongly influences their child's academic achievement. Parents should play the role of "friend" to their child, without placing undue pressure on academic performance. Parents should also communicate frequently and discuss what happens to their child at home and at school; and (4) Tracking is an effective and equitable form of educational management. This perspective again con-flicts with Oakes' (1992) views, but unlike teachers, the parents differ from Oakes' on the issues of both effectiveness and equity.

SIGNIFICANCE

The teachers and parents who participated in this study agreed that tracking is an effective educational practice, though only the parents believed that tracking is equitable. The significance of these findings for curriculum scholars is to alert us to the conflicting values that different groups will hold regarding educational issues; this is especially true in cross-cultural contexts. Curriculum designed to meet social ends must recognize not only Oakes' multiple dimensions of tracking, but also how these dimensions are embedded in specific cultural frameworks. In particular, future research could examine more closely the alignment between cultural concepts of equity and tracking practices. It could be that Taiwanese perspectives on equity are either more collectively defined or given less weight than in Western cultures. Such understandings need further research, but they become increasingly important in efforts to match educational reforms with their cultural context.

Situating tracking and detracking reforms in a specific cultural setting does not invalidate Oakes' (1992) theories or her concerns over the ineffectiveness of tracking practices. Indeed, this study extends her efforts to broaden the perspectives from which we view this important aspect of education. This study also points to an opportunity to enhance the potential benefits and blunt the potential cultural conflicts of tracking in an increasingly globalized world.

REFERENCES

Arlin, M. (1984). Time, equality, and mastery learning. *Review of Educational Research, 54,* 65–86.

Block, J. H. (1974). Mastery learning in the classroom: An overview of recent research. In J. H. Block (Ed.), *Schools, society, and master learning* (pp. 26–29). New York: Holt, Rinehart and Winston.

Bloom, B. S. (1971). Mastery learning. In J. H. Block (Ed.), *Mastery learning: Theory and practice* (pp. 47–63). New York: Holt, Rinehart and Winston.

Noddings, N. (1995). *Philosophy of education.* Boulder, CO: Westview Press.

Oakes, J. (1992). Can tracking research inform practice? Technical, normative, and political considerations. *Educational Researcher, 21*(4), 12–21.

Oakes, J. (2005). *Keep track: How schools structure inequality.* New Haven, CT: Yale University Press.

Spring, J. (1989). *The sorting machine revised.* New York: Longman.

Tyack, D. B. (1974). *The one best system: A history of American urban education.* Cambridge, MA: Harvard University Press.

CHAPTER 3

THE CASE FOR SOCIAL SKILLS TRAINING IN THE PRIMARY SCHOOL CURRICULUM

A Follow Up Study of Attention and Theory of Mind Skills in First Grade Boys

Mary E. McGlamery and Steven E. Ball

The purpose of this study was to determine if boys originally tested during their kindergarten year had gained in theory of mind (ToM) skills. The original study found that boys, who had poor attentional skills, also had delays in ToM functioning. This study focused only on the ToM skills. Surprisingly, there was a significant decline in second-order theory of mind skills from initial kindergarten testing to first grade. The possibility that a shift in focus from relational to more academic endeavors was responsible for the loss suggests possible revisions to first grade curriculum. The implications for curricular changes are discussed.

Starting school is a major milestone for most children. Although many children may have early and varied experiences outside the home environment or may have attended various types of preschool, including day care, the beginning of kindergarten marks the entrance into "real" school, and

Curriculum and Teaching Dialogue
Volume 10, Numbers 1 & 2, 2008, pp. 27–39
Copyright © 2008 by Information Age Publishing

a world of new challenges. According to Entwisle and Alexander (1998), "How well students do in the primary grades matters more for their future success than does their school performance at any other time" (p. 354). As the young primary school student spends the majority of the weekday in this new—and perhaps largely unfamiliar—surrounding, (s)he encounters numerous social challenges. There are routines to be learned, relationships to establish with new adults and classmates, new environments to explore, and ever increasing demands of social expectations.

According to developmental psychologist Jean Piaget, children entering primary school are functioning at the preoperational level. Children in this stage exhibit egocentric tendencies; hence, they see the world from their own viewpoint. Young children may believe that others share their wants, needs, beliefs, feelings and desires. According to Piaget's (1929) theory, it is through interaction with the environment that children move from this egocentric view to an understanding that others are also thinking, feeling beings with needs, wants, and perspectives that may be quite different from their own. This ability to understand the mental states of others and predict behaviors based on that understanding is what Premack and Woodruff (1978) refer to as having a theory of mind (ToM).

The term "theory of mind" was coined by Premack and Woodruff to account for "Sara's" (a chimpanzee in a 1978 study) supposed ability to infer mental states of others and solve problems accordingly. Although Premack and Woodruff worked largely with primates, other researchers soon applied the concept of a ToM to studies of child development. Unlike Piaget's preoperational stage, which ends at roughly 7 years of age, many researchers believe that children as young as 3 years old are able to understand mental states. Young children begin to understand that people may differ in what they know, see, like or want—beliefs that have ties to everyday functioning. By the age of 4, children are beginning to solve problems and draw conclusions about behavior based on false beliefs. Dennett (1978) argued that it is the ability to predict actions based on what a person believes to be true and the predictor knows to be false that more robustly defines ToM skills. The acquisition of this ability is considered to be a turning point in social cognition.

Some researchers such as Shatz (1994) argue that ToM is an ability that generally develops later, appearing sometime after age 4. According to this viewpoint, it is through experience that young children develop a sense of self, as well as through comparison of this sense of self to that of others. As language and the ability to communicate verbally with others develop, children become better able to express internal states. Indeed, as early as age 2, children are able to express their own internal desires and intentions, as evidenced by phrases such as, "Want candy," "Go store," and so forth.

As ToM skills develop, children become aware of the intentions of others. This awareness is crucial to social functioning. Children need a ToM in order to understand that other people are individuals, separate from themselves, who have their own thoughts, beliefs, feelings, wants, needs, and perceptions. A ToM helps make sense of the world and explains why people engage in the behaviors that they do.

For example, interpreting the intentions of someone who spills milk on one's favorite jeans largely determines one's reaction to the event. Dodge and Pettit (2003) found that older preschoolers who are more socially adept at getting along with their peers can judge if an act is intentional or unintentional and gauge their reactions accordingly. This same study found that aggressive children have more trouble assessing intention and are, therefore, likely to react inappropriately to unintentional acts (such as inadvertently spilled milk or accidentally being bumped into while standing in line). Processing social cues, such as intention, is a complex task.

According to Dodge (1993), processing socially relevant information occurs in multiple steps and can prove to be especially formidable to children with poor attention skills. Disruption of the processing task due to attention deficits may result in difficulties for the child in both responding appropriately and monitoring his or her own behavior. A 1986 Dodge study noted that children with attentional difficulties might have a great deal of difficulty in both understanding the perspective of others and assessing intentionality.

There are mixed findings on the role of attention deficits in ToM development. Perner, Kain, and Barchfield (2002) noted that there is some evidence that children with predominately inattention features of ADHD (Attention Deficit Hyperactivity Disorder) experience ToM delays, while other researchers have found no such evidence (Charman, Carrol, & Sturge, 2001). However, problems experienced by children with ADHD are well documented. Kennedy (1999) found that students who met the criteria for Attention Deficit Hyperactivity–Combined (ADHD-C) and Attention Deficit Hyperactivity Disorder–Inattentive Type (ADHD-I) were rated by teachers as exhibiting significantly fewer cooperative classroom behaviors than a control group. Other problems experienced by students with ADHD include peer and teacher rejection (Millich & Landau, 1982), poor academic performance, risk taking and/or anti-social behaviors, such as alcohol and drug use (Barkley, Fischer, Smallish, & Fletcher, 2004), unstable relationships as adults, and diminished job success (Weiss & Hechtman, 1993).

So, how does inattention impact ToM development? In our original research study (McGlamery, Ball, Henley, & Besozzi, 2007), we were interested not only in the relationship between ToM and attention, but also in the multiple relationships bwtween and among ToM, attention, and executive function. This study aimed to answer the following questions:

- Do children with attentional difficulties evidence problems with executive function?
- Do children with attentional difficulties experience a delay in the development of ToM skills?
- Do children with delays in ToM skills evidence problems with executive function?

ORIGINAL STUDY

We administered, via DVD, three ToM tasks of varying difficulty to 67 kindergarten boys in six rural school districts in Northeast Texas. The tasks were administered individually and score sheets of the boys' answers were kept. The tasks were comprised of a false appearance task and two false belief "stories" taken from ToM literature (Baron-Cohen, 1989; Sullivan, Zaitchik, & Tager-Flusberg, 1994). The false appearance task consisted of surprise contents (crayons) in a Band-Aid box. The children were first shown the box and asked to guess the contents from three choices consisting of Band-Aids, crayons, and a large plastic figurine of "Sulley" from the movie, *Monsters* (Lasseter, Docter, Silverman, & Unkrich, 2001). After being shown that the box contained crayons, they were asked, "Now what do you think is in the box?" Next, a voice is heard calling the narrator's name and the children are told, "Hey, here comes my friend. What do you think she will say is in the box?" The final question was, "What did you think was in the box when you first saw it?"

The next two tasks involve narration of two stories. The first is the story of two children, John and Mary, who are playing in the park and encounter an ice cream vendor. John goes to buy an ice cream and discovers that he has left his money at home. The vendor tells John not to worry, that he will be in the park all afternoon. The boy goes home and the vendor decides to move to a new location—the church. On his way to the church, the vendor passes by John's house, sees John, and tells him where he is going. Mary knows that the vendor has moved to the church, but she does not know that the vendor has seen John. Mary goes home and then goes to John's house. She asks John's mother where he is and John's mother says, "He has gone to buy ice cream." Children are asked where Mary thinks John has gone and why.

The second story involves a little boy named Peter, who is celebrating his birthday. Peter's mom bought a puppy for Peter and has hidden it. She tells Peter that he is getting a toy. Meanwhile, Peter, unbeknown to his mom, finds the puppy. When Peter's grandmother calls and asks what Peter thinks he is getting for his birthday, the children are asked what Peter's mother will say and why. They are then asked what Peter is really getting for his birthday. Complete transcripts are provided in the Appendix.

Additionally, self-contained classroom teachers were asked to complete the Behavior Rating Inventory of Executive Function (BRIEF), and the Behavior Assessment Scale for Children–Revised (BASC-2). The BRIEF (Gioia, Isquith, Guy, & Kenworthy, 1996) is an inventory designed to assess executive function in individuals aged 5 to 18. The BRIEF scores are divided into categories associated with executive functioning, such as Inhibit, Shift, Plan/Organize, Working Memory, Monitor, and two composite scores. The BASC-2 (Reynolds & Kamphaus, 2004) is a rating instrument used to measure inattention, conduct problems, hyperactivity, social skills, anxiety, depression, learning problems, and atypicality. These inventories contain questions about the student's observable behavior, which teachers can easily rate on scales ranging from "never" to "almost always." We were primarily interested in the attention, hyperactivity, and composite executive function categories. We found a negative correlation between attention problems, as measured by the attention scale of the BASC-2, and ToM skills, as measured by performance on a series of "false belief" tasks. Our data suggests that children who scored lower on ToM tasks and were identified by teachers as evidencing attentional difficulties were also more likely to be identified by teachers as exhibiting behavioral difficulties.

Provided that ToM is such an important piece of social interaction and positive social interaction in the primary grades is extremely important to future success, we wanted to know if ToM abilities in the students tested had improved throughout the developmental processes. At this point, we were interested only in the developmental stage of ToM skills, rather than in the interaction of attention and executive function with ToM, which was the focus of the first study. For this reason, we chose not to re-administer the two behavior inventories for the follow up study, which is described in further detail in the next section.

METHOD

Participants

Of the 67 boys who participated in the original study as kindergartners, 47 participated in the present study as first graders. Students who did not participate had either moved from the district, did not return a consent form, or returned a consent form with participation permission denied.

Procedure

The students were again shown the three ToM tasks via DVD (see McGlamery et al., 2007). Again, briefly, the tasks consisted of short stories with LEGO characters. The students were asked questions during the DVD presentation of either first-order ("what does x believe") or second-order ("what does x think y believes") tasks. As noted, since ToM development was the focus of this study—rather than the interactions between ToM, attention, and executive function—neither the BRIEF nor the BASC-2 were re-administered.

RESULTS

Participants appeared to improve in first-order ToM abilities ($t(46) = 2.549$, $p = 0.014$), progressing from a mean of 2.13 to a mean 2.47 on the posttest.

Improvement on first-order scores was not correlated with chronological age ($r = -.008$), suggesting that these improvements were not strictly developmental, but possibly attributable to social experiences at home or in school. By contrast, second-order ToM scores actually declined significantly after a year in the first grade ($t(46) = 2.103$, $p = 0.041$), with mean scores dropping from 2.47 to 1.91. The correlation between chronological age and second-order difference scores was not statistically significant ($r = -.132$), again implying that development alone was not the source of the decline.

DISCUSSION

While the advance in first-order ToM skills would be anticipated and hoped for, the decline in second-order ToM scores is somewhat more problematic and, perhaps, speculative. It appears that the children had, possibly through the social interaction provided for in kindergarten, improved in their ability to determine what another might do or say in a given situation. This skill generally precedes second-order ToM skills (e.g., explaining what Mary thinks that John will do). Why the students exhibited a decline in second-order skills is, perhaps, a matter of conjecture. It could be that the original skills were not well established and decline occurred as a natural process of socialization. The notion that children have ebb and flow in abilities is not new. In his keynote address at the International Mind, Brain, and Education Society meeting held in Ft.

Worth, Texas in November of 2007, Howard Gardner spoke of the idea that knowledge at any developmental stage is not a structured whole. Gardner noted that at any one time a child might be at very different stages in his development. The idea that a child may "have" more of a skill one day and less the next does not seem contradictory. Although ToM is seen as a developmental phenomenon, Gardner's ideas may apply. Some individuals may proceed in a somewhat predictable path, while others may garner ToM skills by bits and pieces, gaining a bit here and losing a piece there.

Lave and Wenger (1991) advance the notion of situated learning, which could be applied not only to the acquisition of knowledge, per se, but also to the acquisition of social knowledge. Situated learning views knowledge acquisition as taking place in social relationships involving co-participation. Lave and Wenger refer to a community of practice, whereby participants first learn on the periphery of the community and, as they become more competent, move toward the center of the community. The kinds of social engagements experienced by the learners provide the context for learning to take place. Thus, learning is a process that is impacted by the situation in which learning takes place.

If we apply this concept of situated learning to the transition from kindergarten to first grade, the loss or decline of complex second-order ToM skills becomes more plausible. Transitioning from kindergarten to first grade involves a shift in curricular focus from a community where social skills are generally modeled and addressed both frequently and regularly to the more rigorous academic community of first grade. Children functioning on the periphery of ToM acquisition in kindergarten may well experience a decline in skills in the absence of use and modeling.

It is also worth noting that the transition from kindergarten to first grade is, in and of itself, a difficult one for some children. In a 1998 national survey of 3,600 kindergarten teachers' transition practices, teachers reported that some 48% of students experience moderate to severe problems in transitioning (National Center for Early Development & Learning, 1998). Additionally, the survey indicated that there is often a poor fit between the skills of kindergarteners and the expectations of their teachers. Mastering these new first grade expectations may be a daunting task for the new learner, requiring attention to stimuli very different from those common to the kindergarten classroom and inhibiting development of other, less modeled skills, such as ToM.

Additionally, the original study (McGlamery et al., 2007) noted a correlation between executive function, attention, and ToM skills. These findings may also have implications for the decline of skills. Students who have poor attentional skills and some impairment in executive function (such as problems with working memory, initiating tasks, and planning or organizing materials) may find themselves at a distinct disadvantage in the first grade classroom, where these skills are required.

So, what are the functional implications of ToM skills—or lack thereof? Being able to understand how others think and feel is important in school (and life) in a number of areas, including cooperative activities, moral development, acceptance of differences, resolving conflicts, and positive social actions. Helping students develop ToM skills should prove advantageous in terms of socialization skills as well as in academics. Social skills training has met with some success when used with children with ADHD, autism, and other behavioral disorders. Once again, Entwisle and Alexander (1998) emphasize "How well students do in the primary grades matters more for their future success than does their school performance at any other time" (p. 354). With continuing research on the efficacy of social skills training during the early years, primary school teachers may want to re-think their current curriculum and devise ways for the addition of social skills without the exclusion of academics.

The teaching of social skills need not take time from the regular academic studies. Teachers can choose literary works that emphasize acceptance, promote cooperation, and acquaint students with the customs of different ethnic or racial groups. Providing social scaffolding for students through pairing with a more socially adept peer may also prove to be beneficial. The use of Carol Gray's social stories with children with autism has received a tremendous amount of anecdotal support and may serve as an effective teaching tool for new or different situations. Finally, a variety of formal social skills training curricula are available for purchase commercially. Perhaps most importantly, modeling empathy and perspective taking is easily accomplished during the course of a normal school day, takes no time away from the academic curricula, and may well provide for the most effective gains in social adjustment.

APPENDIX A

Transcript for Band-Aid® Narrative

Hi, there. Today we are going to play a game. It's sort of like a guessing game. See this box? (Hold up band-aid box.) What do you think is in the box?

(Shows items, does not verbally name.)

Crayons Sulley Band-Aids®

(Pause. Count silently and slowly to 5.)

Let's see if you are right. (Open box)

Look! There are crayons in the box!

(Close box)

Now what do you think is in the box?

(Shows items)

Crayons   Sulley   Band-Aids®

(Close the box. Voice off camera calling, "Steve! Steve!")

Hey, here comes my friend Mary. What do you think she will say is in the box?

(shows items)

Crayons   Sulley   Band-Aids®

(Pause)

What did you think was in the box when you first say it?

(Shows items)

Crayons   Sulley   Band-Aids®

Thanks for playing! Good job!

APPENDIX B

John and Mary Narrative

Today we're going to play a game. I will tell you a story and then ask you some questions. This story takes place in a town. Here is the park and some playground equipment. Let's see if you can name the things in the park.

(Point to tricycle) What is this? (Pause) Very good.
(Point to swing) How about this? (Pause) Great.
(Hold up dog) And what do you think this is? Excellent.

Now I will tell you the story. Listen closely.

(Hold up dolls and move them appropriately)

This is John. This is Mary. They live in this town.

(Show Dolls) Which one is John? Which one is Mary?

Here they are in the park. Along comes the ice cream man. (Move van) John would like to buy an ice cream but he left his money at home. He is very sad.

(Put your finger on the ice cream man or motion to him in some way)

"Don't worry," said the ice cream man, "you can go home and get your money and buy some ice cream later. I'll be here in the park all afternoon."

"Oh, good," says John, "I'll be back in the afternoon to buy an ice cream." (Move John & Mary over to the swings)

Prompt Question 1: Where did the ice cream man say to John he would be all afternoon?

(Move John to his house. Leave Mary at the swings)

So John goes home. He lives in this house. (Move John to the house) Now, the ice cream man says, "I am going to drive my van to the church to see if I can sell my ice cream outside there."

Prompt Question 2: Where did the ice cream man say he was going?

Prompt Question 3: Did John hear that?

The ice cream man drives over to the church (move van). On his way he passes John's house. John sees him and says, "Where are you going?" The ice cream man says, "I'm going to sell some ice cream outside the church." So off he drives to the church.

Prompt Question 4: Where did the ice cream man tell John he was going?

Prompt Question 5. Does Mary know that the ice cream man has talked to John?

(Move John to the ice cream van.)

Now Mary goes home. (Put Mary on tricycle to ride to her house.) She lives in this house. (Take off trike, and let Mary "walk" to John's.) Then she goes to John's house. She knocks on the door (Bring Mom to door) and says, "Is John in?"

"No," says his mother, "he's gone to buy an ice cream."

Belief Question: Where does Mary think John has gone to buy an ice cream?

Justification Question: Why?

Reality Question: Where did John really go to buy his ice cream?

Memory Question: Where was the ice cream man in the beginning?

Thanks for playing this game. You did great!

APPENDIX C

Peter and the Puppy Narrative

I'm going to tell you a story about a little boy and then I will ask you some questions. (Motion to house) This is where Peter lives and this (motion to garage) is Peter's garage. (Motion to grandmother) This is where Peter's grandmother lives.

Tonight it's Peter's birthday party and Mom is surprising him with a puppy. (Move dolls appropriately for dialogue).

She has hidden the puppy in the garage. (Open window on garage and show puppy) Peter says, "Mom, I really hope you get me a puppy for my birthday."

Remember, Mom wants to surprise Peter with a puppy. So, instead of telling Peter she got him a puppy, Mom says, "Sorry Peter, I did not get you a puppy for your birthday. I got you a really great toy instead."

Probe Question 1. "Did Mom really get Peter a toy for his birthday?"

Probe Question 2. "Did Mom tell Peter she got him a toy for his birthday?"

Probe Question 3. "Why did Mom tell Peter that she got him a toy for his birthday?"

Now, Peter says to Mom, "I'm going outside to play." On his way to play, Peter goes by the garage to get his bike. In the garage, Peter finds the birthday puppy! Peter says to himself, "Wow, Mom didn't get me a toy, she really got me a puppy for my birthday. "

Mom does not see Peter go to the garage and find the birthday puppy.

First order belief question. "Does Peter know that his Mom got him a puppy for his birthday?"

First order belief question. "Does Mom know that Peter saw the birthday puppy in the garage?

Now, the telephone rings, ding-a-ling! Peter's grandmother calls to find out what time the birthday party is. Grandma asks Mom on the phone, "Does Peter know what you really got him for his birthday?"

Second-order false belief question. "What does Mom say to Grandma?"

Memory aid: Now remember, Mom does not know that Peter saw what she got him for his birthday.

Then, Grandma says to Mom, "What does Peter think you got him for his birthday?"

Second-order false-belief question. "What does Mom say to Grandma?"

Justification question. "Why does Mom say that?"

Thanks for playing. You did great!

REFERENCES

Barkley, R. A., Fischer, M., Smallish, L., & Fletcher, K. (2004). Young adult follow-up of hyperactive children: Antisocial activities and drug use. *Journal of Child Psychology and Psychiatry, 45(2),* 195–211.

Baron-Cohen, S. (1989). The autistic child's theory of mind: A case of specific developmental delay. *Journal of Child Psychology and Psychiatry, 30,* 285–298.

Charman, T., Carrol, F., & Sturge, C. (2001). Theory of mind, executive function, and social competence in boys with ADHD. *Emotional and Behavioral Difficulties, 6(1),* 31–49.

Dennett, D. (1978). Beliefs about beliefs. *Behavioral and Brain Sciences, 1,* 568–570.

Dodge, K. A. (1986). A social information processing model of social competence in children. In M. Perlmutter (Ed.), *Cognitive perspectives on children's social and behavioral development* (pp. 77–125). Hillsdale, NJ: Erlbaum.

Dodge, K. A. (1993). Social cognition mechanisms in the development of conduct disorder and depression. *Annual Review of Psychology, 44,* 559–584.

Dodge, K. A., & Pettit, G. S. (2003). A biopsychosocial model of the development of chronic conduct problems in adolescence. *Developmental Psychology, 39,* 349–371.

Entwisle, D. R., & Alexander, K. L. (1998). Facilitating the transition to first grade: The nature of transition and research on factors affecting it. *The Elementary School Journal, 98,* 351–364.

Gardner, H. (2007, November). *Keynote Address* presented at the meeting of the International Mind, Brain, and Education Society, Ft. Worth, TX.

Gioia, G. T., Isquith, P., Guy, S., & Kenworthy, L. (1996). *Behavior rating inventory of executive function.* Lutz, FL: Psychological Assessment Resources.

Kennedy, M. (1999). A comparative analysis of the social skills of children with attention deficit/hyperactivity disorder. *Dissertation Abstracts International, 60*(04), 1010.

Lasseter, J. (Executive Producer), Docter, P., Silverman, D., & Unkrich, L. (Directors). (2001). *Monsters, Inc.* [Motion picture]. United States: Pixar Animation Studios.

Lave, J., & Wenger, E. (1991). *Situated learning: Legitimate peripheral participation.* Cambridge, England: University of Cambridge Press.

McGlamery, M., Ball, S., Henley, T., & Besozzi, M. (2007). Theory of mind, attention, and executive function in kindergarten boys. *Emotional and Behavioural Difficulties, 12(1),* 29–47.

Millich, R., & Landau, S. (1982). Socialization and peer relations in hyperactive children. In K. D. Gadow & I. Bialer (Eds.), *Advances in learning and behavioral Disabilities* (pp. 283–339). Greenwich, CT: JAI Press.

National Center for Early Development and Learning. (1998, July). *Spotlight #1: Kindergarten Transitions.* Chapel Hill, NC: Author.

Perner, J., Kain, W., & Barchfield, P. (2002). Executive control and higher-order theory of mind in children at risk of ADHD. *Infant and Child Development, 11,* 141–158.

Piaget, J. (1929). *The child's conception of the world.* New York: Harcourt Brace.

Premack, D., & Woodruff, G. (1978). Does the chimpanzee have a theory of mind? *Behavioral and Brain Science, 4,* 515–526.

Reynolds, C. R., & Kamphaus, R. W. (2004). *Behavior assessment system for children II.* Circle Pines, MN: American Guidance Service.

Shatz, M. (1994). Theory of mind and the development of social-linguistic intelligence in early childhood. In C. Lewis & P. Mitchell (Eds.), *Children's early understanding of mind.* Hove, England: Erlbaum.

Sullivan, K., Zaitchik, D., & Tager-Flusberg, H. (1994). Preschoolers can attribute second-order beliefs. *Developmental Psychology, 30(3),* 395–402.

Weiss, G., & Hechtman, L. (1993). *Hyperactive children grown up: ADHD in children, adolescents, and adults* (2nd ed.). New York: Guilford.

CHAPTER 4

PROJECT TEACH

Using Reality Shows as a
Framework for Teaching Methods Courses

Jacqueline Bach

Inspired by a comment made by Madeleine Grumet at the 2006 AATC conference, this study explores the redesigning of English/Language Arts methods course based on the Bravo show, Project Runway. The author considers how an approach can (re)create some of the fundamental assignments in these courses, such as lesson planning. She concludes by providing suggestions for teacher educators wanting to avoid using popular culture as teaching "gimmicks."

When I heard curriculum theorist Madeleine Grumet confess at the 2006 AATC conference that she had not been reading lately because she had been watching the latest season of *Project Runway,* I immediately perked up, as I was an ardent fan of the first three seasons. Grumet proposed that curriculum theory courses should be taught in a manner similar to the show: students would be presented with a real problem and then be asked to provide solutions to that problem.

I am not sure if she thought anyone in the audience would take her comment seriously (although fans of the show readily voiced our agreement),

Curriculum and Teaching Dialogue
Volume 10, Numbers 1 & 2, 2008, pp. 41–53

but I spent quite a bit of time pondering her suggestion. Aware of the criticism surrounding the use of popular television shows, like *Survivor* and *Jeopardy*, as models for delivering content in the classroom (Gustavson & Appelbaum, 2006), I know that "gimmicks" do not necessarily translate into successful learning experiences. A "reality" course might tap into the interests of my students (as well as my own) but not prepare them for the realities of teaching. Grumet's suggestion is somewhat related to problem-based learning (PBL), and I could see how this television-inspired approach might enrich students' engagement with education courses' texts and topics. Because of the opportunities to apply theoretical readings to practical applications, to encourage creative, autonomous approaches to actual classroom issues, and to challenge the traditional roles of teachers and students, *Project Runway* provides a useful, alternative model for teaching education courses.

LESSON WRITING IN EDUCATION METHODS COURSES

There seem to be a few assignments that many colleges and universities typically include in their teacher education courses: the teaching philosophy essay; the field experiences journal; and the teaching unit. In the Methods of Teaching English/Language Arts (one of the courses that I teach), we write lesson plans. Smagorinsky and Whiting's (1995) research of the syllabi used in English methods courses showed that 69% of those instructors required their students to write lesson plans and engage in teaching demonstrations as part of their coursework. Only four out of the 79 syllabi they examined, however, actually required students to teach the lessons they created in their cooperating teachers' classrooms.[1] This finding is understandable considering that many field experience students might find themselves having to use their cooperating teachers' lesson plans for the convenience of their schedules, continuity of the classes' schedules, and consistency in level of expectations. In order to address this limitation, some instructors incorporated into their courses presentations on lesson planning by master teachers or studies of " 'cases' of problematic teaching situations" (p. 16) as a means for exploring writing lessons for different contexts (Smagorinsky & Whiting, 1995). They also found that instructors adopted a "workshop approach," which required students to work in groups on lesson plans in a series of steps, culminating with the presentation and/or teaching of those lessons to their classmates. The limitations with these approaches are similar to the other limitations tied to writing lesson plans in methods courses: unless students are in the field working with a teacher who is able to make space for them to teach those lessons, they are unable to try out their ideas in "real" teaching situations.

Eleven years later, Dickson, Smagorinsky, and a number of leaders in the field of English education (Dickson et al., 2006) presented components of successful English/Language Arts methods courses. Those components included teaching "purposeful observation," holding conversations with the various parties responsible for teacher education programs, and fostering mentor teacher relationships (p. 325). In order to create "exemplary programs," Dickson et al. (2006) proposed that teacher educators—along with their students—should "engage in more provocative research that can help us and our students articulate the ways our work has import, and to use that knowledge to help us continue to improve our programs" (p. 325). Since many English/Language Arts methods instructors require their students to engage in lesson-plan writing (which they should), and students rarely have the opportunity to teach one or more lessons created during their field experiences, two guiding questions emerge:

1. How might PBL be modified to include problems which students feel are "authentic" representations of their experiences in the field?
2. How might PBL, guided by the reality show *Project Runway*, contribute to how teacher educators and their students create meaningful lessons?

Because of the opportunities to apply theoretical readings to practical applications, to encourage creative, autonomous approaches to actual teaching and classroom management issues, and to rethink the roles of teachers and students, *Project Runway* provides a useful alternative model for teaching how to write lesson plans that may not be used in authentic teaching situations.

WHAT IS PROBLEM-BASED LEARNING?

First used by Howard Barrows in the medical field as a strategy for preparing future physicians, PBL continues to make its way into education (Slavkin, 2004; Torp, 2002). Traditionally, in this approach, teachers carefully craft a problem for students to explore. In small groups, students decide on ways to "solve" this problem. In many cases, the teacher, or a group of "experts," acts as facilitators and assist groups with their endeavors. In other words, the point is not necessarily to find the "right" answer but for classmates to work together with their various knowledge, resources, and experiences to create these "solutions." Many scholars have pointed out the positive learning experiences created by PBL in education courses and professional development opportunities (Mikeska, Lundeberg, Koehler, & Weizman, 2007; Mulcahy, 2006; Slavkin, 2004; Torp, 2002). However, the seemingly contrived nature of creating solutions to a problem that is hypothetical and removed from students' concrete experiences keeps students from making meaningful connections with the actual experience of teaching. A *Project Runway* approach, with many of its weekly challenges, including professional design companies and celebrity clients, incorporates "real" problems into its format.

This study is not the first one to attempt to find a variation of PBL that would satisfy both teachers' and students' needs. Chung and Chow (2004) created a framework designed to introduce and ease occupational therapy students into PBL. They found that working with students to revise the use of PBL in their program improved their students' learning experiences. Mulcahy (2006) explores how PBL might produce "capable beginning teachers, self-reflective professionals, and competent" (p. 57). Hardie (2007) merges popular culture with an academic context in order to create a meaningful experience for her graphic design students. They put a particular graphic design manifesto "on trial" and use popular television shows like the BBC's *Judge John Deed* and CBS's *Judge Judy* (Hardie, 2007, p. 217) to create a trial in which students assume various roles. This creative approach addresses many skills than just problem solving. Interested in whether introducing teachers to PBL strategies in professional development courses would move them toward a more student-centered approach to teaching, Mikeska et al. (2007) developed two templates for creating PBLs: a teaching dilemma and a content dilemma. PBL is an interdisciplinary teaching strategy that needs to be modified for every instructor who intends to incorporate it into his/her program.

Thus, it is interesting that so many reality shows are based on authentic problems—albeit out of contrived contexts. Whether one must literally survive, crisscross the world, or maintain sanity in a house with 24-hour surveillance, reality shows are at their best when they focus on "real" tasks. *Project Runway* begins each season with 12–16 contestants who have various experiences in designing and producing clothes. They move to posh New York flats and spend most of the season at the Parsons New School for Design. Each week, the group receives a fashion challenge from the host, supermodel Heidi Klum. They then have between 1 and 2 days to conceptualize, design, prepare, create, and show their original (or often sadly unoriginal) outfits. They are given a certain amount of money and/or resources with which to work, and receive mentoring from Tim Gunn, Chair of the Fashion Design Department at Parsons. They then showcase their creations in a runway show for a panel of judges. After the contestants' designs are judged, they receive very frank—sometimes harsh—comments from the judges.

A winner is chosen, and then rewarded. A loser is also chosen, who is subsequently eliminated from the show (Bach, 2008, p. 154). There are a few restrictions in adapting this format for the classroom: educators may not kick students out of their classes for coming in last during a challenge; they may not offer truly stupendous rewards; and they should not recreate such an intense, competitive atmosphere in their classrooms.

METHOD

Design

Each semester, I teach a methods course on the instruction of secondary English/Language Arts. My students take this course the semester before their student teaching internship. Most are in their third semester of the English education program and have spent between 40 and 60 hours each semester observing teachers and students in diverse school settings. As they progress through the program, they are encouraged to take a more active role in their field placements by designing and teaching lessons in these placements. We then meet 2 hours each week to discuss their experiences and to explore the various methods for teaching English/Language Arts. The university's course catalog asserts that the main objective for the methods student is "to apply instructional strategies." Therefore, much of the work we do pertains to the designing and presenting lessons and units that incorporate various research-based teaching strategies.

Procedure

Collecting and analyzing data collected during teacher research can be especially problematic, and those challenges influenced the collection and interpretation of the data for this study. In his work on the often precarious role of teacher researcher, Hammack (1997) explores the ways in which they might exploit their students for the benefit of their own research agenda, consequently neglecting the needs of their students. In their article on teacher research, Nolen and Putten (2007) recommend that teacher researchers be sensitive to their roles as teachers and researchers, remind their students of their rights, and allow their participants to be active members in the decision-making process at all stages. Even before I began this study, I briefed my students on my motives, how my university's institutional review board's protocol tries to protect their rights as participants in the study, how the data they created for this study was part of their ordinary coursework (it was not extra work), and explained that their grades would not be affected by whether or not they participated in the study.

For this study, participants created three different lesson plans using three different approaches: traditional PBL, components from *Project Runway*, and teacher-led instruction. All three lessons plans began with the district's comprehensive curriculum, which asks teachers to teach mini-lessons on various rules of grammar. According to the curriculum guide, those lessons should improve upon deficient skills exhibited in students' writing. Participants completed pre- and postsurveys on their experiences with PBL and designing lessons. Like Chung and Chow (2004), I used these to assess my students' previous experiences with PBL. After participants submitted each lesson plan and received feedback, they responded to two questions about their experiences with each approach: (a) Describe your experience with this approach to lesson writing; and (b) How does this lesson compare with the other lessons you have written? Using a list of resources I provided for them, they checked off the different resources used in creating their lessons (e.g., the Internet, their cooperating teacher, or their textbooks). During and after class, I made notes based on my observationsm, which I later wrote into fieldnotes based on the recommendations of Emerson, Fretz, and Shaw (1995), and kept copies of the final lessons. Participants also offered feedback on the initial findings of the study.

Keeping my students' needs foremost in my mind, I used anonymous presurveys to ascertain what types of experiences they felt they had missed in writing lesson plans. I then compared those surveys with the postsurveys to determine which approaches worked and which ones left them lackluster. I read and reread their reflections about each lesson approach (which were also anonymous), looking for connections between their responses and the surveys. I also compared the lessons they created with their reflections in search of emerging themes. As codes emerged, I turned those codes into analytical statements, which informed the conclusions I made at the end of my study.

Finally, I member-checked with my students throughout the study by collecting their written responses, listening to informal comments made before and after class, and by discussing my findings with them at the conclusion of the study. Stringer (1996) notes the importance of presenting one's findings so that participants "understand their own experiences in terms that make sense to them" (p. 81). Keeping this advice in mind, I tried to present my findings to my students as they unfolded throughout the semester.

FIRST LESSON PLAN:
TRADITIONAL APPROACH TO PROBLEM-BASED LEARNING

Using the teaching dilemma template for PBL created by Mikeska et al. (2007), I created a fictitious scenario for my students. Using my district's lesson plan template, students created a lesson plan addressing the teaching objective provided in the following scenario:

PBL Focus on Practice Teaching Dilemma:
Instructional Decision Making

Topic: Grammar related to writings completed for 10th grade nonfiction comprehensive curriculum unit.

Context: I began the unit on nonfiction by asking my students to complete activity #5 (A Memorable Event, see page 19 of the comprehensive curriculum). As I read their drafts, I noticed that many of them were having problems with using apostrophes (instead of using them to indicate possessives or contractions, they were using them to make words plural); commas with introductory elements (they are not using them); and making pronouns agree with antecedents.

Objective:[2] Students will be able to identify one or more of these errors and be able to correct them.

My students found that the specific information about this scenario facilitated a smoother start to finding an activity that would address this teacher's need. However, in their written reflections, students characterized their own lessons as "uncreative" and "more boring" than other lessons they had written in previous courses because they were limited to a scenario.

For some, this was the first time they had been asked to write a lesson in a group, and they mentioned that the experience was "strange ... because everyone had either a different opinion or none at all." Lopsided contributions often occur during unstructured group work like PBL, so Faidley, Salisbury-Glennon, Glenn, and Hmelo (2000) have offered suggestions to counteract one or two people dominating the process. They contend that the facilitator should not play an overly dominant role in the problem to be solved but instead focus on solving the problem of the group's dynamics. On the other hand, some students expressed the ease of working in groups from the synergy that resulted from the various contributions of group members. They also found the group approach to be "very laid back" and appreciated the opportunity "to collaborate" because, as one student observed, "more ideas (perspectives) for one project/ lesson make lessons even better." Students also commented on the importance of on-going feedback during the process of writing this lesson, especially feedback from their peers. Overall, the lessons were generated from ideas based on their field experiences, textbooks, and classmates. They were not necessarily "boring" as much as they were more traditionally structured, teacher-centered lessons that include the introduction of the skill, practice of the skill, and assessment of the skill.

SECOND LESSON PLAN: THE "WALK OFF"

Only 4 out of the 79 syllabi examined by Smagorinsky and Whiting (1995) required students to teach the lessons they created in their cooperating teachers' classrooms. Remaining in the same groups, the second lesson plan my students created was based on a *Project Runway* model in which I tried to provide an actual context for my students to consider when writing their lessons. Since Dickson et al. (2006) recommend that methods courses create school partnerships and connect with mentor teachers, I included practitioners outside of my university during this activity. For this challenge, I brought in a practicing teacher from one of the field placement school sites as the "client." Together we created the following challenge:

> Your client has noticed the following trends in her students' writing from the back-to-school letters in which they described themselves as students.
> - Some students might like to do *they're* work in class, but I like to do mine at home in my room.
> - I don't have a specific place *were* I keep my writing, but I have done a lot of it.
> - I was *to* ashamed to ask for help with reading faster.
>
> She then asks you for help in constructing a mini-lesson that addresses the similar errors located in each of these examples to use in class tomorrow. After the mini-lesson, your colleague wants to be able to determine whether or not her students understand the concept covered.
> Your group's challenge is to design and present a 15–20 minute lesson plan that not only identifies the recurring errors in each one of these sentences, but also includes a follow-up idea for tracking your colleague's students' progress.

The judges for this challenge were the "client/teacher," her student teacher, and the district's language arts specialist. The reward for the "winners" was to have their mini-lesson used by the "client" and receive feedback on its effectiveness. Each group presented their lessons to the class and the panel of judges who asked questions about each approach. The judges then deliberated, returned to our class, shared their responses, and announced the "winner."

Students enjoyed not only the immediate feedback, but also "getting to see everyone's take on the same problem." In addition, several students remarked how "proud" they were with their lessons and how "positive feedback ... reaffirms how strong [he/she] thought this lesson was in comparison to [his/her] others." My students also commented on how they incorporated feedback they received on their previous lesson when writing their next lesson. They also noted that oral feedback was "exciting" and helped them think about their colleagues' approaches to the same problem.[3] They also valued the feedback from other teachers because "[it] really made [them] look at it [the lesson] from a different angle."

Although I did not ask for it specifically, three out of the four groups incorporated popular culture into either their lessons or presentations. These lessons focused more on motivation and relating the content to students' needs and interests. Three of the four groups also created visual aids or mnemonic devices that students may refer to throughout the school year, continually reminding them of common spelling and grammatical errors.

THIRD LESSON PLAN DESCRIPTION: A RETURN TO THE BASICS

A common criticism of PBL is that students' previous experiences may not have prepared them for PBL (Pawson et al., 2006). Occasionally, students even expressed a preference for their instructor to lecture. Keeping these criticisms in mind, I designed the final activity according to a traditional way of teaching students to write lessons: I created a step-by-step approach to completing the district's lesson template and showed them an example that I had prepared. These lessons are often evaluated with a rubric created not only for the instructor to use as a grading tool but also as a means to collect various assessment data. Therefore, these rubrics are tied more closely to the professional organization's standards and provide generic feedback as opposed to field-based feedback. It was important to me for students to become familiar with this template, and it did not seem to make sense to let them figure out how to use the form on their own.

I asked my students to identify a grammar concept that they felt could improve their students' writing. For example, I asked them to explore ways to encourage their students to use more gerunds in their essays. For this activity, students—once again in the same group of three—created another mini-lesson addressing the grade level expectations from the district's comprehensive curriculum. Because research shows that PBL leaves out essential information that an instructor can provide, I walked my students through one of the "best ways" to write a lesson, using the template provided by our district and my own objective for using grammar to improve student writing. This time, I explained the concept behind each component of that template and how to match the district's grade level expectations with one's own objectives.

Students commented that they liked having "a clear idea of what was expected" and found the district's template to be user-friendly. However, having to incorporate the district's grade level expectations was a distraction for some of them. Several confessed that "it [was]n't my best or most creative work" or that their lesson was "way too narrow" and "not as fun." One student also commented on the amount of work it took to complete the template. The resources students used for creating this activity were derived mainly from their field experiences observations, their own experiences as a student, and ideas from their classmates.

Once again, these lessons were examples of traditional approaches to teaching grammar.[4] One group did not address the assignment; instead, they created a lesson that focused more on the types of writing (e.g., narrative), rather than on how the understanding of a grammatical concept could improve student writing. Possibly this confusion occurred because my role was neither facilitator nor mentor this time—but instructor— and they wrote their lessons outside of class. I answered questions if they had them, and I did not examine their work until after they turned in their lessons. I suspect this method is the one most commonly used in the traditional instructor-led "teaching" of how to write a lesson plan.

DISCUSSION

In their final reflections, students continually noted the need to "test" out their lesson plans in "real" classrooms. In spite of their 100+ hours completing field experiences in secondary schools, they still felt unsure as to the quality and feasibility of the lesson plans they were creating. While there can be no substitute for designing and teaching a lesson to a group of high school sophomores, pre-service teachers do need authentic opportunities to write lessons and "try them out" before they enter the field full time as student teachers. While a *Project Runway* approach has its limitations, many of its qualities can improve how methods course instructors can help students gain confidence in writing lessons that may not actually be used by them in the field. Based on the written reflections after each activity, the types of lessons created, and my observations, I suggest the following techniques for lesson-writing in methods classes and how a *Project Runway* approach addresses each need:

1. **Students need opportunities to design lessons in groups and individually.** Just as some of the *Project Runway* challenges are individually completed, some are with partners, and some are in groups. Just as in an ideal school setting, teachers too should often

come together to plan lessons and objectives, but ultimately retain a level of autonomy.

2. **Students need opportunities to design lessons for a particular group of students**. As demonstrated in the second approach of this study, the opportunity to interact with a client and determine the needs of his or her students may help teacher candidates address their lessons to a particular audience.

3. **Students should be able to share their "solutions" to the same problem and discuss with experts about their various approaches.** A formal presentation of lessons, coupled with the light-hearted competitive nature of a challenge, engages participants in considering multiple approaches to one problem.

4. **Students prefer a traditional approach to lesson-writing using a particular format, possibly the district's lesson plan template, comprehensive curriculum, and grade level expectations.** While these pieces can easily be included in a challenge and serve to make the experience authentic, this finding stresses what most already know about education—scaffolding works. Part of a challenge/problem might be figuring out how to use these tools. However, studies about most PBL approaches show that students sometimes prefer the lecture. **Students need feedback, preferably immediate, and from more than one source**. Again, the mentor, other classmates' opinions, and a panel of experts from the field contribute to the multiple types and sources of feedback during this variation to PBL. While others have posted student work to Web sites (Chung & Chow, 2004), immediate feedback from the instructor, classmates, and a panel of experts seems to be more valuable to students.

A *Project Runway* approach to teaching methods classes introduces many questions into the field of teacher preparation. How can teacher educators incorporate popular culture into their courses in ways other than critiquing and analyzing, even producing it, or using it as a springboard to talk about the content area or for creating gimmicky-type lessons? Furthermore, if teacher educators successfully implement popular culture into their courses, will their students go on to consider meaningful engagements in their future professions? Finally, how can these approaches be evaluated? One way is to consider what researchers believe is required for building successful education programs and using those criteria as benchmarks. I hope to continue to examine these questions by conducting "provocative research" with my students; next semester, I will ask them to create the challenges.

In previous semesters, I used three types of challenges based on three different templates from the show: the design for a client, the field trip, and the design for a colleague. One of these is an individual challenge and the other two are group challenges. I am constantly aware of Vasquez's (2005) caution not to co-opt our students' interests; however, I find this approach to be not only meaningful but also invigorating. One of my students aptly summarizes the role that popular culture can play in teachers' practices and why I will continue with this approach: "I can't stand being boring, or being bored, so things like this are really fun ... If I ever turn into a boring teacher, I want the authorities alerted immediately." I could not agree more.

NOTES

1. A cooperating teacher is a mentor teacher with whom each field experience student is paired.
2. I left out the final three parts to Mikeska, Koehler, and Weizman's (2007) template because their findings suggested that when students were presented with an explicit teaching dilemma, a focus question, and instructions for creating a product, the final "solutions" were more structured and traditional approaches to learning.
3. The only time my students presented their lessons to one another was in the *Project Runway* approach.
4. The limitation in the variety of lessons might be linked to students' own experiences with grammar. They may not have been exposed to non-traditional ways of teaching grammar before this semester. Because many of them indicated that these lessons came from their own or each other's experiences as students, and I did not ask them in this lesson to create a non-traditional approach this conclusion is likely.

REFERENCES

Bach, J. (2008). Reality shows and problem-based learning. *Academic Exchange, 12*(1), 153–157.

Chung, J. C. C., & Chow, S. M. K. (2004). Promoting student learning through a student-centered problem-based learning subject curriculum. *Innovation in Education and Teaching International, 41*(2), 157–168.

Dickson, R., Smagorinsky, P., Bush, J., Christenbury, L., Cummings, B., George, M., et al. (2006). Are methods enough? Situating English education programs within the multiple settings of learning to teach. *English Education, 38*(4), 312–328.

Emerson, M. E., Fretz, R. I., & Shaw, L. L. (1995). *Writing ethnographic fieldnotes.* Chicago: The University of Chicago Press.

Faidley, J., Salisbury-Glennon, J., Glenn, J., & Hmelo, C. E. (2000). How are we doing? Methods of assessing group processing in a problem-based learning context. In D. H. Evenson & C. E. Hmelo (Eds.), *Problem-based learning: A research perspective on learning interactions* (pp. 109–136) Mahwah, NJ: Elrbaum.

Gustavson, L., & Appelbaum, P. (2006). Youth cultural practices, popular culture, and classroom teaching. In L. Kincheloe (Ed.), *Classroom teaching: An introduction* (pp. 281–297) New York: Peter Lang.

Hammack, F. (1997). Ethical issues in teacher research. *Teachers College Record, 99*(2), 247–265.

Hardie, K. (2007). On trial: Teaching without talking—teacher as silent witness. *Art, Design & Communication in Higher Education, 5*(3), 213–226.

Mikeska, J. N., Lundeberg, M. A., Koehler, M. J., & Weizman, A. (2007, April). *Designing teaching dilemmas for problem-based learning professional development.* Paper presented at the annual meeting of the American Educational Research Association, Chicago.

Mulcahy, D. (2006). The salience of space for pedagogy and identity in teacher education: Problem-based learning as a case in point. *Pedagogy, Culture & Society, 14*(1), 55–69.

Nolen, A. L., & Putten, J. V. (2007). Action research in education: Addressing gaps in ethical principles and practices. *Educational Researcher, 36*(7), 401–407.

Pawson, E., Fournier, E., Haight, M., Muniz, M., Trafford, J., & Vajoczki, S. (2006). Problem-based learning in geography: Towards a critical assessment of its purposes, benefits and risks. *Journal of Geography in Higher Education, 30*(1), 103–116.

Slavkin, M. L. (2004). *Authentic learning: How learning about the brain can shape the development of students.* Lanham, MD: Scarecrow Education.

Smagorinsky, P., & Whiting, M. (1995). *How English teachers get taught: Methods of teaching the methods class.* Urbana, IL: National Council of Teachers of English.

Stringer, E. (1996). *Action research: A handbook for practitioners.* Thousand Oaks, CA: SAGE.

Torp, L. (2002). *Problems as possibilities: Problem-based learning for K-16 education.* Alexandria, VA: Association for Supervision and Curriculum Development.

Vasquez, V. (2005). Resistance, power-tricky, and colorless energy: What engagement with everyday popular culture texts can teach us about learning, and literacy. In J. Marsh (Ed.), *Popular culture, new media and digital literacy in early childhood* (pp. 201–218). London: RoutledgeFalmer.

CHAPTER 5

"I DON'T EAT WHITE"

The Transformational Nature of Student Teaching Abroad

Christine Moseley, Stacey Reeder, and Neill Armstrong

The purpose of this yearlong qualitative study was to describe the transformational learning experiences of three preservice teachers as part of a student teaching experience in San Jose, Costa Rica. This study illustrated the importance of cultural immersion in a foreign country and culture as a means of learning about one's self. The study also illustrated the essential importance of the need for support for the student teachers as they progressed through the experience.

Most educators today are aware of the ongoing demographic changes that are reshaping the fabric of American society. In fact, classroom teachers are probably among those citizens with the most active insight into this significant transformation, as the "world" is appearing in their classrooms in the form of students. At present, more than 20 million United States citizens, or more than one in twelve, are foreign born (Miller & Miller, 1996). Current projections suggest that immigration will continue to add approximately 1 million people annually; at this rate the proportion of minorities in the United States population is expected to rise to 47% by

Curriculum and Teaching Dialogue
Volume 10, Numbers 1 & 2, 2008, pp. 55–71
Copyright © 2008 by Information Age Publishing
All rights of reproduction in any form reserved.

2050, with Hispanics constituting nearly 25% of the total U.S. population. According to Riche (2000), "By 2060, non-Hispanic whites are projected to account for less than one-half of all Americans. By 2100, non-whites and Hispanics are projected to make up 60% of the United States population, with Hispanics alone accounting for 33%" (p. 14). Institutions engaged in the education of classroom teachers in states with changing demographics must accommodate this demographic trend by instituting appropriate changes and modifications to their teacher education programs. A challenge that many teacher education programs face, especially in the Midwest, is limited diversity among teacher education candidates and faculty and access to public schools with large ethnically diverse populations.

It was in this context that the International Student Teaching Project, developed by a large Midwestern land grant university, was implemented in Costa Rica. This project sought to positively impact the preparation of preservice teachers by effecting significant improvements in their ability to develop insights, awareness, and competency when working with culturally different students, especially Spanish-speaking minorities. The original goal of the project was to internationalize the teacher education curriculum by promoting global awareness and understanding, especially in regards to Latin America. Eventually, broader, more holistic goals emerged in the course of the planning process as participants, faculty, and students sought to address issues related to cross-cultural learning, second language acquisition, exposure to globalizing processes, experiential and contextual learning, and appreciation for the perspective of the "other." These many factors coalesced into an opportunity for student teaching participants to undergo a transformative experience that would lead to a perspective transformation and a deep and profound awareness of the constraints that had come to influence their personal worldviews.

THEORETICAL FRAMEWORK

This case study focused on three student teachers' perceptions of the changes in their personal and professional growth as well as in their enhanced global view. The project was based heavily on the theory that international student teaching experiences for preservice educators result in personal growth, an expanded worldview, and increased professional competence (Barnhart, 1989; Mahan & Stachowski, 1987; McKay & Montgomery, 1995; Wilson, 1993). This study also embraced transformative learning, a developmental theory whereby "learning is understood as the process of using a prior interpretation to construe a new or revised interpretation of the meaning of one's experience in order to guide future action" (Mezirow, 1996, p. 162). Transformative learning is concerned with "how learners construe, validate, and reformulate the meaning of their experience" (Cranton, 1994, p. 22). Taylor (1998) defines the purpose of transformative learning as an attempt "to explain how our expectations, framed within cultural assumptions and presuppositions, directly influence the meaning we derive from our experiences" (p. 14).

Perspective transformation explains the process through which adults revise their meaning structures. According to Mezirow (1991), meaning structures are composed of meaning schemes and meaning perspectives. Meaning schemes are smaller components, occur often, and are comprised of "specific knowledge, beliefs, value judgments, and feelings that constitute interpretations of experience" (Mezirow, 1991, pp. 5–6). Meaning perspectives, however, are more encompassing, provide general frames of reference, or world views, and involve "a collection of meaning schemes made up of higher-order schemata, theories, propositions, beliefs, prototypes, goal orientations and evaluations" (Mezirow, 1990, p. 2).

Meaning perspectives are frequently acquired as an individual moves through childhood as he/she experiences meaningful encounters with significant adults. Mezirow (1991) writes that meaning perspectives "mirror the way our culture and those individuals responsible for our socialization happen to have defined various situations" (p. 131). These perspectives become part of an individual's nature and are difficult to change (Taylor, 1998). Thus, meaning perspectives may validate one's life experiences, but they may also distort the reality of these experiences.

At the heart of transformative learning theory is the change in meaning perspective that leads to the development of a new meaning structure. Many times, such development is the result of a disorienting situation "due to a disparate experience in conjunction with a critical reappraisal of previous assumptions and presuggestions" (Taylor, 1998, p. 14). A perspective transformation is "a more fully developed (more functional) frame of reference ... one that is more inclusive, differentiating, permeable, critically reflective, and integrative of experience" (Mezirow, 1996, p. 13).

Perspective transformation as a model for adult learning offers an explanation of the way personal paradigms develop and grow. Mezirow (1996) believes that fostering transformative learning is vital to the promotion of adult development. Facilitating transformative learning incorporates communicative learning which "involves identifying problematic ideas, values, beliefs, and feelings, critically examining the assumptions upon which they are based, testing their justifications through rational discourse and making decisions predicated upon the resulting consensus" (Mezirow, 1995, p. 58). Mezirow (1997) views transformative learning as the essential component of adult education, because it "helps the individual become a more autonomous thinker by learning to negotiate his or her own values, meanings, and purpose rather than uncritically acting on those of others" (p. 11).

The concept of perspective transformation, and consequently, transformative learning, is a key element in the International Student Teaching Project in Costa Rica. An essential program objective is to facilitate a personal change in each student teacher, the reexamination of self, their world, and cultural identity. Mezirow's (1996) theory specifically centers upon how adults make meaning of their life experiences and asserts that "learning is understood as the process of using a prior interpretation to construe a new or revised interpretation of the meaning of one's experience in order to guide future action" (p. 162). This remains the primary objective of the program.

PURPOSE OF STUDY

The purpose of this yearlong qualitative study was to describe the experiences of preservice teachers that were transformational in nature as part of an international student teaching experience.

METHOD

Participants

This study centered on the personal and professional experiences of three student teachers in two different international schools in San Jose, Costa Rica. A case-study design was used as the research approach because it is well suited to describe what happens with the passage of time (Eisner, 1991; Merriam, 1988; Yin, 1989). Participants were selected purposively specifically because they each chose to complete their student teaching field experience in Costa Rica. Throughout this paper, the pseudonyms Teresa, Brad, and Dana are used. Dana was placed in a secondary English classroom, while Teresa and Brad both were placed in elementary classroom settings (second and fourth grade classrooms respectively). All three participants were Caucasian and their ages ranged from 23–28 years. Furthermore, all three student teachers came from rural and homogeneous cultural backgrounds in the same state where they chose to attend college.

Design

To gain different perspectives of changing perceptions—and to establish internal validity (Mathison, 1988)—the researchers gathered individually multiple sources of data prior to, throughout, and following the field experience studied. The primary sources were autobiographical data, reflective journals, pre- and post-interviews, weekly e-mail correspondences, classroom observations, and on-site conferences. In addition, the school directors, principals and mentor teachers supplied data to the researchers through multiple structured observations of the participants' teaching, as well as through weekly conferences with the participants, and in-depth midterm and final written evaluations.

Each participant student teacher was interviewed before the start of the experience. During the student teaching experience, participants kept a daily reflective journal of their teaching experiences that were collected at the end of the experience. In addition to the daily journal writings, each participant was required to correspond a minimum of twice weekly via e-mail to the university supervisor addressing structured questions about the teaching experience, as well as to pose personal questions and thoughts for discussion. The researchers also conducted a minimum of two on-site observations and conferences with each participant, as well as conferences with each mentor teacher and school director. Detailed field notes and written assessments were collected during each on-site observation and conference. Finally, each participant was interviewed individually at the end of the experience and all participated in a final focus group.

Data Analysis

Using the constant comparative method (Strauss & Corbin, 1988), the research team began data analysis following the first interactions with the participants during the semester prior to their experience and continued throughout the study, including a post interview once participants completed the student teaching experience. The team continuously explored data for key ideas and emergent themes in order to develop rich descriptions of the participants' insights and changing perceptions.

Analysis was ongoing and continually informed the data collection process. When the data collection phase was complete, the process of analytic induction was followed, reviewing the entire set of data to identify themes and categories and generate initial assertions within each case. The data was then revisited to refine the themes, and add, collapse, or drop them as necessary. Analytical threads were identified to link the major themes together and to explain the process of change over time. Internal validity, a criterion for rigor when using data collected in a naturalistic setting (Scott, 1991), was established through triangulation (Merriam, 1988)—that is, multiple researchers, multiple sources of data, and multiple methods were used to confirm the emergent findings.

Research Context and Background

This case study followed the experiences of three teacher candidates who student taught for one semester in San Jose, Costa Rica. Initially, the candidates participated in weekly hour-long focus group conversations with the faculty team during the semester prior to student teaching where they explored topics related to the practical considerations of the host country, including religion, climate, politics, education, economy, and food. The weekly seminars also covered materials and resources needed for the classroom teaching, ways to avoid the "ugly American" syndrome, and the logistical elements involved in the journey. In addition, the faculty coordinator provided support in assisting students with making their travel arrangements, applying for passports, and in making arrangements for finances and computer technology. However, these tasks were ultimately the participants' responsibility to complete by the end of this semester.

The faculty team accompanied the teacher candidates for an orientation weeklong visit to the schools and their new "home" and subsequently returned midsemester for another weeklong visit to conduct observations and conferences in the schools. Teacher candidates, in turn, were expected to become involved in all teacher related functions at their school. Selected teachers from the international schools served as mentors for the teacher candidates, either individually or in groups, and often facilitated cultural opportunities.

The university schedule was followed with teacher candidates leaving the United States during the fourth week of the semester, completing a 10-week teaching experience, and returning on the 15th week prior to graduation. The teacher candidates attended a 4-week orientation seminar on campus with other teacher candidates before departing to Costa Rica. This seminar discussed requirements of the student teaching experience and described expectations for evaluation. Thus, once teacher candidates arrived at their teaching sites, they would discover that the components of student teaching, the evaluation models, and support groups were parallel to those of their peers in other field placements. During the 16th week, the teacher candidates also participated in a weeklong seminar back on campus. The seminar provided an opportunity for candidates to discuss issues and requirements of teacher certification, graduation, and professional portfolios.

A unique model chosen for the International Student Teaching Project in Costa Rica included a cultural orientation experience prior to visiting the assigned school and meeting mentor teachers. The teacher candidates and the faculty team arrived in Costa Rica four days prior to the initial school visit as part of a loosely structured experiential learning adventure. This experiential component included a trip out of San Jose, learning how to utilize public transportation to reach a specific region of the country. The objective was for the students and faculty to forge a closer-than-usual bond while interacting with the local culture and environment, gaining insights into the country's geography, history, and its society. Throughout this process, faculty and students engaged in reflective thinking activities and proactive planning sessions in preparation for the students' upcoming classroom experiences. Hopefully, any issues associated with separation anxiety or cross-cultural discomfort were detected, discussed, and eventually resolved before the faculty returned to the United States.

When the orientation adventure was completed, the group returned to San Jose and paid a preliminary visit to the cooperating international schools to meet with the school directors and mentor teachers. The teacher candidates spent a full day at the school with the university supervisors, touring the site and meeting teachers, staff, and students. Teacher candidates also connected with their home-stay families. On the following day, the student teaching experience began. The university faculty team remained for the rest of the week, observing the school alongside the teacher candidates and conferencing with the mentoring teachers. During this time, the supervisors shared with the mentor teachers the university's policies and expectations, and the evaluation process for the student teaching experience. The faculty team returned midsemester for a week-long visit to the schools for observations and conferences. During the second visit, the faculty and participants engaged in another 4-day adventure into the countryside of Costa Rica. This trip allowed faculty and participants to engage in reflective discussions and cross-cultural experiences together.

Research Sites

The student teaching experiences for this study were completed at two international private schools—The American International School and The Costa Rica European School—located in two distinct suburbs of San

Jose, Costa Rica. Both schools have a pre-K–12 curriculum with instruction in English.

RESULTS AND DISCUSSION

The analysis of data revealed four major overarching themes: meeting basic needs, problem solving as daily life, typical student teaching experiences, and working with English Language Learners (ELL) students. The results of this study were organized around the four major themes and presented as excerpts from the original data sets.

Meeting Basic Needs. In the weeks prior to the experience and during the first several weeks in Costa Rica, the major theme evident in all data was meeting basic needs. Our participants were very concerned about not having access to consumer products that they take for granted. One of the participants had a friend promise to mail her each issue of *Cosmopolitan* so she would not miss any issues while in Costa Rica. Both girls had parents mail them bath and body products and American candy, which they could not find to purchase. As the participants moved further into their student teaching, this theme of meeting basic needs became less prominent in the data and eventually faded away. Each participant asked the following questions in a variety of ways and sometimes multiple times:

- What things do I need to pack? How many pairs of shoes should I take? How many bags and how much weight can I take?
- Do we know yet where we will be living? Can I have a key to my room? Will I have a room to myself?
- How do we deal with getting money while we are there? Are there ATM machines in Costa Rica? Banks?
- Will we be able to call home? How? Will phone cards work?
- Can I talk with my host family before I go? Who is my host family?
- Will I have access to the Internet to communicate with family and friends?
- Does San Jose have a Wal-Mart or some similar store for us to purchase the products we need?
- Will I encounter wild animals while there?

These questions and concerns revealed a need on the part of the participants to feel settled and secure prior to the actual experience. The normal questions about the student teaching experience itself were not even asked until they became more comfortable and secure in their surroundings. These comments and concerns also reveal the need for transformational experience—the need for removing oneself from one's "comfort zone" and to experience life as the "other."

Problem Solving as Daily Life. Once the participants were in the beginning weeks of their experience in Costa Rica, the theme of problem solving as daily life began to emerge. In the first few weeks, the participants used only taxis to travel as they required limited language ability and were readily available. Once they became more familiar with their surroundings, they began to inquire about bus schedules and began to read Costa Rican maps. Soon, using available bus transportation, they began to not only travel within San Jose, but also across the country for weekend adventures.

Participants also discovered that all grocery products and directions for cooking written on the outside of those products were in the metric system. The local grocery stores carried far less processed food and more fresh and native grown foods. At first, they were hesitant to try the unfamiliar food and did not know how to cook the local fruits and vegetables. Getting a Costa Rican cookbook was mentioned, but when they checked into that, they realized that the cookbooks were also written using the metric system and in Spanish. All of these issues had to be overcome eventually in order to eat. At first, Teresa expressed a strong dislike for eating any food that was "white in color" during the first meal upon arrival, referring to served ceviche. However, by the time of the faculty visit midsemester, she was not only eating "white," but eating ethnic food of the country that included gallopinto (rice), yucca, and local potato dishes.

The theme of daily problem solving was evident throughout the data collection process while the participants were in Costa Rica. Brad, Teresa and Dana expressed their attempts, successes and failures in problem solving in their daily experiences in the following ways:

Brad: "I realized I have no way to contact Teresa and Dana—do you have their e-mails or what should I do?"

Teresa: "Well, I am so proud of myself today; I took the bus into downtown and was able to make my way back! All in all, it was an adventure, a sometimes frightening experience, but a liberating one knowing that even I could get around this city on a bus."

Teresa: "The battery went out on my alarm clock and I have looked everywhere for a replacement and there is just not one to be found—any ideas?"

Dana: "I am really having a hard time finding resources I need on the Internet and I didn't bring a lot of my books with me to save on space. I am having a hard time making my lessons what I would like. The library doesn't have much for teacher resources. Also, I got here without a disk so I haven't been saving anything, do you want me to go out and buy one or what?"

Each day required problem solving as the participants navigated through life in Costa Rica. Shopping, eating, finding transportation, communicating with home and with one another, finding a much needed Coca-Cola, and communicating with their host families became transformative experiences as they worked in another language as the "other" in a foreign country.

Typical Student Teaching Experiences. The typical student teaching experiences emerged as a theme in the data as we would have predicted. Each participant teacher struggled with classroom management, assessment, time management, and lesson planning issues. The participants shared their experiences in this way:

> Brad: "Math is going well. I started off a little nervous but I am getting better. Today in math we made solid figures (cube, pyramid, rectangular prism) out of toothpicks and clay. It seemed to go very well and I think it helped some of the students to get a better idea of vertices and edges."
>
> Teresa: "I went off to school a little down today because yesterday was a really hard day. My class was really out of control yesterday and we didn't seem to get much done at all. My teacher doesn't really have any class rules in place and there is one boy that yells out often and sometimes kicks – she doesn't seem to know what to do with him."
>
> Dana: "I have some interesting things happening with the seventh grade and the child with autism. I am hoping to talk with you about it when you visit."

Throughout the experience, the participants struggled with the various aspects of teaching, including classroom management, lesson planning, conducting authentic assessment as opposed to traditional assessment, and planning curriculum and content in alignment with expectations. Additionally, they learned that curriculum planning is closely related to the cultures and traditions of the country in which schools are located. It was through these curricula and lesson planning activities and issues that they also began to examine their own cultural identity.

> Dana: "The mother of one of my students came to teach a lesson about the Native Americans who live in the Northwestern

part of the U.S. She was a great teacher with smoked salmon for the kids to try, pictures, and maps…. We may dress up as Native Americans for Spirit Week! I have not asked the students about their prior knowledge, I guess I should have. The ones from the states know interesting things about Native Americans. My teacher calls them "natives," which I find a little weird, but it might be just a language translation. I also have to remember to say North American Native Americans because there are Native Americans here, too."

Teresa: "The Independence Day celebration was unique to Costa Rica. I enjoyed being the spectator and seeing the traditions and pride of people. I think that the 4th of July is one hard Independence Day celebration to beat, but each country celebrates differently. The students dressed in traditional attire and performed dances and skits that told their story. Then we ate "gallo pinto" and "agua dulce"—very interesting, by the way. I think the main difference that I saw in between the two country's celebrations is that Costa Rica's is more of a reflection and remembrance of the past. The day is spent doing things as they were when the country gained their independence. I see our independence day spent more as a celebration of freedom."

Working with ELL Students. All three participants faced the challenge of working with a class of students who speak a language different than English. This remained a central theme throughout the entire data collection process. All three participants were surprised by what they encountered in their students' language learning and the difficulty in making modifications to accommodate the variety of levels within their classrooms. The schools have high expectations for their students to achieve and place little emphasis on making modifications for ELL students. As one administrator stated, "Our students must graduate and compete with others" to be admitted to preferably American universities.

The participants each shared their thoughts and concerns:

Brad: "It is not possible to make one modification for just ELL learners, because there are so many different levels. Of the 12 students in my room, only one is a native English language learner."

Dana: "The students I am working with are really bright, most of them are very smart and the work they are doing in the IB program is amazing, but I am surprised every day at how low their reading levels are. It is just the English thing but it is odd when they read out loud."

Teresa: "We spend a great deal of time having the students work in their journals and then read what they have written out loud. We also have a lot of discussion, more than most second grade classes would. I think this is done so the students are speaking and writing English. I have also tried to add more discussion with them during math learning—having them work in groups and then share with the class. But when they work with a partner, they speak Spanish to each other so it really doesn't help."

Dana: "Last Thursday were the parent/teacher conferences…. By the end of the day, I had visited with 35 sets of parents. Thirty-two of the 35 conferences were in Spanish. This made it more difficult for me, but I preferred this because it helped me in my Spanish. If I teach ELL, then I will need to speak to the parents in Spanish."

Additionally, all three participants expressed their surprise that the students and staff spoke so much Spanish at school. Dana stated:

> I guess I just thought that since we were teaching at English speaking schools that that would be the only language the students spoke, but all you hear all day long is Spanish. They only speak English when they have to in class. I don't know, I was just surprised by this. It is just strange.

This experience was quite different from the way most teachers or teacher educators envision working with ELL learners or making modifications for them. Generally, we envision classrooms with mostly English speakers and then a few students who speak other languages. However, in Brad's classroom, nine different countries were represented by 12 students. Several students in his classroom spoke one language at home with their families, such as Korean or German, they spoke Spanish as they moved about and existed in their community, and they spoke English in the classroom. Brad's realization by the second week in the classroom—that a simple modification would not work because of the tremendous diversity of his students in their language acquisition—was a significant one.

The theme of working with ELL students also became an issue of transformative learning for members of the research team. The research team shared many years of experience supervising student teachers in the United States. However, none of them had supervised student teachers in the context of such diverse cultures and multiple languages. Thus, they learned alongside the participants and were able to model their own transformative learning through critical reflection and rational discourse with the participants. Both faculty and student teachers experienced being ELL learners, in the context as Spanish Language Learners, during the student teaching experience, and left the experience with a greater understanding about what it means to be an ELL learner in classroom, school, and community environments where communication occurs in a different language than one's own.

IMPLICATIONS FOR TEACHER EDUCATION

Not all learners are predisposed to engage in transformative learning, nor do all teachers of adults have transformative learning as a goal for instruction (Taylor, 1998). However, if transformative learning is the goal of adult education, how can it best be fostered? The authors of this study agree with Imel (1998) in considering the role of the teachers and the learner, and of the rational and the affective (as outlined below) for best fostering transformational learning in teacher education.

The role of the teachers. As Taylor (1998) states, "the teacher's role in establishing an environment that builds trust and care and facilitates the development of sensitive relationships among learners is a fundamental principle of fostering transformative learning" (p. 2). The researchers in this study attempted to establish such an environment and relationship of trust and care for the learners from the beginning of the international experience. The informal weekly seminars during the prior semester allowed for participants to express fears and concerns in a nonthreatening environment, as well as to get to know the faculty prior to departure. Some of these meetings included off campus meals and social events. The faculty also corresponded with participants' parents who had concerns and questions about their children traveling to and living in a foreign country. In addition, the faculty traveled with the participants on their first trip into the country, assisting them with accommodations, public transportation, and initial acclimation to their new schools. This initial visit also included a 4-day adventure with the faculty team into the country, allowing students—with faculty support—to begin to experience the culture, people, land, and language that were new to them. This adventure also allowed for intensive, informal conversation among the students and faculty in close quarters.

The midsemester visit by supervising faculty also included another 4-day adventure to some sites outside of San Jose that allowed for extensive, one-on-one reflective discourse through travel and evening discussion sessions. In these discussions, the participants shared what they had learned, expressed their concerns and fears, asked questions and solicited advice from the faculty. In addition, these sessions became excellent opportunities for the faculty to share what this cross-cultural experience meant to them and what they were also learning.

The role of the learner. Taylor (1998) believes that the learner also has a responsibility for creating the learning environment. Student teaching in and of itself is a challenging experience, both professionally and personally. Choosing to student teach in a foreign country with a language and culture very different from one's own is to place oneself at risk and in disequilibrium. During the semester prior to the experience when the students were meeting weekly for cross-cultural discussions, the original group who intended to student teach in Costa Rica numbered ten. By the time of the commitment, only three students elected to pursue the experience. These three students made a commitment towards self-transformation; they embraced the challenges and confronted their own fears and cultural biases in order to enhance their knowledge base about students of diverse cultural backgrounds.

The role of the rational and the affective. Teacher educators need to consider how they can help their students connect the rational and the affective experiences and emotions in which they are engaged (Taylor, 1998). The participant who expressed at her first meal in Costa Rica that she "doesn't eat white" almost went home after her first week. Throughout the orientation seminar and weeks prior to departure, she had taken a leadership role in the group. She arranged for computer technology, organized the "what to take and not take" lists, and read every book she could on Costa Rica. And yet, after only a few days in the country, her fears overcame her. Her affective domain overtook her rational thinking. By being encouraged to acknowledge these emotions and feelings through critical reflection and conversation with others, especially with the faculty team, she was able to overcome her fears and complete satisfactorily the whole experience.

Teacher candidates need to develop cross-cultural interdependency and view themselves from the perspectives of different groups. This means that teacher education programs must allow for opportunities for students to become less ethnocentric and more open-minded. They need those affective experiences that cause them to gain a new awareness of the complexities of the world around them, recognize unique ways to depart from the "way things are done at home," and to see first-hand the strengths and weaknesses of educational systems thousands of miles away. This program placed student teachers in a context in which they did not speak the native language and in an environment in which they could not leave at any time. They were forced to learn how to communicate in order to travel on public transportation, order food in restaurants, and even buy needed household goods at the local stores.

CONCLUSION

The overall objective for this program was for participants in an international student teaching experience to gain a more personal understanding of the true meaning of globalization. It was desired that these participants would engage in a process that would lead them to reevaluate their mental schema and consequently lead to a lasting change in meaning perspective; one grounded in "a more fully developed frame of reference, one that is more inclusive, differentiating, permeable, critically reflective, and integrative of experience" (Mezirow, 1996, p. 13). Such a change implies a greater awareness of global cultural events that lead to improved classroom practices and flexibility. To learn about other cultures and their educational systems, student teachers must experience life in a different setting. In contrast to student teaching in the United States in schools of low-income, ethnically diverse populations, the student teachers in this program could not "leave" the culturally different environment once the school day was over. They remained totally immersed in the culture throughout the experience, moving around the community, communicating with the people, and interacting with their host families, all of whom spoke limited English. However, at the same time, student teachers in these experiences must be encouraged, mentored and guided through this process with adults that they trust. This study illustrates that an international setting in which the student teacher must survive and adapt to a culture different than his or her own supports the importance of cultural immersion as a means of learning about oneself. The study further demonstrates the importance of providing a support team for the student teachers as they progress through the experience. These findings support Mezirow's belief that transformative learning must not only consist of the experience itself, but also opportunities for critical reflection and rational discourse with others.

The changing world as reflected in the diversity of students arriving daily in our classrooms constitutes an increasingly significant aspect of the teaching and learning environment in American public schools. How teachers respond to the challenges they encounter in a pluralistic social and academic milieu is certain to factor strongly into the determination of our society's well being in the near future and beyond. It is imperative that teacher candidates be provided with opportunities and challenges to move beyond their own cultural experiences. Experiences such as those embedded in the International Student Teaching Project in Costa Rica may bring about the necessary transformation needed for teachers to work effectively with a diverse and changing population of students. As Dana concluded, "Costa Rica has been an incredible learning experience that will never be forgotten. It's amazing to think that 2 months ago, we were getting off the plane and clueless as to what we had in store for us."

REFERENCES

Barnhart, R. (1989). The assessment of growth resulting from a student teaching experience in an international setting. *International Education, 18*(2), 5–13.

Cranton, P. (1994). *Understanding and promoting transformative learning: A guide for educators and adults.* San Francisco: Jossey-Bass.

Eisner, E. (1991). *The enlightened eye: Qualitative inquiry and the enhancement of educational practice.* New York: Macmillan.

Imel, S. (1998). *Transformative learning in adulthood.* ERIC Clearinghouse on Adult, Career, and Vocational Education. Columbus, OH. (ERIC Document Reproduction Service No. ED 423426)

Mahan, J., & Stachowski, L. (1987). Feedback from British and Irish educators for improving overseas student teaching experiences. *Journal of Teacher Education, 40*(6), 40–45.

Mathison, S. (1988). Why triangulate? *Educational Researcher, 17*(2), 13–17.

McKay, J., & Montgomery, J. (1995, April). *Changes in perceptions: A comparative study of the experiential learning of international student teachers.* Paper presented at the American Educational Research Association, San Francisco.

Merriam, S. B. (1988). *Case study research in education: A qualitative approach.* San Francisco: Jossey-Bass.

Mezirow, J. (1997). Transformative learning: Theory to practice. In P. Cranton (Ed.), *Transformative learning in action: Insights from practice, New Directions for Adult and Continuing Education* (pp. 5–12). San Francisco: Jossey-Bass.

Mezirow, J. (1996). Contemporary paradigm of learning. *Adult Education Quarterly, 46* (3), 158–172.

Mezirow, J. (1995). Transformational theory of adult learning. In M. R. Welton (Ed.), *In defense of the lifeworld* (pp. 39–70). New York: SUNY.

Mezirow, J. (1991). *Transformative dimensions of adult learning.* San Francisco: Jossey-Bass.

Mezirow, J. (1990). Conclusion: Toward transformative learning and emancipatory education. In *Fostering critical reflection in adulthood: A guide to transformative and emancipatory learning* (pp. 354-376). San Francisco: Jossey-Bass.

Miller, E. W., & Miller, R. M. (1996). *United States immigration: A reference handbook.* Santa Barbara, CA: ABC-CLLO.

Riche, M. F. (2000, June). America's diversity and growth: Signposts for the 21st century. *Population Bulletin,* 1–43.

Scott, M. (1991). Naturalistic research: Applications for research and professional practice with college students. *Journal of College Student Development, 32,* 416-423.

Strauss, A., & Corbin, J. (1988). *Basics of qualitative research* (2nd ed.). Thousands Oaks, CA: SAGE.

Taylor, E. W. (1998). *The theory of transformational learning: A critical review.* ERIC Clearinghouse on Adult, Career, and Vocational Education. Columbus, OH. (ERIC Document Reproduction Service No. ED 423422)

Wilson, A. (1993). Conservation partners: Helping students gain a global perspective through cross-cultural experiences. *Theory into Practice, 32*(1), 21–26.

Yin, R. (1989). *Case study research: Design and methods.* Newbury Park, CA: SAGE.

CHAPTER 6

AT THE CROSSROADS OF PRESERVICE TEACHER EDUCATION, NAEA, AND TERRY BARRETT

Exploring Metaphors of Meaning, Narratives of Hope

Heidi C. Mullins

The purpose of this study was to examine the relationship between preservice teachers and art, as well as art's role in accessing the learners' knowledge communities. These preservice teacher experiences take place in an Art for the Elementary classroom within a university setting. Three preservice teachers explored to several pieces of art and constructed new meanings that challenged their preconceived notions of art as part of their daily lives.

It is misleading to speak of a world as it is, or even a single world. It makes more sense to think of various versions of the world that individuals may entertain, various characterizations of reality that might be presented in words, pictures, diagrams ... each of these symbol systems captures different kinds of information and hence presents different versions of reality. All we

Curriculum and Teaching Dialogue
Volume 10, Numbers 1 & 2, 2008, pp. 73–86
Copyright © 2008 by Information Age Publishing
73

> have ... are such versions ... through them do we gain access to what we
> casually term "our world."
>
> (Gardner, 1980, pp. 92–95)

What does it really mean to be a preservice teacher in an Art for the Elementary classroom at today's university? As a preservice teacher educator,
I find myself asking this question on more than one occasion. Preservice
teachers often come into my classroom with preconceived notions of what
art is and how it is to be "used." One such preservice teacher recently
requested an advising session to let me know that what I planned to teach
in my course over the semester was not going to be of value to her, as she
was teaching first grade and did not understand how art could possibly be
important to children learning to read and write. This encounter was
after the first class meeting in which I had simply handed out the syllabus
and given a course overview. In our advising appointment, I asked her if
she had ever taught first grade. She promptly replied with, "No, but I
have observed a first grade class ... twice." I assured her, based on my
experience as a preservice teacher educator for the past 6 years and having taught in the public school system for more than 12 years, that she
would indeed learn something about art that would help her teach in her
first grade classroom. She did not appear convinced when she left my
office.

Art and art-making are defined as special forms of experience (Dewey,
1980), and these experiences are viewed in multiple contexts. The central
role of this narrative inquiry (Clandinin & Connelly, 2000; Olson & Craig,
2001) is to explore the relationship between the preservice teacher and
art, as well as art's role in accessing the learners' knowledge communities
(Craig, 1995) based on the experiences of preservice teachers, all of which
are occurring in an art for the elementary classroom within a university
setting. The earlier encounter is one example of the misconceptions
preservice teachers have about art, and the types of notions that have
prompted this narrative inquiry and brought me to a crossroads when it
comes to leading students in experiences with art. The crossroads are neither the art for the elementary content nor the variety of learning experiences given to preservice teachers in the art for the elementary classroom.

These crossroads involve dealing with the preconceived notions of
preservice teachers about what art is, and the "knowledge communities"
(Craig, 1995) they access to understand and explore art. These knowledge communities refer to any personal, practical, professional, internal
or external resource that an individual accesses to make sense of their
world; that is, how they come to know, or in this case, how they come to
know art. These crossroads that are encountered lead to many forks in the
road where decisions are made in attempt to disrupt what was previously

understood as an art curriculum in an art for the elementary classroom. Instead, these crossroads make art practice for the elementary preservice teacher reflective, personal, and powerful, changing assumptions and adding to the ever-changing knowledge communities that individuals draw from to make sense of their world.

THE LEARNING ENVIRONMENT

Most preservice teachers are preconditioned by prior education experiences to try to construct the "right" fixed answer, while others, who are more open, will begin to take risks in creating, looking at, talking about, and writing about art without regard for a "right" answer. The processes initiated in this art for the elementary classroom were intended to provoke thought and encourage voice while making meaningful art. As a result, the preservice teacher's experiences became the framework for developing and presenting course content (Wasson, Stuhr, & Petrovich-Mwaniki, 1990). This type of learning environment strives to cultivate preservice teacher exploration in the notions about how they believe things are and present new ways of knowing beyond their own conceptions, which at times creates certain tensions—the crossroads.

I had been consciously aware for some time of the tensions related to art that preservice teachers face in the classroom, such as not feeling creative or artistic, notions of one-way solutions, a desire for, what I call, "boxed content," which requires little or no critical thinking, and the everyday things that surround not only being in the art for the elementary classroom, but the dilemmas that surround the students' everyday lives. These tensions are underlying aspects of art education that need to be brought to the forefront in order to cultivate more meaningful art experiences in the preservice teacher classroom. These tensions involve the curricula of life (Dewey, 1985; van Manen, 1991); curricula which define experiences both in and beyond the classroom. These are curricula that make us who we are and guide us in navigating how we know what we know, and in turn how we respond, learn, and act as human beings.

NAEA AND TERRY BARRETT

This past year (2006) as I was attending the National Art Education Association (NAEA) Conference in Chicago, I was still grappling with my efforts to disrupt preservice teacher notions of art. I attended a session led by Terry Barrett on art and metaphors of life and critically looking at art. I must clarify that I do not know Dr. Barrett personally, though I am very familiar with his literature. Although I am familiar with the literature discussed by Barrett and other art educators regarding the vast rainbow of art-looking experiences available for both students at the K–12 level and in higher education, bringing theory and pedagogy together in the pre-service teacher classroom gives rise to challenges to art instruction where there are often no ready-made solutions. In my case, these challenges arise in a preservice teacher educational setting and the ideas about art they bring with them. Although I feel well-versed in the theoretical and practical aspects of art-looking and art-talking, I often feel uncertain about the perceived "meaningful-ness" of these experiences to preservice teachers.

I expose my preservice teachers to multiple methods of criticism, including the Feldman model (1970) of criticizing art (description, analy-sis, interpretation, and evaluation) and Terry Barrett's (1994) method of criticizing art, which is similar to the Feldman model, only a more inter-pretive approach is used to create more personal meanings. However, as a result of experiencing the session at NAEA with Terry Barrett, I began to "see" interpretation in a new light. Maybe it was the simplicity in which he dealt with the topic or simply the demonstration itself, but as Dr. Barrett asked the participants to engage in looking at art through the use of met-aphor, my teaching pedagogy began to be reshaped, a reshaping that I wanted to take back to my students and explore with them.

In Dr. Barrett's session, he used the photographic works of Stephen Alt-house, a professor of photography at Barry University in Florida. Althouse holds a MFA in sculpture and photography and his philosophy of educa-tion reflects many of my own notions, including the idea that "[my] goal in teaching is to encourage students to discover more about themselves, to allow my students the freedom to search for something meaningful, and to ultimately help them find a truly satisfying form of creative visual expres-sion" (Althouse, 2006, para. 2). After returning from the conference, I had already planned on exploring the "looking at art process" in a more in-depth way (I refrain from using the term "art criticism" because it holds its own set of preconceived formulas that would constrain this paper). This idea fits directly into the curriculum pattern for this semester.

As I personally explored the works of Althouse and considered both his philosophy and the session with Terry Barrett at NAEA in Chicago, I decided how I could best use his works in my course to cultivate student experiences with art to create meaning and displace preconceived ideas about art. I wanted to not only explore Barrett's methods of art and meta-phor as he explained them at the conference, but also add in my own notions of metaphor. I chose to incorporate Dr. Barrett's more interpre-tive notion of metaphor and Lakoff and Johnson's (1980) notion of lived metaphor. When merging these two notions together, looking at a work of art morphed into living knowledge of what art is about.

I had my students, like Dr. Barrett had done at the conference, explore the works of Stephen Althouse. One thing to address here is how my own knowledge communities (e.g., my background, education, and practical and professional knowledge, and the sessions at NAEA) of curriculum-making involves engaging my students and their ability to come to know art and art-making in new ways. This curriculum involved my own under-standings of Terry Barrett's workshop and how I chose to put it into prac-tice. If I "understand what makes up the curriculum of the person most important to [you], namely, [my]self, [my] own narrative, [and as a result, I] will better understand the difficulties, whys, and wherefores of the cur-riculum of [my] students" (Clandinin & Connelly, 1988, p. 31).

THE LOOKING: METAPHORS OF MEANING

The two works I chose to use in my preservice teacher classroom from the many that Dr. Barrett had provided in his NAEA session were *Clamps* and *Clamps With Shroud* (Figures 6.1. and 6.2, respectively). I began with my students by giving a brief introduction about Althouse and his work and then turned the conversation to interpretive metaphor (which is more lit-erary) and life metaphor. Students were asked to work together in groups to define metaphor, and also to give examples of how they use metaphor in their everyday thinking. Lakoff and Johnson (1980) articulate that met-aphor is,

> pervasive in everyday life, not just in language but in thought and action. Our ordinary conceptual system, in terms of which we both think and act, is fundamentally metaphorical in nature. The concepts that govern our thought are not just matters of the intellect. They also govern our everyday functioning, down to the most mundane details. Our concepts structure what we perceive, how we get around in the world, and how we relate to other people. Our conceptual system thus plays a central role in defining our everyday realities. If ... our conceptual system is largely metaphorical, then the way we think, what we experience, and what we do everyday is a matter of metaphor. (p. 3)

As we began to explore the meaning of metaphor, different groups defined metaphor differently. Here are three groups' one-line explana-tions of metaphor:

1. Metaphor means comparing something to something else without using like or as.

Source: Stephen Althouse, copyright 2003. Reprinted with permission (Appendix A).

Figure 6.1.   Althouse's *Clamp*. 42 x 60 inches, pigmented inkjet print.

Note: Stephen Althouse, copyright 2003. Reprinted with permission (Appendix A).

Figure 6.2.   Althouse's *Clamps and Shroud*. 42 x 60 inches, pigmented inkjet print.

2. Metaphor is like saying something that is something else but using other words, like, "she's all that" or "she's a star."

3. Metaphor is a way of seeing characteristics of one thing in another like "she's a diamond." That means she is precious and is important.

In this preservice teacher classroom, metaphor emerged as a way of thinking narratively, which began here and continued to grow over time. This idea is embedded in the presuppositions, the nonverbal aspects, and even the way I use my voice to disclose what I am asking of my students— in this case, exploring metaphor as an act of meaning. There is a direct link between metaphor and symbolism that needs explanation. First, metaphor is present in all language and works by translating a more abstract experience into an experience that is more concrete; secondly, metaphor allows people to understand, think about, and explain abstract concepts through the human body and its experiences where it operates as an organizing tool to create a whole piece of knowledge; and last, metaphor is embedded in the very nature of human thinking, using symbols as identifying signs that create meaning (Lawley & Thompkins, 2000). The students demonstrate this in their definitions of metaphor by revealing metaphor's symbolic nature and abstract ideas rooted in experience.

Metaphor then becomes a mode of thinking narratively, where we translate and transfer knowledge from one domain to another, adding to our personal, practical, and professional knowledge communities. This translating and transferring process progresses to forms of narrative knowing. This type of knowing is situated in the temporal where the use of interpretation comes to the forefront of understanding and explanations are exhibited (Polkinghorne, 1987). This is what I came to discover as I participated in Terry Barrett's session at NAEA.

Explaining metaphor in terms of life was harder for the students. They had a more difficult time relating metaphor to their lives. As I observed and watched the students, I realized that, like them, I am not conscious of thinking narratively through metaphor. I was not as aware as I thought I was of "the little things we do every day ... [where what we] think and act [are] more or less automatic along certain lines" (Lakoff & Johnson, 1980, p. 3). I, like my students, took metaphoric thinking for granted.

According to van Manen (1990), "Nietzsche once observed that all language, and therefore all truth and error is metaphoric in origin" and "virtually every word we utter ultimately derives from some image, thereby betraying its metaphoric genesis" (p. 49). He goes on to say that, "our most prized certainties, our best proven ideas, our most neglected commonplaces must admit to their metaphoric genealogy" (p. 49). Exploring and looking at art with preservice teachers became an experience "by way of metaphor," taking us "beyond the content of the meta-phor toward the original region where language speaks through silence" (p. 49), transcending the obvious. So, instead of struggling with trying to define metaphoric thinking, we as a class decided to see if we could expe-rience it firsthand, identifying when it happened in our art-looking and art-making experiences, making it part of a reflective journey with art. This became our own form of narrative knowing where our experiences validated what we know and how we know it. These "knowings" became personalized forms of understanding that had direct implications on how we each come to view the constructional telling of our lives through engaging with art. How these preservice teachers have come to know them is demonstrated here amidst the interactions with Stephen Alt-house's two works.

After attempting to define metaphor, we continued in the classroom by looking at the works of Althouse, *Clamps* and *Clamps and Shroud*, and began to describe what we saw. The act of describing involves simply nam-ing what you see—the facts. As a class, we analyzed these artworks by observing their underlying elements and principles, and then incorpo-rated the use of meaningful metaphor into our lives through interpreta-tion of the works. Like Dr. Barrett had done in his NAEA session, I began by asking the students to imagine that one of these artworks represented their lives, and to choose one and write about how the work represents their lives. This initiated a multilayered form of narrative inquiry where historical truth becomes obsolete as narrative truth enters into the writ-ings of these students, disclosing how they view their lives, how I view them viewing their lives, and how I as a preservice teacher educator make sense of their learning process, where art experiences become reflective, personal, and powerful.

The purpose of this experience in our class was to help my students recognize that each artwork, no matter what or where, can be experienced on a personal level, and the ways in which we engage with art will always reveal something about how we view our world in relation to ourselves, others, and the unknown. Terry Barrett's ideas of looking at art through metaphor was the first step in approaching the crossroads of preservice teacher perceptions about art, and opened up a dialogic response to how art is experienced. This in turn carried over into our making, talking about, and writing about art as it relates to making meaning. This experi-ence discloses the beginning process of thinking metaphorically, illus-trated through dialogues that grow and change to demonstrate internalized concepts of the crossroads, creating a confluence of art, met-aphor, and life.

NARRATIVES OF HOPE

The first step of this journey through art and metaphor required visual thinking to merge with personal meaning in order to build a relationship between the work and the student/viewer (preservice teacher). It is a process that each student goes through and "no one interpretation is better than any other…and no interpretation is more certain than another," and it is a place where art serves as a "rich repository of expression that allows for a rich variety of response" (Barrett, 1994, p. 9). This process of interpreting for personal meaning is one where the viewer sympathetically and emotionally associates with the work and can reveal the different and contradictory ideas that represent beliefs and values. Here, three preservice teachers, Gina, Ella, and Christi, respond to the works of Althouse, revealing and illustrating something more meaningful in their lives and demonstrating how this beginning metaphoric experience enabled thinking that helped them connect with art while displacing preconceived notions about what art is personally and how it can impact educational purposes.

The following stories deal explicitly with the visual acts of meaning in both looking and making and incorporates ideas of metaphor and gaze as processes where students come to learn about themselves, others, and the unknown inside and outside of the classroom environment. In other words, they come to know what art *is* in terms of creating meaning. These acts of meaning are visually induced by art experiences rendering unique forms of language framed in culture, dependent on time, place, and location as personal expressions of knowledge. These expressions of knowledge demonstrate how the crossroads of preconceived notions of preservice teachers were interrupted and renegotiated through my interpretation of Terry Barrett's session using the works of Stephen Althouse in an art for the elementary classroom. These experiences also helped to foster student connections beyond looking at Althouse, seek out other works for creating more of their own meaningful experiences, and potentially carry these ideas into their future classrooms.

In the initial class discussion when we talked about metaphor, we also discussed how many of the students defined "art as life" and how it is a part of our everyday visual language. When preservice teachers began to incorporate metaphor into the visual, they began seeing art as part of their everyday lives. Art in their everyday lives is now seen as a place that blends metaphoric thinking and literary metaphor in multiple contexts. By understanding that all works of art are meaningful and by critically interpreting works of art, these preservice teachers began to use the personal to make meaning through both content and context inside and outside the work. How they each "interpret those layers of meaning depends on the preconceptions and acceptance of, or resistance to certain ideas or ideologies that the work reveals" (Yokley, 1999, p. 20). The following sections explain how these same three preservice teachers began to redefine the very nature of what art means to them by engaging with metaphors of life, which are built on "knowledge communities" (Craig, 1995), thereby creating new relationships with art.

GINA'S RESPONSE TO ALTHOUSE

Gina's response to Althouse's work, titled *Clamps*, reveals much about how Gina invites art to interact with her knowledge communities and how her world as a curriculum of life interacts with the artwork. Gina's dominant preconceived notion about art was that it held no potential for personal value beyond being "ugly" or "pretty" and that art could not be personally relevant; it "really only means something to the artist." Here is Gina's interpretation and response to Althouse, where she discovers a life connection to the work:

> The strips of cloth represent me as complicated, unorganized, and stuck between two important people, my son and husband who are represented by the clamps. As unorganized as I am, I need the clamps to hold me together to avoid falling into pieces. The old and worn out clamps represent my desire to grow old surrounded by my family. The black background represents my fears, which with the help and support of my family, I fight to conquer. (Journal Entry, March 2006)

Gina integrates her interpretation with her life and her family—her husband and son whom she talks about regularly in class. This expresses an experience for Gina in making personally meaningful connections with the visual, an experience which reveals the daily conflicts that Gina experiences in her life. *Clamps* represents a place of conflict and mediation as part of Gina's world where "thought and feeling are irrevocably intertwined" (Barrett, 1994, p. 11). For Gina, these personal life circumstances are revealed in her interpretation as "guided by human intelligence, that makes unique forms of meaning possible" (Eisner, 1986, p. 57). It is a language, where the private and personal lives of individual students have a public presence (Eisner, 2002). It is where reflection begins, a place that pushes the boundaries of the preconceived notions of art for the preservice teacher. Gina was initially not even aware that she had made a personal connection with the artwork until she shared her experience with the class.

ELLA'S RESPONSE TO ALTHOUSE

Ella's dominant preconceived notion about art was that art only expresses the perspective of the artist and in order to connect with art, you have to know artist's intentions. She quickly abandoned that notion with this experience. Ella chose Althouse's *Clamps and Shroud*, and her response dealt with the spiritual. She internalized her conceptions as equal to her belief system, revealing her moral conceptions of self. Ella's response:

> The shroud represents my life, and the freedom I have to be loose as long as I'm being held by the principles and values of God. The white color of the shroud represents purity, because it requires that I have a pure and trans- parent life in order to be secure. All the wrinkles made by the clamps repre- sent the process of maturity that I go through in my life, which include struggles and suffering. At the same time, the shroud becomes more flexible and loose with time because the pressure at the beginning created a new texture that can be bent. This is like God shaping our hearts and making them more flexible to hear his voice. That's how I see my heart. (Journal Entry, March 2006)

Ella reveals the existential ideas in her curricula of life that she has internalized, built around cultural tradition and beliefs as part of her knowledge communities. In Ella's view, *Clamps and Shroud* marks a way of living rather than the everyday struggles with life. Ella's interpretation leads us to ideas of the communal involvement in her life world. These are voices and influences of her indigenous knowledge communities at work. Ella's indigenous knowledge communities are culturally, individu- ally, and socially embedded in a place where individual meaning-making ascribes symbolic and narrative knowing. This resides within a cyclical awareness of the multiple pieces that make up the whole of her life, to what has been known and experienced to create new understandings in the visual. She is drawing on all of her experience and knowledge as a repertoire for what she will see. She has displaced preconceived notions of art through the personal, no longer believing that she must understand what the artist means to understand or experience the artwork.

CHRISTI'S RESPONSE TO ALTHOUSE

Christi's response to Althouse's *Clamps* revealed a deeper and more per- sonal meaning, a meaning that when shared with the class carried art's power, a transformation not only for Christi, but also for the other preser- vice teachers who engaged with her metaphor. At the beginning of the semester, Christi looked at art as objects that held no personal connection to herself or her world; Christi saw art only in the light of fixed content. She saw the experiences in this class as means for making sure she got the "right" answer, controlling what she could in her education experience, such as her grades.

The transformation in Christi with art came as a result of a bigger transformation in her life—a tragedy. Christi's house burned down during spring vacation, causing her to lose everything except a few things she salvaged out of the fire. Coincidentally, this was during the time of the NAEA conference. She discussed the incident briefly in class during the first week back from vacation. Before breaking down in tears as she apologized for being late, she said that she had to take her husband to work and then casually added, "our house burned down this week." Everyone looked in her direction as she continued to speak. She said, "Everything I owned was in the house except my husband and daughter and our car. My daughter was at a friend's house" She began crying but we casually moved on to discuss Althouse's work. Christi's interpretation of Althouse was her first written response to her tragedy, a tragedy of which she was still in the midst. She described how she felt about her life at that moment:

> I sit here and stare at this picture and I have no connection with it. I see my life squished up in those rags, being pushed to the limit, being torn and shattered. My life right now is out of control. I know I should slow down but I am of afraid of failing. I am the white dirty rag being held up by two screws. The shredded cloths are my feelings being squished and torn. I should let my feelings out and unscrew. Then I could balance my life out so I can fall gracefully and allow both screws to unscrew evenly. I think I should stop running and slow down and think. The wooden blocks represent the world around me that I have to overcome. I sit here and stare at this picture and I know exactly what it means. *Clamps* is a metaphor for my life. My whole college career has had one disaster after another, the most recent being the fire. (Journal Entry, March 2006)

Christi provided a forum for interpreting *Clamps*, allowing for the "individual freedom to meander" (Barrett, 1994, p. 13) through her thoughts and feelings, helping her engage in conversations about the tragedy that had recently happened in her life. Art for Christi became a place of power for her to address the personal issues in her life. In fact, two days after that class, she stopped by my office and proudly declared that it was "really great that art can say so many things." What she understood was that there is more than one way to understand something, and that getting it "right" does not mean there is only one right answer. Art gave Christi a voice.

DISCUSSION

For all three students this experience provided opportunities for making intrinsic choices that involved a language of possibilities. The students took the opportunity to draw on their knowledge communities, exercising individual choice where identity and the relationships and interactions with others helped students "to semiotically discern relationships among sign, symbol, and metaphor ... [to] insinuate concepts" (Yokley, 1999, p. 21). This sequence of classroom events helped to provide a foundation for understanding the influences that impact how preservice teachers understand and see the multiple layers of meanings present in art. In turn, each preservice teacher renegotiated and moved beyond their preconceived notions of art. Students began to recognize that "visual works of art don't become art just in the physical act ... [of making], and in the physical act of observing them; they have to be associated with an understanding, a rationale—an aesthetic [and a knowledge community]" (Chaplin, 1998, p. 293). Art, in all of its forms, is imbued with meaning, and helping my preservice teachers find the meaning for art in their personal and professional lives through metaphor has helped me navigate the crossroads of preservice teacher notions about art. So, thank you Terry Barrett, Stephen Althouse, and the multitude of coordinators, speakers, and participants at NAEA. You make a difference and are adding to the knowledge communities that are changing what we know regarding how we teach and experience art!

REFERENCES

Althouse, S. (Artist). (2003a). *Clamps* [Photograph]. Copyright Stephen Althouse.

Althouse, S. (Artist). (2003b). *Clamps and shroud* [Photograph]. Copyright Stephen Althouse.

Althouse, S. (2006). *Biography*. Retrieved March 28, 2006, from http://www.barry.edu/finearts/photography/faculty/althouse.htm

Barrett, T. (1994). Principles of interpreting art. *Art Education, 47*(5), 8–13.

Chaplin, E. (1998). Making meaning in art worlds. In J. Prosser (Ed.), *Image-based research* (pp. 284–306). New York: RoutledgeFalmer.

Clandinin, D. J., & Connelly, M. (1988). Studying teachers' knowledge of classrooms: Collaborative research, ethics, and the negotiation of narrative. *The Journal of Educational Thought, 22*(2A), 269–282.

Clandinin, D. J., & Connelly, M. (2000). *Narrative inquiry: Experience and story in qualitative research*. San Francisco: Jossey-Bass.

Craig, C. J. (1995). Knowledge communities: A way of making sense of how beginning teachers come to know in their professional knowledge contexts. *Curriculum Inquiry, 25*(2), 151–175.

Dewey, J. (1980). *Art as experience*. New York: Penguin Putnam.

Dewey, J. (1985). Democracy and education. In J. A. Boydston (Ed.), *John Dewey, the later works 1925–1953: Essays, reviews, miscellany, and the public and its problems* (Vol. 2, pp. 235–372). Carbondale: Southern Illinois University Press.

Eisner, E. (1986). The role of the arts in cognition and curriculum. *Journal of Art and Design Education, 5*, 57–64.

Eisner, E. (2002). *The educational imagination*. Upper Saddle River, NJ: Person Education.

Feldman, E. B. (1970). *Becoming human through art: Aesthetic experience in the school*. Englewood Cliffs, NJ: Prentice-Hall.

Gardener, H. (1980). Gifted worldmakers. *Psychology Today, 14*, 92–95.

Lakoff, G., & Johnson, M. (1980). *Metaphors we live by*. Chicago: University of Chicago Press.

Lawley, J., & Tompkins, P. (2000). *Metaphors in mind: Transformation through symbolic modeling*. London: The Developing Company Press.

Olson, M., & Craig, C. J. (2001). Opportunities and challenges in the development of the teachers' knowledge: the development of narrative authority through knowledge communities. *Teaching and Teacher Education, 17*(7), 667–684.

Polkinghorne, D. (1987). *Narrative knowing and the human sciences*. Albany: State University of New York Press.

van Manen, M. (1990). *Researching lived experience: Human science for an action sensitive pedagogy*. London, ON: The Althouse Press.

van Manen, M. (1991). *The tact of teaching: The meaning of pedagogical thoughtfulness*. Albany: State University of New York Press.

Yokley, S. (1999). Embracing a critical pedagogy in art education. *Art Education, 52*(5), 18–24.

Wasson, R. F., Stuhr, P. L., & Petrovich-Mwaniki, L. (1990). Teaching art in the multicultural classroom: Six positions statements. *Studies in Art Education, 31*(4), 234–246.

CHAPTER 7

HOW DOCTORAL MENTORING SUPPORTED A CULTURAL TRANSFORMATION FROM PERIPHERAL OBSERVER TO ACTIVE LEARNER

Learning to Teach and Research From Suzanne Wilson

Yonghee Suh

This article is an autobiographical account of how Suzanne Wilson's work influenced the author as her doctoral advisee. The author follows her own path throughout the doctoral program, and analyzed her intellectual and professional growth as a teacher educator and researcher, using Lave and Wenger's situated learning theory (1991).

In their book, *Situated Learning: Legitimate Peripheral Participation*, Lave and Wenger (1991) wrote that learning is a process of participation in communities of practice; participation that is at first legitimately peripheral but that increases gradually in engagement and complexity. This has

Curriculum and Teaching Dialogue
Volume 10, Numbers 1 & 2, 2008, pp. 87–100
Copyright © 2008 by Information Age Publishing

certainly been the case of me as I have been transformed from a South Korean graduate student to a teacher educator in the United States. I grew up and was educated in South Korea. When I entered the graduate school in the United States, not only did I have to learn about university teaching and research, I also had to learn the norms, values, and expectation of teacher educators and educational researchers—especially those related to "active participation in one's own learning" as Lave and Wenger note. In this article, I will document my own journey to become an educational researcher and teacher educator in the United States, and how I crossed linguistic and cultural borders with mentoring assistance from Suzanne Wilson. I will explain the community of researchers in South Korea and how I learn to socialize and belong to the communities of educational researchers and teacher educators in the United States. I will also describe and explain how Suzanne Wilson, as my academic advisor, challenged and supported me to become a better educational researcher and teacher educator.

BEFORE THE BEGINNING

I first met Suzanne Wilson through her writing in the spring of 1995 when I started my master's degree in South Korea. At that time my professor asked us to read research articles about teaching social studies and history which had been published in the United States and England. That assignment introduced me to Suzanne's early work on history teachers and their subject matter knowledge: "Peering at history through different lenses: The role of disciplinary perspectives in teaching history" (Wilson & Wineburg, 1988). It was a study of four novice social studies teachers with different undergraduate majors, and Suzanne and her colleague wanted to know how the teachers' different disciplinary backgrounds influenced their teaching. To answer this question, they followed these teachers for 3 years, from their entry into the teacher education program to the first year of teaching. They interviewed the four teachers 14 times and observed them on several occasions. Using the data from both interviews and field observations, they reported that teachers brought different disciplinary perspectives to teaching, and those different perspectives affected how they view history, and what and how they chose to teach in history.

At the time I was first reading Suzanne's work, there were two research traditions of history education in South Korea (Song, 1999): It was either theoretical work or quantitative studies based on small-scale surveys. Researchers in the first school did extensive literature reviews, and based on their analysis of previous researchers' findings, proposed new teaching strategies. Those in the second school designed a survey to answer their research questions, conducted the surveys once or twice in a classroom of 30 or 40 students, used SPSS (Statistical Package for Social Sciences) to analyze their data, and reported their results. It appeared that neither researchers in the first school nor in the second school captured what was really going in the classrooms.

I was not the exception. I belonged to the first school. As a middle school social studies teacher and a student of history, I was interested in how secondary history teachers can use artwork such as paintings, photographs, and music created during an historical period to teach students about the history of that time period. Like most master's students at that time in South Korea, for my master's thesis I reviewed both history and history education literature, and tried to rationalize how artwork could serve as a good pedagogical tool in history. However, by the time I finished the thesis, I started to wonder whether or not my rationale was the same as other practicing teachers'. As a teacher, I used artwork when I taught history and had my own rationales for doing so. But that was only one person's experience. I wondered if other teachers of history used artwork, and, if so, why. What kinds of artwork did they use, and how did they use it? What did they teach using artwork? Questions came one after another, but I did not know how to answer them.

Suzanne and her colleague's work appeared to give me a way to answer my questions. Their study was based on theory, and yet documented what was going on in teachers' thinking and in their classrooms. What I loved about her work was the way in which she wrote about the four first-year teachers, Cathy, Fred, Jane, and Bill. Because of her vivid and thick description of these teachers, I felt I was listening to them talk in the teacher's lounge. Cathy, an anthropology major, and Fred, a political science major, suffered from the lack of historical content knowledge. They saw history as a collection of facts and presented history without any contextual knowledge and from only a single perspective. In contrast, Jane, an American history major, and Bill, an American studies major, believed that history is a construction of human interpretation, and taught the same event from multiple perspectives including political, social and cultural perspectives. Jane and Bill also used a variety of sources such as music, novels, and graphs to represent the atmosphere of the given historical period. With all these descriptions, Suzanne explained the complexities of teacher knowledge that is necessary to become a good teacher of history. Teachers' content knowledge is not only about teachers' knowledge of facts and interpretation. It is also about the teachers' beliefs and knowledge involving how knowledge in the discipline is created, refuted and revised.

Her work left me with a desire to know more about how Suzanne and her colleague conducted their research. I soon decided to come to the United States to study with Suzanne. Later, while working on my PhD, I learned that Suzanne's work was from the Knowledge Growth in Teaching Project with Lee Shulman, and that Suzanne and her colleagues conducted research on teacher knowledge across multiple content areas (Ball, 1991; Carlsen, 1991; Grossman, 1990). Later I also learned that she used a case study as her research method for the study (Yin, 1989/2003), but I did not know any of these things back then. In the fall of 1998, I applied for and was accepted into the graduate program at Michigan State University. The acceptance letter informed me that Suzanne would be my temporary advisor. Almost instantly after receiving the letter, I received an e-mail from her. "Hi Yonghee, I am Suzanne Wilson, your temporary advisor. Is there anything that I can help you with?"

CROSSING THE BORDERS

In her review of Larry Cuban's book, *How Scholars Trumped Teachers*, Suzanne (Wilson, 2003b) agrees with a current reform effort that calls for the scholarship of teaching, and argues that the tension between teaching and research does not have to be inevitable. She makes the case that teaching and research should be complementary especially at the university level; in other words, what one does as an educational researcher should inform one's teaching practices, and vice versa. She also documented the cultural clash she experienced while working with a professional development school as a teacher-researcher. Teaching is personal and private, often lacking critical professional discourses between group members. In contrast, research is public and grounded in critical professional discourses such as the peer-review process of research. She concludes that teaching and research inform each other, and that's what she taught me while I was at Michigan State University as her advisee. In the graduate program at Michigan State University, Suzanne emphasizes the importance of teaching to doctoral students' careers, often noting that PhD means doctor of philosophy or teacher of philosophy.

ENTERING THE PROFESSION: LEARNING TO TEACH

I met Suzanne 2 days after I arrived in East Lansing. I remember the night before I met her for the first time. I stayed awake until midnight writing down what I would say to her: How I would introduce myself to her, what my master's thesis was about and my plans for my doctoral dissertation. I thought Suzanne would ask me to talk about my research interest and my plan for research.

Unlike my expectation, Suzanne did not ask even one question about my plan of study. Instead, she asked me where I would be living, whether I had any family members in the United States, and what exercises I would do in my leisure time. I told her I would be living in the graduate students' dormitory for one year, and would then like to move to an off campus apartment. I also told her I had distant relatives in Los Angeles and New York but I had not seen them in more than 10 years. I also told her that I like swimming. While listening to me, she started to draw a campus map on white paper. She showed me where I could find two Korean restaurants and the swimming pools on campus, as well as telling me which swimming pool was the best. She also gave me the e-mail address of her Taiwanese advisee, Phone-Mei, the kindest person I met at East Lansing. Suzanne wanted me to contact her, and ask her what international graduate students' lives were like. She then told me we would meet every other week to talk about my new life at Michigan State University. I left her office, puzzled by why she did not ask me anything about my research interests.

Several years later, I ran into another of Suzanne's graduate student advisees who was also puzzled for the same reason. Suzanne had asked him what exercises he would do when he had time, and told him where to go to play tennis, his favorite sport. She, however, did not ask him what he wanted to do for his research. I smiled. By then I understood why Suzanne had asked me about the exercise I liked instead of my research interests. I knew that doing a PhD is like running a marathon. You do not want to burn out at the beginning or in the middle of the race. To finish it successfully, you have to create a support system that allows you to breathe. Most of all, although I came to the United State as a graduate student who completely focused on my PhD, Suzanne wanted me to learn to live a life beyond my academic studies.

Suzanne also helped me understand another important facet of American academic culture. In addition to emphasizing the importance of teaching in her research, she also supported graduate students in their efforts to learn to teach at the university level. She offered a seminar where graduate students learned how to create a teaching portfolio for future job interviews, and often co-taught with graduate students, something unknown in South Korean graduate school. When I taught an undergraduate course—elementary social studies methods course—in the fall of 2004, Suzanne volunteered to work with me as my supervisor. Suzanne and I spent the summer planning the course. As a peripheral observer, I began by reading as many articles as possible about how to teach social studies methods courses. I collected all the previous syllabi and met with previous instructors. That fall, while I taught, Suzanne observed me teaching from the back corner of the room. Once a week we would meet and discuss what happened in class, and plan the next class.

My teaching, however, did not seem to work. All the tips and prescriptive strategies were not working for me because of something that I had not considered before. The problem was not about what I knew about social studies but the cultural gap between students and me. In South Korea where I grew up, I was not expected to look straight into the eyes of a senior, including teachers. During class, we were not prompted to ask questions. Teachers do not compliment students often, either. Even though I was always a good student, I do not remember my teachers praising me in public or in private. Rather I heard from my mom that I was doing well in school when she came back from once a semester teacher-parent conferences.

My students grew up in a totally different culture. If they were confused about anything, they raised their hands and asked questions. Some of them would also stay after the class to talk about what was going on in their field. They asked questions that, had I been in their place, would have been answered by looking in books rather than asking the teacher. They would sometimes stay simply to chat about what they did over the weekend, and I did not know exactly how to respond. Not surprisingly, I reacted to students as my teachers in South Korea had reacted to me. I did not compliment their work until they did really well. At times I scolded them when their work did not meet my expectation. My students felt my evaluations of their work were harsh, and seemed to be hurt by my straightforward comments on their assignments. Students and I were experiencing a cultural clash. This caused me to become an active participant in my own learning and to relearn the relationship between the teacher and students. To resolve this cultural clash, I had to learn how to interact with students and how to create learning opportunities such as small group and whole group discussion in addition to more traditional lectures.

Although I believed that "classroom discussion and debate—social endeavors—more closely match the ways in which individuals learn or construct their understanding" in their real life situations (Ball & Wilson, 1996), and I wanted students to learn from each other through the discussion, it was not easy for me to learn how to lead a good class discussion. I tended to either let students talk too much or to fish for right answers instead of synthesizing students' responses, finding patterns, relating these patterns to a larger context so that students would learn from each other and from me. Helping students become active participants rather than peripheral observers was new to me.

In his analysis of mathematics teaching, Cohen (1990) wrote that even if the teacher believes she incorporates reform efforts, her teaching practice does not appear to be that different from the traditional practice. He suggested that it was difficult for the teacher to teach in a new way because she had never experienced the new teaching practice that she was trying to implement. To teach as the reform efforts suggest, the teacher needs to relearn from experience. As a novice teacher educator, I was like the teacher in Cohen's study. While I was committed and enthusiastic about learning theories of situated learning and communities of practice, I did not know how to teach given those theories.

After watching me teaching, Suzanne suggested that I needed an alternative tool to communicate with students and new ways to listen to what they thought about the course. She suggested I conduct a mid-term teaching evaluation to identify the students' difficulties and challenges of the class. After gathering students' responses, Suzanne and I created an action plan. We listed ways I would address students' concerns and shared that action plan with them. The first part of the plan was that students and I would develop a system to communicate in and out of the class. I also used ANGEL, an online pedagogical tool, on a regular basis. I followed up the class discussion by summarizing the points we discussed and raising new questions. When my directions were not clear I would ask one or two students to rephrase to make sure we were on the same page. Whenever students were not sure what was going on, they needed to raise their hands and ask me questions. If I made any insensitive comments, they were to raise their hands, and tell me. I told them I would not take it personally. I also told them I have high standards, and I wanted to maintain my standards as they were. However, I would give students an opportunity to rework their assignments. I reminded students that we grew up in different cultures, and because of that, we needed to be proactive in understanding and communicating with each other. I was beginning to learn that effective teaching requires the active participation of both the teacher and her students.

Because open discussion was not part of my "cultural capital" (Bourdieu, 1970/1990), Suzanne also modeled how to lead class discussions. At times we facilitated the class discussion together, and at other times she gave me a signal when students and I talked too much about one topic, so that we moved on to another topic. My responses to students' feedback seemed to work. When I told them I would give them my comments by the end of that week, one female student, who often asked me questions with a frowned look up on her face, raised her hand and responded, "We know you have other things to do, too. Wouldn't it be fair if we give you at least two weeks to return our papers?" By becoming of an active participant in my own learning, I began to learn how to transform my classroom from a teacher-centered one into a more student-centered one and communicate with students.

COMMUNITIES OF EDUCATIONAL RESEARCHERS

Similarly, I also had to relearn how to read, write, think, and eventually take ownership of my own learning from Suzanne during my doctoral program. My years at East Lansing were both exciting and challenging. They were exciting because the courses I took offered me a broad, new perspective with which to look at educational issues such as the purposes of public schooling, and the history of teaching and teacher education in the United States. This, in turn, allowed me to look back and rethink my educational experience in South Korea. I learned that South Korea and American public schooling started as a great equalizer, and yet both public school systems now face the dilemma that it has served to increase inequalities in society (Labaree, 1997). I also learned there are reform initiative cycles, and it is teachers who determine whether or not the reform would be successful. Teachers are the gatekeepers who make decisions about whether the reform will be accepted at the classroom level (Tyack & Cuban, 1997). I also learned that a good research method should be chosen to answer a research question rather than the preference for a certain methodology (Miles & Huberman, 1994). Most importantly, I learned that the field of education is so complex that no one theory can explain all. I felt empowered with this knowledge.

Among the many courses I took, Suzanne's courses were the most fun and challenging. For instance, she taught a required introductory course for all doctoral students in which she reminded us that reading widely is one of the critical components of being a good educational researcher. My classmates and I were required to read a wide variety of texts, including those inside and outside of education, primary and secondary sources, as well as progressive and conservative ones. We read John Dewey's (1902/1991) *Child and the Curriculum* and Jerome Bruner's (1960/1999) *The Process of Education* and at the same time watched an episode of *The Simpson's* and the British movie, *Educating Rita*. We read Horace Mann's (1841/1891) *Fifth Annual Report of the Secretary to the Board of Education of Massachusetts,* and the conference paper Sarah Lubienski presented at the annual meeting of the American Educational Research Association, based on her recently completed dissertation. Suzanne repeatedly asked us to identify the complexities of the purposes of education, and the intended or unintended consequences of these purposes on knowledge, teaching and learning represented in those sources.

In addition, Suzanne taught us that building a learning community with cohorts is as important as reading and writing articles. Learning happens when you work together rather than when you work in isolation. She used to tell us, "I am speaking from my own experience. You will learn from your cohort much more than you will learn from me." She had us read each other's paper. She constantly encouraged us to work in small groups, partnering with someone who shared similar interest such as English or social studies instruction. Outside of the class, she facilitated this by introducing graduate students with similar interests to each other, and encouraging us to learn from one another. She invited the class to her house after my classmates and I finished major writing assignments. The class seemed to continue in her living room, kitchen, and backyard. Over meals Suzanne cooked for us, we discussed issues that we had puzzled over in class. We often found ourselves talking to each other about where we came from, how we met our husbands, wives or partners, and the kinds of research and work we hoped to do after we graduated.

I also relearned how to make an argument and write. In the South Korean culture where I grew up, I was expected to write about the most important parts at the end. I was taught to develop my ideas throughout the paper, and finally end with the main points. Yet what I learned in the United States was the opposite. You state your main points immediately. You write your point as a topic sentence, elaborate and support it with reliable evidence. Then you conclude by restating it (Weston, 1992). In the United States, if you do not state what you want to say upfront, within the first two pages, your reader will be lost. Perhaps no one will even read your paper to the end where you make your key statements. In South Korea, I was trained to read and understand the text rather than to be critical of it. It was easy for me to summarize and discuss the strengths of the author's points. However, it was not easy for me to identify and critique the weaknesses. In doing so, I felt I was rude.

All the courses I took, however, kept pushing me to develop my own thoughts on the readings and to write my own ideas in a logical way. As always, Suzanne was the person who asked graduate students to write more rigorously and to think more critically than anyone else, but she was also the person who gave graduate students the most generous support. In addition to two full pages of comments on the assignments, she encouraged us to read books on writing. They are at times rule books such as *A Rulebook for Arguments* (Weston, 1992), and books on writing such as Stephen King's (2002) *On Writing* and William Zinsser's *On Writing Well* (1976/1998) in which writers make their reasoning visible, illustrating what they are struggling with when they write, and how they resolve those struggles. Suzanne also taught us that to be critical is to respect one's work while at the same time being honest and straightforward about it. She emphasized that as a colleague and as a teacher, you must be generous and kind in offering your support.

When I took Suzanne's introductory course, one of the assignments was to find out about a historical artifact from nineteenth century schooling along with a contemporary counterpart. With these artifacts in hand, we were to identify the purposes of teaching the subject matter, what teachers needed to know to teach it, and what it meant to be a teacher at the time when the two artifacts were created. For this assignment, I took a look at U.S. history textbooks from the early 1900s and from the present. I spent quite a bit of time writing the paper, and by the time I turned it in, I was proud of what I had written. I thought Suzanne would like it, too. And then I received Suzanne's comments:

> You did a good job describing what the textbooks are about but your analysis of the textbooks is not nuanced or complicated. Most of all, I do not really see your thinking in this piece. You need to make your own argument given the reading you did in class and analysis of the artifacts you chose.

I still have that paper and the pages of her comments. Whenever I get stuck in writing, I remind myself of these comments. What do *you* think about this topic? What are *your* arguments?

Writing a dissertation was another task of learning to trust my own judgment to answer these questions. For my dissertation, I did a case study of the three secondary high school history teachers in the United States who used artwork in their teaching of history (Suh, 2006). I began writing the dissertation proposal, doubting myself. Unlike my experience in the early years of the doctoral program, Suzanne did not give me specific directions or suggestions on how to write a dissertation. Instead, she asked me questions, including questions about the logic of every single interview question and every argument I made throughout the chapters. Suzanne also gave me comments to guide my analysis of the data and writing my arguments. For instance, there were two things Suzanne always emphasized. First, as a researcher, I should be generous in listening to and understanding participants (Wilson, 2003b). I still remember a conversation with Suzanne one afternoon in her office. I was reporting what I had found out about the three teachers I was studying. Mark, one of the teachers, was nice and wanted to be supportive of my work, but his teaching simply did not look appealing to me. I told Suzanne that I was not sure if I really liked the way he taught history. Listening to me, Suzanne responded, "Whether you like him or not does not matter. Your job as a researcher is to explain why Mark teaches in such way. Although his teaching may not make sense to you, it must make sense to him." Therefore, my job as a researcher was to listen to the teacher and understand his logic that makes such pedagogical decisions.

In addition, Suzanne taught me that I must use theories to guide my data analysis but to be cautious and not use theories blindly to categorize the teachers and judge their work (Wilson, 2003b). In analyzing the data, I used theories from three perspectives including those of cultural historians, social historians, and postmodern historians. Theories from these discipline of history guided me to see things I would not have seen if I had not used those theories as my theoretical framework. However, using these perspectives was also dangerous. I often found myself trying to fit each of my teachers into one of the three perspectives. Whenever I tended to match the teachers to one of the three, Suzanne would ask me to look for the counter evidence. She would tell me, "It seems you have little boxes in your mind and you are trying to put your teachers in those little boxes." To avoid it, I would need to go back and forth between the theories and data, and again understand the teachers' reasoning behind their decision of what and how to teach history using artwork.

Writing my dissertation was a real test to prove to myself that I was no longer a peripheral observer, but an active participant in my own learning. It showed me that I could use what I had learned from both my coursework and Suzanne to create and answer my own research questions. Because of the cultural differences between me and the teachers, and the language barrier, I worried that there might be subtleties and nuances in the teachers' words and behaviors that either I might miss or misinterpret. My experiences in the doctoral program, however, taught me that when there is a problem, there is always some way to solve it. One way to solve the problem is to ask questions, critically look at your problem, and solve it strategically. Suzanne used to tell me that I should be the one who knows about my own work best, and knows the strengths and weaknesses of it.

Therefore, I developed several strategies to compensate for my weakness as an international researcher who speaks English as a second language and has limited experience in U.S. schools. I interviewed the three teachers and observed them teaching using the arts. First, I designed semistructured interviews so that I could be both flexible and yet have some structure. I learned from the pilot study that when I was focusing on listening, I tended to lose a chance to prompt the teachers to get back to the topic when they were off the topic. By using the semistructured interview, I was able to keep the interview focused on the topic. At the same time, by asking general questions (e.g., Can you tell me what you believed is important to teach in your unit?), I was able to let the teachers talk about their teaching so they could explain what they knew and believe about the content they were teaching.

Second, with the teachers' permission, I audio taped every lesson. While my command of English was competent, there were other times when I wished I could slow down conversations between the teacher and students when I observed. Audiotapes complemented my field notes by recapturing conversations and scenes. They helped me revisit events and discussions, and fleshed out my field notes. As a result, I collected data that I might not have been able to collect otherwise.

Third, I made a promise to myself that I would not take any single incident for granted, and ask questions. I would use literature instead of experience to educate myself about the context. For example, Katie and Mark, teachers in my study, teach interdisciplinary courses following block schedules, thus it might be natural for them to teach art and history together. For me, however, a block schedule was not something with which I was familiar. In South Korea, we do not have block schedules. After learning this, I read every article I could find to learn more about interdisciplinary courses. This eventually helped me figure out why Katie and Ray were comfortable using the arts in their classrooms while Mark worried about time constraints and colleagues' indifference.

Lave and Wenger (1991) note "The mastery of knowledge and skill requires new comers to move toward full participation in the sociocultural practices of a community" (p. 29), and for new comers, learning is something that allows them to ask questions and answer those questions in their own contexts rather than to acquire knowledge that is abstract and general without a context. In that sense, by writing the dissertation, I learned to develop my own knowledge and skills that enabled me to make sense of the teachers and their teaching.

CONCLUSION

When I was asked to write about the influence of Suzanne's *work* on my profession, I automatically thought I would write about how her research —the articles she wrote about teacher knowledge or her book, *California Dreaming*, where she wrote about reform effort in teaching mathematics in California—influenced me. While drafting this paper, I changed my mind. As Suzanne (Wilson, 1995, 2003a, 2006) notes over the years, her work includes *teaching* as well as research. She continues to do research on teachers' growth from the novice teachers to the experienced teachers, and at the same time she mentors graduate students and junior faculty members to grow to become effective teacher educators and researchers.

I end this article by referring to a painting that always reminds me of Suzanne. It is the Mexican muralist Diego Rivera's (1935) *The Flower Carrier*. This painting has three parts: A man, a woman, and a huge basket of pink flowers. The man is carrying a basket of flowers with his two hands grounded on the land. The flowers look beautiful in pink but heavy. He appears to be trying to stand up. The woman stands behind him, helping him load the basket. She supports him with her firm hands and looks at him with calm and grace. Like the woman in Rivera's painting, I know

Suzanne stands by the novice teacher educators-researchers to nurture their intellectual and professional growth as they struggle to lift their heavy loads of learning to become active participants rather than simple peripheral observers in their own learning to teach and research.

REFERENCES

Ball, D. L. (1991). Research on teaching mathematics: Making subject-matter knowledge part of the equation. In J. Brophy (Ed.), *Advances in research on teaching: Teachers' knowledge of subject matter as it relates to their teaching practice* (Vol. 2, pp. 1–48). Greenwich, CT: JAI.

Ball, D. L., & Wilson, S. M. (1996). Integrity in teaching: recognizing the fusion of the moral and the intellectual. *American Educational Research Journal, 33*(1), 155–192.

Bourdieu, P. (1990). *Reproduction in education, society, and culture.* London: SAGE. (Original work published 1970)

Bruner, J. (1960/1999). *The process of education.* Cambridge, MA: Harvard University Press. (Original work published 1960)

Carlsen, W. S. (1991). Subject-matter knowledge and science teaching. In J. Brophy (Ed.), *Advances in research on teaching* (Vol. 2, pp. 115–141). Greenwich: JAI.

Cohen, D. (1990). A revolution in one classroom: the case of Mrs. Oublier. *Educational Evaluation and Policy Analysis, 12*(3), 311–329.

Dewey, J. (1991). *School and society/Child and curriculum.* Chicago: University of Chicago Press. (Original work published 1902)

Grossman, P. (1990). A study in contrast: sources of pedagogical content knowledge for secondary English. *Journal of Teacher Education, 40*(5), 24–31.

King, S. (2002). *On writing: A memoir of the craft.* New York: Pocket books.

Labaree, D. (1997). Public good, private goods: the American struggle over educational goals. American Educational Research Journal, *34*(1), 39–81.

Lave, J., & Wenger, E. (1991). *Situated learning: legitimate peripheral participation.*London: Cambridge University Press.

Lubienski, S. (1997). *Successes and struggles of striving toward "mathematics for all."* Paper presented at the annual meeting of the American Educational Research Association, Chicago.

Mann, H. (1891). *Life and works of Horace Mann.* Boston: Lee & Shepard. (Original work published 1841)

Miles, M., & Huberman, M. (1994). *Qualitative data analysis: an expanded sourcebook.* Thousand Oaks, CA: SAGE.

Song, C. (1999). *Theory and practice in history education.* Seoul, Korea: Hyung-sul.

Suh, Y. (2006). *Using the arts to teach history: teacher knowledge and beliefs.* Unpublished doctoral dissertation, Michigan State University, East Lansing.

Tyack, D., & Cuban, L. (1997). *Tinkering toward utopia: a century of public school reform.* Cambridge, MA: Harvard University Press.

Weston, A. (1992). *A rulebook for arguments.* Indianapolis, IN: Hackett.

Wilson, S. M. (1995). Not tension but intention: A response to Wong's analysis of the researcher-teacher. *Educational Researcher, 24*(8), 19–22.

Wilson, S. M. (2003a). *California dreaming: Reforming mathematics education.* London: Yale University Press.

Wilson, S. M. (2003b). Realizing our rhetoric: making teaching public. *Journal of Curriculum studies, 35*(2), 217–229.

Wilson, S. M. (2006). Finding a canon and core: meditations of the preparation of teacher educator-researchers. *Journal of Teacher Education*, 57(3), 315–325.

Wilson, S. M., & Wineburg, S. (1988). Peering at history through different disciplinary lenses: the role of disciplinary perspectives in teaching history. *Teachers College Record, 89*, 525–539.

Yin, R. K. (2003). *Case study research: Design and methods.* Thousand Oaks, CA: SAGE. (Original work published 1989)

Zinsser, W. (1998). *On writing well.* New York: Harper Perrennial. (Original work published 1976)

CHAPTER 8

THE CON/TEXT OF MARY SHELDON BARNES (1850–1898)

A Hermeneutic Inquiry

Benjamin H. Welsh and Nancy J. Brooks

Research on the life of Mary Sheldon Barnes (1850–1898) has focused mainly on her contribution to the teaching of history. However, this hermeneutic exploration of her child-study scholarship indicates a broader significance for her work. A search for the ostensive, personal, and historical motives behind Barnes's texts points to recapitulation theory as the answer to apparent contradictions noted by previous researchers and the conduit through which her work continues to influence education today.

The tapestry of the genesis of public schooling is so complex that educational scholars may have only just begun to unravel it. This article will further that unraveling by exploring the work of Mary Sheldon Barnes (1850–1898), first female professor of Stanford University. By focusing on particular research and pedagogical texts of Barnes, our aim is to understand both how she formed and was formed by the intellectual and educational milieu of her times. Furthermore, we suggest the possibility

Curriculum and Teaching Dialogue
Volume 10, Numbers 1 & 2, 2008, pp. 101–115

that the influence of her work may continue to linger in current educational thought and practice. We begin by explaining the benefits of hermeneutic inquiry for this type of project, move from there to an analysis of Barnes's texts, and conclude by proposing a resolution for what Monteverde (1999) has called the "conundrum" (p. 35) of Mary Sheldon Barnes.

The philosophical hermeneutics of Gadamer provide the theoretical framework for the exploration of the texts in this study. Although Gallagher (1992) types Gadamer's approach as "moderate," we believe that our project may also be considered critical in that we seek greater insight into our own "pre-understanding," thereby allowing us in some way to transcend our present situation.[1] As Gadamer (1960/1997) notes, "Insight is more than the knowledge of this or that situation. It always involves an escape from something that had deceived us and held us captive" (p. 356). We must acknowledge that while this emancipation represents a place of wider understanding, the nature of understanding is that it is never complete or permanent. We can never escape the limits imposed upon us by our pre-understandings; we will never attain a vantage point from which new questions cease to arise.

Regarding hermeneutic methodology, Laverty (2003) points out that there is no universal set of appropriate procedures, but there is an "obligation to understand the context under which the text or dialogue was being produced and to bring forth interpretations of meaning" (p. 21). Gadamer (1960/1997) proposes that hermeneutics is the art of conducting a conversation, the "art of the formation of concepts as the working out of common meanings" (p. 368). A useful understanding of the text itself is possible only if the text is seen in a limited field of inquiry. If we expect a response from the text, we must limit what we wish to learn from it by addressing specific questions to it. While curriculum scholars have taken up hermeneutic methodology in a variety of ways (e.g., Blumenfeld-Jones, 2004; Brooks, 2000; Reynolds, 1989), we felt the approach of Blumenfeld-Jones provided an appropriate set of questions to pose to this particular set of texts. Like Blumenfed-Jones, our intention was to examine literal curricular texts so that we "might learn who we are as historical beings living in the onflowing stream of thought that comprises our particular field of endeavor" (p. 126). In addition, we desired "an approach that reveals the historical characteristics of curriculum and their direct material presence in the curriculum text itself" (p. 127). Therefore, we decided to explore the texts of Mary Sheldon Barnes by utilizing the concepts of "ostensive, personal, [and] historical motives" (p. 128). In short, this involves a search for (1) explicitly stated reasons why the text was produced, (2) specific, individualized issues that the curricularist has within the field that moved her to conceive of new curricula, and (3) general, historical, sociocultural conditions that create a context for the text. Blumenfeld-Jones emphasizes,

> Of the three motives ... this last may be the most difficult to explicate, but in some ways it is the most significant. Although a curriculum may be the product of the curricularist's imagination, no curriculum emanates idiosyncratically from the person's mind or responds to an isolated tradition. The multiple contexts of the curricularist's decision making not only affect decisions but must find a material presence in the curriculum. (p. 127)

For the work of Mary Sheldon Barnes, we find this last motive to be particularly significant.

GENESIS OF THE PROJECT

Within hermeneutic inquiries, authors and readers are both thought of as being products of a plurality of historical and textual connections, resulting in what Gadamer (1960/1997) describes as a historically effected consciousness:

> If we are trying to understand a historical phenomenon from the historical distance that is characteristic of a hermeneutical situation, we are always already affected by history. It determines in advance both what seems to us worth inquiring about and what will appear as an object of investigation. (p. 300)

Hermeneutic inquiries require, therefore, that researchers recognize their situatedness in this web of textuality. In our situation, the work of Mary Sheldon Barnes was first brought to our attention through Ben's research on educational research methods in the early days of the U.S. public school movement. Approaching the library at the University of Pennsylvania as an archeological site with titles going at least as far back as the late 1700s, Ben went into the stacks in search of the oldest text book on educational research methods that he could find. What he unearthed was *Studies in Education*, a series of 10 research monographs in child-study and the history of education, edited by Earl Barnes (1896-97/1903a), Mary's husband. The series included the two articles of Mary's that we will discuss here, together with several pieces that directly address educational research methods. Sometime later, the two of us discovered that we share an interest in textual analysis and a fascination with the role that scientism has played in curriculum. This project grew from our discussions of the work of Mary Barnes and our interest in exploring her work through a hermeneutic lens.

We see the aforementioned two articles from *Studies in Education* as typical of the work of Mary Barnes. One of these pieces examines the historic sense in primitive peoples, while the second examines the historic sense in children. Each of these articles refer to the other. Following a comparison of the results reported in each, Barnes makes a set of recommendations for teaching history in schools from primary schools through college that drew us to study them because we felt they were eerily familiar. We felt that perhaps we had not only encountered them before, but that we might have been schooled according to them—that Mary Sheldon Barnes' recommendations had become part of our pre-understanding. In addition, we were especially drawn to these two articles—"The Historic Sense Among Primitive Peoples" and "The Historic Sense Among Children"—because of characteristics they exhibit that are apparently contradictory to Barnes' espoused values of scientific "objectivity." Our project focuses on, but is not limited to, an exploration of these two articles that the Barnes's saw as important enough to publish together in several different places at different times—in 1896 in Mary's *Studies in Historical Method, in 1896–97 in Earl's Studies in Education series* and again in 1903 in a bound reissue of *Studies in Education.*

INTRODUCTION TO A CONUNDRUM

Up to now, Mary Barnes has been known for her contributions to the teaching of history and her significance has been limited to her contributions in that field. McAninch (1990) and Monteverde (1999) both acknowledge that Barnes made the application of nineteenth century scientific methods to the study of history "the central focus of her [scholarly] work" (McAninch, 1990, p. 47). In other words, Barnes advocated the use of primary source materials and inductive inquiry, whether she was teaching history at Wellesley College or writing comprehensive history books for junior high students. Thus, she is credited with being well ahead of her time, inasmuch as the push to use primary source material in the teaching of history was still more than half a century away.

However, both McAninch (1990) and Monteverde (1999) point out that while Barnes had the desire and the potential to change how history was taught, it is clear that potential was never realized. McAninch accuses Barnes's work of entailing "a considerable degree of indoctrination" (p. 46) in that it did not challenge students to identify and critically examine the ideological premises of the times, such as faith in a divinely ordered universe and human progress. The picture of Barnes that emerges from Monteverde is conflicted at best. On one hand, she is depicted as being "ahead of her time," pioneering an approach to teaching history that used primary sources and encouraged independent critical thinking. On the other hand, she is portrayed as being unable to critique her own beliefs, including her belief in the primacy of men, which contributed to her invisibility throughout her life and may have prevented her from assuming what Monteverde contends is her rightful place as a historically significant figure in social studies education. In the end, Monteverde cannot explain the paradox—exactly how Mary Barnes could "advocate intellectual open-mindedness" and "fail to subject her own contradictions and assumptions to interrogation" (p. 35) at the same time. Monteverde calls the paradox a "conundrum" that she attributes in a vague way to Mary's "socio-cultural filter" (p. 35).

We propose that a hermeneutic study can offer an explanation for the paradox and a potential resolution of the conundrum. Indeed, we believe a careful exploration of Barnes's work may show that her "socio-cultural filter" was embedded in a theoretical perspective that is directly observable in her work—a theoretical perspective that emerged strongly in educational and psychological research during Barnes's lifetime. Furthermore, we propose that the "direct material presence" (Blumenfeld-Jones, 2004, p. 128) of the age in Barnes's curriculum indicates a broader significance for her work.

QUESTIONING THE TEXT: OSTENSIVE AND PERSONAL MOTIVES

Mary Barnes' (explicit motives for the creation of these texts are expressed in the preface of her 1896 methods book, where she declares she wrote *Studies in Historical Method* for the

> many people who ... would like to be careful and special students and teachers of the subject of history ... especially for the teacher who wishes to specialize his work, and to see the world from this particular point of view. For as the world grows smaller, and time and space condense, our intellectual world grows greater ... in order to have any point of view at all ... we must choose some particular height as our own; do the best we can, it will take a good part of life to attain any high outlook. (p. 1)

This ostensive motive also reverberates with tones of probable personal motives behind Barnes's project. The intellectual world had not long been open to women and it was still closed to all but a few. The details of Mary Barnes' road to Stanford showed her to be an extraordinary woman of her times, who had foregone a woman's traditional role in order to teach, but even more important, to study. Matriculating with the first female class at the University of Michigan, she included a concentration in the natural sciences with the AB (Artium Baccalaureatus) degree she received there in 1874. Later, she would teach at Wellesley and study at Cambridge University before returning home to Oswego at the age of 36 and marrying a former student, Earl Barnes, who was 11 years her junior. That same year marked the publication of *Studies in General History*, the first of three textbooks she would write on the study of history. For the next 6 years Mary accompanied her husband as his career took him from Hoboken, New Jersey, to Cornell University to the University of Zurich and to Indiana University before he received the call to join the Stanford faculty. Throughout this time Mary Barnes continued a life of scholarly research, writing, and publishing But wherever she was and whatever she was teaching or studying, Barnes appears to have never moved very far from her life-long area of interest, curriculum, and pedagogy.

She undoubtedly was influenced in this regard by her father, Edward Austen Sheldon (1823–1897) who served as superintendent of Oswego public schools from 1862 until his death. In 1859 he had introduced the colorful, age-appropriate Pestalozzian-inspired methods and materials to local teachers. In 1867 he founded the Oswego Normal School which quickly developed an internationally recognized Pestalozzian teacher preparation program, attracting visitors from as far away as Japan. Prior to leaving for the University of Michigan, the young Mary Sheldon attended the Normal School, took her degree in classical studies, and taught 2 years in the local schools. Over the next 15 years, she would return periodically to teach at Oswego Normal, where a good part of the students' day was spent observing and practicing in local schools.

This sheds light on another of her comments in the preface to *Studies in Historical Method*.

> The curse of secondary teaching is often the fact that after a year or two it provides no free outlet for the mind; but with the rapid development of departmental and individual work, the day is not far off when every one who chooses to teach, and who can protect himself from the insanity of over-work and the frivolity of scattered work, may hope to make his way out of the deadly treadmill of routine to join the life and motion of the greater world of knowledge. (Barnes, 1896, p. 2)

It is possible that Barnes's personal experience in the classroom had motivated her to find greater intellectual stimulation, as well as to attempt to provide that in her publications for others struggling under the "curse of secondary teaching." It appears possible that her Pestalozzian background contributed to her low tolerance for the mind numbing atmosphere of the majority of schools in her day, with their emphasis on memorization and recitation.

Certainly any discussion of Mary Barnes's personal motives would be incomplete without an account of one very important jog on her path from Oswego to Stanford. Shortly after her graduation from the University of Michigan, her interest in chemistry and physics gave way to a commitment to the field of history. This was most obviously evidenced by her denial of an offer to teach science at Wellesley College. Instead, she waited in order to accept a history post that opened up there a few months later. Clearly, she did not see this as an abandonment of the realm of science, as her particular passion was the "scientific study of human history" (Keohane, 1971, p. 92). Here Barnes found a synthesis of all her academic interests: curriculum and pedagogy, history, and science. For the next two decades, she pioneered the "scientific" or "inductive" approach to history in both the classroom and her scholarship.

By the time she arrived at Stanford she had authored three history textbooks which she considered, in current terms, "developmentally appropriate." During her tenure there she produced curricular and peda-gogical recommendations related to the teaching of history from kinder-garten through college, including the text *Studies in Historical Method*. She also conducted quantitative studies of area school children and wrote and edited articles on a variety of historical topics. Some of them clearly related to what today would be called the history of education, such as the article focusing on Johann H. Pestalozzi and the "historic sense of primi-tive peoples" (Barnes, 1896-97/1903b, p. 29). Her work, published together with the work of her graduate students and her husband, con-tributed to the birth of child study, the widespread research movement spearheaded by G. Stanley Hall.

TEXT AND CONTEXT: SOCIOCULTURAL MOTIVES

As Blumenfeld-Jones (2004) points out, any attempt to understand the ostensive and personal motives of a scholar would be lacking without a consideration of the sociocultural context. In the case of Mary Barnes it is possible to see how she both shaped and was shaped by the intellectual milieu of her times. As to the former dynamic, some of Barnes's work was truly original. Monteverde (1999) characterizes Barnes's approach to teaching history as a synthesis of the object lesson method of Pestalozzi and the "source method" (p. 25) of Leopold von Ranke, the German his-torian famous for his scientific approach to history. Accordingly, Barnes's history books featured primary source material, such as quotations, art reproductions, and drawings of artifacts, followed by numerous questions intended to encourage the reader to interpret the material. Monteverde also notes that minimal amounts of authorial narrative were found in Mary's books, unlike typical history books of the day.

However, certain elements of Barnes's history books seem inconsistent with a scientific (i.e.," objective") approach to history. These inconsistencies are quite noticeable in the blocks of questions that follow the presentation of the primary source material. Monteverde (1999) notes that leading questions such as, "How is Christianity superior [to Islam]?" suggest the presence of an a priori belief in the superiority of White, Anglo-Saxon, Protestant America and the assumption that "modesty, sub-missiveness, and domesticity" (p. 32) were virtues appropriate for women. But the connection that Monteverde does not appear to seriously con-sider is that *both presuppositions were central tenets of recapitulation theory*, "the idea that the child in his or her development must recapitulate the intel-lectual and moral development of humanity epoch by epoch" (Tanner & Tanner, 1990, p. 101). Indeed, it is as if Monteverde overlooked the phy-logeny article, "The Historic Sense Among Primitive Peoples" (1896–97/ 1903a) altogether.

It is understandable. Barnes's (1896-97/1903b) treatment of her sub-ject matter in the "The Historic Sense Among Primitive People," together with the comparison between children and "primitive peoples" (1896–97/ 1903a, p. 47) in "The Historic Sense Among Children," seems outlandish and racist. In these articles tribal cultures are arranged by skin color and demeaning cultural stereotypes (i.e., the darker the skin, the simpler or more "primitive" the culture). However unpalatable such stereotyping and racism are, Gould (1996) points out that they were an essential part of recapitulation theory and could not be separated from it. To exclude the racist aspects of Mary Barnes' articles would be to provide an incom-plete picture of her work. Indeed, the racist article on primitive peoples together with the demeaning comparisons between children and primi-tive peoples in the second article were considered so important to educa-tional research that, as mentioned earlier, they were published at least twice, in *Studies in the Historic Method* (1896) and *Studies in Education* (1896-97/1903a). An examination of these articles is able to suggest the degree to which recapitulation theory permeated the scientific, "objective" schol-arship of the era, in spite of the protest of such esteemed scholars as Dewey (1916). Such an examination may also shed light on what Mon-teverde (1999) calls the conundrum of Mary Sheldon Barnes.

Phylogeny: The Historic Sense Among Primitive Peoples

"The Historic Sense Among Primitive Peoples" (Barnes, 1896-97/1903) opens with the claim that it is an inductive, scientific study of primitive people's "historic sense" (p. 29). It then claims that the "historic sense" is composed of separate elements that should be self-evident when one (i.e., the author, Mary Barnes) looks at recorded history. The elements identified are "a true record," "continuous time," "cause and effect," and "the social unit" (p. 29). What ensues is a two-page critique of the ways in which various tribal cultures, living and dead, from around the world, were known to count and keep track of the past.

The tribal cultures are arranged from those that were considered to be the most primitive to those that were considered to be the least primitive. Using few words, little evidence, and no examples, Barnes (1896-97/ 1903b) effectively dismisses the cultures of the Australian Bushmen, the Veddahs of India, Sandwich Islanders, several American Indian tribes, the Eskimo, and the ancient Mexicans as she ranks them. According to Barnes, the Bushmen was a tribe that could not "count above three, [had] no known traditions of origin, nor any known myths" (p. 30) and therefore had no historic sense. The Veddahs of India, on the other hand, could "count as high as five, [had] a tradition of origin, and worship[ped] their ancestors" (p. 30). The section ends with the ancient Mexicans who were on "another stage of culture" because they "counted on by fives indefinitely ... [and] ... marked months and years by astronomical observations" (p. 31).

Next, Barnes (1896-97/1903b) discusses elements of a variety of cultures, such as ancestor worship, myths, songs, and the Bible, that reportedly corresponded to the elements of the historic sense and suggested to her the order in which the elements emerged. Like the arrangement of tribal cultures, the elements are discussed in a simple-to-complex, inferior-to-superior hierarchy. By the end of the "The Historic Sense Among Primitive Peoples," Barnes seems to believe that she has proven the following about the emergence of the historic sense in human history: (1) the sense of cause and effect is more primitive in more primitive peoples, (2) the notion of continuous time develops after the sense of cause and effect, and (3) the methods of scientific history (and *her* historical methods) develop last of all.

Ontogeny: The Historic Sense Among Children

"The Historic Sense Among Children" is actually a synthesis of four separate statistical studies, and is connected via footnotes and in-text citations to "The Historic Sense Among Primitive Peoples" and other studies found in the volume. The first study summarized in the article seeks to uncover the types of things children are curious about when given a simple story stripped of contextual details that would link it to a particular place or time, such as "date, place, name, or moral." School children, numbering 1,250, from Oakland, Santa Rosa, Napa, and Santa Paula were given the following story to read and respond to:

> There was a king who had a beautiful wife whom he dearly loved. But a fair prince came and took her away to a far country. Then the king and all his men went to fight the prince, who lived in a great city all walled about with stone. For many a day the king and his men tried in vain to enter it; buy, at last, by a clever trick, some of his men got into the city, and burned it to the ground; and so the king got his wife once more. (Barnes, 1896–97/1903a, p. 43)

After reading the story, the children were instructed to write down questions that they had about it. The children's responses became the data for the study. Sample sets of questions are included in the text of the article. For example:

> *Average set from girl of nine.*—Did the king have a beard? How many years was the king married when his wife was taken away? What kind of a dress did the wife wear when she was married? What was the name of the city that the prince lived in? What was the name of the stone that was put around the great city? What was the name of the prince? (p. 43)

The questions are sorted into categories based on what the children asked after reading the story. The categories that were derived from the questions are "who, where, how, why, result, personal detail and feeling, general detail, ethics, time number, and truth" (p. 43). The data from four of the categories, "who," "where," "how," and "why" are displayed in separate line graphs. A fifth line graph, labeled "how-why-result" presents the combined data of three of the categories. The text notes that the results from those three categories are combined because all three concepts are related to "cause and effect." The conclusion drawn from the results is that children are interested mainly in "action" and want to know primarily "persons, places, [and] relations of cause and effect" (p. 47).

The remaining three studies presented in "The Historic Sense Among Children" used similar methods to examine children's "inferences," "sense of evidence," and their preference for first person accounts of history. Generally speaking, these studies conclude that the younger the child, the more he or she favored concrete historical items and first person accounts of historical events, and, by logical extension, the older a child is, the less he or she favors concrete historical items and first person accounts.

Recommendations directly related to the teaching of history are found towards the end of the article. However, these recommendations do not occur without direct comparisons between the historic sense of "savages" and that of children. For example, the first recommendation appears as follows:

> As to the order in which these [elements of the historic sense] appear, we see
> that among savages they appear all together in the rudimentary form of the
> myths of origin, which, unplaced in space, vaguely placed in time, attempt
> to give some true account of the beginnings of man and of the world. Such
> are the tales of Prometheus, of the Under-World of the Zuni, the Midgard
> and Yggdrasil stories of the North.... History, then, appears early as a con-
> sciously separate field of human knowledge. Among children we find the
> same fact. From the age of seven onward we find them inquiring after time,
> cause and effect, the social unit, and the truthful record,—that is, all the ele-
> ments of history lie within the field of the child's curiosity.... [Thus] history
> is a suitable subject for children from the age of seven at least. (Barnes,
> 1896–97/1903a, p. 89)

In the sixth recommendation, Barnes (1896-97/1903a) alludes to *her* scientific historical method, suggesting that it is the superior of the lot and therefore should be reserved for the students in later stages of development. She begins to use her study of the historic sense of "savages" (p. 91) as a source for curriculum content, implying that the best historical material for children in a particular culture-epoch is primary source material generated by tribes, races, or cultures that allegedly belong to the same culture-epoch as the children. In the passage below, she acknowledges that the material belonging to the most evolved culture-epoch (i.e., her period of history in the United States) is still being developed. At the same time, she suggests that the more evolved critical historic sense is developing along with the materials:

> As to the forms of history, we have seen that critical history develops last in
> the history of the race, being preceded by beautiful history, moral history,
> and mnemonic history.... With children we see that history finds natural
> expression in stories, picture, dramatic plays and poems, with or without a
> moral. From both these sets of facts I conclude that we should seek our his-
> tory for children in Plutarch, Homer, and Shakespeare, before seeking it in
> edited documents with notes and criticisms of the modern school of his-
> tory.... [These authors] give us plenty of appropriate material. The scien-
> tific forms [of history] must wait on the development of material, and also
> on the development of the critical sense; that is, until the ages of twelve and
> above. (p. 91).

Perhaps, in Mary Barnes' mind, human beings were evolving in front of her eyes, and through her teaching she was playing an active role in their evolution. Perhaps she saw her history books that were intended for eighth grade children and that covered history from 1000 B.C. to the present (Monteverde, 1999) as contributions to a final superior or scientific chapter of human evolution. This interpretation is supported by material found toward the end of the article in which she seems to be describing her work, and her tendency to focus on primary source material, directly:

> At the age of fourteen or fifteen another sort of work should appear. Original sources should still be used ... these sources should illustrate, however, not the picture of human society moving before us in a long panorama, but should give us the opportunity to study the organization, thought, feeling, of a time as seen in its concrete embodiments, its documents, monuments, men, and books. Now come the statesmen, thinkers, poets, as successors to the explorers and fighters of the earlier period. (Barnes, 1896–97/1903a, pp. 92–93)

Here we also find statements that, at first glance, appear advanced or ahead of their time:

> Sources ... should still be used, but used with reflection; and the children should be encouraged not only to understand and remember them, but to interpret and criticise [sic] them. They should learn to read with increasing accuracy and fulness [sic] between the lines for the life and thought of the people they study, and for the standpoint of the narrator. They may also be led ... to answer the question: How do we know that this is true? (p. 93)

However, in the context of recapitulation theory, terms such as "interpret" and "criticise" inevitably take on meanings that are narrower and more judgmental than the meanings they would carry today in a similar context. In the passage above, Barnes probably does *not* mean children should be encouraged to *analyze* and *evaluate* primary source material on the children's (or material's) own terms. Instead, she is likely stating students should be encouraged to *judge* and *find inferiorities and deficiencies with* primary source material when compared with the accomplishments of Western Civilization, in general, and the United States, in particular, in the way that Barnes, herself, did. Regardless of which interpretation you accept in this particular situation, Mary Barnes' work stands as a clear example of recapitulation theory's direct material presence in the curriculum.

CONCLUSION: THE CONUNDRUM RESOLVED

A consideration of the "historical motive" (Blumenfeld-Jones, 2004, p. 128) of Mary Barnes's work--specifically recapitulation theory—provides a solution to the conundrum identified by Monteverde (1999). Of course, as Wraga (2006) points out, any interpretation of a scholar's career illuminates some dimensions of it and eclipses others. Gadamer's notion of the incompleteness of understanding concurs that no one assessment could sum up the whole truth of Barnes's career or the time in which she lived. We offer this interpretation to both challenge and extend previous considerations of the life and work of Mary Sheldon Barnes and, we hope, to "enhance appreciation of the sheer complexity of the past" (p. 1097).

Monteverde (1999) states that Barnes "suggested that students use primary sources inductively as raw material to construct their own knowledge, conclusions, and interpretations of the past" (p. 18) even as her "tacit worldview ... blinded her to ... paradoxes in her thinking" (p. 19). But, while Barnes's emphasis on primary source material (and de-emphasis on author narrative) may have been innovative, her innovations stopped there. Barnes appears to have been interested in her students' "knowledge, conclusions, and interpretations" only if they conformed to a theoretical framework that was at once sexist, racist, anti-child, nationalistic, and invisible to those who were unaware of it because it was assumed to be true.[2] The ultimate irony in Mary Barnes' life work may not be, as Monteverde suggests, that she encouraged her students to reach for intellectual freedom that she, herself, was unable to obtain, but that Barnes, as a woman in late nineteenth century America, enjoyed unparalleled freedoms in her life that she used to disseminate a "scientifically-based" ideology that reduced women to over-grown, emotional children.

That she did so, however, is almost unremarkable in light of the way recapitulation theory permeated the zeitgeist of her time. According to Ross (1972), the timeframe for child study continued for more than 2 decades, from 1883 when G. Stanley Hall published "The Contents of Children's Minds," until the early 1900s. However, this timeframe does not take into account that recapitulation theory "had been widely accepted as a valid scientific principle from at least the seventeenth century on" (Kliebard, 1986, p. 45). It also fails to note the importance of the decades leading up to Hall's publication, during which recapitulation theory gained currency.[3] Significantly, it also neglects child study's legacy, which is detectable in many "common-sense" public school practices of today (see Egan, 2002), thus accounting for the eerie echo of familiarity we sensed from Barnes's texts.

In the face of the unprecedented worldwide human suffering, socio-political upheaval, and industrial progress, recapitulation theory offered the promise of certainty and order. It offered a place for everyone and everyone a place, within nice, neat "scientifically" revealed twin hierarchies with light-skinned, Northern Europeans at the top of both.

Unfortunately, the theory was little more than a narcissistic projection—a picture of Dorian Gray—that, under the banner of science, at once justified oppression and shielded oppressors from seeing its human cost. Even as the details of recapitulation theory have faded from memory, the *scientism* spawned by the theory has not. Herbert Spencer's unconditional faith in science to solve all social and educational problems lives on today in high-stakes testing, "scientifically-based research," and "adequate" yearly progress. Although the whereabouts of Dorian Gray's picture have long been forgotten, its legacy continues.

NOTES

1. Preunderstanding is defined by (Gadamer, 1960/1997) as the traditions in which our attempts at understanding are embedded. For explication of the potential for philosophical hermeneutics to be emancipatory, see Gallagher (1992) and Kogler (1992/1999).
2. Gould (1996) notes, "E. D. Cope, the celebrated American paleontologist who elucidated the mechanism of recapitulation … identified four groups of lower human forms on this criterion: nonwhite races, all women, southern as opposed to northern European whites, and lower classes within superior races" (p. 144).
3. Beginning in the 1850s, Herbert Spencer (1861/1920) had begun calling for further investigation of recapitulation theory in the series of essays that became his famous book, *Education: Intellectual, Moral, Physical*. In addition, Kliebard (1986) notes the boost that Darwin's work gave to the theory's widespread acceptance.

REFERENCES

Barnes, E. (1896-97). *Studies in education*. Standford, CA: Stanford University.

Barnes, M. S. (1896). *Studies in historic method*. Boston: D. C. Heath.

Barnes, M. S. (1903a). The historic sense among children. In E. Barnes (Ed.), *Studies in education: A series of ten numbers devoted to child-study and the history of education* (Vol. 1, pp. 43–52, 83–93). Standford, CA: Stanford University. (Original work published 1896–97)

Barnes, M. S. (1903b). The historic sense among primitive peoples. In E. Barnes (Ed.), *Studies in education: A series of ten numbers devoted to child-study and the history of education* (Vol. 1, pp. 29–40). Standford, CA: Stanford University. (Original work published 1896–97)

Blumenfeld-Jones, D. (2004). Dance curriculum then and now: A critical historical-hermeneutic evaluation. In W. M. Reynolds & J. A. Webber (Eds.), *Expanding curriculum theory: Dis/positions and lines of flight*. Mahwah, NJ: Erlbaum.

Brooks, N. J. (2000). Re/searching the Reconceptualization: A hermeneutic inquiry (Doctoral dissertation, Oklahoma State University, 2000). *Dissertation Abstracts International, 61*, 3450.

Dewey, J. (1916). *Democracy and Education*. New York: Macmillan.

Egan, K. (2002). *Getting it wrong from the beginning: Our progressivist inheritance from Herbert Spencer, John Dewey, and Jean Piaget*. New Haven, CT: Yale University Press.

Gadamer, H.-G. (1997). *Truth and method* (2nd, Rev. ed.) (J. Weinsheimer & D. G. Marshall, Trans.). New York: Continuum. (Original work published 1960)

Gallagher, S. (1992). *Hermeneutics and education*. Albany: State University of New York.

Gould, S. J. (1996). *The mismeasure of man*. New York: W. W. Norton.

Keohane, R. E. (1971). Barnes, Mary Downing Sheldon. In E. T. & J. W. James (Eds.), *Notable American women, 1607–1950: A biographical dictionary* (pp. 92–93). Cambridge, MA: Harvard University Press.

Kliebard, H. M. (1986). *The struggle for the American curriculum: 1893–1958*. New York: Routledge.

Kogler, H. H. (1999). *The power of dialogue: Critical hermeneutics after Gadamer and Foucault*. (P. Hendrickson, Trans.). Cambridge, MA: MIT. (Original work published 1992)

Laverty, S. M. (2003). Hermeneutic phenomenology and phenomenology: A comparison of historical and methodological considerations. *International Journal of Qualitative Methods, 2*(3), Article 3. Retrieved June 14, 2006, from http://www.ualberta.ca/~iiqm/backissues/2_3final/pdf/laverty.pdf

McAninch, S. A. (1990). The educational theory of Mary Sheldon Barnes: Inquiry learning as indoctrination in history education. *Educational Theory, 40*(1), 45–52.

Monteverde, F. E. (1999). Considering the source: Mary Sheldon Barnes. In M. S. Crocco & O. L. Davis, Jr (Eds.), *"Bending the future to their will": Civic women, social education, and democracy*. Lanham, MD: Rowman & Littlefield.

Reynolds, W. (1989). *Reading curriculum theory: The development of a new hermeneutic*. New York: Peter Lang.

Ross, D. (1972). *G. Stanley Hall: The psychologist as prophet*. Chicago: The University of Chicago Press.

Sheldon, M. D. (1886). *Studies in general history*. Boston: Heath.

Spencer, H. (1920). *Education: Intellectual, moral, and physical*. New York: D. Appleton. (Original work published 1861)

Tanner, D., & Tanner, L. (1990). *History of the school curriculum*. New York: Macmillan.

Wraga, W. G. (2006). Progressive pioneer: Alexander James Inglis (1879–1924) and American secondary education. *Teachers College Record, 108*, 1080–1105.

CHAPTER 9

CITIZENS OF TODAY AND TOMORROW

An Exploration of Preservice Social Studies Teachers' Knowledge and Their Professors' Experiences With Citizenship

Chara Haeussler Bohan, Frans Doppen, Joseph Feinberg, and Carolyn O'Mahony

This study examines preservice teachers' knowledge about citizenship through their performance on the United States Citizenship and Immigration Services (USCIS) Naturalization Test. In addition, the study examined four of the researchers' own conceptions of citizenship based on their professional experiences as social studies educators and personal experiences. The study found that many teachers, particularly at the elementary school level, were unable to answer correctly questions associated with the U.S. Constitution and the different branches of government.

According to the *Civic Mission of Schools Report*, competent and responsible citizens are informed and thoughtful. They participate in their communities, act politically, and have moral and civic virtues (Center for Information and Research on Civic Learning and Engagement [CIRCLE],

Curriculum and Teaching Dialogue
Volume 10, Numbers 1 & 2, 2008, pp. 117–134
Copyright © 2008 by Information Age Publishing
All rights of reproduction in any form reserved.

2003, p. 10). Schools may be the only institutions with the mandate and capacity to reach virtually every young person in the country and help students become virtuous citizens (p. 12).

Research reveals, however, that teachers are often ill-prepared to effectively deliver citizenship education. Two studies in the 1980s found that preservice elementary teachers were unprepared to explain to children how the American government works (Gilmore, McKinney, Larkins, Ford, & McKinney, 1988; Larkins, 1984). In a more recent study involving an elementary education methods course, which focused on the intersection between patriotism and citizenship, Nash (2005) found that participating teachers faced factual as well as conceptual challenges. Such challenges included the inability to consider perspectives beyond a two-sided polemic mode (Bohan & Davis, 1998) and equating patriotism with feelings of love, respect, and loyalty—all of which are demonstrated by saluting the American flag. The teachers had a limited understanding of tolerance, diversity, and multiculturalism. In addition, they failed to suggest that questioning governmental policies or actions could ever be considered as an act of good citizenship.

Whether our nation's teachers have gained sufficient preparation and education to teach civics, however, has been relatively unexplored. The primary purpose of this study was to analyze preservice teachers' citizenship knowledge through their performance on the U.S. Citizenship and Immigration Services (USCIS) Naturalization Test. More importantly, participants reviewed the test items, suggested revisions, and offered insights into their beliefs about citizenship. An additional purpose of this analysis was to explore four of the researchers' own understandings of citizenship based on their professional experiences as social studies educators and their personal experiences as foreign-born residents or as the parent of a foreign-born American. Finally, the researchers explored the relevance and meaning of citizenship for the twenty-first century as the world becomes more globally interconnected (Bohan, 2001).

CIVIC EDUCATION AND CITIZENSHIP

Living in a "marketized civil society" (Torres, 1998), teachers should be competent civic educators. Teachers and students need to be knowledgeable and aware that they have political as well as economic choices to make. The IEA Civic Education Study, a comprehensive study of civic knowledge, attitudes, and experiences of 14-year-olds, found that U.S. students scored significantly above the international mean (Hahn, 2001). Twenty-eight countries participated in this large-scale study (Torney-Purta, Lehmann, Oswald, & Shultz, 2001). The researchers found that

American students scored significantly above the international mean on civic knowledge and also scored above average on measures of civic engagement. More recently, however, the *Civic and Political Health of the Nation* report found that civic engagement of young people is low, they have lost confidence in the government, and their political knowledge is generally poor (Lopez, Levine, Both, Kirby, & Marcelo, 2006). Many factors contribute to this level of disengagement, such as teachers' fear of criticism when discussing controversial issues, the movement for high-stakes testing, and the impact of budget cutbacks on civic education (CIRCLE, 2003, p. 15; Miller, 2007). Whether or not American students gain appropriate levels of civic knowledge is clearly subject to debate. At the same time, the notion of citizenship itself must be examined beyond the simplistic notion of a group of people enjoying limited rights within the context of a given country (Torres, 1998).

A variety of conceptions of *good* citizenship have been identified throughout the citizenship literature. Many educational researchers agree that there is a spectrum of ideas or conceptions about good citizens (e.g., Allen, 1996; Clark & Case, 1997; Westheimer & Kahne, 2004). For example, Westheimer and Kahne (2004) contrast and detail three broad conceptions for citizenship education (including personal responsibility, participatory, and justice-oriented) that were drawn from various program strategies and approaches to democratic education. Westheimer and Kahne caution that "obedience and patriotism" are not necessarily democratic goals and would instead be desirable in a totalitarian regime. Indeed, some of the current citizenship education conceptions are "narrow and often ideologically conservative" and reflect "political choices that have political consequences" (p. 237). Thus, good intentions of educators to facilitate citizenship education are not always realized and may not promote democratic principles.

While most social studies teachers might not agree with Count's (1932) call to build a new social order, they might agree with his wish for a "more noble and beautiful" America (p. 55). According to Barr, Barth, and Shermis (1977), however, most social studies teachers see citizenship transmission as their central role. They seek to instill patriotism, cultural heritage, and traditional political values. Banks (1997) has argued that social studies teachers should also promote cultural democracy conjointly with citizenship education to help their students develop an identity as members of their own "cultural communities, the nation-state, and the global world society" (p. 124). Unfortunately, citizenship education often promotes mainstream national narratives and lacks a global orientation, while highlighting the nation's strengths and other countries' weaknesses (Banks, 1997; Camicia, 2007; Myers, 2006). Yet, promoting conformity to mainstream notions of citizenship is not just an American phenomenon (Astiz & Mendez, 2006; Doppen, 2007a).

In order for teachers to have nuanced understandings of citizenship, they need to be given opportunities to examine their beliefs and knowledge base. Thornton (2001, 2003) has argued that liberal arts professors, who often teach the bulk of teacher preparation coursework, seldom think of themselves as teacher educators, whereas education school professors tend to define their task as limited to pedagogy. Thornton (2003) suggests that, rather than "piling up" content courses by themselves (p. 2), the lines between subject matter and professional education should be blurred (p. 6) and preservice teachers should be required to take courses that are based on what they will be expected to teach (Thorton, 2001, p. 7). Such an approach will allow teacher preparation programs to better prepare their candidates to teach about citizenship. Consonant with this notion of blurring the lines between content and pedagogy, researchers in this study not only sought to find out how the preservice teachers would fare on the USCIS naturalization test, but also grounded discussions about immigration, citizenship, and assessment in the act of taking the test and providing responses.

METHOD

Design

The participants in this study attended universities in Georgia, Ohio, Indiana, South Carolina, and Michigan. During the spring and fall of 2006, the seven researchers administered a test in eight different social studies methods courses. The test consisted of 50 written questions from the 100 that might be asked by officers of the USCIS (2007). Approximately half of the 100 USCIS citizenship study questions were considered very similar or identical to answers for other questions. For example, "How many states are there in the Union?" and "How many stars are there in our flag?" were considered leading questions. In addition, four questions focused on the specific aspects of the flag, such as colors, numbers, and meaning. Thus, the researchers reduced the questions to the most salient and non-redundant 50 questions.

Typically, USCIS officers randomly select ten questions of the 100 to orally examine an applicant's citizenship knowledge. However, given the number of participants in this study, oral examinations were impractical. Instead, each preservice teacher was asked to write an answer for each question. Researchers at each site independently graded their students' tests. After discussing their scores and responses, participants were asked to respond to the following four items:

- Explain whether you think the questions on the citizenship test represent what every immigrant applying for citizenship should know.
- Explain whether you think the citizenship test represents what every American citizen born in this country should know.
- The USCIS is currently revising the citizenship test. Explain, if you were revising this version of the citizenship test, which questions, if any, would you delete and/or change.
- The USCIS is currently revising the citizenship test. Explain, if you were revising this version of the citizenship test, which questions, if any, would you add.

The researchers then reviewed the qualitative written data from the preceding items and participant responses were coded as supporting, disagreeing, or containing elements of both support and disagreement through qualified answers.

Participants

The 206 participants in this study comprised a total of 114 elementary preservice teachers (55%) and 92 middle and high school social studies preservice teachers (45%). Of these, 170 participants (83%) were undergraduate students. While, males made up 26% of all participants, only 11% of whom were in the elementary methods courses versus 45% who were in the middle and/or high school methods courses. The majority (73%) of the participants in this study were traditional students aged 19-24 years, whereas 13% were aged 25–29 years. The ethnic background of the participants was overwhelmingly homogeneous, as 95.6% were Caucasian.

About one-third of the participants (31%) indicated that they had graduated from a rural high school. Another 56% indicated that they attended a suburban high school, and only 13% attended an urban high school. Approximately one-fourth of the participants attended high schools with fewer than 500 students, one-third had 500–1,000 students, almost one-fifth (19%) had 1,000–1,500 students, and one-quarter attended a high school with more than 1,500 students.

Nearly 9 out of every 10 participants (88%) attended a public high school, and only 12% attended a private school. When asked to characterize the level of ethnic diversity in their high school, 69% indicated that their school had "almost none" or "little" diversity. About one-fifth (19%)

of the participants indicated that their high school had "a fair amount" of diversity, whereas 11% suggested it had "very much" diversity.

In this exploratory study, an early childhood methodology researcher was not part of the research team. Therefore, a distinction between elementary preservice teachers and early childhood preservice teachers was not delineated. Future studies should include early childhood methodology courses in order to provide a more comprehensive understanding of all preservice teachers.

RESULTS

Sources of Civic Knowledge

Using a Likert-scale (from not important to very important: 1–4), all participants were asked to assess the importance of sources of information that contributed to their knowledge of citizenship. There were no significant differences between the undergraduate and graduate participants. They ranked extracurricular activities [3.3] as their most important source of information, followed by their college courses, their family and friends and the print media [3.2], civic organizations [3.0], the Internet [2.9], and television [2.8].

Civics Knowledge

Not surprisingly, undergraduate preservice teachers preparing to teach social sciences in high school scored the highest on the test ($M = 91\%$ correct) followed by middle school ($M = 77\%$ correct). Future elementary school teachers scored the lowest ($M = 62\%$ correct). Graduate preservice teachers who took a methods course that included middle and high school social science majors predictably scored between middle and high school preservice teachers ($M = 83\%$ correct). An analysis of the scores showed that out of 50 questions, more than 40% of the middle and high school preservice teachers missed 4–12 items; and more than 40% of the students in the elementary methods courses missed between 17 and 23 items.

In all eight methods courses in this study, nearly every participant answered correctly questions about the American flag, presidential term limits and succession, and voting age. In contrast, more than 40% of the participants could not name the two senators from their state or the Chief Justice of the Supreme Court, nor did they know the number of members in the House of Representatives. In seven of the eight courses, more than

40% of the participants did not know the length of the term of office for a U.S. Senator or the year the U.S. Constitution was adopted. In six courses, more than 40% did not know how many times a U.S. Senator could be reelected. In five of the eight courses, more that 40% of the students were unable to articulate the purposes of the U.S. Constitution, the executive branch, and judicial branch. Finally, in half of the eight courses, more than 40% of the participants did not know how often a U.S. Representative could be reelected, how many justices sit on the U.S. Supreme Court, the name of the building in which the U.S. Congress meets, and that popular sovereignty is the underlying concept of the U.S. Declaration of Independence.

It is apparent that while the participants generally answered correctly those questions related to the American flag and key figures in American history, they struggled with questions related to the broad principles that underlie the U.S. Constitution. Participants also lacked factual knowledge about the composition of the U.S. Supreme Court and U.S. Congress, and were not familiar with contemporary leaders in the legislative and judicial branches.

Beliefs About the Test as an Assessment of Civic Knowledge

Preservice teachers in a number of social studies methods classes across the nation were unable to answer correctly many sample questions taken from the current United States naturalization test. Given the far from laudatory demonstration of citizenship knowledge[1] that these nascent teachers demonstrated, one might expect them to be indignant about the nature of the questions asked of prospective countrymen and women. One might reasonably expect them to suggest that questions on such a test should disclose evidence of the attributes possessed by individuals who contribute to society in a positive way. Yet, when asked if they thought the questions on this test represented what every immigrant applying for citizenship should know, they generally agreed (59% yes, 39% no, 2% no response). However, these results are not as simple as the numbers may suggest. When asked about changing questions for the revised naturalization test, only 34% of respondents agreed unconditionally with the statement that the questions represent what every immigrant applying for US citizenship should know. Conditional responses tended to focus on issues of fairness with teachers contending that most Americans by birth could not answer many of the questions.

Many of the preservice teachers who rejected the test as an effective assessment of what immigrants should know when applying for citizenship (i.e., the "no" responses) also claimed that it was unfair to

expect immigrants to know more than native citizens. Individuals sug-
gested that it was more important to know the laws, be able to speak
English, or be patriotic and loyal to the United States. One future teacher,
Lauren, made the following conclusion:

> Why does a new citizen need to know all this stuff? [Is the USCIS] testing for
> ambition? Ambitious people will study, practice, do well; lazy people will not
> study, not do well? Literacy? Ability to follow societal norms—follow direc-
> tions etc? They [the administrators of the naturalization test] are testing for
> something besides people's knowledge of these ideas.

When the preservice teachers were asked if the naturalization test was a
good assessment of what citizens born in the United States should know,
an overwhelming 81% of the preservice teachers agreed (49%
unconditionally). Conditional "yes" responses were frequently colored by
individuals' performance on the citizenship test they had taken, with a
number of apologetic comments and explanations of how one learns facts
in school and then forgets them, or how the majority of Americans do not
know these facts. Others said it is more important to know political structures rather than the exact dates of historical events. A number of students, who disagreed with the content of the test, were dismayed about
how poorly the test questions assessed one's potential for being a "good"
citizen.

When asked what questions they would eliminate from the current test
and what questions they would add, the preservice teachers had surprisingly few suggestions. However, the questionnaire was given during a class
session, so there was limited class time for highly reflective written
responses. In each of the methods courses, a minority of individuals
determined that the test was effective as it was—there was no need to
change or delete any of the questions. There were also students who were
concerned about the phrasing of particular questions (e.g., as written,
there could be a number of ostensibly correct responses).

When students reflected on the questions that were most commonly
missed, there were individuals who suggested eliminating questions about
the number of senators or representatives and the nature of terms and
term limits. In most groups, individuals suggested eliminating questions
that they perceived as too specific or trivial, such as those pertaining to
details about the flag, holidays, and history. These individuals suggested,
for instance, that it is more important for citizens to understand the purpose of the Declaration of Independence than to know who wrote it. Others suggested that the questions were culturally biased. One participant
stated that it "[seems] like history should not be limited to Jefferson's writing the Declaration or Lincoln's Emancipation Proclamation. Very White,
Anglo-Saxon exam." Other preservice teachers challenged the need for

any questions about U.S. history. They proposed that it is more important for citizens to know how the government works than requiring them to know when documents were signed and what holidays the colonists celebrated.

When asked how they would revise the naturalization test, 71 of the 206 preservice teachers had no suggestions. The other 135 students suggested that immigrants should know about their rights, state-level issues, and current events in the country. A number of them stated that there should be more of a focus on exploring why applicants wish to become citizens. They would like to add questions that would assess if an applicant is "cognitively able" (including being able to speak English) and intent on becoming a good, patriotic citizen (Chebium, 2000). One preservice teacher wrote, "I would add some questions that make you tell how you really feel about the U.S. to me and how you would be loyal." Some suggested adding questions that spoke to an immigrant's ability to assimilate. They would ask questions that would measure the applicant's grasp of American ideals, beliefs, and culture; for instance, "I might ask some questions about cultural dynamics of the melting pot theory that is supposed to be America." Another suggested adding questions that would assess "a person's ability to thrive in the U.S., e.g., laws, the tax system, etc."

Perhaps because of the nature of the questions, few individuals commented on the validity of the test in assessing a person's potential value as a citizen of the United States of America. Only two individuals spoke to this issue, suggesting that instead of taking a test, applicants undertake a service project that demonstrates a desire to become a citizen.

The preservice teachers' responses to these questions are very interesting because, apart from being unable to recall so-called citizenship knowledge (particularly among the respondents preparing to be elementary school teachers), these future teachers regard themselves and each other as "good citizens." According to Sadker and Sadker (2003), people who are teachers tend to want to work with others, they love the classroom environment, they want the respect that being a teacher evokes, they love learning, they want to be creative, they want to make a difference in the lives of others, and they want decent salaries and long summer vacations. In addition, individuals cannot enter the profession if they have a criminal record or if they have other moral blemishes on their official records. Despite the poor performance of some of these students on the naturalization test, they may well be the kinds of citizens we would want living in our communities.

However, what is missing in many of the preservice teachers' responses is acknowledgement of the rights and responsibilities entailed in being an active member in a democratic society. As described, they could be respectable members of any society, including a totalitarian one. What is missing from the majority of the responses and suggestions for changes is the notion that immigrants are requesting to become participants in the world's oldest democracy. In doing so, surely new immigrants should be expected to demonstrate to what extent they are capable and willing to participate in public decision-making (Allen, 1996; Clark & Case, 1997; Westheimer & Kahne, 2004). This is, perhaps, too much to ask of people who may be arriving in a nation with very few belongings, or who are arriving with limited language skills or educational backgrounds. Nevertheless, it seems important that the students—people who will soon be entrusted with educating children on how to participate in a democratic system—be aware that informed participation and willing participants are essential in maintaining a healthy democracy.

I DID IT MY WAY: TO BE A CITIZEN OR NOT TO BE

Interest in studying preservice social studies teachers' conceptions and knowledge of American citizenship by means of the naturalization test was a personally relevant activity for several of the authors. Indeed, three of the researchers were born in foreign countries. A fourth author adopted a foreign-born child. Therefore, four of the researchers[2] had personal and first-hand dealings with USCIS. Strikingly, each has followed a different path with respect to making the decision "to be or not to be" a United States citizen. Despite noticeable differences in experiences, all four demonstrated common themes in their experiences. At the heart of these varied pathways has been the notion of wrestling with what it means to be a citizen of a nation.

Each of the foreign-born researchers hails from a different country around the globe. Frans was born in the Netherlands, Carolyn was born in New Zealand, and Masato was born in Japan (Doppen, 2007b; Ogawa, 2007; O'Mahony, 2007). Chloe, the foreign-born adopted daughter of Chara, came from China. These four individuals share interesting narratives of their journeys to the United States and their encounters with U.S. immigration services. Not surprisingly, the three researchers arrived in the United States as adults in order to further their education. The adopted child, Chloe, came to the U.S. at 13 months of age and had no ability to control her entry into America. Nonetheless, the Chinese government permits abandoned children to be adopted by foreigners (e.g., Americans and other Westerners), because as her orphanage director stated, "They would have better educational opportunities in the United States."

America's renowned educational system attracts people from around the globe to the United States. Yet, a "silent crisis in American education" exists (Friedman, 2007). According to Friedman, the challenges imposed by U.S. immigration policy lead the majority of these scholars to return home. The crisis is particularly pronounced in science because few doctoral students in scientific studies are American citizens, thus the knowledge and scholarship gained in the United States does not remain within American borders. Friedman advocated that foreign-born students be granted automatic citizenship upon earning doctoral degrees as a means to attract these scholars to reside and work in the United States.

Various reasons have led each of the foreign-born researchers in this study to remain in the United States. Two found relationships with American citizens a compelling reason to remain, and all three found opportunities to work in higher education. Each of the three foreign-born adults has grappled directly with the concept of American citizenship. Not only does each of the three think about citizenship in a theoretical manner as a social studies educator, but also each has faced the practical reality of immigration and citizenship processes in the United States.

Frans has consciously chosen to remain a citizen of the Netherlands. After immigrating in 1984, he elected to maintain Dutch citizenship because Dutch law did not allow him to have dual citizenship and he did not want to lose allegiance to the country of his birth. Although Frans understands that since 2003 the Dutch law allows dual citizenship for persons married to a U.S. citizen, he has not elected to become an American citizen. Frans has lived in the United States for more than 20 years, is married to an American citizen, and has two American-born children. Yet, he writes, "Although there are many things I like about the U.S. in comparison to the Netherlands, I am, in essence, still Dutch, even after all these years" (Doppen, 2007b).

On the other hand, Carolyn, who was born and raised in New Zealand, recently became an American citizen when she took the naturalization oath on September 10, 2007 (O'Mahony, 2007). According to Carolyn, four prosaic factors contributed to her decision to become a U.S. citizen. First, she gave birth to a son and does not want her immigration status to raise legal issues for her continued residency if anything should happen to her husband. Second, she wants the ability to be fully involved in American society, including having a voice in the political system. Third, she does not want to be in a vulnerable position as a social studies methods professor. Her former status as a resident alien subjected her to criticism from students. Indeed, shortly after September 11, a student accused her of being "un-American" when she tried to explain why people in the larger world might not agree with American values. Finally, she believes that if she encourages students to be involved in the social, political, and economic aspects of society, she must be similarly engaged (O'Mahony, 2007).

The third researcher, Masato, has also wrestled with the concept of American citizenship (Ogawa, 2007). Like many individuals who come to the United States, he enjoys many aspects of American life and work. Yet, he maintains ties to Japan, his country of birth. Importantly, he does not want to sever his connections to Japan. He and his wife are in the process of applying for lawful permanent residence (commonly known as "green cards"), and would only be able to apply for American citizenship after having resided in the United States for a certain number of years. Masato recognizes several benefits to be gained from American citizenship, such as freedom from worrying about U.S. immigration laws, the ability to vote in elections, and ease of traveling to and from the United States. However, he faces barriers with respect to gaining American citizenship. Although the United States acknowledges the legality of dual citizenship, the Japanese government does not (U.S. Department of State, 2007). Understandably, Masato does not want to lose his identity as a Japanese citizen, the place he was born and had lived for 32 years.

All four foreign-born individuals contended with considerable immigration paperwork because of citizenship and residency issues. For Carolyn, the road to becoming an American citizen was a 7-year journey. Because she initially came to the United States to pursue a graduate degree, Carolyn began with a student visa. Later, she gained an "Optional Practical Training" visa, followed by a Permanent Resident Card (O'Mahony, 2007), and finally she sought citizenship. Carolyn began citizenship paperwork in 2000, and had an attorney assist in the process. Despite her apparent advantages as a highly educated woman, a native English speaker, an American husband, and the assistance of a woman in her church community, she found that there was little flexibility in the system (O'Mahony, 2007). Because of the cumbersome nature of the immigration process, Carolyn is not at all surprised by the large number of illegal immigrants in the United States.

Frans and Masato have had to pursue the paperwork that enables them to work in the United States while they maintain citizenship in their native countries. Frans had to marry in order to remain in the United States, so he was granted a fiancé visa, which required that he marry within 30 days of arrival. He also experienced considerable paperwork. In addition to completing many forms, he had to take a medical exam, prove he did not have tuberculosis and prove he had not engaged in any act of prostitution, and gain clearance for his political sympathies (Doppen, 2007b). Frans had to explain to the immigration official that the Labor Party was a mainstream political organization in Holland. Within a week of his arrival, Frans married and began the process of applying for a permanent alien registration card (which he reports is not green). He encountered further paperwork challenges when applying for a teaching certificate in the state of Florida, as the green card application was held up by the INS (currently USCIS) bureaucracy. His sister-in-law had to sign a form stating that Frans would not become a burden to the state for the first five years of his residence in the United States. If he did become unemployed, his sister-in-law had to agree to financially provide for Frans. After contacting his wife's legislative representatives, Senator Bob Graham (Governor at the time) and Congressman Buddy MacKay, Frans was finally able to procure his green card and teaching certificate. Masato has only begun the process of applying for a green card. Masato, on the other hand, does not have the advantage of an American wife, and faces the dilemma of not wanting to renounce his Japanese citizenship.

With respect to adopting foreign-born children, immigration rules are different. Prior to a change in the law enacted by the Clinton administration, all foreign-born children of American citizens had to follow a similar immigration paperwork path as foreign-born adults, in order to gain American citizenship status. The required paperwork included records of medical examinations, INS documents, police reports, birth and marriage certificates, passports, IRS tax returns, social worker reports, and the certification, authentication, and translation of these documents. The Clinton era legislation, known as the Child Citizenship Act of 2000, and its enactment as law (PL 106-395) allowed for the foreign-born adopted children of American citizens to automatically gain citizenship status (Bohan, 2001), thus bypassing a cumbersome second round of immigration paperwork once the child was adopted. So, Chloe's arrival in the United State meant that she automatically gained U.S. citizenship.

For each of these foreign-born individuals, citizenship has a special and unique meaning. Because of their cross-cultural experiences, they think of citizenship in a broader sense than simply voting or having content-level knowledge typically asked on the naturalization test. For each, citizenship means multicultural competency, global awareness, open-mindedness, but even more importantly, contributing to make the Earth a better place, now, and for the future.

DISCUSSION

Naturalization applicants will begin taking the new revised test on October 1, 2008. The test includes completely new questions that focus on the concepts of democracy and the rights and responsibilities of citizenship (USCIS, 2006a, 2006b). In redesigning the exam, at a cost of $6.5 million, USCIS received assistance from and worked with test development contractors, U.S. history and government scholars, and English as a Second Language experts (Preston, 2007; USCIS, 2006b). USCIS also sought input from a variety of stakeholders, including immigrant advocacy groups, citizenship instructors, and District Adjudications Officers.

According to USCIS, the intention of the new test is to move away from trivia type questions to ones that are more concept-oriented, where applicants must consider concepts such as democracy and the rights and responsibilities of citizens. The new test appears more consistent with the central purpose of National Council for the Social Studies (NCSS), "to help young people develop the ability to make informed and reasoned decisions" (NCSS, 1994, p. 3). Even highly educated applicants may need to prepare more for the concept-oriented questions on the new test. For example, on the old test, applicants were asked, "Who was President during the Civil War?" The question on the new test, however, is, "What was one important thing that Abraham Lincoln did?" Despite these types of changes, there are several questions on the new test, such as, "Who was President during World War I?," that seem to fall short of the concept-oriented goal.

Additionally, some language changes are more inclusive and culturally sensitive, which fits with the NCSS central purpose to prepare citizens for "a culturally diverse, democratic society in an interdependent world" (NCSS, 1994, p. 3). Not only have "colonists" replaced "Pilgrims," but they are also given less attention. Furthermore, there are more questions about slavery and the Civil Rights Movement (Preston, 2007). Yet, according to the British Broadcasting Corporation (BBC), some immigrant rights groups have called the new test an "anti-immigrant measure" and reject the test (BBC, 2006). The Illinois Coalition for Immigrant and Refugee Rights (ICIRR) released a statement calling the test "the final brick in the second wall" (ICIRR, 2007). The group said that the test included "more abstract and irrelevant questions that tended to stump hard-working immigrants who had little time to study" (Preston, 2007). Fred Tsao, policy director for the Coalition, described several new questions—such as, "What is the rule of law?"—as too abstract, arguing that political scientists and philosophers struggle with questions about the rule of law (Brulliard, 2007). As a representative to USCIS, Aguilar stresses that the new test is not meant to be a punitive measure nor is it meant to fail anyone (Preston, 2007). On the other hand, the test is not meant to be easy. Gary Gerstle, a professor of American history at Vanderbilt University, attests that—with studying—most applicants will pass, stating, "Indeed, their knowledge of American history may even exceed the knowledge of millions of American-born citizens" (Preston, 2007). Clearly, the new test is controversial and further investigation by researchers and educators would be timely and relevant.

Building preservice teachers' awareness of the inequities and inherently delicate health of any democracy is important because they will soon be in the position of being able to teach in ways that promote democratic thinking. Social studies instruction is being eliminated in many elementary classrooms so that students can spend more time studying mathematics and language arts. By examining the questions on the naturalization test in social studies methods classes, teacher educators can introduce new ways of thinking about citizenship knowledge to their preservice teachers and, in so doing, affirm the validity and importance of teaching social studies and citizenship education. Westheimer and Kahne (2004) suggest that citizenship education should develop "commitments for civic participation and social justice as well as foster ... the capacities to fulfill those commitments [that] will support the development of a more democratic society" (p. 245). Merely memorizing or identifying facts from history and governmental structure neither foster nor guarantee commitments for civic participation and social justice.

This study created a space for the participants and researchers to discuss what it means to live in a democracy and to examine the conceptions of a *good* citizen. These conversations move beyond simple answers on a test to a broader discussion of both democracy and assessment. How can beliefs be evaluated? Does holding particular beliefs and values necessarily lead to an individual having behaviors that would support a vibrant democracy? What would a vibrant democracy look like? How would a classroom that promoted democratic practices operate? Is it possible to have a democratic classroom when schools are inherently undemocratic? By having participants take the citizenship examination, and by having four researchers examine their own personal experiences with the citizenship process, both groups delved deeply into the core issue of what it means to be an "American." These are exciting conversations that get to the heart of social studies instruction—and young teachers need to have them.

NOTES

1. As defined by U.S. Department of Homeland Security: Citizenship and Immigration Services
2. Although seven researchers are situated in the larger study, their immigration experiences are not salient to this section because they cannot offer first-hand narratives or experiences regarding immigration. In other words, the other three of the seven researchers do not have personal or direct experiences with immigration.

REFERENCES

Allen, R. F. (1996). Introduction: What should we teach in social studies? And why? In B. G. Massialas & R. F. Allen (Eds.), *Crucial issues in teaching social studies K–12*. Belmont, CA: Wadsworth.

Astiz, M. F., & Mendez, G. (2006). Education for citizenship: The Argentine case in comparison. *Education, Citizenship and Social Justice, 1*(2), 175–200.

Banks, J. A. (1997). *Educating citizens in a multicultural society*. New York: Teachers College Press.

Barr, R. D., Barth, J. L., & Shermis, S. S. (1977). *Defining the social studies*. Washington, DC: National Council for the Social Studies.

British Broadcasting Corporation (2006, December 4). U.S. unveils new citizenship test. *BBC*. Retrieved October 22, 2007, from http://www.bbccaribbean.com

Bohan, C. H. (2001). The meaning of citizenship in the 21st century. *Theory and Research in Social Education, 29*(3), 517–523.

Bohan, C. H., & Davis, O. L., Jr. (1998). Historical constructions: How social studies student teachers' historical thinking is reflected in their writing of history. *Theory and Research in Social Education, 26*(2), 173–197.

Brulliard, K. (2007, September 28). New citizenship test to begin next fall. *Washington Post*. Retrieved October 22 2007, from http://www.washingtonpost.com

Camicia, S. P. (2007). Deliberating immigration policy: Locating instructional materials within global and multicultural perspectives. *Theory and Research in Social Education, 35*(1), 96–111.

Center for Information and Research on Civic Learning and Engagement. (2003). *The civic mission of schools*. New York: Carnegie Corporation of New York.

Chebium, R. (2000, July 18). Disabled woman's family says INS denial of citizenship is discriminatory. *Cnn.com*. Retrieved October 8, 2007, from http://archives.cnn.com/2000/LAW/07/18/citizenship.ins.suit/index.html

Clark, P., & Case, R. (1997). Four purposes of citizenship education. In R. Case & P. Clark (Ed.), *The Canadian anthology of social studies: Issues and strategies for teachers* (pp. 17–27). Burnaby, BC: Simon Fraser University Field Relations.

Counts, G. S. (1932). *Dare the school build a new social order?* New York: John Day.

Doppen, F. H. (2007a). Now what? Rethinking civic education in the Netherlands. *Education, Citizenship, and Social Justice, 2*(2), 103–118.

Doppen, F. H. (2007b, September 13). *Written interview questionnaire responses to Chara Bohan*. Transcript deposited at the Social Studies Education Center, MSIT Department, Georgia State University.

Friedman, T. L. (2007, May 23). Laughing and crying. *New York Times*. Retrieved May 23, 2007, from www.nytimes.com.

Gilmore, A. C., McKinney, C. W., Larkins, A. G., Ford, M. J., & McKinney, K. C. (1988). *Preservice elementary education majors knowledge of American government* (Report No. SO 019 805). Atlanta, GA: Mercer University. (ERIC Document Reproductive Service No. ED 305315)

Hahn, C. (2001). *Civic knowledge, attitudes, and experiences of ninth graders in the United States: Results of the IEA Civic Education Study*. Washington, DC: U.S. Department of Education. (ED 458161)

Illinois Coalition for Immigrant and Refugee Rights. (2007). *New citizenship test: Final brick in the second wall.* Chicago: Author. Retrieved October 31, 2007, from http://www.icirr.org

Larkins, A. G. (1984). *Preservice teachers' knowledge of social studies content in the primary grades.* Paper presented at the 64th annual meeting of National Council for the Social Studies, Washington, DC.

Lopez, M. H., Levine, P., Both, D., Kirby, E., & Marcelo, K. (2006). *The 2006 civic and political health of the nation: A detailed look at how youth participate in politics and communities.* College Park, MD: Center for Information and Research on Civic Learning and Engagement.

Miller, J. J. (2007). Can political participation be taught? The civics of student engagement. *Education Week, 26*(24), 36.

Myers, J. P. (2006). Rethinking the social studies curriculum in the context of globalization: Education for global citizenship in the U.S. *Theory and Research in Social Education, 34*(3), 370–394.

Nash, M. A. (2005). How to be thankful for being free: Searching for a convergence of discourses on teaching patriotism, citizenship, and United States history. *Teachers College Record, 107*(1), 214–240.

National Council for the Social Studies. (1994). *Expectations of excellence: Curriculum standards for social studies.* Washington, DC: Author.

Ogawa, M. (2007, September 21). *Written interview questionnaire responses to Chara Bohan.* Transcript deposited at the Social Studies Education Center, MSIT Department, Georgia State University.

O'Mahony, C. (2007, September 17). *Written interview questionnaire responses to Chara Bohan.* Transcript deposited at the Social Studies Education Center, MSIT Department, Georgia State University.

Preston, J. (2007, September 28). New test asks: What does "American" mean? *New York Times.* Retrieved October 7, 2007, from www.nytimes.com

Sadker, M. P., & Sadker, D. M. (2003). *Teachers, schools, and society* (6th ed.). New York: McGraw-Hill.

Thornton, S. J. (2001). *Subject matter in social studies teacher education.* Paper presented at the meeting of the National Council for the Social Studies, Washington, DC.

Thornton, S. J. (2003, Month). *What counts as subject matter knowledge for teaching?* Paper presented at the meeting of the American Educational Research Association, Chicago.

Torney-Purta J., Lehmann, R., Oswald, H., & Schultz, W. (2001). *Citizenship and education in twenty-eight countries: Civic knowledge and engagement at age fourteen.* Amsterdam: IEA.

Torres, C. A. (1998). *Democracy, education, and multiculturalism: Dilemmas of citizenship in a global world.* Lanham, MD: Rowman & Littlefield.

U.S. Citizenship and Immigration Services. (2006a). *Fact sheet: USCIS naturalization test redesign.* Washington, DC: Author. Retrieved February 21, 2007, from http://www.uscis.gov/portal/site/uscis

U.S. Citizenship and Immigration Services. (2006b). *Press release: USCIS issues, questions and answers for the new pilot naturalization exam.* Washington, DC:

Author. Retrieved February 21, 2007, from http://www.uscis.gov/portal/site/uscis

U.S. Citizenship and Immigration Services. (2007). *Civics and citizenship study materials*. Washington, DC: Author. Retrieved February 21, 2007, from http://www.uscis.gov/portal/site/uscis

U.S. Department of State. (2007). *Dual nationality*. Washington, DC: Author. Retrieved October 5, 2007, from http://travel.state.gov/travel/cis_pa_tw/cis/cis/_1753.html

Westheimer, J., & Kahne, J. (2004). What kind of citizen? The politics of educating for democracy. *American Educational Research Journal, 41*(2), 237–269.

CHAPTER 10

SERVICE-LEARNING

What Motivates K–12 Teachers to Initiate Service-Learning Projects?

Marjori M. Krebs

This phenomenological study describes the essence of the service-learning experience for the K-12 teacher, specifically exploring teacher motivations for initiating service-learning in the classroom. The researcher interviewed seven K–12 teachers who had implemented service-learning in their classrooms. Three major themes emerged to describe the essence of implementing service-learning from the K–12 teacher's perspective: (a) connections, (b) resonance in the heart of the teacher, and (c) the right fit with a teacher's philosophy and teaching style.

When I incorporate service-learning in my teaching, I know that I am changing the lives of children and I make a difference in their lives and it empowers them. That empowerment and self-confidence, especially for the child who isn't strong academically, but has other gifts and talents, and seeing that they had not been in the service-learning project, they wouldn't have encountered that self-confidence ... I think, if you just taught your normal day and your normal subjects and did your normal thing, you wouldn't

Curriculum and Teaching Dialogue
Volume 10, Numbers 1 & 2, 2008, pp. 135–149
Copyright © 2008 by Information Age Publishing
135

be giving these kids the opportunity to really shine in ways that some of them can't typically shine. (Nancy, Fifth Grade Teacher)

WHY SERVICE-LEARNING?

In my 14 years of experience as a high school social studies teacher in a Midwest suburban district, I had the opportunity to work with hundreds of students—students who had grand plans for their lives, who worked hard, who were kind to their classmates and teachers, and who generally had positive outlooks on life. I also taught students who did not like themselves or others, who used alcohol and other drugs to ease their pain, and who lived their lives with neither hope nor resilience. I found one particular teaching method that seemed to engage all my students in more meaningful roles in their own education and helped them find a sense of passion and purpose in their lives: service-learning (Aquila & Dodd, 2003; Melchior & Bailis, 2002). This article examines the essence of the service-learning experience from the K–12 teacher's perspective, reporting the results of a phenomenological study of the motivations of seven K–12 teachers to implement service-learning in their classrooms. In the current climate of high-stakes testing and accountability, teachers are becoming more wary of such hands-on, student-centered pedagogy. As noted in the stories from the teachers that follow, this is unfortunate.

Service-learning is an educational methodology that incorporates student preparation, service to the community, and reflection, with links to the academic curriculum (National Commission on Service-Learning, 2002). In addition, service-learning pedagogy also contains four critical phases when implemented in the classroom: preparation, action, reflection, and demonstration/celebration (Kaye, 2004).

By involving my students in service-learning activities, I was able to catch a glimpse of the positive effects these activities had on the lives of my students. This method had a positive impact on their personal development as well as their academic achievement. Especially evident was the newfound motivation and interest in learning among my at-risk, disengaged students.

Shad was a bright student achieving much below his potential in my class. He visited a nursing home each week, where he typically played euchre with three men over the age of 75 and talked with them. One morning, I saw Shad in the hallway. As we passed, he said, "Hey, Mrs. Krebs! I was about to cut school today, but then I remembered, 'Hey, it's service-learning day.' I just knew I had to be here." It was on that day that

I began to truly pay attention to the power of service-learning to change the behaviors and, therefore, change the lives of students.

HOW DO STUDENTS BENEFIT FROM SERVICE-LEARNING?

Researchers report that students derive personal, interpersonal, social, and academic benefits from participation in service-learning (Aquila & Dodd, 2003; Scales, Blyth, Berkas, & Kielsmeier, 2000). In the area of personal development, students report increases in self-confidence, self-esteem, leadership skills, personal decision-making skills (Aquila & Dodd, 2003), career benefits, and spiritual growth (Eyler & Giles, 1999). Socially, students who participate in service-learning report a positive impact on their own social responsibility, civic attitudes, and volunteerism (Scales et al., 2000). Students see themselves as valuable resources in their communities (Eyler & Giles, 1999).

Students who participate in service-learning also report greater academic success (Eyler & Giles, 1999) and experience a positive impact on their feelings toward school and their grades (Scales et al., 2000). In other studies, student writing achievement showed significant improvement (Strange, 2004; Wurr, 2002), especially in their expression and understanding of complex issues. Students at-risk especially benefit from participation in service both through improved academic work and increased leadership skills and experiences (Boyd, 2001; Greenberg et al., 2003).

INCENTIVES FOR TEACHERS

When teachers speak about their experiences in implementing service-learning, they use such terms as "motivational, rejuvenating, purposeful, gratifying, heartwarming, relevant, exciting, and necessary." There are many rich, textural stories to support these terms. What motivates teachers to implement service-learning? What is the essence of the service-learning experience for K–12 teachers? How does service-learning help teachers reach unmotivated and disengaged students? Why do teachers continue to implement service-learning even when they are crunched for time, pressured by testing, and inundated with paperwork?

Much research has been conducted on the motivations and experiences of *faculty* implementing service-learning in higher education (McKay & Rozee, 2004), but there is a gap in the research on motivations for K–12 teachers. In 1998, Giles and Eyler wrote that the key question for the service-learning agenda regarding faculty should be, "What factors explain faculty involvement in service-learning and how they are affected by participation?" (p. 65).

Researchers have revealed that a few of the reasons faculty implement service-learning are that they observe increases in the levels of student learning, especially in the areas of analytical and problem-solving skills (Hammond, 1994), and they personally value experiential learning (McKay & Rozee, 2004). In addition, faculty express the importance of students taking responsibility for their own learning, applying learned concepts in the community, increasing student exposure to social issues, and improving critical thinking and communication skills (McKay & Rozee, 2004). They also see the positive effects service-learning has on achievement and motivation of at-risk students (Boyd, 2001; Greenburg et al., 2003).

If teachers are motivated to incorporate service-learning into their classes, more students will reap these many benefits of participation and will develop a greater sense of passion and purpose in their lives. More students labeled as at-risk will understand the purpose of learning content because that content is connected to problems they see in their own communities every day. With service-learning, students see themselves as part of the solution to these problems. For students to experience these positive benefits in the classroom, the leader of the classroom—the teacher—must choose to incorporate service-learning as a teaching method. Thus, the key to broader infusion of service-learning into the curriculum is in the hands of the teachers.

METHOD

Participants

The participants in this phenomenological study included six teachers in K–12 public schools in Ohio, and me, a former high school teacher. These teachers had between 6 and 30 years teaching experience in urban, rural, and suburban schools, with varying degrees of experience in implementing service-learning in their classrooms, from 1 year to approximately 17 years.

Design

In phenomenology, a researcher conducts studies with several individuals to explore a particular concept or phenomenon and seeks to discover the *essence* of that experience for those individuals (Creswell, 1998;

Moustakas, 1994; van Manen, 1999). For this study, the initiation and implementation of service-learning by K–12 teachers is the phenomenon. To begin, the researcher focuses on the phenomenon of interest—service-learning—and describes it just as it seems. Through continued study of the phenomenon, its varied dimensions are discovered and added to the original descriptions. According to Moustakas (1994):

> We look and describe, we look again and describe, until there is a sense of having fulfilled our intention, of having arrived at a breaking off point, of having a sense of completion or closure, of really knowing what is there before us. (pp. 73–74)

By recording the experiences of others, in essence, *borrowing* them, researchers gain experience and knowledge (van Manen, 1999). In this study, I sought the essence and meaning of the service-learning experience from the K–12 teacher's perspective, focusing on the motivations to initiate service-learning, thus making phenomenology the logical research method to employ.

Procedure

I collected and analyzed data in four phases. *Phase One*, the *Pre-Interview*, included having a colleague interview me in order to achieve epoché. In phenomenology, epoché requires the researcher to set aside beliefs, judgments, and perceptions to focus fully on the experience (Moustakas, 1994). Epoché allows the researcher to look at the experience from a fresh, naïve, open perspective. By expressing my own ideas and experiences first, I was able to then focus on the ideas and experiences of the participants without allowing my own perceptions to cloud my view of their true experiences.

Phase Two, the *Interview*, involved conducting one long, open interview with each participant, which lasted from 1.5–2.5 hours. I audiotaped each interview and recorded personal field notes. In *Phase Three*, the *Post-Interview*, each participant completed and returned the Post-Interview Reflection Form, a simple questionnaire which I mailed to each participant three days following each interview, to capture other ideas or thoughts that emerged following the interview. In *Phase Four, Transcription and Analysis*, I transcribed all interview audiotapes, and coded those transcriptions along with the Post-Interview Reflection Forms using Moustakas' (1994) modifications of the Stevick-Colaizzi-Keen Method of Analysis of Phenomenological Data. This analysis procedure involves considering each individual statement with respect to significance for the description of the experience; listing each nonrepetitive, nonoverlapping statement; clustering these statements into meaningful themes; and synthesizing those themes into a description of the experience as a complete, woven texture—or essence.

RESULTS

The Phenomenon: K–12 Teachers Initiating and Implementing Service-Learning

Three major themes emerged from these interviews that describe the experience of implementing service-learning from a K–12 teacher's perspective: (a) connections, (b) resonance in the heart of the teacher, and (c) the right fit with teaching philosophy and style. These themes all play important roles in motivating teachers to both initiate and implement service-learning in their classrooms.

Theme One: Connections

The most obvious theme that emerged during the coding process was the importance of connections teachers made when planning and implementing service-learning projects. Teachers repeatedly mentioned connections with other teachers, administrators, students, and parents. They explained the importance of connections made with the curriculum, which includes purposeful links between service and academic learning. Finally, teachers reported the important connections made with members of the community, from local to global, through various service agencies and organizations.

The student connection. Teachers explained that the connection with students begins with the planning and preparation stages of service-learning projects. Finding connections between the students and the focus issue of the service-learning project and listening to students before, during, and following the project are important steps in this process. Teachers found it valuable to help students get to know their own individual strengths and weaknesses, as they worked toward completing their projects. Jill, a middle school Family and Consumer Sciences teacher, explains this interaction:

> The direct benefit is coming out of a service-learning project feeling like as a teenager, "I can serve a purpose that is meaningful and everybody's not looking at me like I'm a trouble-maker. I have really contributed." When the students get letters from people that they have met at an agency the

students say, "Oh, they said that about me?" They put those letters in their portfolios and can go back to that and say, "Whoa, I was really helpful!"

Teachers also found service-learning as a meaningful way to connect to their at-risk students. Andy, a middle school social studies teacher, described Jimmy, a student whose mother had characterized as shy. She wanted him to push himself further. Andy seized the opportunity during the planning of their South Africa community program and named Jimmy emcee for the event. Andy noted, "He was nervous at first, and we practiced ... but he just shined through ... Mom was there watching. It just set the tone for the whole year for him."

Students also connect to each other through service-learning. Nancy involves her students in a Grandpals Project, where fifth graders visit a local retirement center once a month, and complete a variety of activities with the residents. During the year, a few of the Grandpals passed away. According to Nancy, "The kids were very supportive of each other; it is emotional because they don't want that [the death of a Grandpal] to happen. The other kids are good about giving support." In Nancy's classroom, service-learning helped to build a true community of learning and caring.

The teacher connection. Connections were also evident among the teachers themselves. Every teacher related at least one story of another teacher who made that project more manageable and enjoyable. It was important for teachers to have their peer teachers assist in planning and working through details. Even overcoming difficulties provided opportunities for teachers to connect to one another. When Jill struggled to find transportation to take her students to their various service sites, she found a positive outcome: "The good thing about struggling with that [transportation] was we would get teachers to volunteer to help us drive and then they got to know what we were doing, so in a round-about way, that was a good thing."

Teachers also connected with each other through the curriculum. When teachers are in team-teaching situations, the benefits of service-learning can be shared more purposefully and directly with students in many different academic areas. Jill was a member of a content-area team in her middle school, for which she noted the following:

> I am meeting with those people [content-area teachers] on a daily basis; they understand what I'm doing and now they've bought into it like crazy, especially the English teachers, and it just became a part of what we do as a team.

Teachers also connect with other teachers through more formalized professional development opportunities. Often teachers develop ideas for projects from connections made with other teachers during these professional development programs. Nancy and Erin gained many of their ideas from attending conferences and talking with other teachers about new ideas. These professional development opportunities broaden teachers' awareness and spark new ideas to implement in their own classrooms.

The parent connection. Through service-learning, teachers also have unique opportunities for meaningful connections with parents, thus providing opportunities for greater communication—for parents to see and understand what is happening in the classroom and to see how the curriculum connects with community events.

Parents often serve as classroom aides during service-learning projects. During Kim's homeless shelter project, parents volunteered to transport food to the shelter and also helped prepare and serve the meals. For Jill's projects, parents provided after-school transportation for middle school students to and from their service sites.

Parent-teacher organizations provided funds for many service-learning projects. For Kim's homeless project, parents purchased pots and pans for food preparation. For Nancy's Grandpals Project, they purchased literature about older adults for the classroom. An integral part of Bonnie's third and fourth grade service-learning projects are the connections with parents and families. At the elementary level, Bonnie believes this connection is a necessity:

> I think with true service-learning, there has to be an investment by the child—by the child, by the teacher, and even by the families ... I think really the most dramatic moments [of service-learning experiences] would probably be shared at home with their families.

When teachers get students involved in real issues in the community, parents respond positively.

The administrator connection. Administrators, like parents, play key roles in making connections with teachers through service-learning. Administrators can provide personal mentoring and encouragement, a framework for professional development, and funding for projects. Through service-learning, administrators are given authentic opportunities to support and appreciate the efforts of their teachers and also provide unique opportunities for school administrators at all levels to connect in positive ways with teachers, students, parents, and the community.

Having district support was imperative for Jill and the success of her projects. As stated by Jill, "The funding support was there. There was already grant writing going on district-wide. There were suggestions for whom to contact, and people to call if we needed something. All I had to do was get on the phone and call."

Teachers reported that administrators also noticed changes in the behavior of at-risk students after their participation in service-learning. Nancy named two students in whom she and her principal saw "phenom- enal" changes when working with older adults. One of her students has had a difficult life, but at Norworth, "All that pizzazz is channeled in a positive way; all of that crankiness, all of that orneriness, all that changes." The principal has also noted changes in students' behaviors. "He goes and he sees the kids—he sees the kids who are the trouble- makers go over there and do good work."

The curricular connection. Another important connection teachers make through service-learning is a meaningful connection to the curriculum, providing opportunities to make academic content more meaningful. Jill described the curricular connections as one of the most important parts of the service-learning experience for her students:

> The whole service piece is really good, and it is even better that we can tie it to the curriculum and make the curriculum more meaningful to the kids and to the teachers—to help the teachers make it more tied to real life.

Nancy explains the importance of including various academic compo- nents in her Grandpals Project:

> The academic piece of the puzzle that goes with the service-learning is the learning that goes along with it. Is it great to volunteer? Yes. The learning through literature, the empathy, and some of the details that go with Alzhe- imer's, or heart disease, or dementia, and then learning what they [the stu- dents] could do. You've got the science part of aging of the body and emotional needs of a person and the isolation that they can feel when they are in a nursing home. So it is tying all those learning processes in.

Through service-learning, teachers can integrate many different subject areas and connect with a variety of other teachers in the building. Through various projects, teachers have incorporated reading, writing, music, art, technology, and other subject areas. According to Bonnie, these types of projects "make learning meaningful and relevant." The academic and personal benefits for students complement each other so that the students grow, mature, learn, and change personally, socially, and academically.

The community connection. School-community connections are rarely more evident than when students are participating in service-learning activities. Students see their own roles in making their community a better place. The retirement center found the service of Nancy's students so valuable that when the school district cut the funds to transport Nancy's students to the retirement center, the center itself donated money to be placed directly in a budget line-item designated for Nancy's student transportation needs.

The media were invited to Andy's cultural public assembly on South Africa, and the students received positive publicity. Andy believes school districts should take greater advantage of these public relations opportunities:

> If we can get kids out in the community and make [the general public] aware of what we are doing, I think it is going to be extremely powerful. I don't think we really get the message out there that we are doing that, you know.

The importance of connections when implementing service-learning cannot be understated. Every teacher interviewed expressed the importance of various connections as primary motivators for implementing service-learning. Teachers are motivated because of connections with other people, namely students who have difficulties connecting to school in general, connections within their curriculum, and in their communities. As I explained in my own interview, "It was because of these meaningful connections that I knew my students learned their content. More importantly, I believe they still remember."

Theme Two: Resonance in the Hearts of Teachers

The second major theme associated with motivating factors in implementing service-learning is the necessity that service-learning resonate in the hearts of teachers. This resonance comes from deep, personal beliefs about the importance of making a positive difference in the world and teaching this belief to students. An internal motivation exists for each teacher—one that stems from the heart. Almost every teacher mentioned the importance of teaching to the heart, and they literally touched their hearts as they expressed these feelings. As Kim put it, "You have got to do things for the goodness of mankind."

Resonance from past personal experiences. Each teacher spoke of a role model who introduced him or her personally to service and almost all participated in service at a young age. One remarkable commonality among the teachers interviewed was the importance of parents, and in particular, mothers, who modeled service for and included their children in service to others. Jill's mother was a member of a Wednesday Club where she and other mothers practiced good deeds around the community. Andy's mother helped him prepare and deliver Easter baskets to the local women's shelter; Nancy's father visited retirement centers advising residents on their legal issues.

At an impressionable age, these teachers personally experienced the deep, personal rewards of service including increased self-esteem, organizational skills, and the positive feelings of making a difference. Now, as teachers, they are more eager to provide these types of experiences for their students.

Resonance from professional development experiences. Through professional development experiences, teachers were able to hone those emotional beliefs into curricular connections for their students. Professional development experiences gave these teachers opportunities to see how service could meet not only their personal desires for service to the community, but also their professional goals of meeting their students' curricular needs.

Through professional development opportunities, teachers were afforded the gift of time—time to connect, to plan, to learn, and to think about potential service and learning connections for making the curriculum more relevant. Participation in these workshops gave these teachers opportunities to reflect on personal experiences and the implementation of service-learning to improve student learning, share roadblocks, and get suggestions from other teachers. Several teachers pursued or are pursuing their graduate degrees focused in service-learning.

Resonance in mentoring and motivating other teachers. Once teachers see the personal and professional benefits of service-learning both for themselves and for their students, they are motivated to share this method with other teachers. This sharing of successful service-learning experiences reinforces the importance of teachers connecting with other teachers. These teachers found service-learning to be so purposeful, helpful, and meaningful, it was as if they *had* to share it with other teachers—a service in and of itself—to other colleagues.

Since these teachers have experienced the benefits of service-learning for themselves and for their students, they are energized promoters of service-learning and consider it a privilege to spread the word about this teaching method to motivate more teachers to implement service-learning for their students, thereby helping other teachers and students find passion and purpose in serving their communities. When Erin was trying to mentor and motivate other teachers, she got support from her own mentor, a college professor for her master's degree program. Erin summarized the advice she received as follows: "It's okay...No one's doing it, but if you start, it will catch on.... If you're doing something good and you know it's good, just do it and if there's good results people will catch on and they'll start doing it."

Teachers who implement service-learning believe that caring and making a difference in the world can be purposefully taught, both to students in their classrooms and to their colleagues next door or across the country. They have experienced the benefits of service first-hand. They, in turn, mentor and motivate others to participate with their students, as well. It is such an important message for them, it is written on their hearts.

Theme Three: The Right Fit With Teaching Philosophy and Teaching Style

The third emergent theme explains the importance of creating a well-balanced, harmonious relationship between service-learning and a teacher's student-centered philosophy and experiential teaching style. The teaching philosophies of the teachers interviewed included the importance of educating children to be functioning members of society, helping students find purpose and meaning in their lives, and connecting to their students and their communities. These teachers see it as their responsibility to create links between learning and purpose, between students and society. Service-learning is more than just a teaching strategy. It touches the core of why these teachers want to be teachers. Kim explained, "Kids have to learn, we as human beings have to learn, to give and share with one another. And what better way to do it than with service-learning?"

Many teachers expressed a deep, personal internal motivation to implement service-learning. Jill concurs when describing her teaching philosophy:

> It has got to be purposeful; I want them to find something that ties into their gifts, their talents, what they are interested in, what they are passionate about, tie it into the real world ... find a way to improve the situation—tying it all together so it is meaningful in their lives.

There is a strong philosophical passion and purpose for service-learning for these teachers. It seems if service-learning were removed from their classrooms, then they would experience a deep void in their passion for teaching as a whole.

Not only does service-learning need to be compatible with a teacher's philosophy, it must also fit the teacher's style. These teachers believe in facilitating learning and providing hands-on, authentic learning opportunities. Flexibility and active learning are key qualities, as well. Erin explains that she is more of a "guide in the classroom, guiding them to discover the knowledge themselves; to let them discover the stuff on their own."

Andy's style is also that of a facilitator in the classroom, providing opportunities for student discovery, hands-on learning in the classroom, and incorporating authentic assessment during and after the project. He believes it is by using these methods that helps him reach the at-risk students in his classes.

The teachers' key words used to describe their service-learning experiences summarize their thoughts; speak to their deep, personal beliefs; explain how they act on these beliefs in their classrooms; and describe The Right Fit between service-learning and their own teaching philosophies and styles:

Jill:	"motivational, rejuvenating, purposeful, a habit of the heart."
Nancy:	"gratifying, heartwarming, self-satisfaction, all the stars are in the right place."
Andy:	"It benefits school, teachers, and community."
Bonnie:	"meaningful, enlightening, relevant, enriching, magical, incredible."
Kim:	"worthwhile, educational, motivational, emotional."
Erin:	"necessary, learning-by-doing."
Marjori:	"meaningful work, connection to the curriculum, motivational, fun."

Teachers who are motivated to implement service-learning believe their jobs are more than just teaching content to students. They are comfortable with hands-on, experiential approaches to teaching and believe they are teaching for the greater good—that they are producing the future leaders of the world who must know about important issues and develop the confidence and skills to solve them. It is a deep, philosophical drive that keeps these teachers going, even when there are no funds for a bus for the field trip.

DISCUSSION

Teachers in this study were motivated to initiate service-learning for both personal and professional reasons. Even though they teach in the pervasive national environment of high-stakes testing and data collection, through implementing service-learning, these teachers found unique connections with their students, with other teachers, with parents, administrators, the curriculum, and with the community. They found service-learning to be particularly important for re-connecting their at-risk students with their desire to value learning. Teachers met personal needs to serve the community and to teach that importance to their students, a need that resonates in their hearts. Finally, service-learning fits their teaching philosophies and teaching styles, being driven to motivate others to implement service-learning because of their own positive connections and personal feelings when implementing service-learning. It also meets an important personal need to make the world a better place—a need present for both students and teachers. Further research is needed using the presented methodologies with teachers in other settings, such as in urban and rural schools, to determine if these themes still ring true.

REFERENCES

Aquila, F. D., & Dodd, J. M. (2003). *Learn and serve Ohio: Annual evaluation report.* Cleveland, OH: Cleveland State University.

Boyd, B.L. (2001). Bringing leadership experiences to inner-city youth. *Journal of Extension*, *39*(4). Retrieved February 15, 2008, from http://www.joe.org/joe/2001augusta6.html

Creswell, J. W. (1998). *Qualitative inquiry and research design: Choosing among five traditions.* Thousand Oaks, CA: SAGE.

Eyler, J., & Giles, D. E. (1999). *Where's the learning in service-learning?* San Francisco: Jossey-Bass.

Giles, D. E., & Eyler, J. (1998). A service-learning research agenda for the next five years. In R. Rhoades & J. P. F. Howard, (Eds.), *Academic service-learning: A pedagogy of action and reflection* (pp. 65–72). San Francisco: Jossey-Bass.

Greenberg, M. T., Weissberg, P., O'Brien, M. U., Zins, J. E., Fredericks, L., Resnik, H., et al. (2003). Enhancing school-based prevention and youth development through coordinated social, emotional, and academic learning [Electronic version]. *American Psychologist, 58,* 466–474.

Hammond, C. (1994). Integrating service and academic study: Faculty motivation and satisfaction in Michigan higher education. *Michigan Journal of Community Service Learning, 1*(1), 21–28.

Kaye, C. B. (2004). *The complete guide to service-learning: Proven, practical ways to engage students in civic responsibility, academic curriculum, and social action.* Minneapolis, MN: Free Spirit.

McKay, V., & Rozee, P. D. (2004). Characteristics of faculty who adopt community service-learning pedagogy. *Michigan Journal of Community Service-Learning, 10*(2), 21–33.

Melchior, A., & Bailis, L. N. (2002). Impact of service-learning on civic attitudes and behaviors of middle and high school youth: Findings from three national evaluations. In A. Furco, & S. H. Billig (Eds.), *Service-learning: The essence of pedagogy* (pp. 201–222). Greenwich, CT: Information Age.

Moustakas, C. (1994). *Phenomenological research methods.* Thousand Oaks, CA: SAGE.

National Commission on Service-Learning. (2002). *Learning in deed: The power of service-learning for American schools.* Newton, MA: Author.

Scales, P. C., Blyth, D. A., Berkas, T. H., & Kielsmeier, J. C. (2000). The effects of service-learning on middle school students' social responsibility and academic success. *Journal of Early Adolescence, 20*(3), 332–358.

Strange, A. (2004). Long-term academic benefits of service-learning: When and where do they manifest themselves? *College Student Journal, 32*(2), 257–261.

van Manen, M. (1999). *Researching lived experience: Human science for an action sensitive pedagogy.* Albany: University of New York Press.

Wurr, A. J. (2002). Service-learning and student writing. An investigation of effects. In S. H. Billig & A. Furco (Eds.), *Service-learning through a multidisciplinary lens.* Greenwich, CT: Information Age.

PART II

CHAPTER 11

THE STORY BEHIND THE PRESENTATION

Forrest Gump and Uncloistered Scholarship

Carl Glickman

In this short, personal essay, Carl Glickman, a featured speaker at the American AATC (Association of Teaching and Curriculum Conference) 2007 annual conference, ruminates on how his career has focused on the purpose of education in a democratic society. After explaining how his interests developed and played out over his career, Glickman concludes that "democracy must be first seen as a practice of learning before it can become a practice of self government. In essence, we cannot close learning gaps until we close participation gaps. And it has to be simultaneously played out at every level of education, starting with ourselves."

This past summer, I was reading the book *Dewey's Dream; Universities and Democracies in an Age of Education Reform* (Benson, Harkavy & Puckett, 2007). At the same time, an old colleague Tony was visiting me at our family home in Vermont. While out fishing, we reminisced about our first years together at Ohio State University and then our coincidental arrival at the University of Georgia (UGA). After 15 years at Georgia, he left for a Big Ten School and I remained for another 10 years (with a brief but

Curriculum and Teaching Dialogue
Volume 10, Numbers 1 & 2, 2008, pp. 153–156
Copyright © 2008 by Information Age Publishing

valuable interlude at Texas State University). While fishing, Tony and I discussed in a joking manner the question of what our respective professional work had amounted to in this later stage in our careers. Days after the successful fishing expedition, I took the question as a focus point in developing a presentation titled *Toggling Between Democracy and Education* that I first gave at the 2007 AATC conference and then later at the John Dewey symposium at the American Educational Research Association on *Uncloistered Scholarship and Community—School Engagement* (Glickman, 2008). The following is my story.

Ever since I served in the Teacher Corps in 1968 during the integration of schools in the rural south, I have been drawn to the role of education in a democracy. Later as a school principal in New Hampshire, our school community worked on the concept of democracy as central to our curriculum and, still later, with my university appointment in 1979, I and colleagues created a network of K–12 public schools in Georgia with this same emphasis. The network grew to over 100 schools and lasted for more than 15 years. We became partners with other major networks including the Coalition of Essential Schools, The Accelerated Schools, The Basic Schools, and The Democratic School Network.

We found a cadre of university faculty across the nation willing to collaborate with public schools on how to assist schools to democratize themselves using the lens of action research, governance and what we have referred to as the *pedagogy of democracy*: connecting the education of students to their larger communities. Over this period, I became un-cloistered in terms of the disciplines I accessed. I held successive appointments in five academic departments at UGA as I kept finding my interest being informed by faculty outside my college in fields such as political science, constitutional law, religion, anthropology, art, music, literature, economics, and history. For 1 year, I took a research leave to become a student at other universities throughout the country where I could visit and sit in on classes in fields far from my own.

I never thought about working outside of my field as abandoning it but rather as building upon it. But, it has led to some befuddlement. I was simply following my intellectual heart by tapping into the ideas and imag-inations of others. However readers of my earlier books on school disci-pline, supervision of instruction, and site based school leadership would become puzzled when they would approach me to speak on one of those earlier topics, and I would politely tell them that I do not do that anymore and instead, I would prefer addressing the issue of education and public purpose.

In still following the same intriguing concept of education and democ-racy since my first year of teaching, the journey has taken me into then unimaginable settings. For example, I am a counsel to the legal team litigating against the state of Georgia for inadequate funding. I have served on the steering committee member of Kids Voting USA, and the National Commission on Service Learning (chaired by John Glenn). I am now on the steering committee of The National Campaign for the Civic Mission of Schools (cochaired by Sandra Day O'Connor), and I am one of the founding conveners of a policy group called The Forum for Democracy and Education which has direct access to presidential candidates for the purpose of influencing federal education policy.

I think of myself more as the Forrest Gump of uncloistered scholarship; I am not particularly smart and I wind up in many improbable situations. I do policy but I am not a policy person, I do history but I am not a historian, I write journalistic essays but I am not a journalist, I do litigation law but I am not a lawyer, I am involved in grass roots community activism but I am not a community activist. In some ways, being uncloistered becomes both challenging and uncomfortable as I know enough about a topic to converse with experts but not enough about their field to be "of the field" and at times, my ignorance shines through in the most basic confusions about names, organizations, and professional language. And, I write more often now to a general audience of educators and citizens via newspapers and Web sites and work with noneducators in local communities as much as I work with educators.

I have been uncloistered throughout my career, always needing to find support from those both within and without; trying to be consistent in my own practice as to what I mean by a democratic education in addressing issues of equality, voice, equity, boundary crossing and identity diffusion, and respectful, thoughtful, and participatory citizenship. How do I provide an education that enables students to be free, to be self governing, and to use their education in ways that make democracy renew in ways better than those of my own generation?

As I move into a more personal realm, let me be very clear that I am neither putting anyone down nor putting anyone up as a model of practice. Dewey did not want disciples but rather, colleagues who would challenge him, and so it is in this spirit that I make these following remarks. John Dewey often did not act in accord with his own writings as Benson, Harkavy, and Puckett (2007) point out. As the director of lab schools in Chicago and at Teacher's College, Dewey's curriculum did not involve students in real work beyond the classroom. Older colleagues of mine who had Dewey as their teacher at Columbia have told me that he was a poor and quite boring instructor. His classes consisted of lecture and note taking and Dewey was nearly oblivious to his students.

So to me, one of the questions of individual responsibility is how does one try to practice what one espouses? Let me be mundane with an example. In all my courses whether for beginning undergraduate students or

PhD seminar students, I stop after the first four or five classes and ask for answers to the following questions

1.   How is this class helping you to learn what you need to learn?
2.   How is this class getting in the way of your learning?
3.   And, what can you recommend to me as the instructor that I should do to make this course better for you and your classmates?

Students answer the questions on their own, meet with each other and discuss, and then submit to me a write up of their responses as a group. I always read the synthesized list back to them before this class ends that night and tell them that I will be back to them by the next class with my responses and my actions. There is nothing earthshaking about asking for feedback and course correction, but most of the students are amazed. Inevitably it comes out that most of them have never been asked how to alter the teaching and learning of a course in order to make it better for them as students.

Of course there are faculty members who do this in ways far beyond what I do, but this experience reminds me, over and over again, that no matter how progressive or intellectual we are in our thoughts and espousals, we can never be better individually or collectively until we learn to listen to those who live lives different from our own. Students should not be forced into a single category of *learner* while instructors hold for themselves the category of the *learned*. We must see people beyond the categories of identity that those in authority put upon them, and to be willing to reason together even when such reasoning pushes all of us into what I call *issues of unease*.

Democracy must be first seen as a practice of learning before it can become a practice of self government. In essence, we cannot close learning gaps until we close participation gaps. And it has to be simultaneously played out at every level of education, starting with ourselves.

REFERENCE

Glickman, C. D. (2008, March). *The John Dewey annual symposium: Uncloistered scholars and community-school engagement.* Presentation at the annual meeting of The American Education Research Association. New York

Benson, L, Harkavy, I., & Puckett, J. (2007). *Dewey's dream: Universities and democracies in an age of education reform.* Philadelphia: Temple University Press.

CHAPTER 12

PERSPECTIVES ON THE PEDAGOGY OF DEMOCRACY

William H. Schubert

Bill Schubert is one of several AATC (Association of Teaching and Curriculum Conference) members asked to participate in a discussion responding to Carl Glickman's conference presentation. Glickman's talk leads him to conclude, in terms of democratic pedagogy that "the most revolutionary thing we can do … is encourage learners, educators, and the general (including oppressed) public to ask and act on basic curriculum questions: What's worthwhile? How can we survive and, beyond survival, how can we live together in a state of personal and public growth on this threatened planet? We must teach directly in such a way that each can become her or his own curriculum director."

It is a challenging pleasure to respond to Carl Glickman's 2007 AATC keynote address, *The Pedagogy of Democracy: Toggling between Education and Community.* I have known Carl since he interviewed me for a University of Georgia professorship which I was offered in 1988. A few years later we spoke together at a John Dewey lecture (symposium) at the Association for Supervision and Curriculum Development. I have been impressed, over the years, with Carl's writings and overall work in educational reform. He is an exemplar of *toggling* among academe, policy, and general public sectors (Glickman, 2003). Such work requires that one be a

Curriculum and Teaching Dialogue
Volume 10, Numbers 1 & 2, 2008, pp. 157–164
157

public intellectual. Carl's editorship of *Letters to the Next President* (2004, 2007) is a principal illustration of such efforts. I commend this. Surely, the discussion it engenders builds community around educational issues.

I recall giving an earlier AATC keynote address in Tulsa in 2002, in which my central message was to keep curriculum questions alive, not just among scholars in the curriculum field or among curriculum leaders in schools, but in the population at large (Schubert, 2003). Furthermore, I was intrigued that early in Carl's address, he referred to a 1974 paper he did on the topic of open education, a term given to progressive practices in the 1960s and 1970s. This sparked my memory of having written about the historical roots of open education in a paper in graduate school that I revised, after receiving my PhD in 1975, and submitted to the American Educational Research Association journal, *Review of Educational Research*. I recall checking with the editor in 1978 and learning that one review of the manuscript was yet to arrive. Apparently, it has not arrived yet, since I still have not heard. If it does arrive, I suspect that it would substantially affect the averages that one finds appended to each published article about dates manuscripts were received, revisions received, and acceptances! However, it would likely be rejected for not having any citations since 1974! There are glitches in even the best of publications. In any case, my thoughts of open education, prompted by Carl, reminded me of an ear-lier era of concern for the topic of his address, as it did for him, quite obviously. I had hoped that he might have said a bit more about the con-nections among re-invigoration of concern for pedagogy and education, education and community in different eras—especially in response to today's reactionary domination of education as represented in Marshall, Sears, Allen, Roberts, and Schubert (2007). As I know, however, from my own after-dinner keynote 5 years ago, one must make decisions to say less and maximize impact for a late evening audience.

Derived from the open education era, and from progressive education in the 1920s–1940s, I see clearly a consistency of emphasis on what Virgil Herrick (Herrick, Goodlad, Estvan, & Everman, 1956) called the *organiz-ing center* of the curriculum. In Carl's address, the progressive heritage is renewed with its emphasis on learner concerns, interests, and crafting a life as an organizing center. Creating a life, perhaps the most neglected and most important, is the heart of education (Willis & Schubert, 1991/2000). It deals directly with what Mary Catherine Bateson (1990) called "composing a life," a process that many today refer to as shaping identity. It is my contention that this is what, deep down, the public wants. It has been called *human interests* by Jurgen Habermas (1971).

My own work with schools and their publics in Chicago illustrates this point. In the late 1980s and early 1990s, when the Illinois State Legisla-ture created Local School Councils (LSCs) for each of the Chicago public schools (approximately 500 elementary schools and 50 secondary schools), to be elected publicly, I was involved in the *training* efforts for these mini school boards. Much that constituted this training consisted of telling newly elected LSC members about how schools work—legally, administratively, and financially. Interest in participation was evident in that some 10,000 ran for these offices, which is inconsistent with Robert Putnam's (2007) highly touted findings that diverse communities withdraw from collective life. Moreover, I was asked to develop training materials and strategies for developing school vision, a topic considered by the inviters to be curriculum-related. This whole training affair made me wonder why training was deemed necessary for LSC members, whereas, other elected officials (mayors, governors, senators, representatives, presidents, vice presidents, secretaries of departments of the executive branch) are not subjected to any official training. It made me worry that the judgment of LSC members, often from diverse lower socioeconomic classes and oppressed racial and ethnic groups, was not to be trusted. In contrast, I wondered, too, if all elected officials needed to be trained—better, to be *educated*. In any case, our university (University of Illinois at Chicago) was somehow selected to collaborate with many different citizens' groups to forge the training.

When I was asked to present on and develop curriculum materials for *vision*, I interpreted it as the essence of curriculum, and I did not pull punches. As Carl Glickman said in conversation with Suzanne Wilson earlier during this AATC conference, it is important to express educational ideas in the most accessible ways, and as I recall, I tried to do this in my work with LSCs. I knew that one of the strategies my graduate students in curriculum said they benefited from the most was my theatrical role-playing of different (often opposing) viewpoints or philosophies about curriculum, that is, about what is worthwhile to learn, know, need, do, be, become, overcome, share, and contribute. I decided to do this for LSCs, and my graduate assistant and experienced community organizer, Margy McClain, translated this into the written materials. Finding others with appropriate experience to democratically present them was another problem, however.

The main point of relevance of this experience to Carl's presentation is that LSC members resonated positively. They told me that the reason they ran for these offices was to consider alternative ways that their children might learn and grow more fully. They were particularly intrigued by my portrayal of Experiential and Critical Reconstructionist positions (see Schubert, 1996, 1997) I role-played, that is, positions built from scholars such as W. E. B. DuBois, Jose Marti, John Dewey, Jane Addams, Carter G. Woodson, George S. Counts, Harold Rugg, Caroline Pratt, Paulo Freire, James B. Macdonald, Dwayne Huebner, Maxine Greene, Michael Apple,

Henry Giroux, William Pinar, Madeleine Grumet, Janet Miller, Jean Anyon, Linda McNeil, William Ayers, Donaldo Macedo, Peter McLaren, William Watkins, Patti Lather, and more. Ideas of such scholars spoke to LSC members' lived plight, oppression, and desire to become. I recall that one LSC member who appeared to be homeless, announced that his appearance must have bothered me, and told the group that it had been caused by a stroke. He went on to say how glad he was to have more alternatives to draw from about teaching and curriculum. He then asked a powerful question that should take us all aback: Why, then, are such alternatives not known or understood by the CEOs of schools, the mayor, the state superintendent of schools, the legislatures and business leaders, and other key policymakers at the local, state, and federal levels. He pointedly asked why I had not told them!! This is the key question of the day.

The work of Carl Glickman constitutes a valiant effort toward generating the level of community and democratic discourse needed for this level of educational deliberation. I commend such efforts, but I am exceedingly worried. As one who has devoted nearly a decade as an elementary school teacher and another 3 decades as a professor, researcher, and consultant, it is difficult for me to express my uneasiness about the future of schools as inspirers of democracy and community. As Barbara Slater Stern, astutely pointed out during the discussion of Carl's keynote address, constitutionally the United States is a republic, not a democracy. I remembered this distinction emphasized by my mother, who taught my high school government class! Today, I am concerned that we are not a republic either. Too many of our *representatives* represent their puppeteers, the barons of business. This makes me worry about how close we are to an oligarchy. Moreover, when I look at school practice, especially in oppressed urban areas, I see preparation for autocracy as the modus operandi.

I know there are schools that serve oppressed populations in democratic ways. I think of Paulo Freire's (1970) work with Brazilian peasants, helping them to become literate by naming their own world. I think of democratic schools portrayed in *Democratic Schools* (Apple & Beane, 2007) and in the democratic work of George Wood (2005). I reflect on schools in Chicago, such as Perspectives Charter School, schools worked with by critical math educator, Rico Gutstein (2006), Telpochcalli Community School of the Arts, the Little Village High School, and an inspiring account of fifth graders in a school in the Cabrini Green housing projects who marshaled political, business, and media attention to an integrated curriculum built around renewing their decrepit school building (Schultz, 2008). I know, too, there are numerous other examples in the school networks that Carl has worked with over the years. These examples are beacons of what might be. Still they are few and far between.

Is hope or depression a more sensible response to this state of affairs? I wonder to what extent attempts to work with high level commissions, blue ribbon committees, and others in powerful positions (as Carl valiantly attempts to do), is an attempt to convert those who are solidly committed to greed, a neocolonialism, and empire building on a global scale. Can such power wielders be converted to practices that see in Deweyan light that democracy is education and education is democracy, that experience is education and education is experience (see Dewey, 1916, 1938)?[1] As I am motivated by this hope, I am simultaneously disgruntled by practices that have overpowered the progressive tradition time and again. To wit, the relative long history of opposition to the public interest, as conveyed in *Gag Rule* by John Lapham (2004), who vividly portrays the stifling of dissent and democracy that dominates our history, especially legal and political support of the nouveau riche oligarchy that arose in the 1890s, and has continued since:

> The emergence of the United states as a world power between the years 1890 and 1920 followed from the domestic political crisis threatening to remove control of the country's wealth and well-being from the custody of its newly ascendant ruling class—the passions of war meant to overrule the motion for economic justice, the band music intended to silence the solo voices of dissent. (pp. 59–60)

In fact, John Nichols (2004) of *The Nation* magazine has published a brilliant anthology of Americans (from founding fathers to present dissidents) who have written in opposition to empire, which he calls *the beast*. Alex Molnar (2005) depicts well how the Wilson administration, in *need* of the economic benefits of war that benefited its barons of wealth, acquired public relations expert Edward Bernays to sway public opinion to support U.S. entry into World War I. For many years, liberals perpetuated the necessity of propaganda (see Bernays, 1928) for their version of *democracy* to alter the public mind. This is even advocated in the widely respected work of Walter Lippmann (see Lippmann, 1963) and soundly criticized by Noam Chomsky (1997), who captured the sordid character of policy making by restating their own term for the public, *the bewildered herd* (p. 22). Bernays became founder of the public relations industry (Chomsky, 2001, pp. 151–52). The augmentation of economic injustice, under the mask of democracy and freedom, is made indelible by Cass Sunstein's (2004) reintroduction of FDR's call for a second Bill of Rights, one that emphasizes economic rights, claiming that the original Bill of Rights provides for political rights, not economic ones. In fact, it was Dewey in a little known *New York Times* piece in 1933, who declared that the propensity of acquisition, which he called the acquisitive society, is the fundamental reason that his progressive pedagogy cannot be actualized. The question before us then, which Carl's presentation evokes, is: Can we have even a semblance of democratic community in a world of imperialistic acquisition?[2]

So, should we continue to direct our efforts toward schools? Or, are they owned by the architects of empire? Should we look again at Ivan Illich's (1970) *deschooling* or John Holt's (1981) *unschooling*? After all, John Bremer (1979) with his sage sarcasm observed that law schools teach law and medical schools teach medicine, but public schools do not teach what it means to be public! I shudder as I ask why we hope that public schools (sponsored by states that are sponsored by a matrix of corporate-political-military power) will be the seedbed of democracy or even of a republic. Is it, I say with trepidation (as I harbor some of this hope, too), because schools are our bread and butter. Without schools there would be no colleges of education, for there would be little support for the need to study education if it were not to perpetuate schools and the sorting machine (see Spring, 1989) that they provide. In fact, if colleges of education predominately called for full-fledged focus on building individual and group identity and concomitant striving for social, political, and economic justice through intimate human relationship, they would likely be seen as threats and discontinued immediately. There are attempts to do so, of course, even when we emphasize teacher education and the desirability of perpetuating standards and accountability that supports not only the multi-billion dollar testing industry, but empire in its full attire.

Perhaps the most revolutionary thing we can do, even if Dewey's (1934) common faith is only heard as a faint cry for survival, is to encourage learners, educators, and the general (including oppressed) public to ask and act on basic curriculum questions: What's worthwhile? How can we survive and, beyond survival, how can we live together in a state of personal and public growth on this threatened planet? We must teach directly in such a way that each can become her or his own curriculum director. As Ann Lopez Schubert said on several occasions, we must all become our own curriculum directors. Over a quarter century ago, we (Schubert & Lopez-Schubert, 1981) wrote that we must imagine and move toward "curricula that are of, by, and therefore for students."[3]

Finally, I thank Carl Glickman for helping me rekindle the thoughts expressed above.

NOTES

1.   I have found, as a student once told me he learned in a philosophy class, one can gain insight into Dewey by changing the word *and* in his titles to *is*.

2. I am beginning to write a book based on this *New York Times* piece, which I see as an unsung microcosm of Dewey's curricular stance.

3. As noted in conversation in the early 1980s with Ralph W. Tyler (Tyler, Schubert, & Schubert, 1986), this is connected with Lincoln's phrase in his Gettysburg Address, though is not found in the U.S. Constitution, as many think. Dewey, too, paraphrased Lincoln's "of, by, and for the people" in *Experience and Education* (Dewey, 1938, p. 29).

REFERENCES

Apple, M. W., & Beane, J. A. (Eds.). (2007). *Democratic schools* (2nd ed.). Portsmouth, NH: Heinemann.

Bateson, M. C. (1989). *Composing a life*. New York: Plume.

Bernays, E. (1928). *Propaganda*. New York: Liveright.

Bremer, J. (1979). *Education and community*. Sheparton, Australia: Waterwheel Press.

Chomsky, N. (1997). *Media control*. New York: Seven Stories Press.

Chomsky, N. (2001). *Propaganda and the public mind*. Cambridge, MA: So. End Press.

Dewey, J. (1916). *Democracy and education*. New York: Macmillan.

Dewey, J. (1933, April 23). Dewey outlines utopian schools. *New York Times*, p. 7.

Dewey, J. (1934). *A common faith*. New Haven, CT: Yale University Press.

Dewey, J. (1938). *Experience and education*. New York: Macmillan.

Freire, P. (1970). *Pedagogy of the oppressed*. New York: Continuum.

Glickman, C. (2003). *Holding sacred ground: Essays on leadership, courage, and endurance in our schools*. San Francisco: Jossey-Bass.

Glickman, C. (2004). *Letters to the next president*. New York: Teachers College Press.

Glickman, C. (2007). *Letters to the next president*. New York: Teachers College Press.

Gutstein, E. (2006). *Reading and writing the world with mathematics*. New York: Routledge.

Habermas, J. (1971). *Knowledge and human interests*. Boston: Beacon Press.

Herrick, V. E., Goodlad, J. I. Estvan, F. J., & Everman, P. W. (1956). *The elementary school*. Englewood Cliffs, NJ: Prentice Hall.

Holt, J. (1981). *Teach your own*. New York: Dell.

Illich, I. (1970). *Deschooling society*. New York: Harper & Row.

Lapham, L. H. (2004). *Gag rule*. New York: Penguin.

Lippmann, W. (1963). *The essential Lippmann: A political philosophy for liberal democracy*. (C. Rossiter & J. Lare, Eds.). New York: Random House.

Marshall, J. D., Sears, J. T., Allen, L., Roberts, P., & Schubert, W. H. (2007). *Turning points in curriculum: A contemporary curriculum memoir* (2nd Ed.). Columbus, OH: Prentice Hall.

Molnar, A. (2005). *Commercialism and the schools*. New York: Routledge.

Nichols, J. (Ed.). (2004). *Against the beast: A documentary history of American opposition to empire*. New York: Nation Books.

Putnam, R. D. (2007). E Pluribus Unum: Diversity and community in the twenty-first century The 2006 Johan Skytte Prize Lecture. *Scandinavian Political Studies, 30*(2), 137–174.

Schubert, W. H. (1996). Perspectives on four curriculum traditions. *Educational Horizons, 74*(4), 169–176.

Schubert, W. H. (1997). Character education from four perspectives on curriculum. In A. Molnar (Ed.), *The construction of children's character: 1997 NSSE Yearbook, Part II* (pp. 17–30). Chicago: University of Chicago Press and the National Society for the Study of Education.

Schubert, W. H. (2003). The curriculum-curriculum: Experiences in teaching curriculum. *Curriculum and Teaching Dialogue, 5*(1), 9–22.

Schubert, W. H., & Lopez-Schubert, A. L. (1981). Toward curricula that are of, by, and therefore for students. *The Journal of Curriculum Theorizing, 3*(1), 239–251.

Schultz, B. D. (2008). *Spectacular things happen along the way: Lessons from an Urban Classroom.* New York: Teachers College Press.

Spring, J. (1989). *The sorting machine, revisited.* New York. Longman.

Sunstein, C. R. (2004). *The second Bill of Right: FDR's unfinished revolution and why we need it more than ever.* New York: Basic Books.

Tyler, R. W., & Schubert, W. H., & Schubert, A. L. (1986). A dialogue with Ralph W. Tyler. *Journal of Thought, 21*(1), 91–118.

Willis, G. H., & Schubert, W. H. (Eds.). (2000). *Reflections from the heart of educational inquiry: Understanding curriculum and teaching through the arts.* Troy, NY: Educators International Press. (Original work published 1991)

Wood, G. (2005). *A time to learn.* Westport, CT: Heinemann.

CHAPTER 13

CONNECTIONS, CONSTRUCTIONS AND COLLAGES

Initiating Dialogues on Diversity in Teacher Education Courses

Pamela B. Thompson and Richard L. Biffle

This article presents the use of learning activities that assisted the initiation of mean-ingful classroom dialogues on diversity in two graduate teacher education courses. The purpose of the article is to highlight the culturally competent practice of dialogic learning activities in a university level classroom, as supported by Freire's (2005) def-inition of dialogue. The authors, who are both engaged in preparing teacher candi-dates, designed hands-on, self-expressive activities that incorporate selected ideas from Banks (2002), Eisner (1994), and Gay (2000).

Currently, teacher preparation programs in the United States are not well prepared to deal with the range of unique needs associated with an increasing population of culturally diverse students (Gay, 2000). National demographics illustrate that nearly 50% of the children who will be in kindergarten within the next 5 years will be children of color from historically underrepresented

Curriculum and Teaching Dialogue
Volume 10, Numbers 1 & 2, 2008, pp. 165–175
Copyright © 2008 by Information Age Publishing
All rights of reproduction in any form reserved.

groups. Data from the American Association for Employment in Education (2006) show that the prospective pool of teachers in bilingual, ESL (English as a Second Language) and the learners of diverse languages categories are all experiencing considerable shortages.

Garcia (2005) in his book, *Teaching for Diversity,* points out that one of the major challenges is the growing cultural gap between students and the teachers who are trained to teach them. Consequently, the ability to harness the strengths of diversity within teacher education programs remains underdeveloped (Biffle, 2006). This continues to be part of an ongoing national discussion and debate related to meeting these challenges. Nationally, teachers are typically not well prepared to deal with the unique needs, challenges and opportunities associated with student diversity (Biffle, 2006); therefore, the task of closing the cultural gap described by Garcia will involve teacher education programs advancing the cultural competence of preservice teachers.

For our purposes, *diversity* is a term that embraces a wide contextual meaning. Differences are recognized as racial, ethnic, and cultural; however, they are also identified in areas such as learning styles, preferences for the organization and management of classroom environments, teaching practices, and the learner's perspective. An apt definition of *cultural competence* is captured by Nuri-Robins, Lindsay, and Terrell (2003):

> For students to learn what their teachers have to offer, they must feel fully appreciated as individuals, within the context of their own distinctive ethnic, linguistic, and socio-economic backgrounds and with their own particular gender, sexual orientation, sensory and physical abilities. [Culturally competent] educators address the issues that arise in the midst of diversity and respond sensitively to the needs of students in ways that facilitate learning. (p. 15)

A culturally competent educator is a professional who embodies an ongoing commitment to acquiring the knowledge, skills, and attitudes that enable communication across cultural perceptions and experiences.

CONNECTIONS: INITIATING THE DIALOGUE

This article highlights selected instructional activities that we developed for our university level classes. The authors' collaborative interest in this topic grew out of a casual conversation where we discovered that we had common goals in our teacher education programs to nurture culturally competent practices in our students, who were soon to find themselves in diverse classrooms. The two graduate level courses in teacher education, which were taught by the authors at separate institutions, were titled

Learning and Cognition and *Diversity in Education*. The purpose of the activities are twofold (1) to initiate meaningful dialogues related to diversity and (2) to offer avenues for our students to reflect upon culturally competent practice. It is our intent that students will begin to make connections between the cultural experiences of their learners and how as teachers, they might influence change in their own classrooms. We need to clarify that our activities are *dialogic*; their philosophic foundations lay in the concept of dialogue and active expression; therefore, before we describe the selected learning activities, we provide the reader with very brief descriptions from the work of Freire (1998, 2005), Banks (2002), Eisner (1994), and Gay (2000) that support our concept of dialogic learning activities.

Banks (2000) points out that there is often confusion about the term *diversity* as it relates to the dimensions of education, observing that in many cases privileged majority groups define the mainstream culture-behavior patterns, symbols, institutions and values. These groups often play a dominant role in determining what is acceptable and unacceptable, what is valued and ignored in curricular content, instructional practice and evaluative measures. Classroom dialogues framed within critical consciousness can address and clarify these cultural issues.

Critical consciousness is the ability to perceive social, political and economic oppression and to take action against those elements. In other words, a culturally competent and critically conscious educator resists instructional methods that would consider the learner as a passive receiver of knowledge.

Dialogue, according to Freire (2005) is not a feel good conversation or a beaten path of certainties and specialties (p. 23). Neither does it rely on mechanistic philosophically imposed guidelines, instead, it engages our pre-service teachers in critical thinking which often calls into question the ways curricula are designed, instructional models are embraced and learners are evaluated.

As we planned our activities, we were looking for meaningful and multisensory approaches that would illustrate personal and unique interpretations of diversity, thus, we were inspired by Eisner's (1994) idea of multiple forms of representation. A form of representation is a private concept made public through self-expression which may take visual, auditory, kinesthetic or tactile shape. Eisner states: "Once the individual makes the transformation from the conception (of an idea) to the representation (of an idea) the qualities that are created in these forms become part of the environment upon which he or she can reflect further (p. 47). By creating instructional activities that encouraged a wide context for understanding diversity, our preservice teachers were able to reflect upon the dimensions of diversity in more significant ways.

In her book *Culturally Responsive Teaching*, Gay (2000) states that we must address the instructional processes included in teacher preparation by way of stimulating intellectual curiosity and modeling strategies of inquiry, critique and analysis, rather than the traditional preferences for rote memory and regurgitation of factual information. Educators who are culturally competent are able to contextualize diversity in multiple perspectives, engage in more ways of knowing and thinking, and to become more active participants in shaping their own learning (p. 35). This shift in practice begins with changing preservice teacher knowledge and attitudes about diversity.

Constructions: Puzzles and Collages

Learning and Cognition is a graduate level course that explores the theoretical concepts underlying learning and cognition and examines applications of mainstream and alternative learning theories. One of the major goals for this course is for students to begin to draw relevant and meaningful connections between the current research on neuroscience (study of the human brain), perception, cognition, and practical instructional approaches in a diverse classroom. The highlighted activity from this class is the *puzzle activity.*

Diversity in Education is a graduate level course designed to engage teacher education candidates in activities and projects that provide the essential foundations for understanding the intersections of culture, instructional practice, and professional development through intentional plans of action. The highlighted activity from this class is the *collage activity.*

The Puzzle Activity

An activity that guides pre-service teachers in *making connections* between the diversity of student learning styles and instructional practice is the *puzzle activity* (Thompson, 2001). The jigsaw puzzle represents an example of subject area content. When students are tasked with the work of constructing the puzzle, they are encouraged to think about their own personal learning style and the contributions that they make to the group effort. At the beginning of the activity students are asked to place themselves in small groups. Each group is given a cardboard jigsaw puzzle. The puzzles vary by number of pieces; 100, 250, 500, and 1000. The groups do not have any choice in what puzzle they receive. There is usually 30 to 45 minutes allowed for students to complete the puzzle. After the allotted time has elapsed, students are asked to stop their work and consider the following introductory question: *In what ways did the experience illustrate diversity in terms of student perspectives and learning styles?* In response to this question, an initial dialogue ensues where students are encouraged to translate their observations of the activity into the context of a K–12 classroom. Students verbally express and examine the activity by drawing major themes around which they can describe diversity in student perspective and styles of learning.

During the Fall 2006 semester, students in *Learning and Cognition* identified four themes that the *puzzle activity* had helped to illustrate diverse student perspectives and learning styles: time, trust, identity and learning environment. The following is an elaboration of these four themes.

Time

We have chosen to share the actual, abbreviated quotations from students in an effort to demonstrate the depth of the discussion that transpired during the post activity dialogue. A brief interpretation follows each selection of student voices.

> *"We knew we could never complete the puzzle in the time we had, so we tried to do as much as we could; however, knowing we would never be able to complete the work in the time allowed was frustrating."*

—Char (1000 pieces)

> *"When you said, five minutes, I said, forget it. There is no way. I'm done."*

—Karie (500 pieces)

> *"I think some people had more experience with putting puzzles together. I do and I like puzzles, but some people in my group did not have as much practice and they didn't put things together as quickly."*

—Miyo (500 pieces)

> *"When we finished our puzzle and looked around, we realized that we were the ones with the least amount of pieces, so we celebrated, because it had been really simple for us. We won!"*

—Meghan (100 pieces)

Students contrasted the time allowed with the number of puzzle pieces required to complete the task. They observed that it was far easier for the group with less puzzle pieces to complete the task; that some groups had individuals who were more adept at completing puzzles; or that some puzzles were easier to construct by the nature of the puzzle image on the box. In other words, it may have been easier to put together pieces of a giraffe than an ocean wave.

As indicated by their identified theme, students observed that time played a significant role in how they were able to complete their puzzle. They were able to connect their reactions to the challenges that some learners, who are not as familiar with the language or the content, may experience when there is not enough work time provided to be successful with an assigned task in a classroom.

While the students who had fewer puzzle pieces to complete their puzzle were able to finish within the time allowed and even introduced an element of competition, another group of students pointed out that those with the more complex puzzles felt frustration because they did not have the ability to complete the puzzle in the time given. They associated this to the frustration learners might experience in an actual classroom setting, when expected to master content within an inadequate amount of time.

Trust

The notion of mistrust and trust became evident by one group's uneasiness with the perceived outcome of the *puzzle activity* itself. Their concern was that the activity would somehow skew what they perceived to be a competitive task for a grade. This possibility provoked a reaction that was uncomfortable for members of the group who even entertained that the professor had set them up to fail, but removing a number of puzzle pieces.

> *"I thought maybe the point of the exercise was for you to observe what we would do if there were pieces missing and we could not complete the puzzle. If that had been the case, I would have been angry."*
>
> —Stephanie (500 pieces)

> *"I felt like the student who is never able to finish, when I saw Meghan's group celebrating, it made me think that it became more of a competition. It was like we were all competing for a grade, maybe?"*
>
> —Mike (250 pieces)

> *"Our group thought, well we just won't be able to finish, it is like we were being set up for failure from the beginning."*
>
> —Char (1000 pieces)

The students equated this experience to the alienation or isolation that some K–12 students may experience when their perspective or ways of knowing may not be recognized or valued in the classroom. The developmental term *self-fulfilling prophecy* entered the dialogue, Self-fulfilling prophecy is recognized as an eventual process where teacher anticipated levels of student achievement can be reflected in student output, but not necessarily illustrate actual student abilities. Unfortunately, as students pointed out, this can manifest itself in low teacher expectations resulting in low student achievement. In an atmosphere of mistrust, learners may be less inclined to achieve the instructional objectives and this, they commented, "has implications for instructional decision making as a classroom teacher."

Identity

Students explored this theme as it related to the self-concept and self-efficacy of learners from diverse cultural backgrounds. By being honest in expressing their own learning styles and approach to the *puzzle activity*, students were able to connect the need for teachers to become well acquainted with the unique learning styles and experiences of their own future K–12 learners.

> *"I'm terrible at this."*
>
> —Scott (500 pieces)

> *"We were trying to work on the border together, but one person in our group did her own thing."*
>
> —Dan (1000 pieces)

> *"It was interesting how people in our group talked about their experiences with puzzles. Some people do puzzles with their children, others don't like puzzles."*
>
> —Bob (500 pieces)

Some students clearly felt uncomfortable during the puzzle activity and equated these feelings to how students will often disengage from the material when unable to draw connections between their own perspectives, realities and knowledge.

Learning Environment

Students were also interested in discussing *where* students worked, in terms of classroom space, furniture, desks, tables, chairs and floors. Interestingly, one group made the observation that they believed that it was often the teacher who had the most important role in determining the physical and emotional atmosphere of the classroom.

> *"There was a lot of talking that was going on in our group too, but what was interesting is that even though we were socializing, we were also getting parts of the puzzle*

completed…. You know when you enter a classroom and you can tell if it is on-task chatter or off task chatter?"

—Karie (500 pieces)

"The floor was where we had decided to work, because there were not enough tables in this classroom, so we moved out to the hallway, where we had more room, but then we felt we had to be quiet, because other classes were being held in other classrooms."

—Selena (250 pieces)

"It was interesting that after you made the announcement that we had only five minutes left, the room got very quiet."

—Bob (500 pieces)

"I think what I will remember about this activity is that we did not have a choice in how many pieces of the puzzle we got, but we did have more of a choice in how we tried to put the pieces together."

—Dan (1000 pieces)

When Dan, offered his comment of *"not having a choice in how many pieces but in determining how the pieces might be put together,"* several students drew connection between the contemporary challenge of linking federal and state mandated performance measures with designing culturally competent lesson plans. This can be further complicated by the necessity to evaluate students whose diverse perspectives and learning styles may not reflect a standard frame of cultural reference or knowledge.

Overall, the themes that emerged from this initial dialogue on diversity: time, trust, identity, and learning environment contributed to student understanding of key components of working with diverse learning styles. These included, the ability of teachers to allow for sufficient time for meaningful learning to occur, the importance of trust in the student-teacher relationship, the direct connection between high expectations and student achievement, the necessity of knowing the learning styles of students in your classroom, and the current challenge of balancing instructional experiences that will address diversity of learner perspective with mandated outcomes.

The Collage Activity

At the beginning of the course, *Diversity in Education*, preservice teachers are tasked with creating a collage. This multi-sensory activity provides students with an opportunity to formulate their emerging professional and personal expressions of diversity through a collage of photographs, gathered images, words and or objects. As the collage projects commence, introductory information related to the definition of collage is the starting point for student construction and design.

While engaged in collage construction, students were encouraged to explore the broadest thinking about diversity and connect these ideas to their own life experiences and learning. The collage emerges as a multi-dimensional landscape of thoughts, words and pictures.

After students complete their collages they are asked to write a reflective statement linking their choice of images, collage technique, and visual expression of ideas, values and feelings related to diversity. As illustrated by the following reflective statements, students were able to display multi-faceted expressions of diversity through the art of collage.

"I chose to put a "mirror" in the center of my collage because I feel diversity is related to perception, not only others' perceptions of us, but our perception of ourselves"

—Rachel

"My collage focuses on what I feel are the biggest diversity issues occurring not only in the U.S. but also around the world today. It focuses on poverty and wealth, religious aspects, the image of women, and race relations"

—Wauneta

"During the construction of my collage, I chose to create a background of multicolored faces, and in doing so came to a … revelation. The more physical space I filled with this background, the more I tended to lose track of the individual faces that made up the image. I wonder, then, if there is a real-world analogy I could make-that diversity might be apparent up close, but as you put greater and greater distance between yourself and the populace the less you see of individual races and creeds, replaced by a … concept of humanity."

—Ari

"Diversity is like a wild garden … there is a pattern … but no uniformity … diversity is like an artist's palette with various colors … or a mask [of] mystery and hidden individuality."

—Erin

This kind of open exchange of information and ideas is crucial to the success and development of instructional strategies that teacher candidates are forming in their minds and practice at this point in their preparation. The nature and quality of the collage activity provides a vehicle for teaching and learning that engages the participants in an asset model of thinking, planning, and voice (personal expression) that helps to shape the people involved in the educational systems, the culture, its traditions values, and future national and local conversations in our schools and classrooms on the topic of diversity.

Concluding Remarks

In summary, the purpose of this article was to present some initial approaches that address the challenges of an educational system that has not kept pace with our rapidly changing demographics. New knowledge about the learning process combined with increased technology and a dynamic cultural reality places new demands on schools. Federal and state mandated content standards continue to increase the demand for educational conformity in learning objectives and outcomes across elementary and secondary grade levels; thus, it becomes essential for educators to be able to challenge the notion that a *one size fits all approach* to curriculum, instruction, and/or evaluation.

The important thing is to design teacher education coursework and programs—in cooperation with schools and their communities—which will prepare teachers to meet these contemporary challenges.

When students can associate their professional descriptions of diversity with their own cultural frame of reference, which comprises a vital system of social values, cognitive codes, behaviors and beliefs, then personal and professional practices emerge as cultural competencies (Thompson & Biffle, 2005). Dialogic activity encourages students to inquire thoughtfully, to seek multiple descriptors of diversity, and to accept, as well as, internalize successful cultural competent practices.

The authors' teaching and research in teacher education continues to explore ways in which dialogue can lead to broader understanding of diversity and how that understanding can translate into a narrowing of the cultural gap (Garcia, 2005). We share a collaborative viewpoint that this is an opportune moment in the history of public education. We invite our colleagues in the field of curriculum, instruction and teacher education to join their voice with ours in this critical on-going dialogue. If teacher educators do not continue this national dialogue in their classrooms, to whom will we cede this responsibility?

REFERENCES

American Association for Employment in Education. (2006). *What is your personal job market: Interpreting the 2006 educator supply and demand research* (Issue Brief No 41). Columbus, OH.

Banks, J. (2002). *Introduction to multicultural education* Boston: Allyn & Bacon.

Biffle, R. (2006). A geo-ethnographic look at a day in the life of a student of color. *AATC Dialogue Quarterly, 8*(1, 2), 193–208.

Eisner, E. (1994). *Cognition and curriculum reconsidered.* Teachers College Press.

Freire, P. (2005) *Teachers as cultural workers.* Boulder: Westview Press.

Freire, P. (1998). *Pedagogy of the oppressed.* New York: Continuum.

Garcia, R. (2005). *Teaching for Diversity.* Bloomington, IN: Phi Delta Kappa.

Gay, G. (2002). Preparing for culturally responsive teaching. *Journal of Teacher Education, 53*(2), 106–116.

Gay, G. (2000). *Culturally responsive teaching: theory, research and practice.* New York: Teachers College Press.

Robins, K., Lindsey, R. & Terrell, R. (2003*) Cultural proficiency a manual for school leaders.* Thousand Oaks, CA: Corwin Press.

Thompson P., & Biffle R. (2005). Defining the new teaching and learning community: From traditional improvisation to narrative community. *International Journal of Diversity in Organizations, Communities and Nations, 4,* 279–288.

Thompson, P. (2001, June). *Putting the pieces of the puzzle together: Diversity in learning styles.* Retrieved June 12, 2001, from www.teachingforsuccess.com

CHAPTER 14

RESISTANCE AT CITY MIDDLE SCHOOL

Critical Race Theorizing in Educational Research

Amy L. Masko

Grounded in critical race theory, I have conducted an ethnographic study to understand how race permeates an urban middle school at three levels: the systemic level, the classroom level, and among youth. This paper will specifically discuss the multiple ways in which resistance is manifested within the school, and how utilizing an oppositional theory provides a framework for examining and discussing resistance and its contributing factors.

In this paper, I will discuss both the literature addressing the role of critical race theory (CRT) in education research and the study's methodology, which utilized CRT as the conceptual framework. I will also describe the school community and the findings as they relate to resistance in the school climate. I will conclude with the study implications for both practice and further research.

Curriculum and Teaching Dialogue
Volume 10, Numbers 1 & 2, 2008, pp. 177–192
Copyright © 2008 by Information Age Publishing

The term "resistance" in education research is often used in relation to resistance theory, whereby some students are driven to actively resist the roles and identities schools provide for them (Collins, 1995). Students engage in oppositional behavior in the form of sustained challenges to authority. This is active opposition, rather than deviance, because the term generally indicates a positive and justified opposition (Collins, 1995). Generally, this term is used to describe behaviors in children and youth that explain their school failure, as Fordham and Ogbu's (1986) notion of Black students resisting school because school engagement constituted "acting White." While these definitions have typically been utilized to explain opposition in youth, in this paper, these definitions describe only the behavior of the administrators and faculty.

Teachers and school administrators did, in fact, engage in active opposition that challenged authority. I would classify this behavior as positive and justified opposition (Collins, 1995). However, the student resistance described in this paper does not fit neatly into this description. While students did engage in oppositional behavior, their opposition cannot be described as resisting school identities. In fact, their opposition was, at times, in response to others denying their school identities. For the purposes of this paper, resistance is defined as engaging in behavior that actively opposes social authority, whether that authority is the actual hierarchical decision-making processes of schooling, a curriculum, or a societal perception.

CRITICAL RACE THEORY

CRT is an oppositional theory, one that resists single-truth claims and instead examines counter-stories in challenging dominant ideology. Utilizing the lens of CRT, I specifically examined my data in search of themes relating to the six tenets described by Delgado and Stefancic (2001): (1) racism is ordinary; (2) the current system of White-over-color ascendancy serves important purposes; (3) race and races are products of social thought and relations; (4) the dominant society racializes different minority groups at different times; (5) intersectionality and antiessentialism are present, whereas everyone has overlapping, conflicting identities and loyalties; and (6) there is a shared minority experience that people of color communicate about race and racism that White people are unlikely to know is present. These tenets taken together can lead us in the field of education to examine the systems of schooling for social justice for children of color through challenging dominant ideology that guides our schooling and by placing experiential knowledge of students and teachers at the heart of educational scholarship on race.

Much of the literature in the field of CRT, which is a legal theory that has recently transcended disciplinary boundaries, balances between situated narrative, based on experiential knowledge, and more sweeping analyses of the law (Tate, 1997). According to Solórzano, Ceja, and Yosso (2000), "Critical Race Theory offers insights, perspectives, methods, and pedagogies that guide our efforts to identify, analyze, and transform the structural and cultural aspects of education that maintain subordinate and dominant racial positions in and out of the classroom" (p. 63).

CRT began in legal studies, but is now considered a transdisciplinary movement (Delgado & Stefancic, 2001; Ladson-Billings & Tate, 1995; Lynn, 1999; Solórzano et al., 2000; Solórzano & Yosso, 2002) and is gaining recognition in education. In 1995, Ladson-Billings and Tate called for race to be theorized in education:

> Over the past few decades, theoretical and epistemological considerations of gender have proliferated. Though the field continues to struggle for legitimacy in academe, interest in and publications about feminist theories abound. At the same time, Marxist and Neo-Marxist formulations about class continue to merit considerations as theoretical models for understanding social inequity. We recognize the importance of both gender—and class-based analyses while at the same time pointing to their shortcomings vis-à-vis race…. By arguing that race remains untheorized, we are not suggesting that other scholars have not looked carefully at race as a powerful tool for explaining social inequality, but that the intellectual salience of this theorizing has not been systematically employed in the analysis of educational inequality. (p. 48)

Tate (1997) expands on this argument, stating that there are omissions and blind spots in education research on race that "suggest the need for theoretical perspectives that move beyond the traditional paradigmatic boundaries of educational research to provide a more cogent analysis of 'raced' people and move discussions of race and racism from the margins of scholarly activity to the fore of educational discourse" (p. 196).

Since 1995, when Ladson-Billings and Tate first challenged the field to theorize race, there have been numerous articles published in the field of education that utilize CRT (see Ladson-Billings, 2005; Lynn, 1999; Masko, 2005a, 2005b; Smith-Maddox & Solórzano, 2002; Solórzano et al., 2000; Solórzano & Yosso, 2002) to analyze educational inequality. Solórzano and Yosso endorse Ladson-Billings and Tate's call that education needs theories that help to better understand those who are at the margins of society, as well as theorizing methods to do so. They suggested a critical race methodology that utilizes storytelling and counter-storytelling as a form of qualitative inquiry aimed at specifically addressing race research

(Solórzano & Yosso, 2002). Indeed, there is a growing momentum for theorizing race in education.

CRITICAL RACE THEORY AND RESISTANCE

CRT is an oppositional theory that challenges majoritarian stories told from the perch of dominance with counter-storytelling, a method that upsets hegemonic truth. It forces the question, *whose* truth? CRT grew out of critical legal studies, as a result of the criticism that critical legal studies did not adequately address the needs of communities of color in the law (Tate, 1997). CRT opposes the historical underpinnings of how race is considered in both law and society, and, in this case, education. It opposes a color blind ideology that is pervasive in the law (see *Brown v. Board of Education,* 1954), and challenges scholars to consider the historical contexts of law in shaping the identity and treatment of African Americans and other people of color (Tate, 1997) prior to the Civil Rights movement.

Consider the constitution, as Derrick Bell had done (Ladson-Billings & Tate, 1995). When the constitution was crafted, African Americans were only considered under property laws. Later, *Plessy v. Ferguson* (1896) led to "separate but equal" laws in the land, which reigned until the Civil Rights Movement, when activists purported a color blind ideology that the courts adopted in the *Brown* verdict. Critical race scholars argue, then, that American society, shaped through law, has a color-coded ideology, where race has historically bore significant weight in legal decisions. It is impossible to maintain a color blind ideology, which has been the underlying philosophy of American society since the Civil Rights Movement, without being deeply aware of the color-coded consciousness that we all assume in this country (Tate, 1997). CRT implores us to deep consciousness of our color-coded national ideology, and it challenges us to resist the liberal civil rights color blind discourse. Furthermore, CRT questions whether this discourse, which is so deeply imbedded in our American psyche, can move the national conversation on equity forward (Delgado & Stefancic, 2001; Tate, 1997).

In the discussion of the findings of my research on how race manifests itself in an urban middle school, I will address the theme of resistance, and posit that the multiple ways in which resistance shows itself in the social and academic milieu of the school is consistent with the role of resistance in CRT. In this way, the praxis of the theory is illustrated.

METHOD

This paper describes an ethnographic study, conducted over a 2-year time span in an urban middle school in a Midwestern community. Ethnographic research tools enabled me to depict the ways in which children and the faculty relate to each other and construct meanings in the classroom and in the school, as a whole, related to race. Issues surrounding race and ethnicity are complex and involved. My research design is based on a "constructive philosophy that assumes reality as multilayered, interactive, and a shared social experience interpreted by individuals" (McMillan & Schumacher, 2001, p. 396).

> What the ethnographer is in fact faced with ... is a multiplicity of complex conceptual structures, many of them superimposed upon or knotted into one another, which are at once strange, irregular, and inexplicit, and which he must contrive somehow first to grasp and then to render. (Geertz, 1973, p. 10)

The marriage of ethnographic methodology with CRT allowed me to view the complexity of race as a conceptual structure within the school. CRT has been compared to postmodernist and poststructuralist criticisms of research and policy that utilize modernist notions of single-truth claims (Jinks, 1997; Lynn, Yosso, Solórzano, & Parker, 2002). In fact, matters of race in the United States are complex and varied, and by providing single-truth models to examine race, researchers are not considering the tapestry of truths that constitute color in this country. Critical race theorists use storytelling and counter-storytelling as a means to explain the reality of people of color in this country, through asset-informed perspectives, not majoritarian stories, which are often based on deficit models (Delgado & Stefancic, 2001; Solórzano & Yosso, 2002).

During the first year of the study I spent time getting to know the school. I did not collect data during the first year. I simply volunteered in the classrooms, getting to know the students and teachers. During the second year of the study, I worked exclusively in two classrooms: two sixth grade world study classes and an eighth grade honors language arts class. I was a participant observer, joining small groups when the students were working in groups, sitting in a desk lined up in a row—not quite in the back, but mixed in with the students. I was in the classes 1 day each week observing the students, teachers, and the enactment of the curriculum. When a teacher was out and the class had a substitute, the students looked to me to help the substitute maneuver the class structure, especially in the sixth grade classes. I once prepared a guest lecture for the honors language arts class on the crisis in Darfur when they were reading *Anne Frank: The Diary of a Young Girl* (1993), connecting the genocide in Darfur to the genocide of the Holocaust. Due to this role as participant observer, the students saw me as an expert voice (similar to their teacher), and often asked my opinion of things they were learning or asked me to read a paper they were writing, but there were also fewer barriers to our relationship owing to my "powerless" role in their classroom. I did not determine their grades or conference with their parents or reprimand their behavior. Therefore, there was a certain amount of ease to our relationship.

Participants

In addition to observing the classroom environment, I also examined the curriculum, collected student writing, and interviewed several teachers, administrators, and students ($n = 12$). A total of eight students were chosen to participate on a deeper level than classroom conversation. I interviewed two sixth graders from first hour world studies, two sixth graders from second hour world studies, and four eighth graders from third hour honors language arts class. I also interviewed both teachers who allowed me in their classrooms for the year and both school administrators. This paper utilizes data obtained only in relation to the administrators, one faculty and three eighth grade honors students. Table 14.1 describes these particular participant demographics.

Design

I interviewed each participant a total of three times during the course of the data collection year. I also followed up with each member checking to ensure that I captured the participants' meanings in my interpretation.

Table 14.1. Participant Demographics

Name*	Position	Gender	Ethnicity
Brian Denny	Administrator	Male	White
Ray VanHook	Administrator	Male	White
Reyna Martinez	Language arts teacher	Female	Latina
Juwan	Eighth grade student	Male	African American
Sarah	Eighth grade student	Female	White
Vanessa	Eighth grade student	Female	Latina

*All names are pseudonyms to protect the research participants' identities.

I interviewed each adult participant three times individually, while I interviewed the students both individually and in focus group settings.

Setting

City Middle School is located in a relatively small, depressed urban center, located in a particularly beautiful geographical area in the Midwestern states. The city, Waterburg, is surrounded by predominately White, upper class tourist communities. Waterburg is a city of approximately 40,000 residents, with over 40% non-White. African Americans are the largest minority group in Waterburg, comprising 80% of the non-White population. The city's unemployment rate was at 12.1% during 2002, and 56% of the population earns less than $25,000 annually (City of Waterburg Demographic Statistics, 2002).

City Middle School, a highly impoverished school located in the heart of the city center, has a population that is approximately 60% African American, 35% Anglo, and 5% Latino and Caldian, with 80% of the students receiving free or reduced lunch (City Middle School Annual Report, 2003). The school building itself is an older building with exposed wood cabinets with glass doors in the classrooms, blackboards with dark stained wood frames, and hardwood floors. There are hand-painted slogans and inspirational sayings on the walls throughout the buildings, such as, "Success is getting up one more time than you fall down." Many of these sayings are quotes from famous people, like Martin Luther King, Jr., Eleanor Roosevelt, and Michael Jordan. Many are antiracist in nature, while others are intended to inspire achievement. The first painted slogan on the wall, "Eracism," is located near a large mosaic art project made by a previous group of students addressing their feelings of racism. The mosaic has tiles that say, "Racism Stinks"; "Erase Hate"; and "Love not Hate," painted by a group of youth with bright colors on white tiles. This first piece of artwork and accompanying slogan sets the tone for the feeling of the school.

RESULTS

Findings of Resistance

The theme of resistance, which is often connected to urban schooling, was prominent in this study (Haymes, 1995). Resistance was present within the administration, in the enacted curriculum and within the students. This resistance was often enacted with good intentions on behalf of the students, and was often complicated in nature.

Administrative Resistance

I would describe both administrators at City Middle School as strong leaders who relentlessly advocated for their students. For instance, they resisted policies and practices that they felt were detrimental to their school community. This resistance was complicated by their compliance. That is, the administration maintained a creative insubordination (Masko, 2006), meaning that they protested practices they deemed detrimental, but if their protests were denied, they complied. In the two years I was in the school, the administration never took a stand that would qualify as insubordination. Yet, they took numerous stands of resistance, and the central administration was often made aware of their resistance. The following are excerpts from two letters. In each letter, both of which were nearly three single-spaced pages, the Assistant Principal Mr. VanHook, refers to "Close the Gap." Close the Gap, or CTG, was a district-wide initiative where representative teachers from each building attended monthly meetings to work toward closing the achievement gap between students of color and White students within the district. In the first letter, Mr. VanHook is reacting to a central office decision to relocate a program from City Middle School to another school within the district:

> Dr. Superintendent:
>
> I am beginning to realize I must not have a clear understanding of the district's Close the Gap initiative. My confusion is an outgrowth of several recent decisions.... Members of the Close the Gap initiative have expressed frustrations over a perceived indifference to their efforts by central office. The frustrations include central office administrators' non-attendance or brief appearances at committee meetings and their apparent superficial attitude to the meetings' importance.... Further, it is disheartening when I hear a central office administrator state that a recommendation to re-locate an educational program was made with no consideration given to how it might impact the culture within either building involved or how it would affect the students and their families.... I ask for clearer definition of the parameters [of CTG]. I am neither disagreeing with these decisions nor questioning anyone's authority to make them.

The second excerpted letter was addressed to the school board in response to a cut in the school counseling staff, from two full-time counselors to one half-time counselor.

To School Board Members:

On Wednesday last, job assignments for next year were given to all TEA members. Based on those assignments [our school] has been reduced by 1.5 counselors.... The .5 counselor will have a caseload of approximately 600 students.... The American Counselor Association recommends a counselor to student ratio of 1:250. This reduction, coupled with the proposal that [our school] will retain the services of a full time media specialist, suggests that a librarian will be more instrumental in raising students' achievement than a counselor. I am interested to know what evidence exists to support this position ... I am advocating for a continuation of the services that will provide the greatest opportunities for all students, but especially minority students, to achieve higher levels of academic success. Given these circumstances, I must ask how these following CTG questions were factored into the decision to reduce [our school's] counseling services by 75%

1. Does what we do serve all our children in a way that achieves excellence and equity?

2. Before decisions are made, have we reviewed the impact on families of different races, ethnicities, economic means and neighborhoods?

3. How can our daily decisions promote a school climate and culture of high expectations for every student?

I do not challenge the authority of those who made this decision; I only seek clarification so I may adequately address the questions from staff and parents this decision has spawned.

It is interesting to note that both letters end with a line that indicates that Mr. VanHook does not "challenge the authority" of the decision makers (the superintendent and school board, respectively). I asked Mr. VanHook if he ever resisted implementing any of the district initiatives or policies. He responded that he always complied, otherwise he would be insubordinate. Mr. VanHook was direct with his dissatisfaction with some district decisions, yet he was cognizant of the hierarchical decision making in schooling practices, and complied with implementing district policies and initiatives. He often openly shared his position with his staff, hence contributing to a resistant climate within the school.

It is possible that Mr. VanHook's dissent with administrative decision making ("central office" as it was referred within the school) may give passive permission for teachers to ignore an initiative or to implement it without passion or follow-through. Further, by sharing his dissent, Mr. VanHook may have also contributed to a resistant climate where teachers felt comfortable to vocalize their discontent with a school practice. While my interaction was limited to two classroom teachers and the two administrators, I can attest that all four of these individuals had resistant dispositions. They were all thoughtful of practices, policies and initiatives, and regularly spoke of shortcomings of schools and schooling practices.

Another form of resistance I regularly saw within the administration and teachers was frustration. The following is an excerpt from an e-mail transcript from Brian Denny, the principal at City Middle School. I sent him the link to a report that indicated that there has been little change in test scores in the state in more than a decade. We e-mailed back and forth that day about educational funding, the resources being put into testing practices, and the injustice of it for urban schools.

> I want to make a difference yet I have spent the last two and a half weeks taking care of administrative busy work BS and then when I finally get the opening of school headaches complete I must manage the [state standardized test]. By the time November hits I will be looking forward to Thanksgiving and Christmas and half the year is gone with little focus on instructional improvement and accountability. I am just a little bitter and frustrated. American education needs to make a commitment to student learning and not political correctness, unionization, time bound promotion of students, with weak instructional practices with little internal accountability in which the best teaching is not rewarded and years of service is. This is fun. Almost therapeutic. Finally lets have high stakes tests which have zero reliability and cultural relevance for our students which will determine funding and promote a greater divide of schools in an era of choice so parents can gain another blame card for [students'] low achievement.

The frustration that Mr. Denny describes was regularly evident among the faculty at the school. Teachers and administrators are faced with having to implement policy that they do not necessarily support. In one study it was found that more than 82% of teachers made sure that test objectives were covered "to a thorough extent" in their instruction and adjusted instructional plans based on students' test scores (Snow-Gerono & Franklin, 2005). Yet, 95% of these teachers indicated that testing created significant tension for them and for their students (Snow-Gerono & Franklin, 2006). So, while teachers experienced tension due to testing requirements, they still complied. In the current American school climate of accountability and reform, educators are regularly faced with the challenge of reconciling their professional educational philosophy with top down educational mandates. The faculty at City Middle School is not immune to the resulting frustration.

When I spoke with Mr. Denny to member check with him about my analysis of resistance, he responded, "[The principalship is like] battling a storm to make sure your students have smooth sailing down the road."

Resistance in the Enacted Curriculum

Ms. Reyna Martinez was given the opportunity to create a pilot honors language arts class for the eighth grade. The intention was to prepare students for the honors curriculum at the high school level. One of the concerns with the program at the local high school was that it attracted mainly White students, even though the school is predominately African American. Ms. Martinez's intent was to develop a program that would be culturally responsive to her diverse middle school students. There were grade requirements to enter and remain in the program. Ms. Martinez consciously sought students of color who met the requirement. As a result, her third period honors language arts class was a mixed demographic.

Ms. Martinez had the academic freedom to create her own curriculum for this honors class. As a result, she resisted the adopted eighth grade literature anthology and instead chose texts that she often described as "juicy," such as John Howard Griffin's *Black Like Me* (1962) and Anne Franks' *Anne Frank: The Diary of a Young Girl* (1993). She also brought in articles for students to read about topics that were relevant to their lives. During a discussion of segregation, while the students were reading *Black Like Me*, Ms. Martinez reminded students of the Jonathon Kozol article they read about apartheid schools, stating, "[Then we] separated by color, today [we] separate by money." She regularly provided reading that connected literature to current events, and required students to engage in evaluative thinking, making judgments that they had to defend, either in writing or in class discussion. At another time, for example, the students were assigned to read a newspaper article about Tookie Williams, the Crips leader who changed his ways while in prison (nominated at one point for a Nobel Prize). He was on death row and the article discussed his upcoming execution and the surrounding controversy. Ms. Martinez pointed out that "Governor Schwarzenegger is deciding his fate. This is juicy."

At one point, the high school English teachers complained because a few of the books she chose were on the high school's reading list—recommended texts for the high school English teachers to choose within their curriculum. Ms. Martinez reported that she felt angry by their complaint. She felt that she should have freedom to choose literature that would be best for her students, and not be confined to district guidelines, even those created by her high school colleagues.

Resistance Within the Students

Resistance within the students at City Middle School took two forms: resistance to societal expectations of low achievement for students of color, and resistance to a multicultural curriculum. The first form of resistance, the resistance of low expectations, was described by two eighth grade students, Juwan, an African American student, and Vanessa, a Latina student. The second kind of resistance was in opposition to a multicultural curriculum, and was described by Sarah, a White middle-class student.

Juwan, an eighth grade honors student described others' expectations of him and his African American friends:

> I have some friends who got into selling drugs and I'm like "You know that's exactly what they expect you to do. Like you supposed to be, like they expect you to be dead by age 21 or so or in prison, you know? They don't expect you to graduate, but you gotta prove 'em wrong. That's the only way you can."

Vanessa echoed Juwan's sentiments, but in regard to academic achievement on the state standardized tests. Vanessa stated, "I don't like it when like on tests they say that Latin people will do bad…. They expect us to do bad; worse than the regular pe- like White people." When I asked who "they" are, she responded, "Like when the papers came out they said what they expected of the different races and stuff and Latins were one of the lowest … I feel kinda angry 'cause they shouldn't really do that. It makes me feel bad." Since she explained how she felt about the articles the newspaper published in regards to predicting the test results, I asked her what she thought when the test results, aggregated by race, were published: "I guess kids respond to what they expect them to do, so they just do that."

Vanessa and Juwan's comments indicate their perception that society ("they" and "'em") holds low expectations for youth of color. Vanessa shares her frustration with the No Child Left Behind policy of publishing achievement data according to ethnicity, which consistently shows students of color performing worse than their White counterparts. She essentially blamed the newspaper for contributing to what she believed to be her community's low expectations for students of color, stating, "I guess kids respond to what they expect them to do." Juwan's comment actually advocates ways to resist low expectations. He advises his friends to quit dealing drugs and to graduate from high school, not because it is in his friends' best interest, but because it is in opposition to what "they" expect. Perhaps Juwan believes that resisting society's low expectations is more motivating to his friends than other arguments he may have employed, such as potential health risks and/or potential adjudication.

Interestingly, this finding is in opposition to Fordham and Ogbu's (1986) suggestion of students of color resisting academics as a form of maintaining Black culture and to defy "acting White." In this case, both Juwan and Vanessa, two honor students of color, actually resist Whiteness through advocating and personally striving for academic achievement.

This form of resistance is supported by the administration. Mr. Denny and Mr. VanHook held an assembly at the start of the second semester, establishing some new policies about celebrating good behavior and chastising the poor behavior exhibited in the school during the first semester. At one point, Mr. Denny described a student from City Middle School who went on to achieve at the University of Michigan. He said, "Well, he got 3 Bs and a C at the U of M. That's awesome. He's a City student doing that well at one of the best schools in the nation. He's a City student." He goes on to remind the students of another former City Middle School student who is attending college:

> You know Robert's sister who comes to see his basketball games? She's in college. She's a City student. She took school seriously. She's in college. We need to highlight those students. Did you see the list in the hall? Those are all City students who are in college.

Mr. Denny refers to a list in the hallway of former students who went on to attend college. The list is not very long. Similar to students in other poor, urban districts, college is often not a reality for City Middle School students. Mr. Denny is trying to resist that narrative by highlighting students who succeeded in high school and are gaining a higher education. His motivational speech, which teeters between chastising poor behavior and inspiring higher achievement, is a form of resisting societal expectations. By highlighting the City students who are attending college, Mr. Denny is providing a counter-story for his students. He is telling them, as Juwan stated, to "prove 'em wrong" and go on to college. However, while it is likely that Mr. Denny's intention is to motivate with a counter-story, he may in fact simply be supporting a majoritarian story. By highlighting the very few students who have attained college, Mr. Denny may be supporting students' beliefs that college is not an attainable goal.

The second form of resistance within the students is evidenced in Sarah. Sarah, a middle-class White student, told me of her frustration with her honors class's focus on issues of race and racism.

> Sometimes it seems like we just focus on race too much sometimes. It's better to just go through life and just treat everybody without even worrying about it and stuff. In school when you like focus on how it's unfair for certain races, it's just like we do it a lot and we know it by now and it's, it's kind of hard for us like if you get pushed around in the hall and stuff, but we just focus on the other end of it. We're always focusing on race and I realize it's a huge issue and stuff and it is something important that we have to talk about, but sometimes she says…. Ms. Martinez does talk about how if any minority is put in school and there is a minority then it's gonna be hard for them, but it seems like we focus on Blacks being the minorities too much

because it's kind of hard for us too. It's kind of hard to find a place in this school. Because some people are kind of mean.

Sarah went on to describe her feelings of blame or guilt that she experiences in Ms. Martinez's class:

In her class, I mean sometimes it feels like there's actually well, I don't know how many white kids there are in her class, but it just feels like we're getting the short end of the stick because we're being.... We didn't personally do anything wrong, but sometimes that's what it feels like. Like we did something wrong, and so we're the ones who should pay for it or something. I don't know, but it feels really weird when you're talking about how the blacks have been treated so poorly. It makes me wonder have they the kids in our class actually been treated like that? Because I know I've been treated like that by some people in my school. It's just confusing because I think that we should be treated the same way and talk about how the whites are sometimes discriminated against, too.

In further explanation of her point, Sarah described a time when students in her class complained that Black history month was only one month. She noted, "I actually said that no other races had any month at all. Women are just as important and they've been discriminated against, too, and they don't even have a month, so why should they complain?

While Sarah's comments indicate a resistance to learning about race and racism, we must recognize that Sarah is an early adolescent. She is clearly dealing with the trials of middle school when she describes some people in her school as "mean." Her comments also indicate the racial tension she feels between African American and White students in her school. However, her resistance to discussing issues of race and racism and her desire that "we should be treated the same way," has limited her ability to recognize that racism is not only an historical event, but one that occurs in systemic ways (such as African American history being relegated to the month of February). Instead, her resistance allowed her to settle into her comfortable Whiteness, in which she has the privilege to ignore the social construction of race (McIntosh, 1988), or to even suggest that discrimination against whites should get as much class time as discrimination against people of color in discussions of race and racism. Sarah's color blind ideology is actually resisting a curriculum that forces her to see herself as raced.

DISCUSSION

There are numerous lessons educators can learn from the administrators, teachers and students at City Middle School. Considering the best inter-

ests of our students and school community in both our administrative policies and curricular choices, taking risks to take a stand and confronting
the status quo are only a few lessons we can take from this educational
community. The purpose of this paper, however, is to examine resistance
in an urban school from the perspective of CRT and to further develop
the CRT praxis by applying the oppositional scholarship to examine the
climate in an urban school. By utilizing CRT in the analysis of my ethnographic data, I was able to examine the theme of resistance from the lens
of an oppositional theory, which I believe provided particularly clear and
focused insights into the climate of this urban school.

The resistance present in the climate of City Middle School is complicated, as we saw with Mr. VanHook's resistant compliance, as well as the
students of color resistance to low expectations and the White student's
resistance to a raced curriculum. Solórzano and Yosso (2002) remind us
that, "Critical Race methodology in education recognizes that multiple
layers of oppression and discrimination are met with multiple forms of
resistance" (p. 22). Indeed, there was a climate of resistance within the
school that was exposed when examined from the perspective of an oppositional theory to study race and racism.

REFERENCES

Brown v. Board of Education. (1954). 347 (U.S.) 483.

City Middle School Annual Report. (2003).

City of Waterburg Demographic Statistics. (2002).

Collins, J. L. (1995, April). *Discourse and resistance in urban elementary classrooms: A poststructuralist perspective*. Paper presented at the annual meeting of the American Educational Research Association, San Francisco, CA.

Delgado, R., & Stefancic, J. (2001). *Critical race theory*. New York: New York University Press.

Fordham S., & Ogbu, J. U. (1986). Black students' school success: Coping with the burden of "acting white." *The Urban Review, 18*(3), 176–206.

Frank, A. (1993). *Anne Frank: The diary of a young girl*. New York: Bantom.

Geertz, C. (1973). *The interpretation of cultures*. New York: Basic Books.

Griffin, J. H. (1962). *Black like me*. New York: New American Library.

Haymes, S. N. (1995). *Race, culture and the city: A pedagogy for Black urban struggle*. State University of New York Press.

Jinks, D. P. (1997). Essays in refusal: Pre-theoretical commitments in postmodern anthropology and critical race theory. *Yale Law Journal, 107*, 499–528.

Ladson-Billings, G., & Tate, W. F., IV. (1995). Toward a critical race theory of education. *Teacher College Record, 97*, 47–68.

Ladson-Billings, G. (2005). Reading, writing, and race. In T. McCarty (Ed.), *Language, literacy, and power in schooling* (pp. 133–150). Mahwah, NJ: Erlbaum.

Lynn, M. (1999). Toward a critical race pedagogy: A research note. *Urban Education, 33*, 606–626.

Lynn, M., Yosso, T. J., Solórzano, D., & Parker, L. (2002). Critical race theory and education: Qualitative research in the new millennium. *Qualitative Inquiry, 8*, 3–6.

McIntosh, P. (1988). *White privilege and male privilege: A personal account of coming to see correspondences through work in women's studies* (Working paper, 189). Wellesley, MA: Wellesley College Center for Research on Women.

McMillan, J. H., & Schumacher, S. (2001). *Research in education: A conceptual introduction* (5th. ed.). New York: Addison Wesley Longman.

Masko, A. (2005a)."I think about it all the time": A 12-year-old-girl's internal crisis with racism and its effects on her mental health. *The Urban Review, 37*, 329–350.

Masko, A. (2005b).Urban children's experiences and teacher pedagogical practices: When it's about race, do adults care? *Curriculum and Teaching Dialogue, 7*, 175–194.

Masko, A. (2006, November). *Seditious surroundings: The climate of resistance in urban schools.* Paper presented on a panel titled Creative Insubordination: Novel Perspectives on the Centrality of Resistance in Standardizing Schools and Identities at the Council for Anthropology in Education at the American Anthropological Association annual meeting, San Jose, CA.

Plessy v. Ferguson. (1896). 163 (U.S.) 537.

Smith-Maddox, R., & Solórzano, D. G. (2002). Using critical race theory: Paulo Friere's problem-posing method, and case study research to confront race and racism in education. *Qualitative Inquiry, 8*, 66–83.

Snow-Gerono, J. L., & Franklin, C. A. (2005, October). *Teachers and testing: Mentor teachers share experiences.* Paper presented at the 23rd Annual Conference Northern Rocky Mountain Educational Research Association. Jackson Hole, Wyoming.

Solórzano, D. G., Ceja, M., & Yosso, T. (2000). Critical race theory, racial microaggressions, and campus climate: The experiences of African American college students. *Journal of Negro Education, 69*, 60–73.

Solórzano, D. G., & Yosso, T. J. (2002). Critical race methodology: Counter-storytelling as an analytical framework for education research. *Qualitative Inquiry, 8*, 23–44.

Tate, W. F., IV. (1997). Critical race theory and education: History, theory, and implications. *Review of Research in Education, 22*, 195–247.

CHAPTER 15

GIVING BEYOND CARE

An Exploration of Love in the Classroom

Kevin Cloninger

This critical ethnography explores the effects of care, love, empathy, and trust in a classroom environment. The study is the result of observing and reflecting on twenty classes over an eight week period in a school for gifted children. Two teachers were also interviewed to help gain insight into the impact of love and care in a classroom. Specific principles defining the impact of love in a classroom environment are identified and ramifications discussed.

1993: A MIDWEST CITY

A short 25-minute drive from the city where I live to the suburbs leads me to yet another day at Ignatius Jesuit High School, a small school in a Midwest city. Located in an ever-expanding suburban area, the school serves a predominately white, affluent community. Today, not unlike other days, I arrive a few minutes late to school. There he is, Mr. Bull, waiting with that same contempt in his eyes. "Card!" he barks. I reach for my wallet to take out my demerit card. After five demerits for being late, each additional lateness entitles you to an automatic "JUG," or "Justice Under God," as the Jesuits called it. In these detentions,

Curriculum and Teaching Dialogue
Volume 10, Numbers 1 & 2, 2008, pp. 193–211
Copyright © 2008 by Information Age Publishing
All rights of reproduction in any form reserved.

students must carry out menial tasks such as rewriting the Declaration of Independence or counting from 500 to 0 by subtracting 2 and adding 1, subtracting 2 and adding 1, subtracting 2 and adding 1…. By now, I had done this so many times I was completely numb to it. After giving me yet another late demerit (my 10th), Mr. Bull looks up at me and asks, "Kid, when are you going to learn?" I sigh, shrug it off, and go on my way to homeroom. I sit down just in time for Channel One to begin to play. The school had recently received a TV in each classroom in exchange for subjecting us to Channel One for 10 minutes each morning. If I had not been late, I would have heard the morning prayer along with a few announcements. In any case, after a few minutes the bell rang and we moved on to our next classes. Leaving the classroom, I realize that I have Mr. Kenson's class this morning. A sophomore English teacher, Mr. Kenson is by far my favorite teacher at the school. He is a former Jesuit brother who had left the order, but who nonetheless still teaches at a Jesuit high school; and I am grateful for it.

After having been in Mr. Kenson's class for several weeks I had decided to take up poetry writing. Mr. Kenson had spent a great deal of energy teaching us how to write a five-paragraph essay with a thesis statement. I had no difficulties with this, but I was more fascinated by ideas and poetry. Today, after situating myself strategically in the back of the classroom, I open my small spiral notebook and call on the muses. The bell rings and Mr. Kenson launches into a class discussion on The Catcher in the Rye. Somewhere in between discussing Holden's preoccupation with "phonies" and Mr. Antolini's potentially homosexual gestures, the class began to grow tense. Feeling a bit uneasy, I stop writing my poetry. The next thing I know, we enter into a discussion of racism in our school. The student body in this predominantly white school is fairly racist. I am impressed with the way Mr. Kenson tries to connect the readings to things he knew were prominent in our lives. "Do you think racism is a positive or negative thing?" Mr. Kenson asks. Most of the students are either tuning him out or sitting there motionless. I am so unpopular with the students in this class that I try not to speak much. Today, however, I raise my trembling hand: "I think it is wrong to be racist." Not the most popular person in the room, many skeptical eyes turn and look in my direction. A little flicker in Mr. Kenson's eyes is enough to make the risk I had taken worthwhile. "Why do you think it is wrong, Kevin?" I respond, "Black people aren't any different from anyone else; they are human beings like the rest of us," with all of the eloquence of a shy 16-year-old, I continue to say, "I think that people just live out here in the suburbs too long and never get to know anyone who is Black." "Anyone else want to say something?" Mr. Kenson asks. The bell rings again. "Saved by the bell," someone said to my left. I stand up, look Mr. Kenson in the eyes, and go on my way.

INTRODUCTION

It has been close to 14 years since this incident in Mr. Kenson's class, but I still remember it as clear as day. That was the day I made a real and long-lasting connection with my sophomore English teacher. I do not know whether it was his courage, his willingness to try to understand our lives, or something else that made me take a social risk and try to help him that day in class. Recently I asked Mr. Kenson what he felt he was doing in his sophomore classes. He told me:

> Part of it is coming from my personal experiences going through high school. One of the joys that I have, in one sense, is teaching sophomores, because in my high school experience I don't remember a damn thing about my sophomore year. I don't know why; there could be all sorts of reasons as to why and I don't want them to have the same kind of experience.... [It is interesting that with you here] some of these guys have not talked like this in a long time. It is not to say, well ... [pauses briefly] It is more to say that students feel that they are being noticed and given attention. That is what sophomores need—all students need. (Interview, May 6, 2005)

Indeed, Mr. Kenson's attention was quite important to me. More importantly, Mr. Kenson made real efforts to create an environment that felt nurturing and loving; it was a place where you could think for yourself. I asked one of his students about his teaching:

Does Mr. Kenson Care About You?

Student: Yeah. I think he has the outside, he wants to kind of appear he doesn't care, but he really does. Like, he wants you to do well in school.

How Does He Show It?

Student: The way he, when we have to turn in papers we have to turn it in through a Web site to make sure we don't plagiarize and that is just to benefit us, really, because he wants us to write our own work. I think his whole class is based on free thinking and thinking for yourself. That is the first thing he taught, the first week of school, is to think for yourself and I think that is how he cares. He is probably the first person in this school who told me to start thinking for myself. (Student interview, May 6, 2005)

What is clear, despite his reserved manner and his slight reluctance to alienate the students by being too open in an all-boys school, Mr. Kenson has certainly had an impact on many students.

RATIONALE AND RESEARCH QUESTIONS

Mr. Kenson's teaching style and his interactions with his students raise important questions for teachers everywhere. What role does love have in the classroom? What role does a teacher's openness with students have in the classroom? These are the questions that have guided this ethnography. This article will explore how the relation between the internal, psychological aspects of the teacher and those of the students affect the learning environment and the culture of a classroom. The major research questions center on an investigation of the effects of love, empathy, care, and trust in a classroom environment. Said differently, how does the teacher's internal state affect the culture in the classroom? What would a culture in the classroom look like if the teacher focused on loving students?

The obvious and recurrent criticism regarding the role of love and empathy in the classroom is that such ideas are "touchy-feely," "soft," or "overly-sensitive." Indeed the criticism is not only misguided but naïve, for it is precisely such an approach that is missing from so many learning environments across the country. A rich philosophical and social legacy, particularly visible in the work of Plato, Gandhi, and Martin Luther King Jr., demonstrate how transformative and powerful this "soft" approach can be. When teachers have the courage to open themselves and show their students love, they help create an ambience of care, trust, empathy, and mutual assistance. Such an atmosphere serves to foster learning and to help students develop their character.

METHODOLOGY

This qualitative study explores facets of love in the classroom. In addition to studying Mr. Kenson and reflecting on my experiences in high school with him, I have chosen to study my own classroom experiences, where I attempted to foster a loving environment. At the time of the study, I was teaching three math classes, and three philosophy elective classes, with children ages 10 to 15. In order to counter some of my own biases as a teacher, I interviewed a colleague with whom I shared the classroom for the year. Mary, the teacher colleague, observed the vast majority of our classes. I have also reflected on my experiences as a student in a loving environment. The memories I have of Mr. Kenson's class still inform many aspects of my teaching. Thus, in addition to reflecting on those experiences, I decided to visit his classroom, where he still teaches sophomore English.

This study is the result of observations and reflections made on 20 classes that I taught at a school for gifted children. The study took place over an 8-week period. I taped every class so that I could transcribe the events. After each class, I recorded in my field log reflections on what had occurred. I also interviewed my old teacher, four of his current students, and Mary, the teacher who had observed my classes for a year. Based on these interviews, my reflections from the entire year (in particular that 8-week period), and my own educational experiences, I have tried to elucidate some of the mechanisms and principles of a loving environment in the classroom.

A BRIEF HISTORY OF LOVE IN EDUCATION

I would develop in the child his hands, his brain and his soul. The hands have almost atrophied. The soul has been altogether ignored.

—(Gandhi, 1972, p. 144)

The ancient Greeks distinguished between three forms of love: *eros, philia,* and *agape.* Plato's *Symposium* discusses *eros,* or desirous love, at length. Contrary to its use in common speech, Platonic love is much more than the abstinence from sex. Plato believed *eros* to be the contemplation of beauty in and of itself. *Philia,* on the other hand, refers to the love shared between friends. People often say, "I like my friends," referring to this type of amicable love. *Agape* refers to a state of unconditional love, like that of a mother for a child or the love of a higher power. Gandhi and Martin Luther King Jr. used *agape* to transform themselves, their communities, and entire political systems. Gandhian nonviolence sought to reconcile differences and injustice through truth and love (Gandhi, 1999). This critical ethnography explores the role of *agape* in schools.

The notion of love and education has been discussed in the literature for years (Goldstein, 1998; Liston, 2000; Liston & Garrison; 2004, McCall, 1989; Noddings, 1992). This literature illustrates the fact that schools frequently disparage talk of love or regard the relationship between a teacher and a student as second to the "serious" work of teaching subject matter. Nel Noddings (1992), speaking not of "love" per se, challenged teachers to "care" in schools arguing that teachers must be more like parents trying to raise a huge "heterogeneous" family. Noddings imagined an entire restructuring of schools to be centers of care that would not only care for students, but model the practices of caring for self, for animals and the environment, for each other, and for subject matter. Since that time, researchers have explored the relevance of "care theory" at many levels of educational practice and theory (Noddings, 2005).

The reader may be asking herself why I have chosen to use the term "love" instead of "care" in this paper. Practically speaking, why use a new term when there is already so much scholarship regarding care? First, I am trying to build on the foundation of "care theory" by looking to principles of Gandhian nonviolence (Gandhi, 1999). Very little has been written on the relevance of nonviolence for curriculum theory and this article attempts to fill that lacuna. Second, there are important differences in the terms that merit scholarly attention. Consider the phrase, "I care for you" and contrast it with the phrase, "I love you." An obvious difference is that of degree; love is fuller or more intense than care. Also, one could question the quality conveyed by both words. Care is sometimes used to connote interest and other times kindness, attention, or compassion (Noddings, 1992). To love something suggests a deeper interest, attention, or compassion; it connotes a stronger desire for connection, communion, and unity.

Other authors have chosen to use the term "love" instead of "care" when discussing classroom teaching. Liston (2000) speaks of the various forms in which love may manifest itself in the classroom. He identifies, "the love of learning" and "the love of inquiry." In a certain sense, teaching is a sharing of love of subject matter, inquiry, and learning with our students. Teaching thus affords us many ways of sharing various forms of love with students. Liston and Garrison (2004) make similar demands to expand a loving role in the classroom, in teacher education, and in dealing with despairing and distraught veteran teachers. Jane Roland Martin (2004) argues that we must acknowledge and rectify the "love gap in educational text." She argues that we have not only forgotten to discuss love in the literature, but we neglect the exploration of love in classroom environments at a time when love is desperately needed.

These authors have addressed the need to explore love and education, but explicitly state that they have only begun to do so. Great theologians, philosophers, scientists, and politicians, for example Plato, Emerson, Gandhi, and Martin Luther King Jr., indicate love to be a key ingredient in the search for happiness, well-being, and nonviolence. In America, the spirit of nonviolence was embodied most powerfully in the life and work of Dr. Martin Luther King, Jr. King was a great admirer of Gandhi and employed his method of active nonviolence, or "*satyagraha*," which is variably translated as "love-force," "soul-force," or "truth-force." King used *satyagraha* to fight his battles during the civil rights movement. People would frequently ask him how it is one could love someone who oppresses him. He would respond simply by saying, "It would be nonsense to urge men to love their oppressors in an affectionate sense. When I refer to love at this point I mean understanding good will" (King, 1991, p. 19). Of the highest form of love, he said,

> *Agape* means understanding, redeeming good will for all men. It is an overflowing love which is purely spontaneous, unmotivated, groundless, and creative.... *Agape* is not a weak, passive love. It is love in action. *Agape* is love seeking to preserve and create community. It is insistence on community

even when one seeks to break it.... In the final analysis, *agape* means a recognition of the fact that all life is interrelated. All humanity is involved in a single process, and all men are brothers. (King, 1991, pp. 19–20)

Agape, this deepest form of love, is the key to the transformation of both the oppressors and the oppressed. King demonstrates how *agape* seeks to build and preserve community and hence culture.

Schools have largely overlooked the relevance of nonviolence in the education of children. Gandhi (1999) said:

Passive Resistance is the noblest and the best education. It should come, not after the ordinary education in letters of children, but it should precede it. It will not be denied that a child before it begins to write its alphabet and to gain worldly knowledge, should know what the soul is, what truth is, what love is, what powers are latent in the soul. It should be an essential of real education that a child should learn that in the struggle of life, it can easily conquer hate by love, untruth by truth, violence by self-suffering. (p. 303)

Gandhi highlighted the importance of helping children to understand love, truth, and nonviolence. He argued that it was more important than their understanding of reading and writing because it would allow them to live happier lives, and to work for social justice and freedom.

This study focuses particularly on what interest love, in the form of *agape*, has in education. Although there are certainly many ways in which *eros* and *philia* are present in education, they have less potential for helping teachers in their daily practice because of their inherent limitations. What is unfortunate is that teachers, while *unconsciously* aware to some degree, are not consciously aware of the power of loving relationships in the classroom. Rarely do teachers realize the effect of such acts of love. Furthermore, the current dialogue in education seems to ignore any aspect of this relationship in teaching and learning environments. Last, the work that has been accomplished in the field has remained theoretical for the most part. In contrast, this study seeks to understand the practical effects of love on the culture of the classroom. The ethnographic approach also allows us to hear student "voices" regarding the role of love in the classroom.

FINDINGS

In this critical ethnography I point out that love's influence in the classroom is both subtle and pervasive. Its influence is felt primarily in terms of the relationships between teacher and student and among students. I will return to this point later when I can develop it more fully, but it is essential to bear this fact in mind as the ethnography proceeds. A classroom is not a distinct culture per se; rather, it is comprised of many sub-cultures. Nonetheless, a classroom culture does have distinct tendencies. For example, a classroom culture demonstrates patterns of behavior, specific acts of speech and language, and shared values and ideals. This article examines each these areas and discuss observations made during this ethnography. Table 15.1 represents a summary of the findings.

The Language of the Classroom

The language used in the classroom to foster a loving environment is first and foremost the language of the students. Here we can take lessons from the late Dr. Martin Luther King Jr., the eminent social scientist, preacher, and activist, who would always speak in the language of those with whom he was speaking. This was one way in which King would express his respect, understanding, and love for those he wished to persuade or lead (Phillips, 2000). This is a subtle aspect of a loving relationship, of course, but it is still an essential element. In the classroom, speaking in the language of the students, or at the very least taking the time to listen carefully to their language is one manner in which a teacher and students convey love. For example, in the fourth and fifth grade philosophy classes that I teach, after reflecting on my field notes, I noticed

Table 15.1.   Principles of a Culture of Love in the Classroom

The language used in a culture of love in a classroom is first and foremost the language of the students.
• Putting oneself in the mind and experiences of the students is essential to demonstrating care.
To cultivate a culture of love in a classroom, one must create a safe place, a safe environment, where students feel that they are both listened to and listening to others.
• In this environment, all students feel that they can speak freely and that what they will say is accepted.
Fostering a culture of love has subtle effects that take place over a long period of time.
• Love's influence in the classroom is both subtle and pervasive.
Love shared between and among students and teachers creates an environment that transforms the meaning and context of all knowledge shared in the classroom.
• The interactions—particularly loving interactions—between class members create a sociocognitive context in which knowledge is imbued with different shades of understanding.
The inner state of the teacher and the students sets a tone for what types of ideas and feelings the students will share or elucidate.
• Teachers frequently overlook the impact their own ideas and feelings have on students.

that in order to understand the ideas and opinions of the students I had to understand the words and the language they used to describe their theories. In one instance, I presented some of the ideas of Miletian and Eleatic philosophers to the students. The Miletian and Eleatic philosophers, such as Heraclitus and Paramenides, were among the first to ask what the world was made of. Much to my surprise, the students moved away from this subject in order to discuss, of all things, the nature of perception—a topic far more complex. One little girl, Suzie, decided that no human being could truly understand the world as it really is and that we had no way of perceiving reality writ large. She decided that the mind and the brain must have something that prevents them from perceiving things in and of themselves and called it the Miletus (she had taken the name of the town where the Miletian philosophers were from and given it a new definition). Of course, it took us all a few minutes to understand what she meant. With the utter certitude of her usual stateswoman-like manner, Suzie said,

> Um, the Miletus does not allow us to understand the world. It is only in dreams that we can see things. The dreams tell us how things are. It is only through dreams that we understand the world and ourselves. Miletus does not allow us to know.

> *What do you mean by Miletus?*

> Suzie: It is what does not allow our brains to understand the world, only our dreams can.

> *So, we have something called a Miletus that blocks us from seeing the world as it is?*

> Suzie: Yes, yes, the Miletus does not allow us to see the world. Our dreams are the way we can understand things. That is why we sleep. (Class recording, April 18, 2005)

After going back and forth like this for some time, the class and I started to understand what she had done. She had taken the word and used it to explain something she had understood. The empathy and ability to listen that we find in this example is an essential feature of a classroom culture impacted by love. By engaging in this practice, a language can develop between teachers and students that conveys meanings that students and teachers have discovered together. From this point forward in the class, all of us began to use "Miletus" to express this aspect of the brain or mind that prevents us from seeing the world as it really is. Indeed, putting oneself in the mind and experiences of the students is extremely important if the teacher wishes to express love and care for his or her students.

To take a different example of the principle, let us consider another event that transpired in class. Suzie commented that she did not believe in good and evil:

> I don't believe that, um, that there is evil. I don't think there is anything called evil because what about the other people.... There is no such thing as evil, 'cause good people, because everyone has good in them. Sometimes they do it for the wrong reason. Now we can do something like that [like war] and sometimes they do it for the wrong reason. Now we can never say, let's say, Mark always does good and Ralph never does good. We can never say that, everyone does good somethings in their life [added for clarity]. (Class recording, May 2, 2005)

I said to myself, "Well this is unusual, I wonder what she means?" The question I had asked was, "Do you believe that there are good people and that there are evil people?" This was in the context of a discussion on war. We had discussed Hitler and Gandhi and we were going deeper into notions of Good and Evil. With more time, patience, and understanding I came to understand that what she really meant was that no person could be either truly good or truly evil, rather people are both. Since all people have aspects of good and evil within them, she said to herself, there is no way such a duality exists. There can only be goodness. In Suzie's words, "I don't believe in evil." In my field notes that week I wrote, "If I didn't take the time to care for them and understand their perspectives I would have missed this entirely."

Patterns of Behavior and Relationships

A number of facets could be examined in both examples given above. Beyond the simple fact of the shared language and speech, there is a set of relationships and behaviors that communicate love among all members of the class. There are at least two different things at work here: being open-minded and being empathetic. David Hansen's (2001) work in this area expresses this well:

> In a previous chapter, I described a teacher's moral sensibility as a disposition of mind and feeling centered around attentiveness to students and their learning. That notion fused intellectual, emotional, and moral aspects of practice. This fusion suggests that open-mindedness yields fruitful human conduct when allied with open-heartedness. Open-heartedness is neither sentimental nor Pollyannaish. Where open-mindedness signals intellectual receptivity, open-heartedness emphasizes emotional receptivity. Both qualities augment human connection and understanding, because

intellectual receptivity may depend upon emotional openness, and vice versa. (p. 52)

Indeed, to create a culture of love, it is necessary to cultivate a classroom climate where not only the teacher is open in both these ways, but also the students. During the interview with my fellow teacher, Mary, I had asked for her impressions of my classes thus far and she responded in the following manner:

It is a safe place for them to discuss things that they have no other place to discuss and also to see whether the people think, you know... A lot of those kids think, think that maybe what they are feeling or worrying about is only their own. So it is comforting to know that other children have the same thoughts, the same worries as they do. (Interview, April 28, 2005)

A little bit later in the interview she continued this same train of thought:

Mary: I think they are more aware in this environment. They are more aware of other people's feelings and other people's thoughts and they are learning to listen which is very important.

Can you say more about that?

Mary: This is so huge because society is in such a hurry these days that children do not have an opportunity to listen and they do not learn that from parents because they don't have the time to listen to them. So this is one big lesson in this class is that they have to listen and if they want other people to listen to them, and they have a lot to say on a subject, in order to have that opportunity they also need to learn to listen to somebody else, which I think is great. (Interview, April 28, 2005)

Thus, to cultivate a culture of love in a classroom, one must create a safe place, a safe environment, where students feel that they are both listened to and listening to others. In this environment, all students feel that they can speak freely and that what they will say will be accepted. Far too often our classrooms quash student participation and alienate students because of a lack of attentiveness, open-mindedness, and "open-heartedness."

In addition to helping students develop empathy, tolerance and understanding, such environments can lead to changes in the character of students. In some sense, when one listens to another deeply over long periods of time we come to understand their thought processes and their innermost feelings. This provides profound opportunities to impart much more than basic information to students in a classroom. That is, if a teacher is willing to extend his or herself in this way. In one particular instance, a child in one of my classes, Jim, was struggling in mathematics because he regarded himself in such low esteem. I explained this to both him and his mother at a parent-teacher conference. Jim was touched that I had taken the time to understand him in this way; that I could help him and his mother understand the situation better. In addition, he could see that I accepted him as he was. At one point in our conversation, I told him that he needed to ease up on himself and allow himself to make mistakes without beating himself up. I reached over and said, "Look Jim, it could be worse," an expression he now regularly uses. Just last week he did poorly on a test in one of his classes. He was telling me about it, laughing with a gigantic grin on his face: "It could be worse." And every time he catches me getting the least bit pessimistic, he'll look at me and say, "It could be worse, Kevin." A culture of love creates learning environments that feel safe and accepting. In such environments, teaching moves beyond the narrow confines measured by standardized testing. They can help both teachers and student learn about themselves and what makes them happy.

Unrecognized Aspects of Classroom Relationships

I mentioned previously that for such loving interactions to take place a teacher must be willing to open herself to her students: this is of course only part of the story. These observations beg many questions. For example, what traits are likely to be present in such teachers? Can such traits be learned or are they innate faculties of the teacher? How are these traits initiated, cultivated, and supported in teachers? To begin to address these questions, it is essential to understand one principle: the teacher's inner state—his or her ideas, feelings, dislikes, judgments, and so forth—sets a tone in the classroom for what types of ideas and feelings the students will share or elucidate. Students feel the state of the teacher and this, in turn, impacts the students at multiple levels, such as their willingness to participate, their psychological state, even their motivation. In my own experiments working with children in schools, I have found that this dimension of the classroom environment is essential to teaching. This principle is not obvious, so let me demonstrate it though an example. In the interview with Mary, she explained this idea in some depth:

I think everybody, every teacher influences the environment of the class. If you are focused, if you are calm, they will feel that and that will influence the others. I have noticed that even when they are very excited that you are so calm in addressing them or when you have to stop them because they need to give somebody else a chance or because they need to stop and think before they talk, you do that in such a calm way that it definitely sets the tone even when they are very excited about an idea. (Interview, April 28, 2005)

Indeed, whether he or she is aware of it, the teacher's inner state influences the learning environment in the classroom. Even if educators do not pay particular attention to this aspect of their teaching it can still influence the tone and tenor of the class. This is another dimension of the "implicit curriculum" pointed out by Eisner (1994). The inner state of the teacher is not explicitly declared, but it does guide and direct learning.

In light of this principle, it is important to understand that teachers do not necessarily need to be taught how to love their students. Every person has an intuitive understanding of love. It is like trying to teach someone how to be calm; we all have some understanding of it even if we do not express it. Likewise, it is not that teachers do not know how to love (in the form of *agape*), but that they are not asked to relate with their students in this manner and are unaware of the importance of it (at least consciously speaking). When a teacher expresses this internal state, he or she is in a position to help elicit from the students an awareness of the love within them. The internal aspects of both teacher and student interact to create a learning environment, and when the teacher develops love and calm within him or herself, he or she can work to help lead students toward a similar inner state.

However, while teachers do have an intuitive understanding of the power of this approach, frequently they do not authorize it to themselves. They feel that it is not an appropriate role for a teacher. Thus, in terms of initiation, cultivation, and support, the key to helping teachers is simply to make them aware of this phenomenon, thereby empowering them and allowing them to work toward intentionally developing a culture of love.

Shared Values and Ideals

Fostering a culture of love has subtle effects that take place over a long period of time. A desire to see quick and fast results immediately dismisses the conditions necessary for establishing a culture of love. As was the case with helping Jim work on a self-accepting attitude, it may take weeks to create an atmosphere of love and understanding in a classroom. In one class I taught to a diverse group of middle-school students (fifth to eighth grade), this work paid dividends in an unexpected way. This class took place about 3 weeks before school recessed for the summer. The subject of the class was the philosophy of religion. I had just spent an exhausting class period trying in vain to get students to finish a project. I walked into the philosophy class to find the students completely self-absorbed and distracted. Rather than just accepting their behavior and trying to move ahead with the subject matter, I took the opportunity to point out their self-absorption in the context of our discussions in the philosophy of religion and growth in self-awareness. Almost impulsively, I told them that they were all being very selfish and that there was simply no way we could conduct the class without them changing their attitudes a bit. What follows is an excerpt from my field notes immediately following the class. Again, please bear in mind that this conversation took place in the context of a philosophy of religion class (the religious references relate to our discussion of Judaism and Christianity):

I hadn't realized that I was unintentionally laying the guilt on pretty thick. However, after stepping off my soapbox I was amazed to see that everyone had become very quiet. Lisa raised her hand and said, "I am sorry Kevin for disturbing your class." The tone and climate of the class immediately shifted to a more calm and introspective one. Elise, serious this time, began to say, "Repent for your sins for you may die tomorrow." "Yes," I responded, "but how many of us actually live that way? How many people actually think about the fact that tomorrow may be their last?" I was astonished when 5 of my 9 students raised their hands. Lisa said, "every night I think about what will happen when I die." "Me too," the other four agreed. Dumbfounded, I decided to take advantage of this teachable moment as the students had tapped into what I consider to be one of the most essential aspects of the religious experience. Jill continued, "I spend hours each night trying to understand what I'm all about exactly, if you know what I mean. I just write and write and try to figure out what I really care about and what makes things meaningful. I worry about my friends and what they think of me." Obviously moved by the candor of their statements, the rest of us just sat back and thought about the experience she was sharing. "You see about a month ago, Alex and Patrick started coming to me for advice about their life and I am still not sure what I have to offer them."

What had begun as the worse class of the year was now transforming itself into the best of my career. At that moment, Lisa added a statement in sympathy with Jill's honesty, "Yeah, me too. I write a lot. Sometimes when I look at what I have written, I find myself saying that I am depressed or crazy. I talk a lot about what my friends think and how good they are and what they must think about me. I am so hard on myself and I think my friends are so much better than I am. They won't miss me when I am gone." Jill leans over puts her hand on Lisa's leg and says, "No Lisa, you are great. You are wonderful and I would miss you sooooo much. Sooooooooooooooooooooo much…. You're great." Kerry chimes in after Jill stops, "You see people put so much pressure on you because you are gifted. I can't wait until I get to Harvard or wherever I am going and I fail so that they see that I am not as special as they think. I will do terrible. Then they will see that I am not perfect and that I am not as special as they think."

The others in the class feel astonished by the statement of this fifth grader and try to comfort her. Feeling that this could turn into a group therapy session I tried to bring the conversation back to the Philosophy of Religion, "You guys, I am very surprised with the turn that this class has taken." They all nodded in agreement. The room had palpably changed. "Do you see what happened when I spent the time to make you think about your thoughts and your actions? The whole conversation shifted in this way. Self-awareness is the essence of the philosophy of religion. Why am I here? What do I have to live for? What will happen when I die? The French philosopher Montaigne once said, 'Philosophy is learning how to die.' Much to my surprise we have stumbled over this profound statement."

Jill said, "Exactly, when I write my thoughts I have to figure out how to understand myself and my life. Sometimes, I think I have problems understanding that." The other students nodded in acknowledgement. "I have to reread my writing sometimes to remind myself of the thoughts I was having and to remember what I had said." Very excited by her statement I added, "Exactly, what philosophers frequently point out to us is that we are not perfect, any of us. We need to accept this fact and realize that we will most likely find ourselves lost on our way in life and that it is O.K. We need to bring ourselves back to the essential questions and not get caught up in the short sightedness of simple pleasures." Jill responded, "Most people get caught up in their day and almost distract themselves from life. They are not at all happy and they just don't want to deal with it. Happiness is something else isn't it?" (Field notes, May 3, 2005)

The class had moved from a very miseducative environment to one that was deeply in touch with the personal lives and feelings of the students in the class. In many ways, the success of this class would never have been possible without the initial work of cultivating a culture of love with those students. Because we had developed an environment that fostered loving concern for all members of the class, the students were able to comfort one another, support one another, and move from their self-absorbed state to one of calm introspection.

As teachers we are often taught to ensure that anytime the class moves off the topic being discussed we should find the quickest possible way to bring them back to the subject matter. I certainly could have employed such an approach in this class, but I would not have helped the students become more self-aware. I would have taught them that in certain ways I was indifferent to their feelings and their lives. Furthermore, had I not directly addressed their selfishness I would have indirectly sanctioned it. The key point for me as an instructor was to realize that over the course of 8 weeks, we had entered into a tacit agreement to respect one another, to listen to one another, to show care for one another, and to leave room for one another. If I had neglected to make them aware of their break with our tacit agreement, and just proceeded with the lesson, I would never have tapped into this rich and deep reservoir of self-awareness in the students.

One might ask whether this type of relationship with students is too intimate, and whether it transgresses certain boundaries that should exist between teacher and student(s). In other words, is this culture of love in a classroom risky? Indeed it may be, but adopting a strictly impersonal relationship with one's students is far riskier. Not a week goes by without a violent incident in one of our schools. Due to a lack of loving interactions in their lives, many children develop cases of depression, sometimes even to the extent of becoming suicidal, and we cannot grant teachers immunity from any responsibility. Ignoring the personal and loving dimensions of teaching excludes incredibly important aspects of a child's education. Students, like everyone, are independent agents and thus we cannot directly blame teachers for their students' progress; however, the classroom is a vital environment for children, and the teacher *does* control that environment, thereby wielding an indirect, though powerful, influence over students' development. With increased levels of violence and depression among our children (Hurst, 2005), it is evident that we must find new approaches to educating them; implementing a culture of love in the classroom may appear risky only in the sense that it is not mainstream, we must rise above these trepidations, because our children are suffering from this existential void.

I was curious to see what the students had felt they learned in the eight-week class described in the previous paragraph. Jaimee, a student who has a gift of expressing her thoughts and ideas responded in the following manner:

> I learned a lot about my self and who we are, and how we define our self like the one day we had the huge discussion about Jill keeping a notebook and keeping awake at night about death. (Class recording, May 12, 2005)

Teaching a class like this involves risks, but if students leave having gained experiences like this one, the risk is worthwhile.

Love Creates a Sociocognitive Context

Another interesting aspect in a culture of love is that love shared among teachers and students creates an environment that transforms the meaning and context of all knowledge shared in the classroom. That is, while you may cover the same material in two different classrooms, loving and caring interactions between teachers and students create a sociocognitive context in which knowledge is imbued with different shades of understanding. Take, for example, the vignette just discussed. What started off as a reprimand informed our discussion of the class's subject matter, which included discourse on self-awareness and self-actualization. When the students realized that the tacit agreement we had entered into during the class required them to be less self-absorbed, they made a connection between that and "learning how to die." They were led to ask themselves, "What if I die tomorrow and I had been as selfish as I was in this class?"

The same would be true, for example, if we had a class on injustice in political systems. Criticism of an unjust political system would be informed by the love felt by all in the classroom. If there is a substantial, meaningful relationship between teachers and students, violence will appear far more detrimental than if a teacher is more domineering or autocratic. The message is clear: the relationships that exist among all members of a class powerfully impact the manner of education, and thus the actualization of loving relationships teaches lessons as, if not more, important than the focus of curricula. There are obvious parallels between this conclusion and the work done on creating communities in classroom—such as Dewey's notion of creating a democratic model for later life in the classroom—though the emphasis in a learning community like the one I tried to create in my own classroom is one of love and understanding.

FINAL THOUGHTS

There are obvious parallels between the culture of love described in this paper and Noddings's (1992) work on caring. While Noddings's desire to reinvent the schools by transforming them into centers of caring is appealing on a number of levels, the sort of love described in this paper expands on the notion of care by broadening it and deepening it. Love motivates one to care for another; without this faculty, care would be an empty vessel, a messageless bottle drifting at sea. When a teacher opens up and cares for a student, he conveys a message of love. Indeed, this message transcends issues of subject-matter and curriculum by attending to the spiritual aspects of the child. In this sense, whether it is expressed in centers of care or in schools dominated by the liberal arts curriculum, love addresses the deepest aspects of the human being. We can teach lessons, have students memorize facts, study challenging and rigorous curriculum and still attend to this dimension of the classroom. One could teach a lesson on evolution or the civil war, while at the same time teaching about love. It is precisely the universality of its message that leads all cultures and peoples to search for love. This universality is important for it allows one to teach simultaneously about subject matter and teach in an implicit or indirect way about love. In other words, we can educate both the heart and the mind.

It has been interesting to reflect on how my own teaching and the culture I have attempted to cultivate in my classroom is similar to that of Mr. Kenson. In many ways, I have more explicitly focused on this dimension of teaching than Mr. Kenson had. However, I find Mr. Kenson's reluctance to be more explicitly open with the students interesting. It is clear that his students feel he cares for them, yet he does not overtly declare his love. Mr. Kenson's reservation does not prevent him from communicating to his students that he loves and cares for them. As Mr. Kenson himself expressed, it is very important for students, particularly young boys, to see adult men who are open in this way; otherwise, we merely propagate a culture of intolerance and repression. These observations of Mr. Kenson confirm for me that many teachers do foster environments of love in their classroom, yet they do so somewhat unintentionally. They are guided by their care and concern for the students, without recognizing it as a dimension of the education they are providing them.

Fostering a culture of love demands courage and dedication. It takes tremendous strength to be "soft" in this way. Gandhi and Martin Luther King Jr. encouraged us to love our enemies. Gandhi asked us not to be attracted to (*eros*) or like our enemy (*philia*), but to love them (*agape*)—to see past their problems and love them as another human being in a spirit of brotherhood. Gandhi spoke frequently on this topic:

> I have found that life persists in the midst of destruction and therefore there must be a higher law than that of destruction. Only under that law would a well-ordered society be intelligible and life worth living. And if that is the law of life, we have to work it out in daily life. Whenever there are wars, wherever you are confronted with an opponent, conquer him with love. In this crude manner I have worked it out in my life. That does not mean that all my difficulties are solved. Only I have found that this law of love has answered as the law of destruction has never done (Gandhi, 1972, p. 78)

In many ways, the principles of non-violence and nonviolent social resistance have many things to teach us as educators, including the importance of love in enacting meaningful change in people and communities. Oftentimes such ideas are characterized as idealistic, out of touch, or too passive or submissive. Earlier on in this paper I had quoted Martin Luther King Jr. (1991) who responded to this criticism:

> *Agape* is not a weak, passive love. It is love in action. *Agape* is love seeking to preserve and create community. It is insistence on community even when one seeks to break it…. In the final analysis, *agape* means a recognition of the fact that all life is interrelated. All humanity is involved in a single process, and all men are brothers. (pp. 19–20)

It is this type of active love that is needed to cultivate a culture of love in a classroom. It is also an essential part of helping our schools to achieve many of its highest ideals. If we really want our schools to encourage ideals like democratic citizenship, multicultural understanding, as well as compassion and nonviolence, it is essential that we focus more intentionally on this dimension of love in the classroom. The principles of a culture of love in a classroom identified in this critical ethnography will hopefully give teachers and administrators some guidance in creating such environments, but ultimately, teachers and administrators need to have the courage to live in this way. If we seek to foster a culture of love in a classroom, teachers must follow the advice left to us in Gandhi's oft-quoted statement, "We must be the change we wish to see in the world."

REFERENCES

Eisner, E. (1994). *The educational imagination: On the design and evaluation of school programs* (3rd ed). New York: Macmillan.

Gandhi, M. K. (1972). *All men are brothers: Life & thoughts of Mahatma Gandhi as told in his own words* (K. Kripalani, Ed.). New York: World Without War Pub, UNESCO.

Gandhi, M. K. (1999). *The essential writings of Mahatma Gandhi* (R. Iyer, Ed.). New York: Oxford University Press.

Goldstein, L. (1998). Teacherly love: Intimacy, commitment, and passion in the classroom life. *Journal of Educational Thought, 32,* 257–272.

Hansen, D. T. (2001). *Exploring the moral heart of teaching: Toward a teacher's creed.* New York: Teachers College Press.

Hurst, M. D. (2005). Mental-health disorders gain foothold during teenage years. *Education Week, 24*(41), 12.

King, M. L., Jr. (1991). *A testament of hope: The essential writings and speeches of Martin Luther King, Jr.* (J. M. Washington, Ed.) New York: Harper Collings.

Liston, D, (2000). Love and despair in teaching. *Educational Theory, 50,* 81–102.

Liston, D., & Garrison, J. (2004). *Teaching, learning, and loving: Reclaiming passion in educational practice.* New York: RoutledgeFalmer.

McCall, A. (1989). Care and nurturance in teaching: A case study. *Journal of Teacher Education, 40,* 39–44.

Noddings, N. (1992). *The challenge to care in schools.* New York: Teachers College Press.

Noddings, N. (2005). Care and moral education. In H. Shapiro, P. Svi, & E. David (Eds.), *Critical social issues in American education: Democracy and meaning in a globalizing world* (3rd ed. pp. 297–308). Mahwah, NJ: Erlbaum.

Phillips, D. (2000). *Martin Luther King: On leadership.* Lebanon, IN: Time Warner Business Books.

CHAPTER 16

ENACTED CURRICULUM AND THE SEARCH FOR IDENTITY

Angst and the Cuban Search for Meaning after the Cuban Revolution

David Callejo-Perez

This article examines angst as a defining matter for the ever changing Cuban experience both on the island and abroad after 1959. The article includes an examination of angst from its infancy to today, using the words and stories of writers who attempt to assign meaning to being Cuban through their work. There is hope that within the schooling and its curriculum there are still gray spaces where individuals can address the concepts of social justice and equality. We can educate learners through the use of critical narrative. Additionally, by referencing traditional authors in comparison to Cuban authors, teachers and curriculum developers might be able to incorporate Cuban literature to illustrate required themes while appealing to the multiple identity issues of diverse minority students.

Curriculum and Teaching Dialogue
Volume 10, Numbers 1 & 2, 2008, pp. 213–231

INTRODUCTION

On a cold Monday night in Beatrice, Nebraska, I discovered my Cuban-ness. At a high school auditorium, I heard "Dos Gardenias," played by *Valle Son*, a *Son* group from Pinar del Rio wearing Gap clothing and touring in the United States (Carillo, 1948/2000). The band and I spent several days speaking about identity; Miami, the United States, and of course, Cuba. We spoke of my family on the island, my mother's stay in political prison, and how cold and windy Nebraska was. What we experienced was a conversation about living similar/parallel pasts (although we never met); similar ethnic realities, and uncertain futures which, as Cubans, we share. What I experienced was the terse existence of angst within a culture. Angst dominates Cuban culture. In this article, I argue that creativity in Cuban literature and poetry is driven by the angst of separation and the attempt by two nations to create a singular cultural hegemony by examining the vital role of angst in literature created by the post-1959 separation and the embargo that caused an expression driven by perception and language as forces of creation. This discussion is important because addressing our racial identity in the curriculum requires individualizing it within the school curriculum through the arts and literature that define our cultural identity (Cubanness). Additionally, by referencing traditional authors in comparison to Cuban authors, teachers, and curriculum developers might be able to incorporate Cuban literature to illustrate required course themes while appealing to identity issues for their minority students.

Identity and Curriculum for Schools

Society, especially in the United States is concerned with place and past, especially regional and racial identities as witnessed by the rise of genealogy searches and the attempt at recreating our immigrant pasts. Schools, busy with acculturation and assimilation do not honestly deal with these problems in their curricula. As an outcome of the civil rights era, individual racial identity was methodically placed at the forefront of American culture before community equity, creating spaces for the women's, Chicano, and other similar movements. As a nation we have always faced problems of race and have had to invent new forms of expression from which to define the new meanings of identity. Louis Castenell and William Pinar (1993) state that it is an "understatement to observe that issues of race are paramount in contemporary curriculum debates in the public sphere" (p. 2). They suggest that curriculum is "racial text" because debates about what we teach youngsters are "debates over who we perceive ourselves to be, and how we will represent that identity, including what remains as 'left over,' as 'difference' " (p. 2). Thus curriculum implies understanding the "American national identity, and vice versa" as racial text (p. 2). Race and identity are terms that are constantly changing; race grows out of the individual's past, for example, "Black" from slavery, whereas identity comes from how the individual deals with her past, and what role society assigns that past.

As repression of identity was lifted by social changes, so too did schools respond, allowing marginalized groups to identify with symbols separate from the dominant social culture. Thus, Hispanic Americans in a quest for their Hispanic identity, no longer saw themselves as extremities of Europeans, ultimately leading to a new definition of self as Latino. First, in society, individuals are always subject to an autobiographical experience that attempts a separation from a dominant political and social structure that oppresses individual freedom and identity. Therein lays the appeal of the literary character's struggle for independence in current society. Second, the individual search for identity in terms of the larger base of knowledge and tradition comes to fruition in attempts to discover themselves as black or feminine or worthy in the face of the closed society of the United States. This discovery finds a receptacle in marginalized groups, particularly for women and persons of color. Third, schooling has traditionally marginalized the importance of these groups as well as providing a place for these groups to exist. In the traditional literature they find there is no place for them. However, there is literature that demonstrates that others too have tried and become ostracized for their attempts to become free from the social order. Educators need to understand the struggle and use the curriculum to assist students in their quest for identity. Understanding the Cuban struggle is a step in that direction.

Angst as Theoretical Approach to Identity

Angst has become a defining matter for the ever changing Cuban experience in the island and abroad after 1959. In the short post-Revolutionary period, the Cuban experience revolves around the angst of separation between competitive national identities both in Cuban and abroad. This phenomenon results from nationalism and separation that defines Cubanness and its definitions of race and class. Although attempts are made to bridge the separation, the question of defining Cuban remains a pervasive issue. Recently, literary, musical, and artistic bridges have reopened the debate of angst. They have also exposed separation as more perceived than real. However, it still has very real consequences, generating expression that drives the creativity necessary to compose music, write literature, and make art across borders to include both communities, and to redefine Cubanness as a community (Anderson, 1991). Attempts such as this still fall under the umbrella of the "embargo (also more perceived than real);" which has become important in still another presidential election. Talks about the embargo have also revived a tension of what will drive Cuban identity on the island and in the United States if the angst supported by the embargo no longer existed thereby collapsing the mainstay of identity.

Enacted Curriculum and Race: A Hispanic Problem

Today's educational segregation is more about individual identity than about either race or ethnicity. We no longer call it segregation; even fail to recognize it as such. Traditional notions of identity generally manage to marginalize, or segregate, certain sections of our society. This disproportionately affects minorities, especially Hispanics. The problem is twofold with the marginalized being invisible; they are not only the minority, but also are also predominately racial minorities. In a time when minority students are just starting to make some progress in their struggle to compete in the classroom and the workforce, notions of identity could serve to nullify present progress in self-efficacy, and perhaps place minority students at a greater disadvantage. Although research in the area of self-efficacy has been substantial over the past 30 years, and the process of labeling and evaluating race has been going on for some 40 years, little research has been done in an attempt to localize the result of group identity on individuals or even on subgroups. In other words, where do I belong as a Cuban within Hispanic culture—much of it dominated by larger Hispanic groups (Mexican and Puerto Rican)?

In order to survive a history of institutional neglect in schools, minority students draw on various cultural and linguistic skills, knowledge, contacts, and abilities nurtured in their home communities that emphasize they maintain self-efficacy to provide agency to maneuver through institutional barriers. Nevertheless, the students still have to compensate for their educational experiences (see Delgado-Gaitan, 2001; Yosso, 2005, 2006). Literature is one avenue to assist individuals in that exploration and compensation.

Historical Account of literature

Cuban literature has always been prolific, both on and off the island; many authors regularly traveled between the Havana and New York,

Madrid, or London. Most Diaspora writers have made their homes in the United States, leading to a constant conflict between the culture on the island and that of the United States. Notable exceptions included Guill- ermo Cabrera Infante, who lived in London. As such, Cuban literature seems to be rooted in complex issues that set themselves within the shift- ing landscapes. As Pamela Smorkaloff states, "the meanings of exile and revolution are not what they were, yet they still hold (Smorkaloff, 1999, p. ix). Many works, including Ruth Behar's (1995) *Bridges* began conver- sations across the span between writers on the island and those in exile. Christina Garcia (1992) exemplifies the underlying force driving Cubans' identity. In *Dreaming in Cuban*, she addresses a young woman's quest to find her identity as a Cuban and most of all as a woman. Like a siren in a Xavier Cugat song, she is oppressed by the dominant male culture and the overwhelming need to find her Cuban roots on the island. Her search is complicated by the embargo. As this article is being written, the United States is seeking to soften the power of the embargo, thereby, opening trade with the island. I offer that the lifting of this embargo will throw Cuban identity into a tailspin; because as Cristina Garcia writes, it is the need to know where one came from that drives her protagonist's journey to Miami, and to Cuba.

The tailspin or fear exists more so in the loss of the span, the loss of the angst; the loss of the ability to use separation as motivating force whether or not it directly relates to Cuba. Young writers like Carlos Manzano, are recapturing their grandparents' fears that they would lose their Cuban- ness if there were no embargo. In fact, what occurs is search for further Cubanization—an act that had already occurred on the island as a result of the Angolan war. As Don Burness demonstrates, Angola like Cuba has had similar histories; and like Cuba and United States, the Angolan war has become as dominant in Cuban culture on the island as Vietnam did in the United States. Also, a connection to the past has opened conversa- tions into the Cuban-African history and influence on literature both on and off the island (Burness, 1996).

At this stage is important to introduce two viewpoints. The first of Cuban identity as seen through Benedict Anderson's (1991) concept of *imagined community* is useful; *imagined* because although the members of the community might not know each other, "in the minds of each lives the image of their communion" and *community* because, "regardless of the actual inequality and exploitation that may prevail in each, the nation is always conceived as a deep, horizontal comradeship" (pp. 6–7). The second, in *Five Roads to Modernity*, where Liah Greenfeld (1995) empha- sizes that sovereignty of a particular group is based on an individual's identification within a people, to which s/he is loyal. Nationalism is a social construct that emerges out of a group's contact and interaction with other groups. Proximity favors more interactions among a particular set of individuals, who develop a similar mentality and perception of reality. Changes brought about by development and overall structural context; accentuate some groups' expectations as opposed to others. An elite shape these expectations and reinterprets sovereignty based on the uniqueness of that particular group, which assumes the character of a collective individual possessed by a single will. Some individuals emerge from the collectivity as interpreters of the single will. The reinterpretation of the idea of sovereignty leads a group transformed into a nationality to try to change the social and political structure.

Cuban identity has begun to incorporate previously ignored minorities and their cultural contributions; because of the influence of "ethnic identity" learned in the United States. Lebanese, Chinese, Jews, and Yucatan Cuban minorities are now accepted as legitimate Cuban cultures. One such example is Evelio Grillo (2000), who remembered that for all relationships and cultural sharing with White Cubans when the school bell rang, he headed to the "colored" classroom and that ended his confusion about what he was, in the United States he was Black. In 2002, in the 100th year of Cuban independence, two celebrations, one in Miami and one in Havana, revealed greatly the crowds and cultures of both lands and, importantly, the differences in the racial makeup of the two places, one White and one not. In the twenty-first century, the majority White Cuban population of Miami has had to accept the racial discrimination that existed on the island.

Imagine Identities: A History

The events between 1898 and 2002 have served to strengthen the resolve of Cuban literature, specifically American Intervention, 1959, and the Diaspora and wars of the last 30 years. The first 20 years of the century produced disillusioned works of Cuban identity resulting from the Spanish American War. In the 1960s and 1970s, literature became more retrospective with an eye looking toward the past through new lenses. Island writer such as Alejo Carpentier (1978) and Jesus Diaz (1987) used the 1959 Revolution as the genesis of their prose, themes, and protagonists. Cuban American writers also use 1959 to mark their departure; and until recently, works from this Diaspora have looked toward the past with a hope for a return to the island. Thus, Cuban American writers have explored collective consciousness developed in the United States, distinct from Cuba yet driven by the events on the island.

The realities of writers on and off the island are the same—race and intergenerational conflict dominate. Literary critics such as Ben Heller

(1998), address Cuban writers' "ideas about the creation and development of culture" (p. 11)." He believes that the poet Jose Ledezma, like many other Cuban writers, experiences assimilation, resurrection and generation in his writing. Vera Kutzinski's (1993) *Sugar's Secrets* explores race and eroticism in Cuban literature as a case study to the role of cultural production from the point of view of race. The overwhelming notion driving race and eroticism is the masculinity of literature and the silenced woman, themes unexplored until recently. Edward Said (1978) and Toni Morrison (1987) have both emphasized that dismissing representations of identity (racial or otherwise) as myths is to underestimate their power in determining the voice of those explored. One issue emerging in this literary simulation is that of violence, and celebration of it, including viewing women, specifically women of color, as figures of male pleasure. This genre has also been critically examined through Cuban painter and cartoonist Victor Patricio de Landaluze.

The idea of Cuban writing/literature then comes from setting oneself at the cross-section of the historical and literary interpretations of the New World, the relationship between past, present, future in myths, tales, faith, and so forth. Miguel Barnet (2001) stated that all Cubans, no matter their location, hold an obsession with 1959. The year shapes and informs the hermeneutics of perceptions, and creates an ethno-nationalism (Greenfeld, 1995). The relationship is one where conversation about history, and how one views Cuba in the history of world undergirds the uniqueness of Cubans in relationship to other Hispanics, especially in the United States.

U.S. Cuban Literature: A Historical Precedent

Cubanness is revived after the Cuban Revolution of 1959 in the United States by the immigrant's re-storying of Cuba. Grandparents' memory of their experiences in Cuba played a crucial role in the formation an image of Cuban life for young exiles. Elders cautioned that after 1959 Cuba was no longer Cuban. But, instead of creating a hate for Cubans, they fostered a love of place for the young 20-year-olds who sought a connection to the island and its culture. Instead of fighting what their children were learning in American schools, Cubans infused Cuban culture into their daily lives, creating a natural avenue for the existence of two simultaneous cultures. The favorable treatment of Cuban immigrants by the Justice Department combined with Castro's alliance with the USSR forced dismemberment between the island and exiles. The primary makeup of the exodus was a large, white middle-class professional population. Today, Cubans form the third largest Hispanic population in the United States, rank highest in per capita income (especially those born in the United

States whose income is actually $50,000 to $48,000 more than Whites born in the United States); have the highest divorce rate, highest percentage of citizenship, highest percentage of college educated persons, and highest rate of ethnic groups behind Jews and Japanese (Pew Hispanic Center, 2006).

The migration to the United States forced the exiles to adapt to American culture without feeling part of the United States. The first groups were largely made up of professionals in their 30s and 40s and teenagers brought to the United States under the *Pedro Pan* program in the early 1960s (Conde, 1999). The third group, *generation ñ* (A Cuban variant for Generation X) grew up in the 1970s and 1980s, adopted American values and norms while relearning the politics of becoming Cuban in the United States (Grenier, Perez, Sun, & Gladwin, 2007; Leland & Chambers, 1999). The re/invention of the culture centered on the value of what was perceived as Cuban. The foil to Cuban culture was American acculturation, learned via schooling, media and friends. The two forged a new form of Cubanness with values associated with the United States, and supported by the state superstructure, and a Cuban way of life supported by the exile community.

The success of Cubanness lies in the uniqueness of the Cuban community. Unlike counterparts in California (Mexicans and African Americans), Cubans have not formed coalitions in their quest for political empowerment. Cubans identified with the conquerors not the conquered. In this view, the United States "helped" against the Spanish, whereas Mexicans see the American Southwest as part of Mexico, and African Americans were enslaved, Cubans were assisted. This condition leaves those other two ethnic groups with the feeling of being marginalized by the United States. But, Cuban migration was seen as temporary by many since efforts directed toward the island would lead to the overthrow of Castro. Along with this belief in returning came the connection between families in Cuba and the United States. Cubans arrived at the height of the Civil Rights Movement and greatly benefited from the Civil Rights Act (1964). Although early Miami was not welcoming, overwhelming numbers and political empowerment helped. Early on signs such as "No Dogs, No Cubans," adorned many Miami-Dade County establishments. Accompanying this early resentment came the demographic relocation of Cubans to places outside Miami-Dade County (e.g., Union City, New Jersey; Chicago, Illinois; and Atlanta, Georgia). Also, within Miami Cubans were segregated in parts of the city. This area later became known as Little Havana and is still the home of the *Calle Ocho* festival. These events led to a galvanization of politics and a protective barrier from the other groups in Miami, allowing political ties to develop among Cubans. They were able to attend school with other people who were going through similar experiences at both home and in the classroom.

The ethnic development of Cuban children occurred as they attended schools with their own people; shared culture and ethnic nationalism of the home environment; and explored notions of self in the classroom and common areas. They were able to construct their own language and rituals. Peers lived at home with grandparents that spoke only Spanish, had mothers who for the first time worked outside the home, and balanced American pop culture with Cuban norms and values.

Revisiting Identity: Angst as a Motivator

In the early 1990s Cuban American writers explored issues of memory, a false myth in the construction of the imagined community off the island. The genre was one of testimonial (a movement largely credited to Michael Barnet, 2001), for example, *Rachel's Song*, where the rebirth of the Race War of 1912 was explored. The works of Oscar Hijuelos, Roberto G. Fernandez, Jose Kozer, Virgil Suarez, and Cristina Garcia promote levels of Cuban connections toward the idea of what it means to be Cuban from the point of view of exiles who do not have access to the island except through the testimonials of others, including family members and experiences learned through their acculturation into the Cuban Diasporan culture. There is a sense among this new generation similar to that of Alice Walker (1992) as she transcends the ideal of slave narrative to that of writing for women. This is illustrated by the success of Garcia as a feminist writer, one who voices the angst of women. Also, the writing of Ruth Behar (1993, 1995), who in discovering her own Cubanness, opened a discussion on the Cuba of non-Spanish Cubans. The reconnection of these writers to the past imagines Cubanness on two planes; one, a museum of the past but dynamic in its own development and the other, perceived as different from the past yet influenced by its own attempt to reinterpret the past. Virgil Suarez (1996) for example, tells the story of a *Marielita* who finds everything he had run away from in Miami; race and class prejudice, a pre-Revolution ideology in Cuba (pp. 240–261). In California he works as a painter for a Cuban, with whom he observes the hierarchy of Cubans.

Estrangement and separation also reflect the literature of the Cubans who remained on the island. As I write this article, I know I write as a Cuban in the United States, and view writing on the island as different. For example, as stated earlier, I believe the Angola campaign plays as large a role in Cuban literature than the separation. Second, issues ignored under Castro's rule, such as homosexuality and gender discrimination are becoming part of Cuban identity. Also, the influence of other cultures into Cuban literature through alternative media (Internet) and travels outside of Cuba for university studies or work has influenced the genre. Cuban literature from the island has always tackled the issue of displacement/return, always seeing the imperial frontier as an overwhelming force driving identity. Smorkaloff (1999) write that we need to examine Cuban literature not as produced on the island or in the exile, but as coming from a tradition that was reinterpreted by two cultural events that occurred in 1959, immigration and revolution. Both are unique genres, yet all roads point to 1959 as a literary nexus, like Faulkner and Hemingway in modern American literature.

Cuban Literature: Reclaiming Cuban Identity in Cuba

Another reality of Cuban literature has been the ability of publishing from the United States and abroad to become the dominant force. Between 1959 and 1979, there were almost 1,000 published works by Cuban authors, mostly from Miami, Spain, and New York. The relative invisibility of Cuban writers on the island coupled with the economic power of publishers in the United States led to their anonymity. Further, in order to rebuild a Cuban identity opposed to 1959, Cuban literature experienced a renaissance through the reissuing of books published prior to 1959 that built and extracted a new Cuban canon, reissuing Martí, Carpentier, Casal, and others. Notably missing was Nicolas Guillén as well as any authors not supporting a particular point of view. It is not until the 1980s that publishing in the island begins to make an impact on the world market. In fact, there has become a steady outpouring of literature, reinforced by a thirst for Cuban culture worldwide. The push to expand the world market for Cuban culture to match the production from Miami and New York has led Cuban writers, musicians, and playwrights especially through Canada, Spain, and London has led to increased artistic production.

It is hard to imagine Cuban literature without Carpentier's influence, especially in the 15 years after 1959. His Cuban novel is couched in terms of world issues, those of humanity rather than the placed-based writing that dominated other Cuban works; similar to those of Southern writers in the United States, such as Robert Penn Warren, Richard Wright, and of course, William Faulkner. In their works, we find issues of race, class, and identity all based on local interpretations and dominated by the Lost Cause. Cuba's Lost Cause was the War of Independence, a chance to make a different culture and society, and replace colonialism with liberation; yet failing to do so in the face of the United States and its economic hegemony.

The constant burden of that moment is a battle between independence and colonization; *criollo* and Cubanness; and race and national identity.

These dichotomies were exacerbated by the ease of travel between New York and Havana, opening the way for influences from abroad. This aided the Cuban exploration of issues such as identity; existential existence from a Cuban point of view at the cost of retarding the development of race identity and class in Cuba. These issues would not be explored in depth until the 1980s. But Carpentier (1933, 1978) looked toward the French Revolution for motivation; its issues of justice, humanity's attempt to reinterpret reality, and attempts to link philosophy and historiography to the Caribbean, not just to Cuba. Alongside Carpentier's vision are Jose Lezama Lima and his affirmation of the cultural context from which Cuba exists, like that of Eudora Welty in the U.S. South. Like Welty, Lezama Lima looks toward the past in a romantic tone.

The switch from these tomes to that of the testimonial novel of the island occurred in the 1960s in the works of Reinaldo Arenas, Rene Mendez Capote, and Miguel Barnet. In this case, the authors' cries are those of liberation after years of dictatorship, and are enlivened by the hopes under Castro. There is a romantic connection to other movements in Latin America, specifically that of Allende in Chile. For example, Reinaldo Arenas' *El Mundo Alucinante* (2004) is set in the memories of the future, where he searches for identity in the past.

Now I switch to focus on two topics, Afro-Cuban Literature and the Angolan war as driving forces of the Cuban renaissance on the island. In these we see issues of race, class, and identity that were placed aside in search for one identity tied to the past. This is an attempt to displace the dominance of 1959 and the Diaspora away from the island's works. At the same time, it points to the reliance of the Diaspora on Cuba as a driving force for creativity and on Cuba's attempt to disassociate itself from the Diaspora. In other words, angst of separation might be more of an issue for the Diaspora and not for writers on the island. The search for the "Cuban" is still important and there are still connections between thee two cultures and the search for a consciousness around identity even under the shadow of the United States. However, issues in Cuba—immersed in the everyday life of the island—are not seen outside by Diaspora writers who themselves are trying to reassess and revisit their own issues with identity amidst the negotiation between being Cuban in the United States, being American, and looking toward the island for inspiration. Angst then is seen differently, one through the frustration of being Cuban with little access to Cuba, driving the creativity of the arts; and the other being Cuban constantly under American shadow and historic past while trying to deal with their own issues of identity and answering questions of separation.

Capturing Diversity—Ethno-Cubanism

Compounding the competition to define what Cuba literature and ulti-mately Cuban identity is the impact of race on the genre. Although, Cuban identity is not easily defined, race remains central to its meaning. This is the case that exists within the literature. Afro-Cuban literature faces two issues; first a long battle in becoming part of not only the His-panic canon but also that of Cuba itself, and second, how can understand-ing the role of Afro-Cubans in literature help us understand the role of race within Cuban identity. The cases exists on two levels, first the impact of Afro-Cuban literature on Cuban identity and second the impact of it on Angolan writers—discussed later as existing between the lines of iden-tity—who do not see themselves as being impacted by the Diaspora but rely heavily on Afro-Cuban literature. In fact, it is not until the 1940s when the works of Arturo Torres-Rioseco (1942) and Pedro Henriquez Ureña (1947) were published despite the fact that Afro-Cuban literature had its renaissance between 1926 and 1938. These works did not become part of the cannon after World War II. Afro-Cubanism was mostly in the form of poetry; with essays as the second most popular form of expres-sion. Afro-Cuban legends and myths found their true nature in the short story. Lydia Cabrera, using French surrealism in her collection explored legends and myths of Africans (Rodriguez-Mangual, 2003). The book was first released in French, appearing in 1940 as *Black Tales From Cuba*. In reality, Afro-Cuban literature has always reflected the fragile position of Afro-Cubans on the island.

With U.S. intervention in 1898, the fragile multiethnic and multiclass union formed during the Cuban War of Independence dissipated, destroying Jose Martí and Antonio Maceo's dreams of Cuban unification, and ultimately plummeting Cuba into a race war in 1912 (Fermoselle, 1972). Cuba was unique in its birth as a nation because of its racial makeup (Whites outnumbered Blacks) and its proximity to the United States (Helg, 1990, pp. 37–70). In Cuba sugar was king and all society centered on the hegemony of sugar. Antonio Benítez Rojo (1986) states that:

> The sugar plantation was not only an agricultural mechanism; it was the basis for a whole system of power relations that presupposed the stability of a society characterized by its abrupt segmentation: First, a small dominant element, the other a large, dominated one, with a monopoly of power in the hands of the first. (pp. 12–13)

Race in Cuba was a "direct consequence of the degree to which slavery and its exigencies had affected the total social structure" (Martínez-Alier, 1989, p. 2). Afro-Cuban men and women slave or free, had to conform to the expectations placed on them by the dominant White sector and at the same time they had to adjust themselves to other Blacks (p. 98). Organization of the Black race was the major obstacle in Blacks' quest for equality in Cuba due to the "marked absence of common identity" (pp. 73, 75). A constant preoccupation with becoming lighter led many Blacks to look to the White race for guidance instead of the Black race. In fact, "race was often used as a symbol for other socially significant cleavages in society" (p. 16) that caused a division between blacks in their quest to become part of society.

Keeping this in mind, we must begin to question the role of Black literature on the Cuban canon. For example, Nicolas Guillén, the best known Afro-Hispanic author used starkly realistic portraits of urban life to represent a schism between the Eurocentric canon and the Black poetics. The story of Guillén's words is remarkably close to those of Derek Walcott (1990), and his quest for negotiating Black and White identities. Similar to both, is the work of Frantz Fanon (1952), and his search for living freedom while living on the margins in *Black Skin, White Mask*. Early representations of Afro-Cubanism, beyond those of Fernando Ortiz (1995), were by Francisco Calcagno's (1863/1887) *Los Crimenes de Concha*, where he describes Afro-Cubans as sexual animals, savages, and more susceptible to vice. Alejo Carpentier's (1933) *Ecué-Yamba-O!* becomes the defining work of Afro-Cuban representation in the Cuban novel. The relative acceptance into the Cuban canon of Afro-Cuban works led to an invisibility taken for granted in studies until the 1970s. In the 1970s a number of poetry anthologies opened new interpretations toward Black literature in Cuba. In 1993, Vera Kutzinski's work *Sugar's Secrets* also reopened the door for exploration of the unique texts in the Afro-Cuban Diaspora. In Kutzinky's work, Black discourse is explored as a unique and separate experience that challenges the notion of racial harmony in Cuban myth.

It is not until the 1960s that Guillén becomes a fixture in the Cuban canon; and not until Anderson Imbert and Eugenio Florit's 1970 anthology is Guillén generally accepted in Latin America. This in turns leads to Afro-Cuban literature as shifting to what Edward Mullen (1998) calls race neutral terminology that stresses ethnic heritage. However, along these lines is the adoption of Nancy Morejón, a post-Revolutionary writer and Juan Francisco Manzano's slave narrative within Cuban anthologies. Ironically enough, Guillén is now a member of the canon, a synoptic discourse he tried to disassociate himself from during his life. This, the de-emphasizing of the Black narrative, is one aspect of Cuban writing on the island that directly is influenced by the attempt of Cuban writers to not deal with the Diaspora to the United States. Whereas, in the U.S. writers' accounts greatly incorporate the Black narrative as a romanticized other; or as a cultural integration of Cuban ethnicity; island writers are much more conscious of race. In other words, when speaking of race, the point of view outside Cuba is that of the detached foreground of Cuban myths about race, whereas on the island, for many writers it is a reality of racism and diversity in thought that is explored as a colonial reality remarkably similar to that of other African populations.

Nicolas Guillén, who embodied both race and the intergenerational conflicts as he constructed and debunked myths of Blackness and identity, also impacts the racial identity of Cubans. Guillén hoped to break the false myths of Blacks, while using their own myths and lore to tell their story (White, 1993). His choices speaks to his influence on the Angolan generation writers. Angola, because of the 20,000 troops sent there, plays a significant role in the Cuban mind that is unique and not a result of the Diaspora. Like Guillén, these writers create myth and move away from the conflict with the United States toward that of Angola. Missing is still the feminist presence (because of war), but still present is race, magnified by not only the writers themselves but also, by the place.

Angola as Angst: Refocusing the Cuban Novel

Angola was a 10 year war fought mostly by young Cubans, born after 1959, with very little connection to the issues surrounding the Diaspora and the Revolution. Many were influenced by a combination of historical and social factors that existed beyond the Diaspora-island argument; and in turn their experiences, like those of the younger Cuban writers in the U.S. emerges out of a system they are not part of. These young writers were impacted by the music of Bob Dylan and the poetry of Jack Kerouac. They also relied on the literary tradition of Afro-Cubans and the realities of living in Cuba and fighting in Africa. In other words, no meaning is immediately present to itself, which means that as these authors acquired identity by being differentiated from other social realities then they could not refer to themselves as first. Thus, to be separated from their Cuban identity and reality established by the Diaspora and the Revolution—and in order to gain their own identity—these writers had to travel to war torn Angola to find an outlet to produce their own meanings. For them, the Diaspora and the Revolution was for the older generations, they; like those who lived in the Vietnam era and U.S. Cuban Generation ñ, created a unique definition of *Cubanness* that ultimately served to influence other writers in their search for their own identity.

Joel James Figarola's (1980) *Hacia La Tierra del Fin del Mundo*, takes the reader on a description of war and resistance in Africa similar to George Orwell's description of Burma and Barcelona. The meaning of Cuban comes from the war and angst of choosing among Cuba and family and duty to state and individual identity. Like Joel James Figarola, Waldo Leyva, Victor Casaus, Antonio Conte, and Benito Estrada Fernandez; Rafael Carralero, a short story writer gained his greatest fame writing about the Cuban experience in Angola. In his prize winning collection of short stories, *Tiro Nocturno*, Carralero explores Cuban experiences in Angola while he refuses to define what Angola constitutes (Carralero, 1978). Unlike James Figarola, Carrralero rarely speaks of Angolans. For him Cubans speak a language while Angolans a dialect. There is an almost colonial nature to his work that can be translated as bitterness to the experience masked in the stories of war and brotherhood. Like Joseph Conrad, his Africa is a place, an idea that only serves to reflect the protagonists. Carralero's sarcasm is in stark contrast to the duty described by James Figarola. Carralero paints a picture similar to that painted by Oliver Stone (1986) in *Platoon*, of brotherhood survived in the violence of the jungle. In James Figarola and Carralero, there are distinct takes on Angola, both examining Angola as a result of the Revolution, but one seeing it as unquestioned duty, like the novels *All Quiet on the Western Front* (Remarque, 1928) with the morality of the *Red Badge of Courage* (Crane, 1895); while the latter, like Joseph Conrad (1999) in *Heart of Darkness*, sees the war as an individual's quest to remain alive and how they fit within world politics. However, for these Cuban authors Angola serves as a backdrop to their identity as Cubans, angst comes from remaining true to Cuba and not from the separation to the United States. In that sense they impact young Diaspora writers who also face their realities of growing up in the United States and who see Cuban literature as Spanish and African.

Conclusions: Identity and Literature of Cubanness

The problem for today's Cuban identity lies in the assumption that we have made: separation, and the angst caused by it, part of shared meanings. Therefore, shared narratives should provide an inspired reason for Cubanness. Yes, we all interpret Jose Martí's dream for Cuban liberation but only insofar as they relate to ourselves, and not to the larger collective mindset. The role of Benedict Anderson's imagined community enters into the equation of interpretation. Although all Cubans can relate to the oppressed state, whether abroad against Castro or in Cuba against the embargo, it is only relevant to their state of being, not to any other person's. The importance of individuality makes it easy for all of us to see ourselves as Cubans, but we cannot see anyone else in that character. In other words, cultural identity does not allow us to see others; it is not about you, it is about me. It was the Angolan generation that allowed us to see that as people we are more than the Diaspora and the Revolution.

Cuban literature has always dealt with race and construction of social roles, although it has rarely explored the power of individual identity as it transcends the island through the revolution, and leads to distinct attempts to create identity abroad and on the island. As Cuban society changed, so did identity and culture, a fact lost on most Cubans in the United States. Many have not dealt with the changing nature of Cuba like those Cuban authors did with the construction of social roles in post-Revolution world of the island. Thus, the critics of Cubans abroad have a point in stating that Cubans have not dealt with that change on the island. The construction of individual identity is now based on separation, whether you are Cuban in or outside the island.

Reasons abound for the differences in attention toward the African and European pasts of Cuba, but some include class; Cuban immigrants were nine times more likely to have a high school degree than people on the island; they were three times more likely to have a White-collar profession and three times more likely to come from a metropolitan area, mainly Havana. Also, they were about 80% White as compared to the island which was about 60% White. According to John Ogbu (1992), there are two types of immigrants in the United States, conquered and those that arrive of their own will. Ogbu claims that schools discourage ethnic behavior and force children of conquered groups to accept the dominant ideology. For the first time Afro-Cubans and *Marielitas* (1980s boat lift Cubans, referred to as *lumpen* by Castro) also began to distinguish themselves from the first wave of Cuban immigrants, as well as the rest of society. These groups of Cubans had experienced discrimination from the earlier generations because they were Castro's lumpen (Castro word for the undesirables of society, poor, Blacks, and sexual minorities). Thus by 2007 race, more than ever, has become a central issue in Cuban identity.

Schooling is an institutional representation of the society that encompasses it. The nature of change in schools as a response to the social milieu of the repression of Hispanics in our society has not been properly addressed. As curriculum is nationalized and standardized, it has excluded aspects of individual identity, forcing marginalization through the public policy of integration. Although the media tells us that we have similar needs and wants, Castenell and Pinar (1993) believe that "all Americans are racialized beings; knowledge of who we have been, who we are, and who we will become is a story or text we will construct" (p. 8). This article addresses some of the issues of Cuban identity. There is hope that within the schooling and its curriculum there are still gray spaces where individuals can address the concepts of social justice and equality.

We can educate learners through the use of critical narrative. Many of the authors mentioned in this article give us places to start.

REFERENCES

Anderson B. (1991). *Imagined communities*. New York: Verso.

Imbert, A., & Florit, E. (1970). *Literatura Hispanoamericana: Antología e introducción historica, Edición Revisada* [Hispanic American Literature: Anthology with Historical Introduction, Rev. ed.]. Toronto: Wiley.

Arenas, R. (2004). *El mundo alucinante* [A hallucinating world]. Barcelona, Spain: TusQuets.

Barnet, M. (2001). *Rachel's song*. Willimantic, CT: Curbstone Press.

Behar, R. (Ed.). (1993). *Translated woman: Crossing the border with Espreanza's story*. Boston: Beacon Press.

Behar, R. (Ed.). (1995). *Bridges to Cuba* [Puentes a Cuba]. Ann Arbor, MI: University of Michigan Press.

Benítez Rojo, A. (1986). Power/sugar/literature: Toward a reinterpretation of Cubanness. In C. Mesa-Lago (Ed.). *Cuban studies 16* (pp. 12–13). Pittsburgh, PA: University of Pittsburgh Press.

Burness, D. (1996). *On the shoulder of Martí: Cuban literature of the Angolan war*. Colorado Springs, CO: Three Continents Press.

Calcagno, F. (1887). *Los crimenes de Concha* [Concha's crimes]. México, DF: Impresora Económica. (Original work published 1863)

Carillo, I. (1948. Dos Gardenias [Recorded by Valle Son]. On *Son de Cuba* [CD]. Whitehorse, YT, Canada: Caribou Records. (2000)

Carpentier, A. (1933). *¡Ecué-Yamba-Ó!* [Lord, May You Be Praised]. Madrid, Spain: Colibrí.

Carpentier, A (1978). *El arpa y la sombra* [The harp and the shade]. Mexico, DF: Fondo de Cultura Económica.

Carralero, R. (1978). *Tiro nocturno (Cuentos)* [a shot in the dark]. Miami, FL: Baquiana.

Castenell, L. & Pinar,W. (1993). *Curriculum as racial text*. Albany, NY: SUNY.

Civil Rights Act of 1964. CRA, Title VII, Equal Employment Opportunities. 42 US Code Chapter 21.

Conde, Y. (1999). *Operation Pedro Pan*. New York: Routledge.

Conrad, J. (1999). *Heart of darkness*. New York: Penguin Books

Crane, S. (1895). *The red badge of courage*. New York: Appleton.

Delgado-Gaitan, C. (2001). *The power of community: Mobilizing for family and schooling*. Boulder, CO: Rowman & Littlefield.

Diaz, J. (1987). *Las iniciales de la tierra* [The beginnings of the world]. Madrid, Spain: Ediciones Alfaguara.

Fanon, F. (1952). *Black skin, White masks*. New York: Grove City Press.

Fermoselle, R. (1972). *Black politics in Cuba: The Race War of 1912*. Ann Arbor, MI: University Microfilms International.

Garcia C. (1992). *Dreaming in Cuban*. New York: Ballantine Books.

Greenfeld, L. (1995). *Nationalism: Five roads to modernity.* Cambridge, MA: Harvard University Press.

Grenier, G., Perez, L., Sun, S. C., & Gladwin, H. (2007). There are Cubans, There are Cubans, and then there are Cubans: Ideological diversity among Cubans in Miami. In M. Montero-Sieburth & E. Melendez (Eds.), *Latinos in a changing society* (pp. 93–111). Westport, CT: Greenwood.

Grillo,' E. (2000). *Black Cuban, Black American: A memoir.* Houston, TX: Arte Publico Press.

Helg, A. (1990). Race and class in Cuba and Argentina. In A Knight, R. Graham, & TE. Skidmore (Eds.), *The idea of race in Latin America, 1870-1940* (pp. 37–70). Austin, TX: University of Texas Press.

Heller, B. (1998). *Assimilation/generation/resurrection: Contrapuntal readings in the poetry of Jose Lezama Lima.* Lewisburg, PA: Bucknell University Press.

Henriquez Urena, P. (1947). *Historia de la cultura en la America Hispanica* [Cultural history in Hispanic America]. Mexico, DF: Fondo de Cultura Economica.

James Figarola, J. (1980). Hacia la tierra del fin del mundo. In *Toward the place at the end of the world.* Santiago, Cuba: Editorial Oriente.

James Figarola, J. (1972). *Los Testigos (Cuentos).* Santiago, Cuba: Editorial Oriente.

Kutzinski, V (1993). *Sugar's secrets: Race and the erotics of Cuban nationalism.* Charlottesville, VA: University of Virginia Press.

Leland, J., & Chambers, V. (1999, July 12). Generation ñ. *Newsweek, 134,* 52–58.

Martínez-Alier, V. (1989). *Marriage, class and colour in nineteenth-century Cuba.* London: Cambridge University Press.

Morrison, T. (1987). *Beloved.* New York: Vintage.

Mullen, E. (1998). *Cuento Hispanico.* Columbus, OH: McGraw-Hill.

Ogbu, J. (1992). Understanding cultural diversity and learning. *Educational Researcher,* 21 (4).

Ortiz, F. (1995). *Cuban counterpoint: Tobacco and sugar.* Durham, NC: Duke University Press.

Pew Hispanic Center. (2006, August 25). *Cubans in the United States fact sheet.* Washington, DC: Pew Research Center. Retrieved on May 8, 2008, from www.pewhispanic.org.

Remarque, E. M. (1928). *All quiet on the western front.* New York: Little Brown.

Rodriguez-Mangual, E. (2003). *Lydia Cabrera and the construction of an Afro-Cuban cultural identity.* Chapel Hill, NC: University of North Carolina Press.

Said, E. (1978). *Orientalism.* New York: Pantheon Books.

Smorkaloff, P. (1999). *Cuban writers on and off the island: Contemporary narrative fiction.* New York: Twayne.

Stone, O. (Writer/Director) (1986). *Platoon* [Motion picture]. United States: Orion Pictures.

Suarez, V. (1996). Headshots. In V. Suarez & D. Posey (Eds.). *Little Havana blues: A Cuban-American literature anthology* (pp. 240–261. Houston, TX: Arte Público Press.

Torres-Rioseco, A. (1942). *Epic of Latin American literature.* Berkeley, CA: University of California Press.

Walker, A. (1992). *The color purple.* New York: Harcourt Brace.

White, C (1993). *Decoding the Word: Nicolas Guillen as maker and debunker of myth*. Miami, FL: Ediciones Universal.

Walcott, D. (1990). *Omeros*. New York: Farrar, Straus, & Giroux.

Yosso, T. J. (2005). Whose culture has capital? A critical race theory discussion of community cultural wealth. *Race Ethnicity and Education*, *8*(1), 69–91.

Yosso, T. J. (2006). *Critical race counterstories along the Chicana/Chicano educational pipeline*. New York: Routledge.

CHAPTER 17

LEVERAGING *ECLECTIC ARTS* AS A RATIONALE FOR MULTIPLE MODES OF INQUIRY

Brian D. Schultz

This article provides a theoretical basis for applying Schwab's (1971) notion of eclectic arts as a rationale and a justification for using a multiplicity of modes for conducting educational inquiry. By describing the nature of my research, detailing the need for a metamethodology, framing modes of inquiry that apply, complement, and interconnect to the research on my classroom, as well as discussing implications for policy and practice, the argument provides opportunities for reflection, change, and transformation.

INTRODUCTION: A METHODOLOGICAL DILEMMA

When seeking to make meaning about my classroom teaching experience, I ran into a methodological dilemma. No single methodology or framework seemed to be appropriate to articulate my experiences while teaching and learning in a fifth-grade classroom. I intended to reconstruct my thought processes, provide vivid descriptions, make student voices prominent, and interpret my experiences in the classroom space with students. I

Curriculum and Teaching Dialogue
Volume 10, Numbers 1 & 2, 2008, pp. 233–250
Copyright © 2008 by Information Age Publishing
All rights of reproduction in any form reserved.

longed for a methodological framework that would allow me to do all that I desired while using narrative vignettes and storytelling to not only chronicle, but analyze the classroom's pursuits of theorizing together while we engaged in an authentic, integrated curriculum centering on the students' priority concerns (Schultz, 2008). Although there were vast data ranging from public documentation and classroom artifacts, to student journals, and a daily reflective teacher journal, the means by which to conduct my intended inquiry was not as simple as selecting a single approach and following its parameters or guidelines.

This article is intended to provide a theoretical basis for applying Schwab's (1971) notion of eclectic arts as a rationale and a justification for using a multiplicity of modes for conducting educational inquiry. By describing the nature of my research, detailing the need for a metamethodology, framing modes of inquiry that apply, complement, and interconnect to the research on my classroom, as well as discussing implications for policy and practice, the argument in this article may provide opportunities for reflection, change, and transformation.

THE NATURE OF MY RESEARCH

The nature of my research is qualitative and interpretive. Specifically, I wanted to make meaning about a phenomenon of interest. Qualitative-based research focuses on gaining insight about a particular phenomenon. In the examination of a phenomenon of interest, qualitative and interpretive research aims at providing a detailed account of what is being studied. The goal of this type of research is not to generalize or predict about particular groups in a positivistic sense, but rather to "interpret how the various participants in a social setting construct the world around them" (Glesne, 1999, p. 5). Qualitative and interpretive research inherently details a particular situation, describing how the actors engage in activities in the context of their setting and make meaning.

Bogdan and Biklen (1998) offer five key characteristics of qualitative research in their book *Qualitative Research in Education*. These five features characterize qualitative research with the following hallmarks: naturalistic, descriptive data, concern with process, inductive, and meaning. The naturalistic component of this research mode has "actual settings as the direct source of data and the researcher is the key instrument" (p. 4). The descriptive data feature focuses on trying "to describe what a particular situation or view of the world is like in narrative form" (p. 5). Rather than describing results in numbers and statistics as in quantitative research, the data that are gathered "take the form of words or pictures ... contain quotations ... in search for understanding" (p. 5). Qualitative research also focuses on process. The qualitative researcher wants to gain understanding of how the data are gathered and the story behind how the subjects make meaning about their world rather than simply striving for preconceived results or products. The investigators allow theory to emerge "from the bottom up" (p. 6) in an effort to inductively analyze the data. They "do not seek out data or evidence to prove or disprove hypotheses," (p. 6) but rather enter a research situation trying to discover meaning. This particular attribute of a qualitative study takes a closer look at "participant perspectives" (Erikson cited in Bogdan & Biklen, 1998, p. 7) essentially focusing on "how different people make sense of their lives" (p. 7).

Although these are features that Bogdan and Biklen (1998) describe as inherent to qualitative research, they note, "all studies that we should call qualitative research do not exhibit all traits to an equal degree" (p. 4), but have characteristics that distinguish them from quantitative studies. There are many different methods to conduct research in the qualitative paradigm described above. Pinar, Reynolds, Slattery, and Taubman (1995) note that as research in education has become increasingly qualitative, qualitative research has become a somewhat generic reference or "an umbrella term which includes all non-quantitative work" (p. 52). In an effort to explain why I chose the methodological approach to my inquiry, a description of the methods utilized to describe the phenomenon I am interested in portraying must be provided. I have selected several different qualitative methodologies that I felt best work with my research study. I do not believe that any one mode of inquiry would suffice as a sole way of making meaning and inductively portraying my phenomenon of interest. The following modes of inquiry best fit my study: ethnography, auto-biography, and portraiture. In addition to these main approaches of inquiry, my research also incorporates and borrows from other methodologies including: life history (Goodson, 1992), case study (Stake, 1997), and teacher/action research (Lytle & Cochran-Smith, 1992; Schubert & Lopez Schubert, 1997).

I have chosen to apply multiple modes of inquiry (Schubert, 1975) in an effort to "generate a conscious sensitivity among those who create and use research so that (they) might discover the degree that each mode best serves particular research purposes" (Schubert, 1980, p. 23). Since any one mode of inquiry would not allow me to tell the phenomenon of theorizing with students to develop an integrated and authentic curriculum in an urban classroom, application of Joseph J. Schwab's *The Practical: Arts of Eclectic* (1971) from his second essay on practical inquiry in curriculum was utilized. This application constructed a meaningful framework that justified the need to combine different theories and approaches to my particular research. Embracing these eclectic arts enabled me "to discover research modes that most productively serve the massive problems confronting the daily flow of students into schools" (Schubert, 1980, p. 23).

THE NEED FOR METAMETHODOLOGY

Since all the modes outlined above have differing parameters as essential features associated with them, it is necessary to match, adapt, and tailor them so as to ultimately create a sort of metamethodology that supports the aim of my particular research and generates a course of action that fits my priority concerns and needs. In Schwab's (1969) first essay on practical inquiry, he was critical of what he termed the reliance on the theoretic. Schubert interpreted Schwab's denunciation as "more a misapplication of research technology" (Schubert, 1986, p. 297) than a condemnation of theory. Schwab (1969) believed that in order to avoid having a "researcher detached from situations" and making the mistake of trying to come up with "lawlike generalizations that can be published" (p. 1), the researcher needed to look at the actual state of affairs of the given phenomenon. In response to the many misinterpretations of his critique of the curriculum field, Schwab outlined a method for applying a multiplicity of theories to given curricular situations so that practical inquiry in curriculum could be achieved (see Block, 2004 for discussion about why Schwab may have been widely misinterpreted). He argued that "theories of curriculum and of teaching and learning cannot, alone, tell us what and how to teach, because questions of what and how to teach arise in concrete situations loaded with concrete particulars of time, place, person, and circumstances" (Westbury & Wilkof, 1978, p. 322). In continuing his argument, Schwab stated that "theory ... contains little of such particulars" (p. 322) but can be resolved by leveraging "pluralities of theories" where each may contribute "its own useful light on the subject treated" (p. 322). Schwab (1969) outlines these eclectic arts as a way of remedying the "moribund" situation:

> The problems posed by these complications can, however, be solved by other means. First, the particularities of each practical problem can be sought in the practical situation itself, the search guided by resources much richer that any one theory can afford. Second, in each instance of application of a borrowed theory to a practical situation, incongruities can be adjusted by a mutual accommodation. Third, restricted subject and limited treatment so characteristic of behavioral theories can be transcended by using more than one such theory. (p. 10)

Essentially, these eclectic arts are a prerequisite to practical inquiry as Schwab (1969) promotes. Schwab was criticized, as was Dewey, in regards to his assertions for the need of practical inquiry rather than focusing on theory alone. Just as Dewey (1916) had posited that learners move from the psychological to the logical, Schwab emphasized the need to move from the theoretic (not a condemnation of theory) to the practical as a necessary step to enhancing the curriculum field. Schubert (1986) offers his interpretation (and clarification) of Schwab's arts of eclectic:

1. The capacity to *match* theoretical or disciplinary knowledge and perspectives to situational needs and interests.

2. The capacity to *tailor and adapt* theoretical or disciplinary knowledge and perspectives to situational needs and interests. (This is necessary because extant theories only account for a small proportion of phenomena in the world, thus, making matching a limited strategy.)

3. The capacity to *generate alternative courses of action* and to anticipate the consequences of such action for moral good. (This is necessary because extant theories are irrelevant to much of the world's phenomena even if they are tailored, adapted, combined, stretched and modified in all conceivable ways.) (Schubert, 1986, p. 297, emphasis and parentheses in original)

As Schwab, and later Schubert have offered eclectic arts for solving curriculum problems, I find them appropriate to establishing methodology for inquiry. Schwab suggested that in order to solve practical curriculum problems, "one must be steeped in literature and direct experience" (Schubert, 1986, p. 297). In addition to having an awareness of literature and experience, the matching, adapting, and generating may only exist with a direct recognition of social location and positionality during the process (Schultz, 2007). These eclectic arts scaffold a means to apply different research methodologies to my particular research interest. In examining relevant methodological approaches in qualitative research, I sought to match existing theories of educational research to the particular situation. Several existing theories, including ethnography, autobiography, and portraiture, related to my phenomenon of interest, but there was a need to adapt and tailor these to fit the given situation. I immediately echoed Schubert's (1986) sentiments, "each … treats only a portion of the complex field from which educational problems arise" (p. 323), concluding that no singular method could solely be applied to my research situation. An alternative course of action was achieved by blending complementary theories together while anticipating methodological consequences. Using this as a basis, I selected parts of methodologies that fit best, while discarding properties that did not work within my context.

By applying Schwab's (1971) eclectic arts, I began to resolve the curricular inquiry dilemma of my study not fitting a particular methodological conversation. I developed a metamethodology that suited the research I sought to conduct since it is tailored to meet my needs by making use of existing theories and applying specific attributes to my particularities.

Since my research resembles several different established modes of inquiry, I offer a short description of each methodology I matched and adapted so that emergent metamethodology from the eclectic arts framework can be better explicated. Through the short description I offer my understanding of the strengths and reasons for selection, while at the same time pointing out shortcomings and the need to find other relevant modes to fit the needs of my inquiry. As I muddle through to conceive my approach, I offer my own matched, adapted, and alternative courses of action for this qualitative research methodology so that I could better interpret and make meaning of the world around me.

ETHNOGRAPHY

One of the more commonly applied methods of qualitative research is ethnography. Harry Wolcott (1997) has been widely accepted as one of the preeminent educational ethnographers. Wolcott's definition of ethnography has been utilized and accepted as a benchmark in educational research. Wolcott describes ethnography as a "picture of the 'way of life' of some identifiable group of people" (p. 329). He prescribes this type of research as one "particular form of qualitative/descriptive research" that is associated with the "mindwork that must occur during and after fieldwork" (p. 328). The role of the ethnographer is successful creation "in attributing aspects of culture to the group under study" (p. 329). Wolcott readily admits, "the ethnographer walks a fine line" in pursuit of meaning to "learn about, record, and ultimately portray the culture of that other group in order to deepen understanding about the different ways human beings have resolved the problems by being human in the first place" (p. 329).

Although the primary methods of data collection for ethnography are participant observation and interview, the ethnographer is "not guided by a specific set of techniques," but is engaged in an "inquiry process" to answer the question, "What is going on here?" (Spradley cited in Short, 1991, p. 104). During this inquiry process using these approaches, the ethnographer must not become too distanced from the group being studied, but simultaneously needs to become intimately familiar with the group as to make warranted interpretations of facts based on the group's culture. Ethnography stresses that the ethnographer is the "research instrument" as well as the means for collecting the data (Janesick, 1991, p. 103; Wolcott, 1997, p. 329). The ethnographer is "there to stay—to become, for a while, part of the local scenery" and ultimately "enhance human understanding" (Wolcott, 1997, p. 332). Ethnography aims to "resolve the tension between involvement and detachment" (p. 333). Instead of attempting to remove biases in an effort to be objective, the ethnographer willingly embraces their subjectivity in pursuit of meaning making of a group's culture.

Utilizing methodology rooted in cultural anthropology widely accepted by the educational research community, ethnography enables a researcher to learn his subject's culture by careful observation, interview, cultural interpretation, and intense description. This can be accomplished by what Eisenhart (2001) describes as "living the immediate experiences of those stud[ied]" (p. 16). The ultimate goal is to understand the ways of seeing, thinking, and doing so that interpretations may be about the "everyday life of persons" (Fox cited in Wolcott, 1997, p. 329) and offering what Maxwell (1992) terms "kinds of understanding" (p. 279) of the particular group being studied. By remaining fixed and focused on the research and culture of the group, the ethnographer can achieve goals.

Wolcott (1997) asserts that all data described in the ethnographic analysis must be pertinent and useful, and be directly related to the case and its particulars in respect to questions and problems being examined. He posits that it is not possible for an ethnographer to include all data as they would neither be feasible nor targeted, but it is part of the responsibility of the researcher to divulge information that would persuade and influence outcomes and findings. Particular to my situation, I brought in issues of race, positionality, and my dominant worldview since it plays an important role to the meaning of the situation. As Eisenhart (2001) concludes, "Ethnographers have long recognized the potential danger to others when intimate details of (subjects') lives are revealed in ethnographic accounts" (p. 16). Ethnographers must promote a "realist approach to validity" (p. 16) by leaving out the details so meaning can be made and the research has a purpose of informing and promoting understanding. This is essential to understanding what it means to conduct ethnographic research based on first hand, personal involvement. Wolcott acknowledges the "fine line" between going too far into the subject's culture or what he describes as having "gone native" by too much active involvement in the group being studied (p. 333). At the same time the researcher cannot be a distant observer "labeled as aloof" or "superficial" out of touch with the reality of his subject (p. 333). Ethnographers must keep "focuses of appropriate attention" while being cognizant of what is "noticed and left unnoticed" during a particular account recognizing constraints "of focus of attention are never absolute" (Erickson & Shultz cited in Eisen-hart, 2001, p. 17).

Although I sought to provide thick ethnographic description through my inquiry, I question if I crossed the line for true ethnographic research by violating one of Valerie Janesick's golden rules for ethnographers by studying my own group. Janesick asserts, "if you are a member of a group you may be so close to it that you may miss much of the nuance of the social dynamics and critical factors that outsiders pick up on more readily" (Janesick, 1991, p. 115). Since I actively participated in the inquiry, ethnography alone did not satisfy my quest for an approach that would allow meaning generation for this study. Although a significant amount of the data was gathered from participant observation and interviewing, I fear that I crossed the line between involvement and detachment. Because my perspectives and inherent personal stake in the outcome of the phenomenon being studied was problematic, I elicited other valuable qualitative modes, in addition to employing ethnographic practices, to gain a more complete understanding and portrayal, and to give more meaning to the investigation.

In order to combat closeness to the subject matter, I have sought out complementary methods to ethnography. Since the storytelling inevitably occurred from my point of view, autobiographical inquiry, which uses many similar ethnographic approaches to conduct research, allowed me to delve deep into the narrative meaning and perspective. In addition, ethnography alone did not allow me to look reflexively on my own educational experiences outside of this case; the autobiographical approach allowed me to seek my own personal meaning from my practice.

AUTOBIOGRAPHICAL METHOD, *CURRERE*, PERSONAL PRACTICAL KNOWLEDGE, AND TEACHER LORE

Using Schwab's (1971) notion of eclectic arts, and my concern that ethnography alone would not satisfy the necessary mode of inquiry to generate and satisfy meaning-making to interpret my classroom experience, I felt that autobiographical inquiry served an important role. William Pinar and Madeleine Grumet created the concept of *currere* in the 1970s to "understand curriculum as autobiographical and biographical text" (Pinar et al., 1995, p. 518). *Currere* is the Latin verb form of curriculum and is defined as:

> To run the course of: Thus *currere* refers to an existential experience of institutional structures. The method *currere* is a strategy devised to disclose experience, so that we may see more of it and see more clearly. With such seeing

can come deepened understanding of the running, and with this, can come deepened agency. (Pinar & Grumet, 1976, p. vii)

This concept of autobiographical inquiry "seeks to understand the contribution academic studies makes to one's understanding of his or her own life. The student of educational experience takes as a hypothesis that out of any given moment he is a 'biographical situation'" (Pinar & Grumet, 1976, p. 51). This conceptualization further describes the idea of tracing past experiences to better understand the relation to present and future experiences. Essentially, autobiographical inquiry seeks to answer the abstract question of "What has been and what is now the nature of my educational experience?" (p. 52).

Since the research is specifically geared toward my own understanding of my classroom practice, I was forced to wrestle with my own individual experience (Grumet, 1981). Contrary to the idea of seeking to remove the anonymity and generalization common with positivistic modes of inquiry, the autobiographical framework described what is apparent through a reflexive lens in search of "intensifying one's own experience of education" (Grumet, 1981, p. 118), or as William Ayers (1990) asserts, "understanding the situation from within" (p. 272). This approach to research provided an avenue for me to best describe my decisions about theorizing with my students through the course of my teaching, as well as my previous professional and educational experiences. The autobiographical lens is an "act of self-creation and potentially transformation" (p. 274) as Ayers describes that provided me to best make sense of and reflect on the situation by "contributing more details, more instances, and more cases" (p. 275) from "an insider's view" (p. 271). This approach is significant to portraying my lived experience in my classroom. I was able to introspectively tell my curriculum experiences through the use of *currere*.

In addition, this approach encouraged me to revisit past experiences that existed outside of "intricate complexities of one case" in a "bounded system" (Stake, 1997, p. 405) inherent to ethnography and case study method. Autobiographical inquiry created opportunity for me to delve deep into my own understanding, experiences, and "self-knowledge" (Graham, 1991, p. 3) to better realize why I engaged in certain activities with my students during the course of a school year, and to also take a closer look and try to realize the effects of previous experiences on my current classroom approaches and pedagogy. Not only did I discover what has influenced me, I also was better positioned to trouble what I choose to reveal through autobiographical methods.

Furthermore, by using autobiography I embraced my subjectivity in "what we notice, what we choose to tell, and how we tell what we do" (Grumet, 1990, p. 324). Since autobiography, as Grumet (1981) posits, "is a reflexive cycle in which thought bends back upon itself and thus recovers its volition" (p. 118), I was able to retreat to my past experiences to better understand actions in the present and potentially in the future. This methodology "invites me to struggle with those determinations" (p. 324) so that a more clear understanding could be made by "constantly combining and recombining" my ideas "in provocative new ways" (Graham, 1991, p. 3).

My autobiographical inquiry also resembled elements of personal practical knowledge (Connelly & Clandinin, 1988) and teacher lore (Schubert & Ayers, 1992) in many instances. Although not adhering to either methodology explicitly, I found that the research on my classroom practice and *currere* is a narrative account of a teacher's lived experience, and shares many traits common to those offered by Connelly and Clandinin and Schubert and Ayers. Connelly and Clandinin emphasize "that teachers routinely enact theories of teaching and learning in their daily classroom activity" (Pinar et al., 1995, p. 557). Through this interaction, teachers develop what they call personal practical knowledge. Clandinin's (1985) definition offers insight and hopefulness for me to better understand my teaching practice:

> the body of convictions, conscious or unconscious, which have arisen from experience ... and which are expressed in a person' actions. The actions in question are all those acts that make up the practice of teaching, including its planning and evaluation. Personal practical knowledge is knowledge which is imbued with all the experiences that make up a person's experiential history, both professional and personal. (p. 362)

Through this application of this narrative strand of autobiographical inquiry, I was best able to engage in "reconstruction of experience" (Connelly & Clandinin, 1990, p. 245) to formally come to understand my life's experiences through my classroom, struggle to achieve meaning and understanding of actions I took within the context of my classroom, and to ultimately improve the learning condition for my students, thus, improving my own teaching and learning practices (Connelly & Clandinin, 1990). I became cognizant that I reconstructed the meaning in my classroom to seek out moral good as Dewey (1916) and Schwab (1971) asserted were essential to classroom practice. This mode of inquiry was a means for me to gain insight "from personal experience via a process of reflection in which storytelling is the key element" (Connelly & Clandinin, 1988, p. 16) where I was able to reconcile meaning from other experience.

Through the narrative account inherent to personal practical knowledge, I inevitably ascribed to a form of what Schubert and Ayers (1992) call *Teacher Lore*. Through storytelling, I "attempt[ed] to learn what teachers learn from their experience" (Schubert, 1991, p. 207) and was best able to contemplate "the experiential knowledge that informs (my) teaching or the revealed stories about (my) practical experiences" (p. 208). Since much of my research focuses on the relations I had with my doctoral studies in curriculum and how I interacted with my students based on what I was exposed to in reading about curriculum theorizing, I hoped to better understand and develop meaning about my engagement in curricular activities that were developed by me in "daily interaction with students" (p. 210). I created vivid, detailed accounts of my lived experiences and attempted to go from the familiar to the unfamiliar (Grumet, 1978) through a teacher lore approach to understanding. My teacher lore-oriented, autobiographical accounts followed the Deweyan rationale that purports "teachers as creators of curriculum theory (who) can illuminate understanding of curriculum, teaching and the educative process" (Schubert, 1991, p. 208). As a result of this notion, I was able to examine ways in which I came to theorizing with my students in the classroom and better understand the underlying meaning surrounding my practice to better myself and offer an account of one teacher's story of theorizing with students about what is most worth knowing.

Although the autobiographical lens, in addition to ethnography, offers a great deal in search of the appropriate mode of inquiry, I felt the need to account for ways I described certain aspects or portraits of the story I felt necessary to tell. In trying to describe the essence (Lawrence-Lightfoot, 1983) of the players and situations of my particular classroom experience, I saw the methodology of portraiture offered considerable insight to the meaning-making potential of this phenomenon.

PORTRAITURE

Borrowing features from ethnography, case study, and autobiography, portraiture encourages a researcher to "capture the richness, complexity, and dimensionality of human experience in social and cultural context, conveying the perspectives of the people who are negotiating those experiences" (Lawrence-Lightfoot & Hoffman Davis, 1997, p. 3). Pioneered by Sara Lawrence-Lightfoot over the last 25 years, this method of inquiry seeks "to combine systematic, empirical description with aesthetic expression, blending art and science, humanistic sensibilities and scientific rigor" (p. 3). Portraiture provides the researcher a way to go beyond the ethnographic account or the autobiographical rendition associated with the previous forms of inquiry detailed "to record and interpret the perspectives and experience of the people they are studying, documenting their voices and their visions—their authority, knowledge, and wisdom" (p. xv) through an artistic, aesthetic lens. The subsequent portrait developed is negotiated meaning that is tailored to the images created through the investigation by the researcher and the subject. Portraiture-based inquiry allowed me to dialogue with students in an effort to more completely reveal the "meaning and resonance" (p. 3) that emerges from trying to understand the lived experiences in the cultural context of the classroom that has social location and race inherent to its function. By engaging in this reflexive dialogue between the portraitist (myself) and the subjects (my students), the research went beyond ethnography and autobiography to promote "the subjects to feel seen" (p. 8). The resultant portrayal was a combination of empirical data collection coupled with an interpretive artistically-laden components (Eisner, 2001). This approach is consistent with Eisner's (1994) arts-based inquiry to enhance meaning of educational research and attendance to gain structural corroboration to "gather data and information ... establish[ing] links that eventually created a whole that is supported by the bits of evidence that constitute it" (p. 237).

Similar to ethnographic research in "moving beyond the surface image" (p. 4) and its use of "thick description" (Geertz, 1973, p. 6), portraiture goes further in attempting to represent the aesthetics in an effort to "discover forms of representation that would capture the fluidity and complexity of the living world" (p. 6). Lawrence-Lightfoot (1983) argues that creating portraits has close ties to autobiographical research as the autobiographical voice and perspectives of the researcher become intrinsically involved in the portrait.

The historical roots of portraiture as a means for educational inquiry have evolved through various influences over the past two centuries in an effort to bridge science and art. Inspired by the writing and practices associated with John Dewey, W. E. B. DuBois, and more recently Clifford Geertz, Lawrence-Lightfoot sought to combine empirical research with an artistic form of inquiry. As a means to merge artistic interpretation with purposeful social science research, she offers a method that blends aesthetics with empiricism promoting a narrative account to emerge that seeks broader meaning. Clearly defining her method as a "resistance to many of the dominant canons and preoccupations of social science" (Lawrence-Lightfoot & Hoffman Davis, 1997, p. 8), Lawrence-Lightfoot illuminates understanding by blending art and science. Lawrence-Lightfoot and Hoffman Davis offer that a major reason for developing this alternative mode was to counter the "general tendency of social scientists to focus their investigations on pathology and disease rather than on health and resilience" (p. 8) that focuses on the "relentless scrutiny of failure" (p. 9). On the contrary, portraiture highlights what is hopeful and good when creating meaning. Lawrence-Lightfoot asserts, "Portraiture resists this tradition-laden effort to document failure" (p. 9) so common to the social sciences, allowing for a focus on "promise and potential" (p. 9) by focusing on how goodness emerges in the cultural context and seeking to define what is morally good from the actors' perspective. Hallmark to this form of inquiry is that the researcher refrains from the imposing views of what goodness entails, but instead invites plurality of meaning to emerge from the actors, seeking to "identify and define the actors' perspective" (p. 9) of what goodness is in their context.

Portraiture enables the researcher to "deepen the conversation" as Geertz (1973) asserted was a tenant of ethnography (p. 29), thus the purpose of portraiture going beyond the academy in educational research to reach a wider audience including practitioners. Lawrence-Lightfoot and Hoffman Davis (1997) suggest portraiture is an "attempt to move beyond academy's inner circle, to speak in a language that is not coded or exclusive, and to develop texts that will seduce readers into thinking more deeply about issues that concern them" (p. 11). The idea of portraiture, as in the other forms of qualitative research described, is not to generalize but as Lawrence-Lightfoot argues is to potentially create dialogue opportunities and influence social transformation (p. 11). Through the "developing of a narrative that is both convincing and authentic" and "recording the subtle details of human experience" the researcher conducting portraiture "seeks to document and illuminate the complexity and detail of a unique experience or place, hoping that the audience will see themselves reflected in it, trusting that the readers will feel identified" (p. 14). Rather than promoting generalization, Lawrence-Lightfoot describes a process that through the "single case ... the reader will discover resonant universal themes" (p. 14) that apply to them and may encourage reflection, transformation, and change.

Lawrence-Lightfoot and Hoffman Davis (1997) describe the process that encompasses the making of a portrait. Just as in ethnographic research, the researcher is seen as an instrument in obtaining the complex information gathered and the process of the data gathering is critical to developing the portrait. Hoffman Davis argues that a process emerges through the making of a portrait that "requires careful, systematic, and detailed description developed through watching, listening to, and interacting with the actors over a sustained period of time, the tracing and interpretation of emergent themes, and the piecing together of these themes into an aesthetic whole" (p. 12). This is done to ultimately portray an authentic standard that captures "the essence and resonance of the actors' experience and perspective ... through action ... in context" (p. 12). The framework Lawrence-Lightfoot and Hoffman Davis offer focuses on process for the researcher to create the portrait. The key features of this portraiture process include: context, voice, relationship, emergent themes, and aesthetic whole. The context element of the portraiture process essentially sets up the "reference point, the map, the ecological sphere" (p. 41) to understand the experiences of the actors in their particular setting. In keeping with the dynamic dialogue associated with portraiture that is forever evolving, Lawrence-Lightfoot asserts that the researcher is "sketching herself into the context" (p. 50) in order to reveal the perch and the perspective embracing the concept; the portraitist is a critical component of the contextual setting.

The portraitist employs the use of voice as it provides a backdrop for the perspectives of the actors as well as the researcher. In an account that features an autobiographical lens, voice has a particularly strong role. The researcher "moves from thin to thick description ... which seeks meaning" ((Lawrence-Lightfoot & Hoffman Davis, 1997, p. 105) and is strongly influenced by their own preoccupation and interests. This is not to say that the researcher must avoid showing their perspective, but instead ought to be purposeful and conscious so as not to drown out the voices of their subjects and their engagement in activities—something I felt was key to interpreting my classroom.

The central feature of the portraiture process is relationship. In developing the relationship to create the depiction, the portraitist "searches for what is good, for what works, for what is of value" (Lawrence-Lightfoot & Hoffman Davis, 1997, p. 158) rather than seeking out an idealized telling of the situation. Although the relationship building is key to creating meaningful stories that embrace the complexities embedded within the situation, a researcher must acknowledge that they must adhere to boundaries, whether due to external factors such as time or space or due to internal struggle with emotional balance and empathetic limitations.

Emergent themes allow the portraitist to reflect on data collected, bringing their interpretations to the forefront in the process. Through a thematic analysis, the researcher examines the ideas to resonate out of the data. The researcher then needs to identify patterns that "become[s] the central activity of synthesizing, sorting, and organizing data" (Lawrence-Lightfoot & Hoffman Davis, 1997, p. 214). The themes are gathered through five modes of analysis: repetitive refrains, resonant metaphors, institutional and cultural rituals, triangulation, and revealing patterns.

Through the process associated with portraiture, an aesthetic whole will emerge as Eisner (1994) promoted for artistically-crafted inquiry. This part of the process promotes the authenticity of the final portrait and promotes the ongoing dialogue rich with complexity of the meaning made by the portraitist. The portraitist is blending art and science, capturing the aesthetic complexity of the human experience through rigorous inquiry.

IMPLICATIONS FOR POLICY AND PRACTICE

By combining parts of the various methodological approaches to educational inquiry using the eclectic arts framework (Schwab, 1971) a more complete interpretation could be revealed. Not only did combining methodologies allow for multiple modes of inquiry to be incorporated as a basis for this particular metamethodology, but multiple voices, sources of data, and perspectives were revealed through ethnography, autobiography, and portraiture inherent to my storytelling and the authenticity of the story itself. The resultant methodological approach demonstrates a rigorous, qualitative, interpretive framework that offered interpretation and description focusing on understanding rather than exploration of final truths or one correct answer (Ellsworth, 2005; Greene, 1995). Using these differing approaches for my research, I was able to highlight in a rich and meaningful way how the autobiographical experiences and those experiences centered on a classroom project relate and continue to affect my classroom practice. Furthermore, this eclectic research design approach showed the potential of purposefully answering Ellworth's (2007) provocative question: "What might become thinkable and do-able if we stop treating curriculum/teaching theory and practice as separate domains of academic research?" (p. 80). Beyond this particular usage, there are wide implications of leveraging eclectic arts as a rationale for multiple modes of inquiry to both practice and policy. These include making research more pertinent, applicable, and approachable for those engaged in classroom practice; going beyond triangulation of methods and challenging assumptions in mixed methodological approaches providing an avenue for others to invent metamethodologies that fit their given research situations; and as a means to creating the researcher as a conduit for inquiry camps to interact and engage with one another.

For many classroom teachers, the notion of research is inapplicable, removed, or is seemingly irrelevant to their daily practice with children in schools. This situation is nothing new, as Robinson (1998) clearly articulates, "the limited contribution of research to understanding and improvement of educational practice is the mismatch between educational research methodologies and the generic features of practice" (p. 17). Using the Schwabian eclectic arts framework can begin to alleviate this problem and allow classroom educators the means and ability to think about what is most appropriate for them to make meaning about their classrooms. When teachers are enabled to be more reflective about their practice, they have the means to improve their abilities to reach students, thus, improving their learning and achievement.

The use of eclectic arts as a rationale for multiple modes of inquiry also raises the possibilities of bringing "research camps" together. Too often, notions of "disciplined inquiry" (Shulman, 1981, p. 5) force methodological conversations to be relegated to research silos, separated by the singular research paradigm or methodology being utilized. The prospects of using a curricular framework such as the *Arts of Eclectic* for conducting research using multiple modes on areas related to classroom practice, curriculum theorizing, and more broadly defined educational research has great possibilities.

Not only does it go beyond the triangulation of individual methods (Massey, 1999) to develop informative research that is trustworthy and valid, it points to the potential of combining methodologies to promote rigor, authenticity, and increased validity especially when research discoveries are "convergent, inconsistent, and contradictory" (Mathison, 1988, p. 13). Further it transcends common assumptions of mixed methods (Cresswell, 2003; Tashakkori & Teddlie, 2002) because it permits and guides the researcher to match, adapt, and generate an appropriate and meaningful course of action that fits their specific situation instead of being forced to adhere to an approach or methods that may be problematic in their research setting or the particular phenomenon being examined. This theoretical framework has the potential to complement and build on the educational research by bringing these various research conversations together. The inquiry itself allows the researcher to invite different methodological frameworks to engage with each other and work in harmony. Researchers have the potential of becoming conduits for bringing the different orientations together, as they seek to make their inquiries practical not only for themselves, but for their participants as well.

REFERENCES

Ayers, W. C. (1990). Small heroes: In and out of school with 10-year-old city kids. *Cambridge Journal of Education 20*(3), 269–274.

Block, A. (2004). *Talmud, curriculum, and the practical: Joseph Schwab and the Rabbis.* New York: Peter Lang.

Bogdan, R., & Biklen, S. K. (1998). *Qualitative research for education* (3rd ed.). Boston: Allyn & Bacon.

Clandinin, D. J. (1985). Personal practical knowledge: A study of teachers' classroom images. *Curriculum Inquiry, 15*(4), 361–385.

Connelly, F. M., & Clandinin, D. J. (1988). *Teachers as curriculum planners: Narratives of experience.* New York: Teachers College Press.

Connelly, F. M., & Clandinin, D. J. (1990). Stories of experience and narrative inquiry. *Educational Researcher, 19*(4), 2–14.

Cresswell, J. W. (2003). *Research design: Qualitative, quantitative, and mixed methods approaches* (2nd ed.). Thousand Oaks, CA: SAGE.

Dewey, J. (1916). *Democracy and education.* New York: Free Press.

Eisner, E. W. (1994). *The educational imagination: On the design and evaluation of school programs* (2nd ed.). New York: Macmillan.

Eisner, E. W. (2001). *The educational imagination: On the design and evaluation of school programs* (3rd ed.). Upper Saddle River, NJ: Merrill Prentice Hall.

Eisenhart, M. (2001). Educational ethnography past, present, and future: Ideas to think with. *Educational Researcher, 30*(8), 16–27.

Ellsworth, E. (2005). *Places of learning: Media, architecture, and pedagogy.* New York: Routledge.

Ellsworth, E. (2007) What might become? What might become thinkable and doable if we stop treating curriculum/teaching theory and practice as separate domains of academic research? *Journal of Curriculum and Pedagogy, 4*(1), 80–83.

Geertz, C. (1973). *The interpretation of cultures.* New York: Basic Books.

Glesne, C. (1999). *Becoming qualitative researchers: An introduction.* New York: Longman.

Goodson, I. F. (Ed.). (1992). *Studying teachers' lives.* New York: Teachers College Press.

Graham, R. J. (1991). *Reading and writing the self: Autobiography in education and the curriculum.* New York: Teachers College Press.

Greene, M. (1995). *Releasing the imagination.* San Francisco: Jossey-Bass.

Grumet, M. (1978). Songs and situations. In G. Willis (Ed.), *Qualitative evaluation* (pp. 274–315). Berkeley, CA: McCutchan.

Grumet, M. (1981). Restitution and reconstruction of educational experience: An autobiographical method for curriculum theory. In M. Lawn & L. Barton (Eds.), *Rethinking curriculum studies* (pp. 115–130). London: Croom Helm.

Grumet, M. (1990). Retrospective: Autobiography and the analysis of educational experience. *Cambridge Journal of Education, 20*(3), 277–282.

Janesick, V. J. (1991). Ethnographic inquiry: Understanding culture and experiences. In E. C. Short (Ed.), *Forms of curriculum inquiry* (pp. 101–120). Albany, NY: State University of New York Press.

Lytle, S. L., & Cochran-Smith, M. (1992). Teacher research as a way of knowing. *Harvard Educational Review, 62*(4), 447–474.

Lawrence-Lightfoot, S. (1983). *The good high school: Portraits of character and culture.* New York: Basic Books.

Lawrence-Lightfoot, S., & Hoffman Davis, J. (1997). *The art and science of portraiture.* San Francisco: Jossey-Bass.

Massey, A. (1999). Methodological triangulation, or how to get lost without being found out. In M. Massey, & G. Walford (Eds.). *Explorations in methodology: Studies in educational ethnography* (Vol. 2, pp. 183–197). Stamford, CT: JAI.

Mathison, S. (1988). Why triangulate? *Educational Researcher 17*(2), 13–17.

Maxwell, J. A. (1992). Understanding and validity in qualitative research. *Harvard Educational Review, 62,* 279–300.

Pinar, W. F., & Grumet, M. R. (1976). *Toward a poor curriculum.* Dubuque, IA: Darnell Hunt.

Pinar, W. F., Reynolds, W. M., Slattery, P., & Taubman, P. M. (1995). *Understanding curriculum: An introduction to the study of historical and contemporary curriculum discourses.* New York: Peter Lang.

Robinson, V. M. J. (1998). Methodology and the research-practice gap. *Educational Researcher, 27*(1), 17–26.

Schubert, W. H. (1975). *Imaginative projection: A method of curriculum invention.* Unpublished doctoral dissertation, University of Illinois, Urbana-Champaign.

Schubert, W. H. (1980). Recalibrating education research: Toward a focus on practice. *Educational Researcher, 9*(1), 17–24, 31.

Schubert, W. H. (1986). *Curriculum: Perspective, paradigm, and possibility.* New York: Macmillan.

Schubert, W. H. (1991). Teacher lore: A basis for understanding praxis. In C. Witherall, & N. Noddings (Eds.), *Stories lives tell: Narrative and dialogue in education* (pp. 207–233). New York: Teachers College Press.

Schubert, W. H., & Ayers, W. C. (1992). *Teacher lore: Learning from our own experiences.* New York: Longman.

Schubert, W. H., & Lopez Schubert, A. L. (1997). Sources of a theory for action research in the United States. In R. McTaggart (Ed.), *Participatory action research: International contexts and consequences* (pp. 203–222). Albany, NY: State University of New York Press.

Schultz, B. D. (2007). Problematizing race: Complicating good liberal intentions. In S. Leafgren, B. D. Schultz, M. P. O'Malley, A. Mahdi, J. Brady, & A. Dentith. (Eds.), *The articulation of curriculum and pedagogy for a just society: Advocacy, artistry, and activism* (pp. 93–105). Troy, NY: Educator's International Press.

Schultz, B. D. (2008). *Spectacular things happen along the way: Lessons from an urban classroom.* New York: Teachers College Press.

Schwab, J. J. (1969). The practical: A language for curriculum. *School Review, 78,* 1–23.

Schwab, J. J. (1971). The practical: Arts of eclectic. *School Review, 79,* 493–542.

Shulman, L. S. (1981). Disciplines of inquiry in education: An overview. *Educational Researcher, 10*(6), 5–13, 23.

Short, E. C. (1991). *Forms of curriculum inquiry.* Albany: State University of New York Press.

Stake, R. (1997). Case study method in educational research: seeking sweet water. In R. M. Jaeger (Ed.), *Complementary methods for research in education* (pp. 401–414). Washington: American Educational Research Association.

Tashakkori A., & Teddlie, C. (Eds.) (2002). *Handbook of mixed methods in social and behavioral research.* Thousand Oaks, CA: SAGE.

Westbury, I., & Wilkof, N. (Eds.). (1978). *Science, curriculum, and liberal education: Selected essays.* Chicago: University of Chicago Press.

Wolcott, H. (1997). Ethnographic research in education. In R. M. Jaeger (Ed.), *Complementary methods for research in education* (pp. 327–353). Washington: American Educational Research Association.

CHAPTER 18

A ROMANCE WITH NARRATIVE INQUIRY

Toward an Act of Narrative Theorizing

Jeong-Hee Kim

The purpose of this article is to identify some of the challenges that narrative inquiry faces in the current political era and find ways to overcome them. I engage in an act of, what I call, narrative theorizing, which is an intentional process of questioning and interrogating the nature of narrative inquiry that may undermine its potentials. The article reaffirms the importance of narrative research in teaching and learning by suggesting that doing narrative research is a poetizing and sacred act transcending the limit of doing research.

Bruner's (2002) rhetorical question, "Do we need another book about narrative, about stories, what they are and how they are used?" (p. 3), reflects how popular narrative research[1] has been over the last decade. As Bruner noted, there has been a proliferation of narrative works across disciplines and around the world. The current popularity of narrative research is an effort to move away from positivism, the traditional epistemological paradigm that views the very nature of knowledge as objective and definite. Narrative research challenges and problematizes the nature

Curriculum and Teaching Dialogue
Volume 10, Numbers 1 & 2, 2008, pp. 251–267
Copyright © 2008 by Information Age Publishing
251

of knowledge as objective and questions unitary ways of knowing (Polkinghorne, 1988). Therefore, using narrative, educational researchers intend to interrogate the dominant view of education and try to reshape our understandings of education and schooling through the lived experiences of teachers or students (Clandinin & Connelly, 2000; Munro, 1998).

Narrative research is cross-disciplinary and its applications now extend beyond a research methodology, utilized as a pedagogical tool in teaching and learning (Conle, 2000a; Denzin & Lincoln, 2005; Riessman & Speedy, 2007). More recently, the use of narrative as curricula and pedagogical strategies has been explored in the field of teacher education (Conle, 2003; Coulter, Michael, & Poynor, 2007). There are also studies that describe how significant narrative inquiry is in helping prospective teachers make connections between the students' lives and the classroom, and understand the interrelationships between narrative, pedagogy and multiculturalism (Clark & Medina, 2000; Grinberg, 2002; Phillion, He, & Connelly, 2005). Through the burgeoning of publications in recent years, narrative inquiry is truly enjoying a "renaissance" across the social sciences, including the field of education (Josselson, 2003, p. 3).

In spite of such popularity, however, I, a self-proclaimed "narrative researcher," still sense that "narrative inquiry is a field in the making" (Chase, 2000, p. 651). Furthermore, the so-called narrative turn is not so empowering in the current era of No Child Left Behind. As Barone (2007) points out, narrative research seems to be in danger of marginalization since the National Research Council recently called for evidence-based educational research that uses "rigorous, systematic and objective procedures to obtain valid knowledge," such as "experimental or quasi-experimental designs" (Maxwell, 2004, p. 3). This political context does not provide a comfortable research environment for emerging narrative researchers who try to establish their research agenda in academia. In an interview conducted by Clandinin and Murphy (2007), Amia Lieblich, an influential narrative researcher, affirms this not-so-friendly political environment surrounding narrative research in the following quote:

> I would be very careful in advising people to go only in their narrative or qualitative way. I would make it very clear that with all the richness and the real complexity that one can touch with this matter, there are also many, many risks and dangers involved in pursuing this manner of research. (p. 640)

It is paradoxical that doing narrative research is such risky business considering the popularity of narrative. Elbaz-Luwisch (2007) also posits that although narrative inquiry has already made a significant contribution to the development of such a public language, much more work is needed, and the task is a long-term one. According to Elbaz-Luwisch, narrative inquiry, indeed, confronts a range of problems resulting from the difficulty of presenting a complex, layered, and dynamic reality within the politically charged research arena.

The purpose of this article is to identify some of the challenges that narrative inquiry faces in the current political era and to find ways to overcome them. I engage in an act of, what I call, *narrative theorizing*. Theorizing, according to van Manen (1990), is the "intentional act of attaching ourselves to the world, to become more fully part of it, or better, to *become* the world" (p. 5). *Narrative theorizing*, then, is an intentional process of questioning and interrogating the nature of narrative inquiry that may undermine its potentials. The ultimate goal of *narrative theorizing* is to look for possibilities that will lead narrative research to re-establish and reaffirm its significance as a research methodology and a pedagogical tool in teaching and learning in the current political context.

In the following article, I first identify some of the problematic issues of narrative inquiry that are raised in the literature. These issues include: (1) the narcissistic nature of narrative inquiry; (2) the lack of narratology in narrative inquiry; and (3) the question of art or research? Then, I discuss possibilities to address such challenging issues, which include: (1) engaging in narrative inquiry as Bakhtinian novelness; (2) transforming lived experience to lived theory; (3) considering narrative research as an aesthetic inquiry; and (4) imagining the implied readership as a fusion of horizons. And finally, in the conclusion, my commitment to doing narrative research is reaffirmed, for doing narrative research means more than doing research, that is, it is a *poetizing act* and a *sacred act*. Now, I first turn to the problematic issues of narrative inquiry.

PROBLEMATIZING NARRATIVE INQUIRY

Narcissistic Nature of Narrative Inquiry

Narrative research is "up close and personal in that it involves in-depth study of particular individuals in social context and in time, and it requires a highly sensitized and self-reflective inquirer rather than a set of objective, impersonal skills" (Josselson, 2003, p. 4). This aspect of narrative inquiry, however, may lead to a sense of narcissism if caution is not used. Behar-Horenstein and Morgan (1995) criticize placing extreme emphasis on teachers' personal meaning, exaggerating the significance of the writer, and having a tendency to confer an unwarranted level of authenticity upon teacher experience seem to reward narcissism. This narcissism is what Patai called "nouveau solipsism" (Hatch & Wisnewki, 1995). In their report of a summary analysis of surveys that were sent to a group of narrative scholars, Hatch and Wisniewski observed the following:

> Based on our review of manuscripts over several years, we see a strong tendency among scholars to reflect on their work and their place in it rather than to do the work, a tendency Patai has labeled "nouveau solipsism." (p. 131)

I confess that my work is not free from this criticism and I also observed this tendency in some of the proposals that I had reviewed in the last several years for the Narrative and Research SIG (Special Interest Group) of the American Educational Research Association (AERA).

Moreover, this narcissistic tendency may lead to the possibility of romanticizing the protagonist. Munro (1998) reveals her uneasy feeling about engaging in narrative while studying women teachers' life history narratives in relation to cultural politics and the teachers' resistance. Her concern was that narrative research had the possibility of romanticizing the protagonist and, therefore, reifying notions of a unitary subject/hero and notions of subjectivity as unitary, essential and universal. Here, stories are reduced to objects, thereby reifying a positivist view of knowledge. Bowman (2006) also states that membership in the narrative community entails courage and considerable risk to the extent that its interests are also seen as "self-indulgent" diversions rather than sources of professional knowledge. Hence, a cynical question is often raised: Is anyone's story just as worthy as anyone else's? (Barone, 2007).

Lack of Narratology in Narrative Inquiry

To explore this issue, I borrow the French term, *narratologie* (narratology), coined by Tzvetan Todorov, who used the word in parallel with *biology, sociology,* and so forth. Narratology denotes "the science of narrative" (Herman, 2005), and it is a theory that helps us to understand, analyze, and evaluate stories (Bal, 1997). Narratology in narrative inquiry with regards to education, then, means using a theory as an intellectual tool to interpret a narrative text that takes place in an educational context.

The lack of narratology in narrative inquiry has been pointed out among educational researchers. According to Behar-Horenstein and Morgan (1995), while the use of story has become an emergent power in educational research, stories currently do not offer a political or theoretical foundation from which to create new understandings. Brinthaupt and Lipka (1992) valorized the proliferation of narrative studies of the self as an object of scientific study, but they also pointed out some of the difficulties that may arise when attempting to integrate the differing theoretical, methodological, and developmental perspectives into narrative inquiry. Clandinin and Connelly (2000) also acknowledged the academic concern that "narrative inquiry is not theoretical enough" (p. 42).

In a similar vein, Conle (2000b) argues that "the inquiry in narrative inquiry" (p. 190) has not been seriously investigated, especially by novice narrative researchers. Conle's point is that before engaging in telling stories, one needs to think about the ways in which such a story is an inquiry. She portrays narrative inquiry as belonging to more than one realm, that is, there are two voices speaking simultaneously: the narrator's voice that presents the case and the theoretical voice that conceptualizes what is presented. These two voices may not be compatible, but they can be beneficial because "narrative inquirers will benefit from a theoretical understanding of the process they are engaged in; and those who are used to theoretical discourse may benefit from lending an ear to experiential testimony" (p. 194).

Unfortunately, many narrative researchers seem to fail to make their methodological and theoretical approaches transparent enough to help their audiences know explicitly how they reached their conclusions (Hollingsworth & Dybdahl, 2007). Therefore, the challenges that narrative researchers may encounter are, as Bowman (2006) states, how to achieve the rigor that professional respectability demands without sacrificing the openness that narrative inquiry requires, and how to communicate the means by which the work at hand achieves this balance. Unless narrative inquirers address these challenges, narrative inquiry will remain a "professional oddity without real transformative power" (p. 13).

Art or Research?

Narrative inquiry, also known as arts-based research, is sometimes understood by researchers as being inseparable from literary art forms. According to Conle (2000b), however, this kind of view requires more careful consideration because it either "leads to the dismissal of narrative inquiry as viable research or else its fictional character is praised as arts-based research" (p. 58). In fact, some researchers criticize narrative inquiry for its tendency of being art rather than research, which seems based primarily on talent, intuition, or clinical experience (Lieblich, Tuval-Mashiach, & Zilber, 1998). Richardson (1996) also pointed out that although researchers who employ arts-based research may be labeled as good writers, the question remains as to whether they are "doing research."

Short stories, biographies, autobiographies, poetry, novels, and plays have been incorporated into narrative inquiry over the years for the study of educational experiences.[2] However, there has been a tension within the area of arts-based research and the use of alternative forms of representation (Piirto, 2002). Debates about the place of these nonacademic forms of writing (i.e., art as research) took place at AERA more than a decade ago (Eisner, 1995; Phillips, 1995), and still continue today. Bowman (2006) sums up these debates in the following statement: "As long as narrative inquiry is perceived as airy-fairy, artsy-fartsy, hippie-dippie, its advocates will continue to wrestle with significant narrative issues both in their research and in their bids for promotion and tenure" (p. 13). Hence, here arises another cynical question: "That's a good story, but is it really research?" (Ceglowski, 1997, p. 198).

LOOKING FOR POSSIBILITIES

Thus far, I have identified some of the challenges or concerns that narrative inquiry confronts. These challenges might contribute to placing narrative inquiry in danger of further marginalization (Barone, 2007) in the politically charged research arena (Elbaz-Luwisch, 2007), unless we narrative researchers scrutinize those challenges in order to find ways to overcome them. In this section, I will discuss some possibilities that narrative inquirers should consider in addressing these concerns. The possibilities include: (1) engaging in narrative inquiry as Bakhtinian novelness; (2) transforming lived experience to lived theory; (3) considering narrative research as an aesthetic inquiry; and (4) imagining the implied readership as a fusion of horizons.

Engaging in Narrative Inquiry as Bakhtinian Novelness

To overcome the possibility of unintentionally promoting the self-indulgent, narcissistic nature of narrative inquiry, I suggest that we incorporate Bakhtinian novelness in our narrative work. Bakhtin developed three major theories of the novel: polyphony, chronotope, and carnival. Polyphony refers to "a plurality of independent, unmerged voices and consciousness" (Bakhtin, 1963/1984, p. 6). In the polyphonic novel, different languages are used and different voices are heard without having one voice privileged over the others. The polyphonic novel produces no final, complete truth, but unfinalizable partial and tentative truths evolving from the interaction among participants whose voices are equally valid. Chronotope pertains to time and space. For Bakhtin, adding voices is not enough to promote genuine dialogue. For the voices to reflect believable individual experiences, they should be put in particular times and particular spaces. Chronotope allows the experiences to be looked at from historical and social perspectives. Finally, carnival, according to Bakhtin, is a concept in which everyone is an active participant, openness and different cultures are celebrated, hierarchy is invisible, and norms are reversed, like in popular festivals. In the carnivalesque novel, counter-narratives are celebrated with equal value. One formal and privileged way of life or way of thinking is discarded whereas differing views and styles are valued. In the carnival, voices of the marginalized or silenced are promoted and respected.

Incorporating Bakhtinian novelness of polyphony, chronotope, and carnival into our researched stories makes it possible for us to avoid developing a self-indulgent, narcissistic text, preventing our narrative work from becoming a mere "soap-box" (Wolcott, 1994). That is, we can avoid romanticizing the protagonist in our research analysis, who often becomes a mode for saying what we want to say and not really listening to what is being said (Munro Hendry, 2007). We can also counteract the skepticism that "narrative researchers risk a backlash because they seem to think that anyone's story is just as worthy as anyone else's" (cited in Barone, 2007, p. 463).

Using Bakhtinian novelness also helps us focus on the voices of disadvantaged lay people. As Bakhtin (1975/1981) says, "the novel's roots must ultimately be sought in folklore" (p. 38). At its core reside personal experience and free, creative imagination. The move toward narrative research in education, indeed, has resulted in part from the long overdue recognition of the sound of silence or voices that have been excluded from the kinds of positivistic research texts (Barone, 2007). The purpose of novel narratives, then, is "to stimulate critical thinking by opening up possibilities for critique and to provoke multiple interpretations, rather than lead the reader to a solitary conclusion" (Rosiek & Atkinson, 2007, p. 508). Examples of such novel narratives can be found in Barone (2001), Tanaka (1997), and Kim (2006).

Transforming Lived Experience to Lived Theory

Narrative research that employs Bakhtinian novelness would contribute to providing multiple perspectives for the reader, thereby accomplishing the promise of narrative as a form of democratic research. Multiple voices, however, as Greene (Ayers, 1995) pointed out, could contribute to a meaningless cacophony of individual interests. Hence, we need to seriously deliberate what the multiple voices might mean by incorporating the narratology, a theoretical inquiry aspect, into data interpretation. Eisner (1991) contends that storytelling without explicit interpretation or theory is insufficient. According to Eisner, although a descriptive dimension of an educational researcher would provide readers with vicarious experiences of events, educational significance of what s/he has described should be provided along with explicit interpretation employing social science theory for the sake of "satisfying rationality, raising fresh questions, and deepening the conversation" (p. 95).

Goodson (1992) also argues that stories in narrative inquiry should be used only as a starting point of a process of coming to know, and they should be extended by a theory to be connected to the larger society to help us understand the meaning of the individual lives and interrogate the historical, social, and political world in which they are embedded. Traditionally, theory is associated with authority, which may make the story overshadowed and perhaps devalued by the authority of theory. Hence, theory needs to be incorporated into an ongoing experiential narrative, so that theory can be transformed by experience to become *lived theory* (Conle, 1999). In *lived theory*, there is no clear line of separation of where the story ends or where the personal theorizing begins, and thus, the expanded story continues (Conle, 1999). In her later work, Conle (2000a) makes the following argument:

> The incorporation of theory into narrative inquiry can over-power an experiential narrative unless the theory in turn becomes a part of the story. After all, our encounters with ideas, readings, and theories are experiences as well and the meaning we make of them can become part of our narrative. (p. 58)

When lived experience becomes lived theory, we are theorizing the lived experience of the protagonists. Thus, lived theory grounded in the protagonist's lived experience promotes dialogical relations between reality and theoretical concepts. It becomes a beginning of an inquiry, rather than a "boundary to inquiry that hampers efforts to discover, for example, practices that will provide the desired changes" (Anyon, 1994, p.127). Lived theory is organic and ontological; it is not bound to a metanarrative. It is constantly in the process of evolving and recurring while *traveling* from place to place and from person to person.[3]

When lived theory is interwoven in lived experience, we are bridging the lives and stories of individuals with the understanding of larger human and social phenomena (Hatch & Wisniewski, 1995). Lived theory becomes socially or politically useful (Anyon, 1994) in that it will be of help in serving the public interest rather than serving primarily the interests of those who produce the theory. Therefore, narrative research in which lived experience becomes lived theory can work to create social change not in a way that a theory would impose a totalizing view, but in a way that the theory would acknowledge the complex narratives, which connect the daily life of the protagonist and larger educational, societal issues. Narrative research, then, can be more than a descriptive kind of inquiry; it becomes interventionist in the sense that it involves questions of social justice and change (Clandinin, 2007).

Considering Narrative Inquiry as an Aesthetic Inquiry

Now, what can be done to prevent narrative research from being dismissed merely as an art that is a fringe undertaking, a species of "frill" (Bowman, 2006)? According to Gadamer (1988), artistic experience can produce a certain kind of knowledge that is different from epistemology. Gadamer writes:

> Artistic experience is a mode of knowledge ... certainly different from that sensory knowledge which provides science with the data from which it constructs the knowledge of nature, and certainly different from all moral rational knowledge and indeed from all conceptual knowledge, but still knowledge, i.e. the transmission of truth. (p. 87)

In this sense, narrative inquiry as arts-based research produces a mode of knowledge since it transmits truths (multiple, partial truths) to the reader through an artistic experience. This kind of knowledge should be distinguished from the traditional, positivistic research that focuses on enhancing certainty with a goal of producing absolute truth. Indeed, narrative research that generates an artistic experience as a mode of knowledge is an aesthetic inquiry in which the aesthetic is integral to the research in helping our reader with his/her cognitive, perceptual, emotional, and imaginative understanding of the world (Greene, 2001). Bresler (2006) calls this kind of qualitative research "*aesthetically based research,*" which places aesthetics at the heart of both artistic experience and qualitative research. It enables the reader to see how research relates aesthetically to knowing, understanding, and perceiving the world in which lived experience takes place. It also provides the reader with aesthetic experience through which the reader can participate vicariously in situations beyond his/her practical possibilities (Eisner, 1995).

Narrative inquiry as an aesthetic inquiry has to do with alternative forms of representation of research, such as short stories, poetry, novels, or visual ethnography. If the aim of our research is to serve the public interest and its well-being, as noted in the theme of the 2006 AERA conference, then these alternative forms of representation should be encouraged and promoted as they appeal to the nonresearch public rather than the educated elite (Dunlop, 2001). For instance, the novel provides a more widely accessible form that can extend its findings to a large, interdisciplinary community of discourse, providing opportunities for multiple perspectives and multiple readings. Artistic representations, such as fiction and poetry, play a pivotal role in our conceptualizations and re-conceptualizations of meaning and knowledge in human lives and in the broader currents of our society (Dunlop, 2001). Narrative inquiry as an aesthetic inquiry can push the boundaries of the qualitative research landscape by honoring art and multiple aesthetic perspectives (Mello, 2007). Therefore, as Eisner (1995) contends, we should create the possibility for an intellectual climate where this kind of contribution is not excluded and we should further encourage ways to engage in this kind of work.

Imagining the Implied Readership as a Fusion of Horizons

Narrative research as an aesthetic inquiry that adopts the concept of Bakhtinian novelness to generate lived theory should have a final feature that turns to the reader. Bruner (2002) calls it a coda, the reader's retrospective evaluation of what it (the research text) all might mean. According to Bruner, a coda is a feature that returns the reader from "the there and then of the narrative to the here and now of the telling, and to the future of the telling" (p. 20). It is a feature that invites readers to have ongoing, dialogic conversations to explore the persistent research question of what is good for the public's well-being. The coda feature, which invites the reader to become a part of narrative research, can be further elaborated by the concepts of Wolfgang Iser's (1974) *implied reader* and Hans-Georg Gadamer's (1988) *fusion of horizons.*

Implied reader refers to the reader's actualization of the potential meaning of the text, which is possible through the active reading process. The implied reader can be an independent character of the story by being actively involved in the dialogue, interpreting the text from his/her own vantage point and discovering a new world to which he/she is not accustomed. Therefore, a narrative research text gives the reader an opportunity to acquire a new horizon. Gadamer (1988) writes, "To acquire a horizon means that one learns to look beyond what is close at hand – not in order to look away from it, but to see it better within a larger whole and in truer proportion" (p. 272). As the reader develops a new horizon, he/she is in the process of a fusion of horizons, which is an indication of understanding that occurs as a constant negotiation between oneself and otherness. Through a fusion of horizons, the reader can participate in empathic understanding where both the horizon of self and that of others are continuously under adjustment while simultaneously upholding differences (Gadamer, 1988).

Hence, by imagining the reader in the process of fusing his/her horizons, a narrative research text can provide a coda to help the reader surmise what it all might mean, challenge their taken-for-granted ideas about educational phenomena, and ultimately expand their horizons. Narrative inquiry that embraces the *implied reader as a fusion of horizons* does not endorse the traditional research paradigms that aim to provide a final answer, nor does it approve the protagonist's narcissism and romanticism. By appealing to the reader's imagination and participation in the reading, narrative research encourages various interpretations and possibilities that will bring about social and educational change.

MY ROMANCE WITH NARRATIVE: A CODA

To engage in an act of *narrative theorizing*—as I attempted to do in this article—is my constant effort to establish a devoted and healthy romantic relationship with narrative inquiry. Such an effort is delineated here by identifying some problematic aspects of narrative inquiry that may undermine its importance, such as its narcissistic nature, the lack of narratology, and the question of art or research. My suggestions—engaging in narrative inquiry as Bakhtinian novelness, transforming lived experience to lived theory, considering narrative inquiry as an aesthetic inquiry, and imagining the implied readership as a fusion of horizons—are just some of the possibilities that would help narrative research achieve the rigor that the field of educational research demands without giving up its original postmodern complexity, ambiguity, and openness. Therefore, these suggestions are not complete as there are other issues of narrative inquiry that need to be addressed, including issues of trustworthiness, fidelity, voice, power relations between the researcher and the researched, ethical issues, and more.

Before I conclude my article, I want to return to the Bruner's question that was cited in the introduction of this paper: "Do we need another book about narrative, about stories, what they are and how they are used?" (Bruner, 2002, p. 3). Bruner answers this question affirmatively in the following statement:

> What we know intuitively about stories is enough to get us through the familiar routines, but it serves us much less well when we try to understand or explain what we are doing or try to get it under deliberate control.... To get beyond implicitness and intuition, we seem to need some sort of outside hoist, something to take us up a level. (p. 4)

Indeed, we need this "hoist" that would transcend our present state of narrative inquiry within the current political arena. This requires narrative researchers to collectively and continuously deliberate what it means to be a narrative researcher. The current political context, especially with the passage of the No Child Left Behind (NCLB) Act of 2001, calls for the use of *scientifically based research,* a phrase used 111 times within the text (Barone, 2007), as a prescription to improve the American public educational system. Barone poignantly points out that the NCLB context pushes for a return to the "gold standard," which threatens the legitimacy of the work of educational researchers who are not engaged in such "*scientifically based research.*" Barone continues, "the deepening chill in the political climate may signal the need for an examination of the current status of this narrative approach to educational research and for reflecting on its future course" (p. 456). This chilling political climate against qualitative research, and narrative research in particular, forces us narrative researchers to seriously think about the reasons why we do what we do.

What should be noted, despite the political oppression against narrative research, is that there are more and more researchers, including practitioners, who employ narrative not only as a research methodology but also as a pedagogical tool in teaching and learning. This goes to show that the power of narrative inquiry reaches beyond the field of research methodology. It has a transformative impact on teaching and learning, including curriculum, professional development, and teacher education (Ayers, Quinn, Stovall, & Scheiern, 2008; Conle, 2000a, 2003; Connelly, He, & Phillion, 2008; Coulter, Michael, & Poynor, 2007; Smith, 2008). Narrative research is indeed a "theory/practice/reflection cycle of inquiry" (Smith, 2008, p. 65) that contributes to the advancement of educational research on research methodology, methods, teaching, and curriculum.

Therefore, I will continue my romance with narrative even though I know that narrative research will never be the "*scientifically based research*" that the current political research arena promotes, and in consequence my research might never be as well regarded as traditional research by the politics of academia. However, I am determined to continue my engagement with narrative because to me, doing narrative research means more than doing research. It is a *poetizing act* and a *sacred act* that goes beyond doing research.

To me, doing narrative is a "poetizing act" (van Manen, 1990, p. 49), in that it creates a metaphor that makes it possible for the researcher to transcend the limit of doing research. Van Manen quotes Virginia Woolf to explain the *poetizing act*:

> By the bold and running use of metaphor, the poet will amplify and give us not the thing itself, but the reverberation and reflection which, taken into

his [sic] mind, the thing has made; close enough to the original to illustrate it, remote enough to heighten, enlarge, and make splendid. (Woolf cited in van Manen, 1990, p. 49)

Doing narrative research as a poetizing act creates a metaphor that gives narrative its "loft beyond the particular" (Bruner, 2002, p. 25), which has such reach that a personal trouble becomes a public plight. This loft beyond the particular is what makes well-constructed narrative research so powerful and so essential. Doing narrative research, therefore, provides me with an opportunity to implement such a poetizing act through which I can transcend the limit of doing research that applies to only a particular situation, and through which I can also transcend my authority as a researcher to become a humble, empathetic subject who thinks with those whom I research.

Through this transcendence, doing narrative research becomes a "sacred act" (Munro Hendry, 2007, p. 495). Munro Hendry quotes Laurel Richardson to expound the meaning of "sacred":

What might I mean by "sacred space?" I know it is not "innocent space" but a space where, minimally, four things will happen: (1) people will feel "safe" within it, safe to be and experiment with who they are and who they are becoming; (2) people feel "connected"—perhaps to each other, or a community, or nature, or the world they are constructing on their word processors; (3) people feel passionate about what they are doing, believing that their activity "makes a difference"; and (4) people recognize, honor, and are grateful for the safe communion. (Richardson cited in Munro Hendry, 2007, p. 496)

Munro Hendry (2007) argues that doing narrative research is a sacred endeavor in which research is considered "not as a scientific act but as a spiritual act, one that honors the sacredness of our humanity" (p. 496). Thus, research becomes more than a site of knowledge production, rather it is a site of communion where the researcher and the researched are interconnected in such an inquiry. Munro Hendry contends that there is no future in narrative research unless we "radically transform our notion of research in ways that honor the sacredness of our humanness" (p. 496).

Alas, narrative research will never be "scientifically based research," hence, it takes a risk of being further marginalized in the current political circumstances. Further, narrative research itself confronts inherent challenges and problems that need to be overcome. What I learned from the narrative theorizing that I attempted in this article is that my romantic partner, narrative research, is not a saint that I can put on a pedestal. However, through its humane nature, it empowers me as a teacher, researcher, and human being who is in the process of *becoming*; therefore, my romance with narrative inquiry perseveres.

NOTES

1. In this article, the term, narrative research, is interchangeably used with the term, narrative inquiry.
2. See also Mello (2007) and Rosiek and Atkinson (2007) for more exemplary narrative works using alternative forms of representation.
3. See Bayoumi and Rubin (2000) for Edward Said's traveling theory.

REFERENCES

Anyon, J. (1994). The retreat of Marxism and socialist feminism: Postmodern and poststructural theories in education. *Curriculum Inquiry, 24*(2), 115–133.

Ayers, W. (1995). Social imagination: A conversation with Maxine Greene. *International Journal of Qualitative Studies in Education, 8*(4), 319–328.

Ayers, W., Quinn, T., Stovall, D., & Scheiern, L. (2008). Teachers' experience of curriculum: Policy, pedagogy, and situation. In F. M. Connelly, M. F. He, & J. Phillion (Eds.), *The SAGE handbook of curriculum and instruction* (pp. 306–326). LA: SAGE.

Bakhtin, M. M. (1984). *Problem of Dostoevsky's poetics*. Minneapolis: University of Minnesota Press. (Original work published 1963)

Bakhtin, M. M. (1981). *The dialogic imagination: Four essays by M. M. Bakhtin*. Austin, TX: University of Texas Press. (Original work published 1975)

Bal, M. (1997). *Narratology: Introduction to the theory of narrative* (2nd ed.). Toronto, Canada: University of Toronto Press.

Barone, T. (2001). *Touching Eternity: The enduring outcomes of teaching*. New York: Teachers College Press.

Barone, T. (2007). A return to the gold standard?: Questioning the future of narrative construction as educational research. *Qualitative Inquiry, 13*(4), 454–470.

Bayoumi, M., & Rubin, A. (Eds.). (2000). *The Edward Said reader*. New York: Vintage Books.

Behar-Horenstein, L. S., & Morgan, R. R. (1995). Narrative research, teaching, and teacher thinking: Perspectives and possibilities. *Peabody Journal of Education, 70*(2), 139–161.

Bowman, W. D. (2006). Why narrative? Why now? *Research Studies in Music Education, 27*, 5–20.

Bresler, L. (2006). Toward connectedness: Aesthetically based research. *Studies in Art Education, 48*(1), 52–69.

Brinthaupt, T., & Lipka, R. (Eds.). (1992). *The self: Definitional and methodological issues*. Albany: State University of New York Press.

Bruner, J. (2002). *Making stories: Law, literature, life*. New York: Farrar, Straus and Giroux.

Ceglowski, D. (1997). That's a good story, but is it really research? *Qualitative Inquiry, 3*(2), 188–205.

Chase, S. (2000). Narrative Inquiry. In N. K. Denzin & Y. S. Lincoln (Eds.), *Handbook of qualitative research* (pp. 651–679). Thousand Oaks, CA: SAGE.

Clandinin, D. J. (Ed.). (2007). *Handbook of narrative inquiry*. Thousand Oaks, CA: SAGE.

Clandinin, D. J., & Connelly, M. (2000). *Narrative inquiry: Experience and story in qualitative research*. San Francisco: Jossey-Bass.

Clandinin, D. J., & Murphy, M. S. (2007). Looking ahead: Conversations with Elliot Mishler, Don Polkinghorne, and Amia Lieblich. In D. J. Clandinin (Ed.), *Handbook of narrative inquiry* (pp. 632–650). Thousand Oaks, CA: SAGE.

Clark, C., & Medina, C. (2000). How reading and writing literacy narratives affect preservice teachers' understandings of literacy, pedagogy, and multiculturalism. *Journal of Teacher Education, 51*(1), 63–76.

Conle, C. (1999). Why narrative? Which narrative? Struggling with time and place in life and research. *Curriculum Inquiry, 29*(1), 7–32.

Conle, C. (2000a). Narrative inquiry: Research tool and medium for professional development. *European Journal of Teacher Education, 23*(1), 49–63.

Conle, C. (2000b). Thesis as narrative or "What is the inquiry in narrative inquiry?" *Curriculum Inquiry, 30*(2), 190–214.

Conle, C. (2003). An anatomy of narrative curricula. *Educational Researcher, 32*(3), 3–15.

Connelly, F. M., He, M. F., & Phillion, J. (Eds.). (2008). *The SAGE handbook of curriculum and instruction*. Los Angeles: SAGE.

Coulter, C., Michael, C., & Poynor, L. (2007). Storytelling as pedagogy: An unexpected outcome of narrative inquiry. *Curriculum Inquiry, 37*(2), 103–122.

Denzin, N., & Lincoln, Y. (2005). Introduction. In *The Sage handbook of qualitative research* (pp. 1–29). Thousand Oaks, CA: SAGE.

Dunlop, R. (2001). Boundary bay: A novel as educational research. In A. Cole, G. Knowles & L. Neilsen (Eds.), *The art of writing inquiry* (pp. 49–70). Halifax, Nova Scotia: Backalong Books.

Eisner, E. (1991). *The enlightened eye: Qualitative inquiry and the enhancement of educational practice*. New York: Macmillan.

Eisner, E. (1995). What artistically crafted research can help us to understand about schools. *Educational Theory, 45*(1), 1–7.

Elbaz-Luwisch, F. (2007). Studying teachers' lives and experience: Narrative inquiry into K-12 teaching. In D. J. Clandinin (Ed.), *Handbook of narrative inquiry: Mapping a methodology* (pp. 357–382). Thousand Oaks, CA: SAGE.

Gadamer, H. (1988). *Truth and Method* (G. Barden & J. Cumming, Trans.). New York: Crossroad.

Goodson, I. (Ed.). (1992). *Studying teachers' lives*. New York: Teachers College Press.

Greene, M. (2001). *Variations on a blue guitar: The Lincoln Center Institute lectures on aesthetic education*. London: Teachers College Press.

Grinberg, J. G. A. (2002). "I had never been exposed to teaching like that": Progressive teacher education at Bank Street during the 1930's. *Teachers College Record, 104*(7), 1422–1460.

Hatch, J. A., & Wisniewski, R. (1995). Life history and narrative: Questions, issues, and exemplary works. In A. Hatch & R. Wisniewski (Eds.), *Life history and narrative* (pp. 113–136). London: The Falmer Press.

Herman, D. (2005). Histories of narrative theory (I): A genealogy of early developments. In J. Phelan & P. Rabinowitz (Eds.), *A companion to narrative theory* (pp. 19–35). Malden, MA: Blackwell.

Hollingsworth, S., & Dybdahl, M. (2007). Talking to learn: The critical role of conversation in narrative inquiry. In D. J. Clandinin (Ed.), *Handbook of narrative inquiry* (pp. 146–176). Thousand Oaks, CA: SAGE.

Iser, W. (1974). *The implied reader.* Baltimore: Johns Hopkins University Press.

Josselson, R. (2003). Introduction. In R. Josselson, A. Lieblich, & D. McAdams (Eds.), *Up close and personal: The teaching and learning of narrative research* (pp. 3–12). Washington, DC: American Psychological Association.

Kim, J. H. (2006). For whom the school bell tolls: Conflicting voices inside an alternative high school [Electronic Version]. *International Journal of Education and the Arts, 7,* 1–21. Retrieved December 9, 2007, from http://www.ijea.org/v7n6/

Lieblich, A., Tuval-Mashiach, R., & Zilber, T. (1998). *Narrative research: Reading, analysis and interpretation.* Thousand Oaks, CA: SAGE.

Maxwell, J. (2004). Causal explanation, qualitative research, and scientific inquiry in education. *Educational Researcher, 33*(2), 3–11.

Mello, D. M. (2007). The language of arts in a narrative inquiry landscape. In D. J. Clandinin (Ed.), *Handbook of narrative inquiry: Mapping a methodology* (pp. 203–223). Thousand Oaks, CA: SAGE.

Munro Hendry, P. (2007). The future of narrative. *Qualitative Inquiry, 13*(4), 487–498.

Munro, P. (1998). *Subject to fiction: Women teachers' life history narratives and the cultural politics of resistance.* Philadelphia: Open University Press.

No Child Left Behind Act of 2001, Public Law 107-110, 20 U.S.C., § 390 et seq.

Phillion, J., He, M. F., & Connelly, F. M. (Eds.). (2005). *Narrative & experience in multicultural education.* Thousand Oaks, CA: SAGE.

Phillips, D. C. (1995). Art as research, research as art. *Educational Theory, 45*(1), 1–7.

Piirto, J. (2002). The question of quality and qualification writing. *International Journal of Qualitative Studies in Education, 15*(4), 431–445.

Polkinghorne, D. E. (1988). *Narrative knowing and the human sciences.* Albany, NY: State University of New York Press.

Richardson, L. (1996). Educational birds. *Journal of Contemporary Ethnography, 25*(1), 6–15.

Riessman, C. K., & Speedy, J. (2007). Narrative inquiry in the psychotherapy professions. In D. J. Clandinin (Ed.), *Handbook of narrative inquiry: Mapping a methodology* (pp. 426–456). Thousand Oaks, CA: SAGE.

Rosiek, J., & Atkinson, B. (2007). The inevitability and importance of genres in narrative research on teaching practice. *Qualitative Inquiry, 13*(4), 499–521.

Smith, T. (2008). Fostering a praxis stance in pre-service teacher education. In S. Kemmis & T. Smith (Eds.), *Enabling praxis: Challenges for education* (pp. 65–84). Rotterdam, the Netherlands: Sense.

Tanaka, G. (1997). Pico College. In W. Tierney & Y. Lincoln (Eds.), *Representation and the text* (pp. 259–299). Albany: State University of New York Press.

van Manen, M. (1990). *Researching lived experience: Human science for an action sensitive pedagogy*: State University of New York Press.

Wolcott, H. (1994). *Transforming qualitative research: Description, analysis and interpretation*. Thousand Oaks, CA: SAGE.

CHAPTER 19

BIRDS OF A FEATHER?

COMMUNITIES OF PRACTICE AND KNOWLEDGE COMMUNITIES

Mark Seaman

In recent years, two distinct theories concerning communities have emerged in regard to group efforts to improve practice: communities of practice (Lave & Wenger, 1991; Wenger, 1998a) and knowledge communities (Craig, 1992, 1995). This work compares the two theories so that educators may better understand their similarities and differences should they choose to utilize such communities in their research and/or practice.

INTRODUCTION

Seventeenth century poet John Donne (1967) wrote that "No man is an island, entire of itself; every man is a piece of the continent, a part of the main" (pp. 100–101). The notion that man, as a social creature, needs others to live and learn is certainly not new to our culture's way of thinking. When one shares commonalities with others, communities are formed. As dynamic organizations, different communities explore

Curriculum and Teaching Dialogue
Volume 10, Numbers 1 & 2, 2008, pp. 269–279

different commonalities and work in different ways. While no two communities are alike, some tend to take on similar characteristics in regard to their structure, operation, and goals. Quite often, the goal of a community is improvement: neighborhood development, public community service, or improvement of practice. In recent years, two distinct theories concerning communities have emerged in regard to group efforts to improve practice: communities of practice (Lave & Wenger, 1991; Wenger, 1998a) and knowledge communities (Craig, 1992, 1995). On the surface, it would certainly be easy to believe that these two theories are basically the same—two new terms describing the same age-old ideas. However, the two concepts share more differences than similarities. The purpose of this work is to explore the two theories, their common traits, and their distinct characteristics so that others may better understand the two concepts should they choose to utilize such communities in their research and/or practice. The delineation between the two models is signifanct to those studying communities, their role in the educational process, and their impact on professional practice.

COMMUNITIES OF PRACTICE

The term "community of practice" was collaboratively coined by Jean Lave and Etienne Wenger (1991) in an effort to provide a perspective on learning and knowing within a social context. This was done while the two where studying apprenticeship and situated learning. At that time, they defined a community of practice as "a set of relations among persons, activity, and the world, over time and in relation with other tangential and overlapping communities of practice" (p. 98). Subsequently, Wenger (n.d) has provided the following definition: "Communities of practice are groups of people who share a concern of a passion for something they do and learn how to do it better as they interact regularly" (para. 1).

Communities of practice exist in organizations, government, education, associations, the social sector, international development, and online communities. In other words, they are everywhere. Recognition of their existence allows the members of the community to transcend the formal structures listed above and focus on improving the practice that defines the community and brought about its existence. It is this shared practice that differentiates the community of practice from other communities. A community of practice consists of members that share more than simply an interest; a community of practice shares expertise, competence, learning, activities, discussions, information, tools, stories, experiences, and a knowledge base. A community of practice not only shares knowledge; but also it creates, organizes, revises, and passes on knowledge among the members of the community.

Wenger (1998a) describes following three dimensions of community as they relate to community of practice:

1. mutual engagement (how the community functions)—"people are engaged in actions whose meanings they negotiate with one another" (p. 73).

2. a joint enterprise (what the community is about)—the community's "negotiated response to their situation ... in spite of all the forces and influences that are beyond their control" (p. 77).

3. a shared repertoire (what capability the community has produced) —"Over time, the joint pursuit of an enterprise creates resources for negotiating meaning" (p. 82).

In terms of community, these three commonalities provide the formation, the cohesion, and the goal of a community of practice.

As stated above, the concept of communities of practice had its beginnings in the study of apprenticeship and situated learning. In the time since the naming of this social phenomenon, the concept has by embraced by the corporate world as businesses become more interested in knowledge management. It has quickly become a leading theory in instructional design.

KNOWLEDGE COMMUNITIES

The conception of knowledge communities occurred as Cheryl Craig was writing her doctoral dissertation. Within a context of school reform research, Craig was looking for a term that explained her relationship with Tim, a teacher who served as a participant in her qualitative narrative inquiry. She has continued that line of research as she looks to investigate knowledge communities in the current educational climate (Craig, 1998, 2001, 2003; Craig & Olson, 2002; Olson & Craig, 2001).

Knowledge communities are bound together by what Connelly and Clandinin (1988) have termed "personal practical knowledge" which they define as "a particular way of reconstructing the past and the intentions for the future to deal with the exigencies of a present situation" (p. 25). When teachers express their personal practical knowledge through stories, they share their narrative knowledge. This concept is closely related to both experiential learning and reflective practice: "education, in this view, is a narrative of experience that grows and strengthens a person's capabilities to cope with life" (p. 27). People share their personal practical knowledge as a way of reflecting, a way of knowing, and a way of bringing meaning to others' stories.

The process of sharing stories and writings with a community of writers benefits all members of the community (Gregory, 1990; Pithouse, 2005). In a quest to improve practice, members of a knowledge community share stories so that their professional growth "is *necessarily* enriched through conversation and critique within a ... community of scholars" (Samaras, Hicks, & Garvey Burger, 2004, p. 910). The structure provided by a knowledge community is designed to improve reflection by providing feedback, collaborating, and finding new solutions to problems.

The notion of knowledge communities is closely related to Fish's (1980) theory regarding interpretive communities. Such interpretive communities do not have preestablished responsibilities:

> It is interpretive communities, rather than either the text or the reader, that produce meanings and are responsible for the emergence of formal features. Interpretive communities are made up of those who share interpretive strategies not for reading but for writing texts, for constituting their properties. (Fish, 1980, p. 14)

Contributions from members of a knowledge community help story and re-story experiential narratives while shaping their meaning. Knowledge communities take advantage of a tacit knowledge-in-action (Schön, 1983) that is rooted in the experiences of its members and the context of their own work. Much of a community's personal practical knowledge (Connelly & Clandinin, 1988) is shared through narratives among colleagues and peers, with members filling with remembrances from their own experience, possibly including alternative versions of the same events.

This concept of shared knowledge was articulated by John Dewey (1916) as he connected community with knowledge and education. He writes that "education consists primarily in transmission through communication. Communication is a process of sharing experience until it becomes a common possession" (p. 9). In addition illustrating the practicality of shared knowledge, the above passage also connects the terms "community" and "communication." This connection is not surprising considering that both words share the Latin root *comunis* (meaning "common" or "general"). There can be no community without communication.

In the case of knowledge communities, this communication is based in the telling of stories. Building on the methodology of narrative inquiry (Clandinin & Connelly, 1990), knowledge communities share knowledge through "a process whereby data is represented as a series of stories that [are] constructed separately, then exchanged" (Craig, 1995, p. 153). These stories are subsequently reflected upon and then responses are shared.

Though primarily based in educational settings, knowledge communities can transcend disciplines in and among organizations that share beliefs that narrative knowledge can be shared in order to improve individual practice.

SIMILARITIES

While these two concepts differ greatly, they do contain some similarities. One such similarity concerns leadership roles within the communities. In both communities of practice and knowledge communities, leadership comes from inside the community. Wenger (1998b) asserts that internal leadership is diverse and has an "intrinsic legitimacy in the community" (p. 7). Leadership roles may exist formally or they can emerge informally, meaning that leadership exists even if it is not officially recognized by the members of the community. This formality and informality of roles extends not only to leadership, but to all roles within the community.

Another similarity between the two concepts is that both recognize that a community is distinct from a network. Networking is about developing relationships; communities of practice and knowledge communities are about developing and sharing knowledge. While an organizational chart of both networks and communities might look similar, the difference between the two is the purpose of the group.

Communities of practice and knowledge communities are also alike in that they share the view that external organizations may legitimize participation in the community. Wenger (1998b) puts it this way: "Organizations can support communities of practice by recognizing the work of sustaining them; by giving members the time to participate in activities; and by creating an environment in which the value communities bring is acknowledged" (p. 7). In knowledge communities, the organization is normally a school; however, knowledge communities can exist anywhere as can communities of practice. Organizations that formally recognize the communities that exist within and among the subgroups within that organization benefit from those communities and the communities benefit from the support of the organizations.

DIFFERENCES

There are more differences than similarities between the concepts of communities of practice and knowledge communities. For one, the concept of communities of practice emerged from business group practices whereas the concept of knowledge communities emerged from the educational community. This does not mean that they are now exclusive to those disciplines. Indeed, the two concepts would work well in any organization. However, their origins lie in two distinct institutions.

Communities of practices develop informally and are emergent, knowledge communities can be created either informally or formally. While both concepts acknowledge that communities can emerge from within an organization, knowledge communities can also be formed purposefully and by the organization itself. For example, a school principal may decide to form a group from specific teachers on his campus for the purpose of sharing teacher knowledge. While this would meet the definition of a knowledge community, it would not be a community of practice.

While members of communities of practice may be either core members or peripheral members, there is no such distinction in knowledge communities. Communities of practice consist of both core members, such as members of a city council, and peripheral members, such as community leaders that attend city council meetings. In the concept of knowledge communities, all of these group members would have equal standing in regard to shared knowledge.

Communities of practice work collaboratively; knowledge communities can work collaboratively and/or cooperatively. In collaboration, all members share a common goal and all contribute to meet that goal. In a cooperative project, all members have specific tasks that individuals must complete. These complete tasks, when put together as a whole, contribute to the final product or goal. For example, when working on a school's budget, the finance committee may use a collaborative process in which all committee members have input on all aspects of the budget or they may use a cooperative process where all departments are responsible for only their own portion of the budget. One is not necessarily better than the other; just simply two different ways of approaching a problem or question.

Communities of practice are informally bound by what members do as well as what they know; knowledge communities are informally bound by what they know. In other words, communities of practice have a shared practice where knowledge communities have a shared knowledge base. An example: a community of practice about architecture would be limited to those in the practice of architecture; a knowledge community centered on architecture might also include sculptors and/or engineers. Members of communities of practice are practitioners with a shared competence or practice; members of knowledge communities are persons with shared interests or goals.

Members of knowledge communities assume that all knowledge is constructed narratively; communities of practice do not necessarily make that assumption. That does not mean that communities of practice do not assume that some knowledge is constructed narratively—the concept simply allows for other way of constructing knowledge and building a knowledge base around which practice can be improved. In research terms, communities of practice can produce quantitative and/or qualitative data; knowledge communities are strictly in the qualitative realm. Communities of practice promote active, conceptual thought; knowledge communities promote reflective though expressed through narrative.

When studying and analyzing communities, the primary unit of analysis concerning communities of practice is the community itself. Conversely, the primary unit of analysis in knowledge communities is the individual. Therefore, the main goal of communities of practice is to improve practice or collectively redefine practice where the primary purpose of knowledge communities is to improve the individual member's practice. For communities of practice, the knowledge they construct as collective unit can in turn impact the definition of the practice and/or modification of the practice. A member of a knowledge community is more concerned with improving individual practice in hopes that sharing the knowledge that led to that improvement will lead to others' improvement.

Members of a community of practice believe that learning is a social process; members of a knowledge community believe that learning is both a social and personal process. While both concepts take into account that it is life itself that is the main learning event, members of a knowledge community take a more personal, reflective turn on life events when constructing knowledge. This is not to say that members of a community of practice are not reflective, they simply are more concerned with acting on their thoughts as they relate to their practice.

Finally, a community of practice follows specific stages of development and knowledge communities can exist indefinitely, sometimes lying dormant. Wenger (1998b) states that there is a life-cycle for communities of practice: potential, coalescing, active, dispersed, and memorable (see Figure 19.1). While not all communities of practice follow these stages, most do. However, knowledge communities do not follow any pattern or cycle. In fact, the relationship may be dormant if there is no current exchange of knowledge. This implies that the relationship can be resumed when members of the community have new knowledge to share or are in need of new knowledge.

The similarities and differences outlined in this work are summarized in Table 19.1.

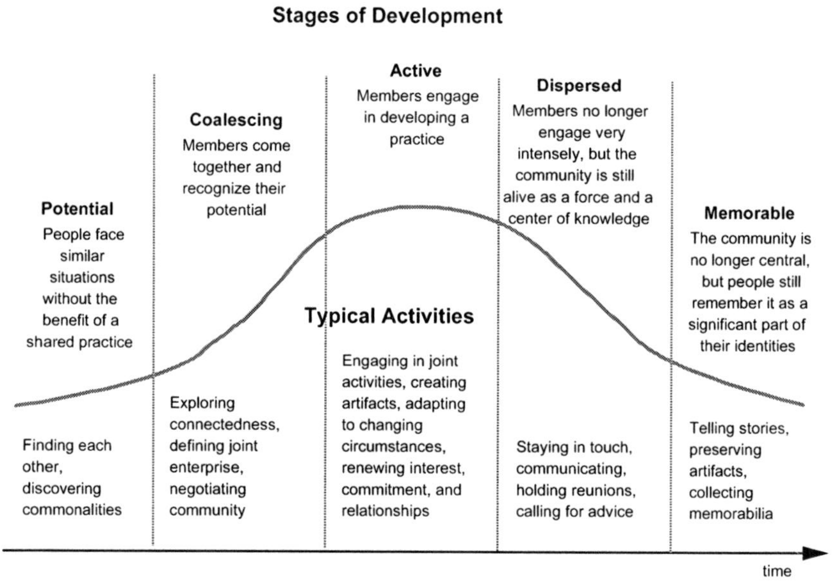

Stages of Development

Source: Wenger (1998b, p. 3).

Figure 19.1.   Stages of development for communities of practice.

IMPLICATIONS FOR PRACTICE

As seen in Table 19.1, there are more differences than similarities between communities of practice and knowledge communities. In any community, a program is secondary to the personnel. It does not matter if a group of people is considered to be a community of practice or a knowledge community; the most important resource is people sharing a common desire to improve.

Both concepts are certainly useful and worthy of use, research, and analysis. Communities are ideally formed for the purpose of improvement. Members of any community may also be members of other communities sharing different stories and purposes and will most likely join other communities at some point. Membership in a knowledge community completely depends on context. Interestingly, members of the community may or may not know each other or their contributions or even be aware of how many people are in this community. This anonymity actually strengthens the community by allowing members to speak freely without concerning themselves with others' opinions.

**Table 19.1.   Summary of the Similarities and
Differences Between Communities of
Practice and Knowledge Communities**

Communities of Practice	Knowledge Communities
distinct from a network	distinct from a network
organizations may legitimize participation	organizations may legitimize participation
roles within the community may be formal or informal	roles within the community may be formal or informal
leadership comes from inside the community	leadership comes from inside the community
informal, emergent	can be either formally or informally created
Collaborative	collaborative and/or cooperative
informally bound by what members do and what they know	informally bound by what they know
exists to improve practice or collectively redefine practice	exists to improve individual practice
community believes that learning is a social process	community believes that learning is both a social and personal process
primarily based on business practices, but adaptable to other settings	primarily based in educational settings
individuals may be either core members or peripheral members	no distinction between core and peripheral members
members do not necessarily assume knowledge is constructed narratively	members assume that knowledge is constructed narratively
primary unit of analysis is the community	primary unit of analysis is the individual
members are practitioners with a shared competence or practice	members are persons with shared interests or goals
active, conceptual	reflective, textual
community follows specific stages of development	community may lie dormant

In terms of practice, knowledge communities may be better suited to a school setting in which the goal is to improve individual teacher practice. The philosophy of the school faculty in this situation would need to be one which believes the individual classroom teacher is the strongest influence on a students' learning. In this case, goals of the school are better served by effective teachers that work together to improve practice.

However, there are schools where the foci of the school may be the school climate or culture, discipline management, or higher scores on standardized tests. These schools may be better served with the communities of practice model because of that concept's focus on the improvement of the community as a whole. In today's culture of accountability, many schools feel they must adopt a business approach to education in which the students' test scores are the product. For this situation, a community of practice model would work well for improving the community as whole.

As with any educational practice, there is no "one size fits all" approach to building and utilizing community. Leadership in each school will need to give some thoughtful consideration to which approach to use. Regardless of preference, the fact remains that both concepts have their merits and their place. As long as there is knowledge to be shared, both will continue to thrive, whether or not they are named as communities of practice or knowledge communities.

REFERENCES

Clandinin, D. J., & Connelly, F. M. (1990). Narrative experience and the study of curriculum. *Cambridge Journal of Education, 20*(3), 241–253.

Connelly, F. M. & Clandinin, D. J. (1988). *Teachers as curriculum planners: Narratives of experience.* New York: Teachers College Press.

Craig, C. (1992). *Coming to know in the professional knowledge context: Beginning teachers' experiences.* Unpublished doctoral dissertation, University of Alberta: Edmonton.

Craig, C. J. (1995). Knowledge communities: A way of making sense of how beginning teachers come to know. *Curriculum Inquiry, 25*(2), 151–75.

Craig, C. J. (1998). The influence of context on one teacher's interpretive knowledge of team teaching. *Teaching and Teacher Education, 15*(4), 397–411.

Craig, C. J. (2001). The relationships between and among teachers' narrative knowledge, communities of knowing, and school reform: a case of "The Monkey's Paw." *Curriculum Inquiry, 31*(3), 303–330.

Craig, C. J. (2003). School portfolio development: a teacher knowledge approach. *Journal of Teacher Education, 54*(2), 122–134.

Craig, C. J., & Olson, M. R. (2002). The development of teachers' narrative authority in knowledge communities: a narrative approach to teacher learning. In N. Lyons & V. LaBoskey (Eds.), *Narrative inquiry in practice: Advancing the knowledge of teaching.* (pp. 115–129). New York: Teachers College Press.

Dewey, J. (1916). *Democracy and education.* New York: Macmillan.

Donne, J. (1967). Devotions upon emergent occasions. In H. Gardner & T. Healt (Eds.), *John Donne: Selected prose* (pp. 100–101). London: Oxford University Press.

Fish, S. (1980). *Is there a text in this class?: The authority of interpretive communities.* Cambridge, MA: Harvard University Press.

Gregory, C. (1990). *Childmade: Awakening children to creative writing.* Barrytown, NY: Station Hill Press.

Lave, J., & Wenger, E. (1991). *Situated learning: Legitimate peripheral participation.* New York: Cambridge University Press.

Olson, M., & Craig, C. J. (2001). Opportunities and challenges in the development of teachers' knowledge: the development of narrative authority through knowledge communities. *Teaching and Teacher Education, 17*(6), 667–684.

Pithouse, K. (2005). Self-study through narrative interpretation: Probing lived experiences of educational privilege. In C. Mitchell, S. Weber, & O'Reilly-Scalon (Eds.), *Just who do we think we are? Methodologies for autobiography and self-study in teaching.* (pp. 206–217). New York: RoutledgeFarmer.

Samaras, A. P., Hicks, M. A., & Garvey Berger, J. (2004). Self-study through personal history. In J. J. Loughran, M. L. Hamilton, V. K. LaBoskey, & T. Russell (Eds.), *International handbook of self-study of teaching and teacher education practices* (pp. 905–942). Boston: Kluwer Academic.

Schön, D. A. (1983). *The reflective practitioner: How professionals think in action.* Basic Books.

Wenger, E. (1998a). *Communities of practice: Learning, meaning, and identity.* New York: Cambridge University Press.

Wenger, E. (1998b). Communities of practice: Learning as a social system [Electronic version]. *Systems Thinker, 9*(5). Retrieved April 17, 2006, from http://www.ewenger.com/pub/pub_systems_thinker_wrd.doc

Wenger, E. (n.d.). *Communities of practice: A brief introduction.* Retrieved April 24, 2006, from http://www.ewenger.com/theory/index.htm

BOOK REVIEW

TRANSDIMENSIONAL CURRICULUM

A Review of *The SAGE Handbook of Curriculum and Instruction*

Robert Boostrom

I have been reading a book about the field of curriculum—*The SAGE Handbook of Curriculum and Instruction* (hereafter referred to as "the *Handbook*" or "the Connelly *Handbook*"). What follows is a review of what I have learned about the state of the curriculum field from this reading. This is not a summary or synopsis of the *Handbook*; that would be an impossible task for a book so expansive and many-colored. It is instead the story of my interaction with the *Handbook* and in that sense only does it do any justice to the material.

For the sake of disclosure, I point out that I served as a consulting author for chapter 10 of the *Handbook*. And, as the *Handbook* is deliberately positioned to be the heir to *The Handbook of Research on Curriculum: A Project of the American Educational Research Association* (hereafter referred to as "the Jackson *Handbook*"), I should also add that I was connected to the Jackson *Handbook* in a similarly tangential way. In the spring of 1989 I was

Curriculum and Teaching Dialogue
Volume 10, Numbers 1 & 2, 2008, pp. 281–300
Copyright © 2008 by Information Age Publishing
All rights of reproduction in any form reserved.

a student in a course co-taught by Philip Jackson and William Pattison "that focused on the dual question of how to organize such a handbook and what its contents might look like" (Jackson, 1992, p. ix). Then, in the last stages of the Jackson *Handbook*, I did some minor editing of final drafts. So, when I talk about *The SAGE Handbook of Curriculum and Instruction* and about its avowed predecessor, *The Handbook of Research on Curriculum: A Project of the American Educational Research Association*, I have been a minor participant in the projects as well as an observer.

AN OVERVIEW AND A PROCEDURAL NOTE

The *Handbook* contains 26 chapters divided into three parts—Curriculum in Practice, Curriculum in Context, and Curriculum in Theory. The arrangement "is intended as a symbol of how this complex field is given life and moves forward" (Connelly, He, & Phillion, 2008, p. xiii). And the part titles—with the *in* significantly present—were chosen "to symbolically avoid one of the field's worries, which is that the form of theoretical writing called curriculum theory could become somewhat independent of curriculum" (Connelly et al., 2008, p. xiii). That is, the practice of curriculum—practice in all its forms—is the intended focus of the *Handbook*. The book is arranged as it is to show that the field of curriculum begins with practice—that, without practice, there is nothing about which to theorize or study.

Despite this emphasis on practice, Part I: Curriculum in Practice actually has fewer chapters than either of the other two parts, and it contains about the same number of pages as Part III: Curriculum in Theory, which is a bit over half the number of pages in Part II: Curriculum in Context. Whether or not these differences in the size of the parts are significant is something I will return to later.

At more than 600 pages (or 3 pounds) for its 26 chapters, the *Handbook* is a large volume, but nowhere near the 1,000+ pages (or 7+ pounds) in 34 chapters of the Jackson *Handbook*. Still, the Connelly *Handbook* is explicitly intended to be "authoritative" and "comprehensive" (Connelly & Xu, p. 517). Especially, it is intended to be "inclusive" and to illuminate "practical places on the landscape" rather than to be "academic" like the Jackson *Handbook* (Connelly et al., 2008, p. xii).

Such talk raises an obvious question: does the *Handbook* succeed in its aim? Is it authoritative, comprehensive, and inclusive? Instead of tackling this obvious question, I will assume that the range of participants involved in the *Handbook* guarantees that the *Handbook* is authoritative, comprehensive, and inclusive. So I ask instead, what does the *Handbook* tell me about the state of the field of curriculum? This is the focus of my review.

Before I can turn to this focus, however, a procedural matter has to be addressed: am I reviewing one book or 26 chapters? Is the *Handbook* a single, unified work? Or is it a collection of disparate articles? Are the chapters summable, corroborating and building up a single image? Or do they convey discrete visions? Connelly and Xu seem to want to embrace both possibilities. They say each chapter is "a different portal into the landscape of curriculum studies" (p. 517), implying that while each chapter conveys a unique perspective, the chapters are unique perspectives of a single field. Each chapter has its own identity, but together they add up to something.

I am not sure that this position is entirely tenable. Consider the three chapters in Part III that deal with curriculum history—"What The Schools Teach: A Social History of the American Curriculum Since 1950" (chapter 23), "Curriculum Development in Historical Perspective" (chapter 24), and "Curriculum Theory Since 1950: Crisis, Reconceptualization, Internationalism" (chapter 25). There are many points of comparison among these chapters, but here is one that illustrates why I am uncertain about whether or not the chapters are summable. Null says (chapter 24) that the reconceptualist (Pinar) and sociological (Apple) critiques of curriculum are situated within "widespread acceptance of curriculum development" which is a "powerful contributor to curriculum and teaching" (p. 489). Pinar agrees (in chapter 25) about the widespread acceptance: "versions of Tyler's protocol [for curriculum development] have remained in wide circulation in United States public schools" (p. 491); but he replies, in essence, so what? The "wide circulation" has occurred despite the "intellectual fate" of Tyler's version of curriculum development, which is to say that, from Pinar's perspective, the *critique* of curriculum development is both more intellectually valuable and more substantive and effectual than the *practice* of curriculum development. So, while Null says that curriculum practice in schools marches on, Pinar says yes, but this is not what we are interested in.

There are two different histories here (and Franklin & Johnson offer a third history in chapter 23), but the authors are not contributing elements that can be combined, because, despite their common starting point (curriculum development has been critiqued, but it continues), they still do not have enough in common to add their arguments together. In one version curriculum development has been (and remains) a significant endeavor for curriculum scholars; in the other version curriculum development was a dead end, if not a stillbirth. When Null, Pinar, and Franklin and Johnson talk about the history of the field of curriculum, they point to different landmarks and salient events. They mean different things by "history" and different things by "the field." These are certainly "different portals," but the portals do not open onto the same "landscape of curriculum studies."

For now, though, I want to leave this question of the summability of the chapters open. As I discuss the *Handbook*, I will move freely from one chapter to another, attempting to highlight connections between them. The *Handbook* was, after all, designed, not randomly thrown together. The topics of the chapters were *chosen*, and the authors were *selected*. The book is the result of a plan.

At the same time, I need to be alert against uncritically assuming that words always mean the same thing, and I encourage readers (of this essay or of the *Handbook*) to keep that caveat in mind.

TRANSDIMENSIONAL CURRICULUM

One of my first responses as I read the *Handbook* was a recollection of the science fiction television series *Dr. Who*. "The Doctor" travels through time and space in what looks like a 1950s era British police box. The craft is called the TARDIS, and one of its startling features is that the TARDIS is bigger on the inside than it is on the outside. Asked to explain this anomaly, the Doctor says that the device is transdimensional (or dimensionally transcendental), meaning that its inside and outside exist in different dimensions.

The field of curriculum, as portrayed in the *Handbook*, is also transdimensional. There is seemingly less to say about the field as a whole than there is to say about its constituent elements. For instance, Connelly et al. note (2008) that "the massive 49-chapter *Handbook of Research on Multicultural Education*" is "a larger volume than this handbook of curriculum and instruction, for which multicultural curriculum is one of its topics" (p. x).

But in saying that curriculum is transdimensional I don't mean the field can be endlessly analyzed into finer and finer examinations of smaller and smaller bits, nor that the field can be inexhaustibly interpreted. Both of these are true, but they are true of any study, not just the study of curriculum.

What I mean when I say that curriculum (as portrayed in the *Handbook*) is transdimensional is that elaborating the field leads to broader vistas. The field of curriculum begins with what is taught in schools, and it leads to a contemplation of all of human existence. In the first chapter of Part III, Schubert sketches the scope of the field:

> culture, language, socioeconomic class, race, ethnicity, gender, sexuality, body and appearance, religion or belief, ecology, globalization, imperialism,

and more. These factors are increasingly perceived as curricula in their own right, not just forces that inhibit or facilitate curriculum in schools. (p. 399)

At the end of Part III, in chapter 26, Connelly and Xu conclude the *Handbook* with the "continuity of being in the Confucian way of knowing" and a vision of "the world, the cosmos … conceived of as an open system" (p. 528).

And curriculum seems to be an expanding cosmos. The Connelly *Handbook* may be smaller than the Jackson *Handbook*, but its scope is larger. In fact, the transdimensional nature of curriculum suggests a different explanation of the *Handbook*'s structure from the one that Connelly et al. (2008) offer. Theory comes last, not only because curriculum begins with practice but also because curriculum moves toward theory.

With the structure of the *Handbook* in mind, I begin with the practice of curriculum, the central theme of Part I, after which I move to the topic of diversity, the central theme of Part II. This discussion leads me to consider conceptions of knowledge and then progressivism as they are taken up in the *Handbook*. Finally, I look at the place of teachers in the *Handbook*, and close with some final thoughts.

PRACTICE

If we want to see curriculum in practice, where do we look?

I suspect that for most people, the answer would be that to see curriculum in practice, we should look in schools. The *Handbook*, however, amends this answer by "[s]tarting with a practical conception of curriculum focused on the experience of curriculum as it appears in schools, policy discussion, and public discourse" (Connelly et al., 2008, p. xiii). In other words, practice is not limited to studies of the "planned curriculum" or the "taught curriculum," but includes studies of the "intended curriculum." It is not limited to shaping or studying what teachers teach in P–12 schools, but is instantiated in analyzing (or influencing) state and national decision making and in critiquing society.

The assertion that the practice of curriculum encompasses diverse activities is so obvious and familiar that the underlying insight may be missed: when Connelly et al. (2008) speak of "curriculum as it appears in schools, policy discussion, and public discourse," the word *it* should be *they*. Whatever "curriculum" is in policy discussion and public discourse, there is something else that goes by the name of "curriculum" in schools. And not only are these various forms of curriculum practice distinct from one another, they may not even influence one another. As Westbury says (p. 58), "many of the issues and disputes around curriculum documents

... stem from images of school and schooling that have no direct, immediate bearing on what most schools do." The practice of curriculum at the level of policy may "play a major role in forming the citizen," it may institutionalize "the narratives that constitute the collective memory," it may "shape individual's [sic] relationships with their natural and social environments" (Westbury, p. 59), but this is not the practice of curriculum embedded in the "[w]orking practices of teachers" that are "shaped primarily by day-to-day realities at their workplace, their habits, and their views about what is practical" (Levin, p. 20).

Even when we speak about the practice of curriculum at, say, only the level of policy, we often conflate different practices. Apple argues (p. 37) that a "set of national or state standards or core knowledge" may be defended on the basis of the content it contains, or it may be used "to stimulate an ongoing and educative debate over what and whose knowledge should be declared official in every nation, region, community, and school." The former practice (attributed by Apple to Hirsch & Ravitch) represents the attempt to impose content, the latter represents "the very process of democratic deliberation over what should be taught" (Apple, p. 37). Both practices are concerned with standards or core knowledge, but they are not the same activities. They are two different ways of practicing curriculum. Deng and Luke (in chapter 4) echo the same distinction, arguing that "researchers and policy makers ... tend to view defining and conceptualizing the subject matter as if it were merely a logical and epistemological rather than a normative and sociopolitical phenomenon" (p. 79). Deng and Luke thus provide labels for two different forms of practicing curriculum at the level of policy—logical and epistemological versus normative and sociopolitical—neither of which may have much to do with the day-to-day curricular decisions made by classroom teachers.

And the practice of curriculum at the level of policy is splintered, not only by different notions of "defining and conceptualizing the subject matter," but also by ignorance of other curriculum practices. Levin argues (in chapter 1) that "many of the scholarly discussions of policies and politics do not reflect the realities of government" (p. 9). The fundamental reality, says Levin, is that "[e]verything in government occurs in the shadow of elections" (p. 9). At the surface, this observation sounds like Deng and Luke noting that defining and conceptualizing the subject matter is a sociopolitical phenomenon, but Levin's point is not that curriculum policy makers are engaging in democratic deliberation. It is rather that "[g]overnments try to do everything at once because that is what citizens and voters require of them" (p. 10). Debates over issues such as the presence of calculus in Ontario's Grade 12 mathematics curriculum (pp. 20–22) are less about defining and conceptualizing subject matter than about satisfying voters that their concerns have been heard.

Curriculum scholars may discover that calculus is for many Ontario parents "symbolic of advanced skills and global competitiveness in the Ontario economy" (p. 21), but this normative perspective of calculus is irrelevant to the policymaker who seeks to end the public debate, not to conceptualize calculus.

The practice of curriculum operates yet again differently when the focus shifts from state and national standards and core knowledge to school systems. For Welner and Oakes (in chapter 5), "The entire schooling system might itself be considered a curriculum structure" (p. 94), and from this perspective, bell schedules, social promotion, and detracking reforms exemplify ways in which curriculum is practiced. Means (in chapter 7) shifts the scene from physical structures to "technology's potential for transforming what and how students learn" and the possibility of offering "entire school programs over the Internet" (p. 136). This discussion unintentionally raises the question whether the *Handbook*—or any bound volume—could ever serve as a "comprehensive" and "inclusive" review of the literature in the era of the Internet. But this question is only an instance of larger-scale questions. If knowledge became (as Dewey described it) "fluid" at the start of the twentieth century, has it now become plasma? And if teaching and learning are no longer physically located because all knowledge is accessible everywhere, how does such a fundamental change in our ways of knowing affect the practice of curriculum? Means says that teachers must be involved in "participatory design activities" (p. 140), but this sort of talk suggests that the focus of the discussion has returned to "conceptualizing the subject matter as if it were merely a logical and epistemological phenomenon" (Deng & Luke, p. 79). Can all of these levels and scenes of curriculum practice be integrated?

Fullan (in chapter 6) says yes. In answer to the question, "What would it take to have the school-community level, the district level, and the policy or government levels to develop in concert?" Fullan offers the "tri-level solution," in which "leaders at the school, district, and state levels [set] up a system that incorporates six major elements: assessment literacy, school and classroom organization, classroom teaching, professional learning communities, intervention and assistance, and homeschool and community partnerships" (p. 119). But as the other chapters in Part I argue (or imply), the assumption that curriculum practice is the same thing at the school, district, and state levels (to say nothing of the classroom level) may simply be a misunderstanding of the work that curriculum people do. What these chapters suggest is that there is no good reason to believe that curriculum work at one level affects curriculum work at another; even within levels curriculum workers may not be able to communicate with and influence one another. Where Fullan argues that evidence and "our knowledge of implementation" (p. 121) can lead ultimately to changes in classrooms, Levin says that "even where there is a substantial body of knowledge, research evidence will not trump political pressures" (p. 19). Policy makers and those who seek to shape curriculum policy engage in different sorts of curriculum practice, and neither may have much effect on what goes on in classrooms.

RESPONDING TO DIVERSITY

"Responding to learner diversity," says Ainscow (in chapter 12) is "the biggest challenge for education systems around the world" (p. 254). Evidence of the size of this challenge lies in the structure of the *Handbook*. Part II: Curriculum in Context takes up 46% of the book (11 of the *Handbook*'s 26 chapters), and the dominant theme of Part II is diversity. Luke's introduction to Part II sounds the call: "In these chapters, we find this movement in curriculum studies—in the critical reappraisal of issues of inclusion for cultural and linguistic minorities, indigenous peoples, migrants, and communities that historically have been marginalized in the formation of school knowledge" (p. 145). The implications of this critical reappraisal are also clear to Luke: "There is a unanimity of voice on the need for a curriculum politics rebuilt around issues of equity, recognitive and redistributive social justice (Fraser 1996), and democratic education" (p. 145). The chapters in Part II bear out Luke's claim of unanimity of voice.

First, there is unanimity that certain populations have been excluded from the practices of curriculum. Often the populations under consideration are children whose lives have been deprived of any connection to their school learning: "immigrant students enter curriculum situations with knowledge and experience historically ignored in education" (He, Phillion, Chan, & Xu p. 223). But other populations working at other practices of curriculum have been denied inclusion: there has been, for instance, "only marginal attention to theory and practice generated from the work and lives of people of color [in practitioner research]" (Cochrane-Smith & Demers, p. 263). Or, even if practice at the level of the intended curriculum has become more inclusive, the effects have not been felt in classrooms: "We recognize that much important scholarly work that challenged the dominant canon emerged. [But no] systematic work developed to fundamentally change the work curriculum does in our schools" (Ladson-Billings & Brown, p. 154.)

Second, there has been unanimity that this exclusion causes children to suffer. They "languish" in schools: "we cannot leave the marginalized, the most vulnerable, and the most impoverished of our students languishing while theorists toss around heady semantics that take no action toward social change" (Nieto, Bode, Kang, & Raible, p. 194). They have been deprived even of the fundamental human characteristic of thought: "the most profound loss [felt by the poor, disadvantaged, or oppressed] is being deprived of the right to think" (Ayers, Quinn, Stovall, & Scheiern p. 317).

Third, there is unanimity that inclusion improves the quality of life for everyone: "schools that tap into local knowledge and seek the wisdom of the Indigenous community become wise schools" (Deyhle, Swisher, Stevens, & Galvan, p. 340).

The unanimity of response to diversity is both obvious in Part II (numerous additional examples could be offered) and puzzling. The chapters cite a wealth of research into "issues of inclusion for cultural and linguistic minorities, indigenous peoples, migrants, and communities that historically have been marginalized in the formation of school knowledge" (Luke, p. 145). The breadth of this curriculum work—art curriculum (Nieto et al., pp. 186–188), "colorblind classroom discourse" (Nieto et al., pp. 188–190), cultural preservation for immigrant children in a Canadian school (He et al., pp. 228–231), the Enabling Education Network linking groups around the world (Ainscow, pp. 246–247), teacher education curriculum and social justice (Cochrane-Smith & Demers, pp. 273–276), teacher groups (Craig & Ross, pp. 295–296), Freedom Schools and their spiritual heirs (Ayers et al., pp. 314–316), language immersion programs (Deyhle et al., pp. 338–340), and "the quiet revolution in schooling developing in a large number of nations" (Farrell, p. 374 ff.)—speaks of the myriad ways in which inclusion is accomplished. These efforts might be celebrated. But despite unanimity of perspective in the *Handbook* and the wealth of research on responses to diversity that promote inclusion, the language of the authors who discuss the literature is filled with words like *marginalization, resistance,* and *revolution,* and the outlook for the future ranges from a somewhat forced optimism ("there are spaces of hope and possibility," [He et al., p. 231]) to dire urgency. "We must take sides," insist Ayers et al., (p. 321), "This is a time of crisis and suffering. It is a time to act."

In chapter 8, Ladson-Billings and Brown review literature on cultural diversity and end their chapter in despair. "Thus, Woodson's ... words still ring true," they write,

> The same educational process which inspires and stimulates the oppressor with the thought that he is everything and has accomplished everything worth while, depresses and crushes at the same time the spark of genius in the Negro by making him feel that his race does not amount to much and will never measure up to the standards of other peoples. (p. 169)

How can so much work have been done to support inclusive schooling and so much unanimity of perspective have been achieved (in the *Handbook* at least) about the advantages of inclusiveness, only to decide that matters have not changed in the 75 years since Woodson wrote those heavyhearted words?

The answer, as Ladson-Billings and Brown express it, is that "the mainstream United States curriculum functions as a default against which all efforts to challenge it either fail or are incorporated in ways that fail to result in real change" (p. 154). The mechanism of this default, they argue, lies in the way that diversity is treated in the literature on schooling and teaching.

> We were also struck by the way the literature elides over notions of race, class, and language. Instead, we regularly encountered discussions of diversity without a grounding in the social and material reality of what diversity means in the midst of highly stratified societies. (p. 168)

Diversity tends to be seen in the literature as a singular condition rather than as a variety of possible diversities: "linguistic, racial, gender, class, or ability difference is regarded as the same" (p. 166). And this vagueness about the conditions of diversity is exacerbated when words like *urban*, *poor*, or *immigrant* are "understood to be proxies for racial others" (p. 168). With the issue of diversity confused by conceptual inexactitude, it's not surprising that discussions of diversity don't lead to changes in classrooms.

But are these critiques of the way that diversity is treated in "the literature" supportable? The evidence Ladson-Billings and Brown offer for their argument comes from a literature review they conducted. Using the descriptors "cultural diversity" and "curriculum," 67 items were identified (from the ERIC, JSTOR, and Education Full-Text databases) and reviewed. These provide the sample of curriculum literature that Ladson-Billings and Brown find to be "eliding … race, class, and language." It is this literature that does not deal with "what diversity means in the midst of highly stratified societies."

I admit that I doubted the findings of this literature review. It seemed incredible to me that "the literature" could be so different from what was presented and cited in the *Handbook*. So I asked a graduate student (and high school English teacher), James Hamilton, to do a similar review. I changed the descriptors to "curriculum" and "practitioner," and he identified (from ERIC and Education Full-Text) 98 full-text items, which he reviewed for several terms (among them, "diversity," "critical race theory," and "culturally responsive teaching"). He found that "diversity" was addressed in 48 of the items, but (as Ladson-Billings & Brown found) the treatment was conceptually vague, with few implications for classroom practice.

In their literature review, Ladson-Billings and Brown also found that "only five [of the 67 pieces of literature] provided specific definitions for the term curriculum" (p. 165), which inhibits, they suggest, "substantive discussions about what is to be taught and learned in schools" (p. 168). The term *curriculum* tends to be taken as a vague but unproblematic reference to content matter (which was also true in the items James Hamilton reviewed for me), rendering invisible variations in curriculum levels (intended, planned, taught, and received curricula), and making it difficult to connect notions of race, class, and language with classroom practices.

This disjunction between the curriculum work represented in the *Handbook* and that reviewed by Ladson-Billings and Brown may be what Connelly and Xu have in mind when they write, "writers in the broad field [of theoretical curriculum scholarship] have been marginalized in the United States and are not part of mainstream curriculum reforms" (p. 523). Or it may be that marginalization is just a temporary condition and that the *Handbook* offers an image of what mainstream curriculum is becoming.

KNOWLEDGE

The centrality of knowledge to the field of curriculum would be hard to deny. (There is a chapter in the Jackson *Handbook* called "Conceptions of knowledge.") If the question is not Herbert Spencer's "What knowledge is of most worth?" it is the popular variant "Whose knowledge is of most worth?" Either way, it is as necessary for workers in the field of curriculum to ponder the nature of *knowledge* as it is for them to ponder *diversity* or *curriculum*.

Regarding knowledge, Deng and Luke (in chapter 4) argue for "the pluralist premise," saying "it would be theoretically naïve for curriculum practice to institutionally embrace a singular approach to knowledge to the exclusion of others" (p. 70). They discuss methods of categorizing knowledge, beginning with Aristotle's groupings—theoretical, practical, and productive—and arriving at "three conceptions of knowledge"—"a disciplinary conception of knowledge that construes human knowledge in terms of canonical academic knowledge contained in various intellectual disciplines ... a practical conception of knowledge that construes knowledge in terms of knowing what to do in practices and actions ... [and] an experiential conception of knowledge, focusing on the social and cognitive, dispositional, and practical elements entailed in making sense of the phenomena of everyday life" (p. 69). After treating these three conceptions of knowledge, they add that "[t]here are, of course, other ways of conceptualizing knowledge or ways of knowing" (p. 69), among them "knowledge formation … as always the product of identifiable class, gender, and racialized relationships of power" (p. 70).

I highlight this alternative from among the several that Deng and Luke list because of its prominence in the *Handbook*. Nieto et al., for instance, talk about weaving postmodernism and multicultural education in art education to expand "notions of curriculum for what counts as art, who count as artists, and by extension what counts as knowledge" (p. 188). He et al. speak of the "knowledge and experience historically ignored" in the education of immigrants (p. 223). Deyhle et al. argue that the struggle to reclaim "Indigenous knowledge … may also mean defining for themselves what constitutes an educated Native American" (p. 343). Schubert asks if "schools are largely reflections of messages that assert domination by an opulent minority" (p. 412). And in the *Handbook*'s most extensive exploration of the notion of knowledge as the product of class, gender, and race, Ladson-Billings and Brown discuss "four forms of multicultural knowledge"—"marginalizing knowledge" that distorts reality, "invisibilizing knowledge" that obscures "social and cultural heritage," "expanding knowledge" that adds "voices and faces of color" but "fails to disrupt the ideology of White supremacy," and "deciphering knowledge" that "pushes teachers to help students excavate and analyze the discursive moves around race, class, gender, difference, and otherness that are always already present in texts" (p. 156).

At first glance, it may seem that the *Handbook* presents unanimity of perspective on the nature of knowledge and ways of knowing (as was true in the case of the response to diversity), but the shift from "What knowledge is of most worth?" to "Whose knowledge will be valued?" does not speak to the nature of knowledge at all. To say, for instance, that indigenous knowledge should be valued in schools tells nothing about whether that knowledge is disciplinary, practical, or experiential, of if a different set of categories is needed to classify it, or even if the processes of classification and categorization can be meaningfully applied to the Indigenous knowledge. To speak of "marginalizing knowledge" (the example given by Ladson-Billings and Brown is that the "marvelous civilization of Ancient Egypt" [p. 156] is discussed without relating it to the rest of Africa) is not to take any stand about the nature of knowledge. The term "marginalizing knowledge" (like the other terms Ladson-Billings & Brown list) is not a way of categorizing knowledge. It is, instead, a way of talking about how content is used in classrooms, and in this it is similar to the *Handbook*'s many other references to knowledge as an expression of class, gender, and race. The *Handbook* pays a great deal of attention to the sorts of things that are included in the subject matter of schools (what counts as knowledge), but almost no deliberate attention to the nature of knowledge itself. (Compare, for example, the treatment of knowledge in a recent issue of *Educational Theory* [Volume 58, Number 2, 2008] that is entirely devoted to "epistemology and education.")

So, while it may seem that the *Handbook*'s stand on knowledge exhibits the same unanimity seen in its stand on responding to diversity, most of the references to knowledge are an extension of the response to diversity, not a treatment of the nature of knowledge or ways of knowing. As a result, it isn't possible to say how most of the writers (much less the *Handbook*) conceive the nature of knowledge or ways of knowing. And it may be that this represents a purposeful distancing of the field of curriculum from epistemological questions that are not explicitly contextualized within the frame of diversity.

PROGRESSIVISM

John Dewey is cited in the *Handbook* more than any other writer. Most of these citations are brief acknowledgements, part of the academic tradition of saying the names. But at a few places in the *Handbook*, his ideas are more important than the citation. In the introduction to Part I, Westbury (p. 1) says: "The animating questions that lie behind all curriculum making—"What do we want to do, and why?" and "How can we do it?"—were Dewey's questions." And not only did Dewey put the question for us, says Westbury, he had the answer as well. "His conclusion about his situation must also be our conclusion: 'Our difficulties ... come not from paucity or poverty [of aspiration] but from the multiplication of means clear *beyond our present powers of use and administration*' [italics added]" (p. 1).

It was Dewey's (2001) insight, says Westbury, that, if we are concerned about what goes on in schools, "the conditions that underlie and regulate the contact between the teacher and child and between teacher and teacher" (p. 2) are more important than our "aspirations." Curriculum change depends, not on an intellectual position or a movement (say, progressivism), but on the conditions of schooling (the organization of classrooms, subjects of study, teacher education, and so forth) that become, as Dewey would say, "organic parts of the education whole" (cited by Westbury, p. 1).

Still, it is Dewey-as-progressive (Dewey as thinker and aspirer) who figures most prominently in the *Handbook*. "Dewey's influence—never absent from the field—is now pervasive," says Pinar (p. 502), "and progressivism is resurgent." Hansen, Anderson, Frank, and Nieuwejaar argue (p. 450) that the "many ... progressive channels" that have impacted curriculum "are inconceivable" without Dewey's work.

In fact, the inclusion in the *Handbook* of chapter 22, "Reenvisioning the Progressive Tradition in Curriculum" makes the strongest commentary on the significance of progressivism and Dewey. Usually, progressivism is seen as an alternative to some other educational perspective ("traditional" education perhaps). Apple notes (p. 35), for example, that Hirsch and Ravitch have argued that progressive educators should (for the good of the schools) return to a "serious academic curriculum for all children," demonstrating that at least some educators not only see an alternative to progressive educational thinking but would actually prefer the alternative. In the *Handbook*, however, there is no complementary chapter to "Reenvisioning the Progressive Tradition in Curriculum." Progressivism is not merely "resurgent" (as Pinar says); it is triumphant.

The vision of progressivism in chapter 22 develops from looking at the work of Ralph Waldo Emerson, W. E. B. DuBois, Jane Addams, and, of course John Dewey. In each of them, Hansen et al. find the common theme of democratic culture. For Addams this means that curricular aims come from people's lives. "[Jane Addams] prioritizes philosophy over theory in the conduct of life.… This standpoint renders curriculum work a profound intellectual and moral art in which specific theories play bounded, contextualized roles but do not themselves define educational aims. The latter must be set by human values and hopes—in short, by a philosophy of life" (Hansen et al., p. 447). For DuBois it means that education creates human beings: "education's primary aim is what [DuBois] dubs begetting human souls" (p. 449). A democratic education enables each of us to develop a philosophy of life, and in doing so, to recognize the call to enable others to do likewise.

> For the kind of growing, democratic society [Dewey] held in his sights, persons need an education that not only equips them to realize fully their talents but that also helps them perceive how important it is for others to have those opportunities, too. (p. 453)

And this vision of democratic education defines progressive education. "[I]ndividual and societal improvement through effective educational institutions remains," say Hansen et al. (p. 454), "an enduring aim of those who consider themselves to be working within the progressive tradition."

I want to make two points about this discussion of progressivism that I have so briefly sketched. First is the universality of the goals espoused by these exemplars of progressivism. Will anyone speak against "individual and societal improvement through effective educational institutions?" I do not think so, though there are doubts about the possibility of fulfilling these aims. Schubert, for example, is led to wonder if there is not an air in Dewey that is just too positive, too male, and too White in his assumption that all problems can be resolved by human intelligence and that all oppositions can and should be integrated. (p. 394)

But Schubert does not doubt the desirability of "individual and societal improvement through effective educational institutions." He merely raises questions about our competence to achieve the aims and about the limitations of human intelligence to transcend human contexts. If progressivism means both being in favor of improving individuals and society and believing that effective educational institutions can bring about this improvement, we all (Hirsch & Ravitch included) have some of the progressive in us. There are doubters that schools work for good in this way, those who fear that schools are largely concerned, not with democracy, but with asserting "domination by an opulent minority" (Schubert, p. 412), but this suspicion of schooling (commented on by Jackson (1992) in the Jackson *Handbook*, p. 9) is overwhelmed by optimism in the power of education (in both handbooks).

My second point about the discussion of progressivism in chapter 22 concerns its implication for our understanding of knowledge and ways of knowing. The experiential conception of knowledge (to use Deng & Luke's language from chapter 4) presents implications for curriculum "that many progressive educators [find] inspiring" (Hansen et al., p. 451) because of the emphasis on the dynamism of the child rather than on the apparent stasis of the curriculum. For many of the teachers I work with, references to Dewey or to progressivism immediately evoke the phrase "hands-on learning" along with a vague sense that all learning issues from doing something. Hansen et al. acknowledge the experiential dimension of progressive learning, but note that by itself it represents a misunderstanding of Dewey. Summarizing Dewey's position, Hansen et al. argue that "learning is impossible ... without there being something to learn.... [T]his something in schools must be rich expressions of humanity's evolving accomplishments in the arts, humanities, mathematics, and sciences" (p. 451). For Dewey, progressive learning depends on recognition of the ineluctable union of child and curriculum, two terms for a single process. The disciplinary and practical conceptions of knowledge are as much a part of progressive learning as is the experiential conception of knowledge. At least, this is the case being made on Dewey's behalf in chapter 22 of the *Handbook*, and I suspect it is consistent with the views of other authors in the *Handbook* besides Hansen et al. When, for instance, Pinar says, "Social and subjective reconstruction cannot occur without academic knowledge" (p. 502), he implies the intersection of the disciplinary, the practical, and the experiential. But I cannot tell from the *Handbook* to what extent this view of knowledge permeates the field of curriculum and the more explicit descriptions of knowledge as an expression of class, race, and power.

THE PLACE OF TEACHERS

As I wrote earlier, the *Handbook* begins with "a practical conception of curriculum," and for most people, the first practice that will come to mind in connection with curriculum is the practice of teaching. As I take up the issue of the place of teachers in the *Handbook*, I have two questions in mind. First is "How are teachers depicted in the *Handbook*?" Second is "What does the *Handbook* offer to help teachers in their work?"

The depiction of teachers in the *Handbook* is not easily characterized. They are central players in the work of schools: "teachers are the key to more inclusive forms of education" (Ainscow, p. 240), even though they have also been seen as mere "managers of efficient instruction of material that was handed down" (Apple, p. 36). They are products of ill-defined and unappreciated preparation programs: "teacher education does not appear to have well-developed signature pedagogies in the manner of other professions" (Craig & Ross, p. 295), and this may be because "research on teacher education has been marginalized for many years, and there is no conclusive evidence about outcomes or impacts of particular education program structures, curricula, or pathways" (Cochrane-Smith & Demers, p. 264). Like in the movies, teachers are often heroic: "The work of Jerry Lipka (1998) and a group of heroic Yup'ik teachers exemplifies this kind of strategic plan [for language revitalization]" (Deyhle et al., p. 339). They are thoughtful and hardworking advocates for social change: "Today, we are enriched by educators who followed the spirit of Cobb's Freedom Schools and the historic work of John Dewey.... La Escuela Fratney, a public elementary school in Milwaukee, is a fountain of these ideas [for seeking good for society in the individual differences among children].... [T]he second graders were talking about Lake Michigan, and ... [t]heir wise teacher Bob Peterson, pursued the question ["Who owns the water?"] to its outer limits" (Ayers, p. 316). In fact, there is a danger "that the literature available on [the teachers in these alternative schools] is generally so highly laudatory as to convey the impression that they are all paragons of pedagogical virtue" (Farrell, p. 386). Of course, there are researchers who "talk about the persistent superficiality of teacher learning ... 'disconnected from deep issues of curriculum and learning, fragmented and noncumulative' " (Fullan, pp. 114–115), but it is also said that researchers should "experience teachers' lives as they are lived" because they "might be moved, then, to listen more closely to teacher voices, to learn from them, and to take action" (Ayers et al., p. 309).

So, the condition of teachers lies somewhere between de-skilled managing of prepackaged curricula and heroically showing researchers what teaching is all about. The range of these characterizations reflects the reality of teachers' lives. Individual teachers may be more heroic or more de-skilled, but all these characterizations probably describe all teachers' lives to some extent.

On balance, then, though teachers are depicted rather positively in the *Handbook*, they are not seen as fully and thoroughly possessing their profession, which makes all the more surprising the answer to my second question, "What does the *Handbook* offer to help teachers in their work?" The answer is, not very much.

If teachers in general are mostly like the teachers with whom I have worked for the last 15 years (and I suspect that this is so, at least in the United States, though I cannot guarantee it), there are three topics that will come to mind when they think about "curriculum"—school subjects, textbooks, and standards. None of these three topics receives extensive treatment in the *Handbook*.

The Jackson *Handbook* contains nine subject matter chapters and one chapter on the "extracurriculum." The recommendation for including these chapters came from the students in the seminar that Jackson and Pattison taught, in which the organization of the handbook was discussed. The Connelly *Handbook* contains no subject matter chapters. The "Introduction" explains: "Readers of this handbook interested in curriculum studies as a whole need to be aware that specific curriculum subject matters, such as social studies, reading, and mathematics are not treated" (Connelly et al., 2008, p. xiii).

There is one extended reference to textbooks in the *Handbook*. Apple argues (p. 26) that in schools the textbook is "the official arbiter of official knowledge." He notes that "80-90% of classroom and homework assignments 'are textbook-driven or textbook-centered'" and that textbooks are "in many places, in essence, the curriculum." But after this acknowledgment that for teachers, the curriculum is a textbook, there is no further discussion of the subject of textbooks in the *Handbook*.

The *Handbook*'s index contains no listing for "standards" as such, though one page is cited under "curriculum planning and standards," where Apple (p. 28) disputes the "faith that somehow the establishment of standards will serve as an adequate guide for reforming curriculum." Drawing on a study of "the production of Missouri's state standards" Apple says, "Ultimately, the standards became a form of symbolic politics, signaling that something was being done but having little transformative potential." The use of standards to develop the enacted curriculum in classrooms (the sort of concern I expect teachers to have) is not discussed in the *Handbook*.

The absence of school subjects, textbooks, and standards conforms to Connelly et al.'s (2008) presumption that, while the intended audience for the *Handbook* is "the practitioner, policymaker, and researcher," the "principal readers" are likely to be "graduate students, teacher educators, and curriculum researchers" (p. xii). This is not to say that the book ignores the needs and interests of teachers. It is rather an acknowledgement that curriculum researchers need teachers more than teachers need curriculum researchers.

Support for this assertion can be seen in the *Handbook*'s shortest but most telling chapter, "Hidden research in curriculum." In this chapter, Enns looks at "an alternative stream of inquiry in curriculum that is mostly hidden to curriculum researchers," the sort of research that is "characteristically intended for dealing with an in-house, practitioner-focused problem and is reported at this level" (p. 431). Enns draws on his experiences as a curriculum policy researcher to make his case, but anyone who has had any connection with practitioner research will readily recognize what Enns has in mind and be able to supply additional examples.

It may be research "commissioned and carried out by university-trained researchers according to RFPs [Requests for Proposals] carefully monitored by the funders" (p. 436), or it may be smaller-scale research carried out by "educational jurisdictions' own research professionals" (p. 437). Whoever the researchers are, the key features of this sort of research are, first, that it is not retrievable through the usual databases (hence "hidden"), and second, that "experienced educators who are users of hidden research have more trust for the usefulness of these sources in making real, classroom-level change, than for any other common form of inquiry" (p. 437).

Reading this chapter, I recalled a student of mine, whose action-research master's degree project was an investigation of a reading program employed in the schools of the district in which she worked. Upon completion, she presented her findings to the superintendent and administrators, as well as to the school board. This reading program had been studied in many other schools by "research professionals," but the administrators of her school system preferred to trust the local research by the local teacher. Her research was used for making classroom-level decisions, and, like the examples presented by Enns, it is "hidden" from the research community and from other practitioners.

The preference of educators for this hidden research suggests a provocative interpretation of the assertion of Connelly and Xu that curriculum scholars "have been marginalized in the United States and are not part of mainstream curriculum reforms" (Connelly & Xu, p. 523). If there is a "divide between the academic field and the public schools" (Pinar, p. 502), if "scholarly work that challenged the dominant canon" has failed "to fundamentally change the work curriculum does in our schools" (Ladson-Billings & Brown, p. 154), if the "field of curriculum studies has been critiqued … for being an elitist intellectual pursuit that is out of touch with the realities of schools" (Nieto et al., p. 176), the reason for the divide may be as simple as this: the work of practitioners (teachers, administrators, policymakers) does not require the understanding of curriculum that curriculum scholars seek.

For the teacher, the practice of curriculum constantly demands an answer to the question, "What do I do Monday morning when the children walk into the classroom?"—and ideally this answer will take into account district and school curriculum standards, state testing requirements, available materials, the school and classroom's socioeconomic context, individualized instruction, the school schedule, the happenings of the previous week, upcoming holidays, current events, the weather, and a thousand particulars of the students' lives. But the teacher's aim is not to understand these things; it is to act. A progressive curriculum scholar who ignores these realities becomes the "romantic progressive," capable only of "impotent rhetoric without real world impact" (Connelly & Xu, pp. 523–524). It is possible, of course, for a teacher to embrace a progressive (or other theoretical) understanding of curriculum while at the same time attending to the realities of school life, but the understanding is not required. A de-skilled manager of prepackaged curricula can run a classroom. But "scholars who sometimes need to distance themselves enough from practice and context to theorize both practice and context as curricula in a larger social sense" (Schubert, p. 392) cannot both distance themselves from practice and context *and* run a classroom.

FINAL THOUGHTS

I have said nothing, directly, about Joseph Schwab, although he is the second-most-cited author in the *Handbook*, and chapter 14 is entirely devoted to his influence on succeeding generations of curriculum scholars. Schwab casts a shadow across the *Handbook* in all the places and in all the ways that the authors of the chapters ask, "Is it possible for curriculum scholars to make a practical difference?" (Connelly & Xu, p. 520). His 40-year-old criticism of the lack of the practical in curriculum work still stings, even while the accommodation to that criticism—embracing the effort to understand curriculum as an instance of the practical—has found acceptance.

The unease that lingers from Schwab's old criticism reveals how deeply the authors of the *Handbook* care about schooling. They critique and challenge it, despair and hope for it, seek reforms and alternatives, fear the worst and hope for the best. They cannot help but wonder why their work has not changed schools. There is a kind of indignant disbelief in the realization that "[w]hat we have come to understand about human learning has almost nothing to do with how schooling continues to be conducted" (Farrell, p. 371). And the line could be emended to say that schooling continues despite what we have come to understand about poverty, race, gender, language, immigration, tracking, retention, technology, globalization, and our own history.

This universe of concerns suggests another topic I have not yet raised in this review—the moral dimension of the field of curriculum. The term *moral* does not appear in the index, but curriculum work is nevertheless seen throughout the *Handbook* as a moral endeavor aiming at "individual and societal improvement through effective educational institutions." As the book closes, the moral nature of curriculum work merges with its transdimensional quality. Curriculum inquiry, say Connelly and Xu (p. 531), is a way of "bridging values across cultural, ethnic, and religious borders and boundaries to provide an education that works best for all children.... [U]nrolling like a Chinese hand scroll painting, [curriculum inquiry embraces and reveals] diverse ways of knowing and being."

In the end, the *Handbook* teaches that, in their transdimensional way, the practices of curriculum continue to unfold.

REFERENCES

Connelly, F. M., He, M. F., & Phillion, J. (Eds.). (2008). *The SAGE Handbook of Curriculum and Instruction*. Los Angeles: SAGE.

Jackson, P. W. (ed). (1992). *The Handbook of Research on Curriculum: A project of the American Educational Research Association*. New York: Macmillan.

Curriculum and Teaching Dialogue would like to thank the following reviewers for all of their help:

Leigh Ausband, EdD, University of North Carolina at Charlotte
Blake R. Bickham, EdD, Mesa State College
Chara Bohan, PhD, Georgia State University
Robert Boostrom, PhD, University of Southern Indiana
Diane Brown, Oklahoma State University
Linda Brown, MA, CAPM, University of Texas at Austin
Susan C. Brown, EdD, University of Central Florida
India Broyles, EdD, University of New England
Lynn M. Burlbaw, PhD, Texas A&M University
David M. Callejo Perez, EdD, West Virginia University
Mary Beth Cancienne-Acgtblu, PhD, James Madison University
Kathryn Castle, PhD, Oklahoma State University
Cheryl J. Craig, PhD, University of Houston
Stacey Elsasser, EdD, Union College (KY)
Christine Finnan, PhD, College of Charleston
Lyn C Forester, EdD, Doane College
Alan Garrett, PhD, Eastern New Mexico University
Janice Huber, St. Francis Xavier University
Chrystal Johnson, PhD, Purdue University
Jeffrey S. Kaplan, PhD, University of Central Florida
Andrew Kemp, EdD, Northern Illinois University
Carol Klages, PhD, University of Houston- Victoria
J. Randall Koetting, PhD, Marian College
Marcella L. Kysilka, University of Central Florida
Douglas McKnight, PhD, University of Alabama
Mark Malaby, PhD, Ball State University
Amy L. Masko, PhD, Grand Valley State University
Heidi Mullins, EdD, University of Arkansas at Little Rock
Christy M. Moroye, PhD, University of Iowa
David W. Nicholson, PhD, Concord University
Pat Obenauf, PhD, University of West Virginia
Lynda Park, University of Indiana
Michelle Sharpswain, PhD, Saint Xavier University
Margaret Schimmoeller, EdD, Randolph University

Candice Schlein, PhD, University of Oise at Toronto
Gretchen Schwarz, PhD, Oklahoma State University
Mark L. Seaman, EdD, Candidate, University of Houston
Mindy Spearman, PhD, University of Clemson
Pamela Thompson, PhD, University of Hawaii at Hilo
Barri Tinkler, PhD, Shepherd University
Jeanne L. Tunks, PhD, University of North Texas
P. Bruce Uhrmacher, PhD, University of Denver
William R. Veal, PhD, College of Charleston

ABOUT THE AUTHORS

Neill Armstrong is an assistant professor and coordinator of field experience in the Department of Secondary Education & Educational Leadership at Stephen F. Austin University in Nacogdoches, Texas. He teaches both graduate and

Jacqueline Bach is an assistant professor of English Education in the Department of Educational Theory, Policy and Practice at Louisiana State University.

Steven E. Ball is an associate professor in the Department of Psychology and Special Education at Texas A&M University-Commerce, Commerce, Texas.

Richard L. Biffle III is an associate professor of education, and chair of the Department of Education at the University of Hawai'i at Hilo. He has enjoyed a wide variety of experiences during his 25 year career in the field of education, including many teaching and administrative assignments in education and multicultural/bilingual education programs throughout the United States and overseas.

Chara Haeussler Bohan is an assistant professor of social studies education at Georgia State University in Atlanta, Georgia. She can be reached at cbohan@gsu.edu.

Robert Boostrom is professor and chair of teacher education at the University of Southern Indiana. His most recent book is *Thinking: The*

Foundation of Critical and Creative Learning in the Classroom (Teachers College Press). He has been U.S. editor/executive editor of *The Journal of Curriculum Studies* since 1997. In 2007 he was elected as president-elect of AATC.

Nancy J. Brooks is assistant professor of curriculum and foundations, Ball State University. Her research interests include critical analysis of curriculum texts and emerging curriculum trends.

David M. Callejo Pérez currently teaches curriculum studies and coordinates the doctoral program in Curriculum and Instruction at West Virginia University. He coedited *Pedagogy of Place* (2004) and *Educating for Democracy in a Changing World* (2007) and wrote *Southern Hospitality* (2001) and *Life of a School* (2007).

Kevin Cloninger is the president of the Anthropaideia Foundation and a doctoral student in Curriculum and Instruction at the University of Denver.

Frans H. Doppen is an assistant professor of social studies education at Ohio University in Athens, Ohio. He can be reached at doppen@ohio.edu

Joseph R. Feinberg is an assistant professor of social studies education at Georgia State University in Atlanta, Georgia. He can be reached at jfeinberg@gsu.edu.

Alan W. Garrett is professor of education foundations at Eastern New Mexico University and was president of the American Association for Teaching and Curriculum during 2006–2007. He currently serves on the board of his local school district. His interests include educational and curriculum history and curriculum studies.

Jeong-Hee Kim is an assistant professor of curriculum studies in the Department of Secondary Education at Kansas State University. Her research interests include: curriculum theory, narrative research, and teachers as researchers.

Marjori Krebs, EdD, is an assistant professor in the Department of Teacher Education at the University of New Mexico.

Amy L. Masko is an assistant professor of English education at Grand Valley State University in Allendale, MI.

Mary E. McGlamery is an assistant professor in the Department of Curriculum and Instruction, College of Education, at Angelo State University, San Angelo, Texas.

Christine Moseley is an associate professor of interdisciplinary studies at the University of Texas at San Antonio in San Antonio, TX. She teaches graduate and undergraduate courses in science education and environmental education. Her research focuses on the beliefs and knowledge of preservice teachers have of the environment.

Dr. Heidi C. Mullins is an assistant professor in art and art education at Eastern Washington University.

Carolyn O'Mahony is an associate professor of social studies education in at Oakland University in Rochester, MI. She can be reached at omahony@oakland.edu.

Stacy Reeder is assistant professor of mathematics education in instructional leadership and academic curriculum at the University of Oklahoma in Norman, Oklahoma. She teaches both undergraduate and graduate level mathematics education courses and her research focuses on emergent mathematics curriculum and the evolution of mathematics teachers pedagogical practices.

Karen L. Riley is distinguished research professor and distinguished teaching professor of Education at Auburn University Montgomery. A graduate of The University of Texas at Austin, her research interests include the politics of education, history of education and curriculum history. She is the author of *Schools behind Barbed Wire* and the editor of *Social Reconstruction: People, Politics, Perspectives*. Dr. Riley is also the series editor of *Studies in the History of Education* with Information Age Publishing.

William H. Schubert is professor of education, coordinator of the PhD program in curriculum studies, and university scholar at the University of Illinois at Chicago (UIC). There, his teaching has been recognized with the College of Education Distinguished Scholar-Teacher Award and the UIC Excellence in Teaching Award. Having published more than a dozen books and over 150 articles, he received the American Educational Research Association Lifetime Achievement Award in Curriculum Studies (2004) and the Mary Anne Raywid Award (2007) from the Society of Professors of Education for distinguished scholarship in the field of education.

Brian D. Schultz is an assistant professor of education at Northeastern Illinois University in Chicago. His research focuses on students and teachers theorizing together, developing integrated curricula based on students' priority concerns, and curriculum as social action. He is particularly interested in encouraging preservice and practicing teachers to create democratic and progressive educational ideals in historically marginalized neighborhoods. Prior to his role at Northeastern Illinois, Brian taught fifth grade in Chicago's Cabrini Green. change to: He has a new book, *Spectacular Things Happen Along the Way: Lessons from an Urban Classroom* (2008).

Mark Seaman is an assistant professor in the Department of Secondary Education and Educational Leadership at Stephen F. Austin State University in Nacogdoches, Texas.

Yonghee Suh is an assistant professor of Indiana University-Northwest. Her research interest includes social studies/history teaching, teacher knowledge and a comparative study.

Dr. Pamela B. Thompson is an assistant professor of education at the University of Hawai'i at Hilo. She has been in the field of education for 17 years, teaching at the elementary, middle school and collegiate levels. Dr. Thompson has designed and implemented art curricula for both a Montessori elementary school and a middle school program. She has also served as an administrative director of a teacher education program and a human rights education program.

Benjamin H. Welsh is visiting professor at Alfred University where he teaches foundation courses in the Division of Education. The Barnes' research methods are his next research project.

Kai-Ju Yang is curriculum studies doctoral student at Indiana University Bloomington. Her research interests focus on tracking and mathematics education.

CALL FOR MANUSCRIPTS

Curriculum and Teaching Dialogue

The Journal for the
American Association for Teaching and Curriculum

TYPES OF MANUSCRIPT SUBMISSIONS

Selected Conference Papers

These papers must have been presented at the annual conference held in October of each year. The length must not exceed 20 pages double-spaced or 5,000 words including references. Manuscripts in this category must be postmarked by October 31, 2008.

Open Submission Papers

These papers do not have to be presented at the annual conference, but must be on topics related to teaching and/or curriculum. The length must not exceed 20 pages double-spaced or 5,000 words including references. Manuscripts in this category may be submitted any time.

Book Reviews

Reviews of books related to the teaching or curriculum fields will also be welcomed. The length must not exceed four pages double-spaced or 1,000 words. Manuscripts in this category may be submitted for review at any time.

Dialogue Column

This column will be open for anyone who wishes to respond to previously published *CTD* manuscripts or presentations at AATC conferences. The length must not exceed four pages double-spaced or 1,000 words. Manuscripts in this category may be submitted for review at any time.

Letters to the Editor

These will be selected at the discretion of the Editor.

All manuscripts will be reviewed by the Editorial Board.
Accepted manuscripts will be published annually.

Curriculum and Teaching Dialogue

GUIDELINES FOR SUBMITTING A MANUSCRIPT

- 1 original hard copy of manuscript with title of manuscript, submission category, name(s) of author(s), full mailing address, telephone number, fax, and e-mail address on the cover page
- 1 abstract of no more than 75 words
- 1 biography of each author, 50 words or less
- 1 electronic copy of manuscript, abstract, and biography (in Word format) sent via e-mail: ctdjournal@jmu.edu
- 12 pt. font, double-spaced, page limit according to category
- References in APA style
- IBM compatible, Word format (disk to be sent if manuscript is accepted)
- Tables, figures, and graphs attached at end of manuscript, with specific program used to create them noted and with place in manuscript indicated by [insert Table X here].
- 1 self-addressed stamped envelope for notification of manuscript arrival

Please submit both Electronic Copies and Hard Copies.

Submit Electronic copies to: ctdjournal@jmu.edu

Hard Copy Mailed to:

Dr. Barbara S. Stern, Editor
Curriculum and Teaching Dialogue
Department of Middle, Secondary, and Math Education
James Madison University
MSC 6912
Harrisonburg, VA 22807

Questions can be sent to e-mail address: ctdjournal@jmu.edu

Printed in the United States
127639LV00002B/9/P

9 781593 119898